The Government and Politics of the European Community

Second Edition

Neill Nugent

MACMILLAN

First published 1989 by
THE MACMILLAN PRESS LTD
Houndmills, Basingstoke, Hampshire RG21 2XS
and London
Companies and representatives
throughout the world

ISBN 0–333–55798–0 hardcover
ISBN 0–333–55799–9 paperback

A catalogue record for this book is available
from the British Library.

First edition reprinted 1990 (twice), 1991
Second edition 1991
Reprinted 1991, 1992 (with new postscript), 1993, 1994

Printed in Hong Kong

Series Standing Order

If you would like to receive future titles in this series as they are published, you can
make use of our standing order facility. To place a standing order please contact your
bookseller or, in case of difficulty,write to us at the address below with your name
and address and the name of the series. Please state with which title you wish to
begin your standing order. (If you live outside the United Kingdom we may not have
the rights for your area, in which case we will forward your order to the publisher
concerned.)

Customer Services Department, Macmillan Distribution Ltd
Houndmills, Basingstoke, Hampshire RG21 2XS, England

Contents

List of Tables, Figures, Exhibits, Documents and Maps   vii

Preface to the First Edition   ix

Preface to the Second Edition   x

List of Abbreviations   xi

Map of the Member States of the European Community   xiv

PART ONE: The Historical Evolution

    Introduction   2

1 The Post-War Transformation   5
2 The Development of the Community   34

PART TWO: The Institutions and Political Actors
of the Community

    Introduction   60

3 The Commission   61
4 The Council of Ministers   100
5 The European Parliament   129
6 Community Law and the Court of Justice   166
7 The European Council   193
8 Other Institutions and Actors   210

PART THREE: Policies and Policy Processes of the
Community

    Introduction   242

  9 Community Policies   244
10 Policy Processes   273
11 The Budget   313
12 Agricultural Policy and Policy Processes: A Detailed
    Study   335
13 National Influences and Controls on Community
    Processes   364

14 Conclusion: Present Realities and Future Prospects   382

Postscript: The Treaty on European Union   397

*Chronology of Main Events in the Development of the European
Community*   409

Selected Further Reading   419

Index   426

List of Tables, Figures, Exhibits, Documents and Maps

Tables

1.1 Membership of Western and Western European organisations   20

3.1 Directorates General and Special Units of the Commission   67

3.2 Procedures to be used in respect of the Commission's implementing powers   85

4.1 Principal factors determining the progress of a proposal through the Council   113

5.1 The year in Parliament: 1989   135

5.2 National arrangements for the 1989 elections to the European Parliament   143

5.3 Elections to the European Parliament: voter turnout   144

5.4 Political groups in the European Parliament after the 1989 elections   148

5.5 Standing committees of the European Parliament   159

6.1 Cases brought before the European Court of Justice since 1953   184

10.1 The decision-making structure of European Political Co-operation   277

10.2 Number of infringement proceedings initiated between 1986 and 1989 classifed by member state, legal basis, and stage of proceedings   302

11.1 The 1990 Community Budget   318

12.1 Annual average percentage changes in agricultural support prices in Ecus and national currencies   361

Figures

4.1   Rotation of Council Presidency between the states
       and seating arrangements in Council meetings   125
8.1   Organisational structure of COPA   231
10.1 Main stages in the making of Council legislation   292
12.1 Outline of the different price levels and the levy and
       refund system for a full market regime product.   344

Exhibits

4.1   A Council of Ministers meeting: items considered and
       decisions taken   116
5.1   Extracts from a European Parliament Committee
       Report   162
6.1   A Commission Regulation   170
6.2   A Council Directive   172
8.1   An Opinion of the Economic and Social Committee   216
12.1 Package agreed by Ministers of Agriculture,
       December 1986   352
12.2 Major decisions taken as part of the 1986/87 Farm
       Price Review   360

Documents

2.1   Treaty establishing the European Economic
       Community: contents   43
11.1 Extracts from the Interinstitutional Agreement on
       Budgetary Discipline and Improvement of The
       Budgetary Procedure.   321

Maps

13.1 Attitudes to membership of the EC   378
13.2 Feelings on whether membership of the EC has been
       beneficial   379

Preface to the First Edition

The aim of this book is to provide an introduction to the government and politics of the European Community. I hope it will serve both as a useful text for students and as a readily understandable guide for the general reader.

The book is divided into three parts. In Part One the historical evolution of the Community is explored: from pre-Second World War tensions and hostilities between the states of Western Europe to present-day co-operation and integration. Part Two focuses on the institutional structure, and the associated political actors, of the Community. In Part Three, the policy output of the Community, and the processes which produce that output, are considered. It is hoped that, having read all three parts, plus the conclusion, the reader will have a good understanding of why and how the Community has developed, how it works, and what it does.

Many people working in the institutions of the Community, and in national capitals, provided information and advice without which I would have been unable to write this book. To them I express my genuine thanks. For their detailed comments on the manuscript I am extremely grateful to Simon Bulmer, John Gibbons, and Vincent Wright. For his encouragement and helpful advice I must also express my debt to Steven Kennedy of the publishers.

Finally, I would like to thank my family. My daughters Helen and Rachael were often patience personified, and endured endless requests to 'keep the noise down' when I was writing. My wife Maureen, in addition to suffering the added domestic burdens which fell to her because of my involvement with the book, did a superbly efficient job in typing the manuscript.

Any responsibility for errors in the book remains, of course, mine.

November 1988   NEILL NUGENT

Preface to the Second Edition

It is customary for second editions of books on aspects of modern government and politics to appear about five years after the first edition. Such a timetable would have suited me nicely with this book. However, developments in the European Community are unfolding at such a pace, and so much has happened since the first edition was completed in 1988, that I decided a second edition ought to be produced in advance of the usual schedule.

In writing this second edition I have concentrated on four things. First, I have updated where that was necessary. Second, I have examined and explained some aspects of the Community in greater detail than in the first edition: Community legislative processes for example, and the implementation of Community law. Third, I have incorporated more tables, figures, and exhibits. Fourth, I have corrected a few mistakes which appeared in the first edition.

As a result of these changes the book has been lengthened. No chapter has been left untouched, and most have been subject to a considerable amount of rewriting.

Again I must thank the many people working in Community institutions and in national capitals who provided me with information. Wolfgang Gaede of the Council of Ministers and Gary Titley MEP were especially helpful. I would also like to take this opportunity of thanking Tom Kennedy of the Court of Justice, and David Lowe and Michael Shackleton of the European Parliament, who really ought to have been thanked in the Preface of the first edition. Steven Kennedy of the publishers was again very helpful and encouraging. My wife, Maureen, did a wonderfully quick job in preparing the typescript and I am extremely grateful to her, and to my children, Helen and Rachael, for all their help and support.

January 1991

NEILL NUGENT

List of Abbreviations

ACP	African, Caribbean, and Pacific Countries
ASEAN	Association of South-East Asian Nations
BEUC	European Bureau of Consumers' Associations
BRITE	Basic Research in Industrial Technologies for Europe
CAP	Common Agricultural Policy
CCP	Common Commercial Policy
CCT	Common Customs Tariff
CDU/CSU	German Christian Democratic Union/Christian Social Union
CEEP	European Centre of Public Enterprises
CEFIC	European Chemical Industry Federation
CEN	European Committee for Standardisation
CENELEC	European Committee for Electrotechnical Standardisation
CET	Common External Tariff
CFP	Common Fisheries Policy
COPA	Committee of Professional Agricultural Organisations
COREPER	Committee of Permanent Representatives
CSF	Community Support Framework
CSCE	Conference on Security and Co-operation in Europe
CSP	Confederation of the Socialist Parties of the European Community
DC	Italian Christian Democratic Party
DG	Directorate General
DRIVE	Dedicated Road Infrastructure for Vehicle Safety in Europe
EAGGF	European Agricultural Guidance and Guarantee Fund
EBRD	European Bank for Reconstruction and Development
EC	European Community
ECOFIN	Council of Economic and Finance Ministers

ECSC	European Coal and Steel Community
Ecu	European Currency Unit
ED	European Democratic Group
EDA	Group of the European Democratic Alliance
EDC	European Defence Community
EEA	European Economic Area
EEB	European Environmental Bureau
EEC	European Economic Community
EES	European Economic Space
EFTA	European Free Trade Association
EIB	European Investment Bank
EMS	European Monetary System
EMU/Emu	Economic and Monetary Union
EP	European Parliament
EPC	European Political Co-operation
EPP	European People's Party – Federation of the Christian Democratic Parties of the European Community
ER	Technical Group of the European Right
ERDF	European Regional Development Fund
ERM	Exchange Rate Mechanism
ESC	Economic and Social Committee
ESF	European Social Fund
ESPRIT	European Strategic Programme for Research and Development in Information Technology
ETUC	European Trade Union Confederation
EUL	European United Left
Euratom	European Atomic Energy Community
EUREKA	European Programme for High Technology Research and Development
EUROFER	European Confederation of Iron and Steel Industries
FCO	Foreign and Commonwealth Office
FDP	German Free Democratic Party
FRG	Federal Republic of Germany
GATT	General Agreement on Tariffs and Trade
GDP	Gross Domestic Product
GDR	German Democratic Republic
GNP	Gross National Product
IEA	International Energy Agency
IGC	Intergovernmental Conference
IMF	International Monetary Fund

IMP	Integrated Mediterranean Programme
JET	Joint European Torus
JRC	Joint Research Centre
LDP	Federation of Liberal and Democratic Parties of the European Community
LDR	Liberal Democratic and Reformist Group
LU	Left Unity
MCA	Monetary Compensation Amount
MEP	Member of the European Parliament
NATO	North Atlantic Treaty Organisation
NCI	New Community Instrument
OECD	Organisation for Economic Co-operation and Development
OEEC	Organisation for European Economic Co-operation
OJ	Official Journal of the European Communities
PCF	French Communist Party
PCI	Italian Communist Party
PDB	Preliminary Draft Budget
PHARE	Poland and Hungary: Aid for the Restructuring of Economies
RACE	Research and Development in Advanced Communications Technologies for Europe
RBW	Rainbow Group
R & TD	Research and Technological Development
SCA	Special Committee on Agriculture
SEA	Single European Act
SEM	Single European Market
UK	United Kingdom
UN	United Nations
UNCTAD	United Nations Conference on Trade and Development
UNICE	Union of Industries of the European Community
USA	United States of America
VAT	Value Added Tax
WEU	Western European Union

Member States of the European Community

Founding members (1952 ECSC; 1958 EEC and Euratom)

First enlargement (1973)

Second enlargement (1981)

Third enlargement (1986)

Incorporation of the territory of the German Democratic
Republic into a united Germany (1990)

PART ONE

The Historical Evolution

Introduction

No political system or organisation can properly be understood unless it is set in its historical and operational contexts. The structure and functioning of government institutions, the nature and dynamics of political forces, and the concerns and conduct of those who exercise power do not happen as a matter of chance. They are shaped and are constantly being remoulded by evolving forces and events.

Though a relatively new organisation, the European Community (EC) is no less subject to these dictates than are long established nation states and, like them, its nature cannot be appreciated without reference to its historical sources or to the world in which it functions. Thus, the Community is often criticised for being weak in structure and quarrelsome in nature, with far too much bickering over matters such as the price of butter and not enough visionary thinking and united action to tackle unemployment, regional imbalances, and other major problems. Unquestionably there is much in these criticisms, but that the Community should find harmonious collective policy-making difficult is not surprising to anyone with a historical perspective. For before they became members of the Community the now twelve member states made decisions for themselves on most matters. It is not easy, especially for those which, until relatively recently, have been great powers or which believe themselves to be different or to have special interests, to have to cede sovereignty by transferring decision-making responsibilities to a multinational organisation in which other voices may prevail. An explanation and understanding of what the EC is, and what it has and has not achieved, must recognise this. The Community must, in other words, be seen in the context of the forces that have made it, and are still making it. Some of these forces, notably ones of increasing economic interdependence, have served to push the states together. Others, and long established assumptions regarding the importance of national independence and sovereignty

2

are very much amongst these, have resulted in progress towards co-operation and integration being slow, difficult, and far from continuous.

The sovereignty issue may also be used to give another, rather different, example of the importance of both historical background and contemporary operational context in explaining and evaluating the EC. Many of the Community's opponents and critics subscribe to the view that the nation state, not an international organisation, is the 'natural' supreme political unit. They argue that insofar as transferences of power to Brussels, Luxembourg and Strasbourg – the three main seats of the Community's institutions – undermine national sovereignty, they should be resisted. But what proponents of this view all too often fail to recognise is that the member states of the Community were seeing their sovereignties being steadily eroded long before the EC was established, and since it was established they have seen their sovereignties further eroded by forces that are not a consequence of Community membership. Whether it is because of movements in financial markets, transfers of capital within multinational corporations, changing trade patterns, or superpower military dominance, virtually all West European states have become increasingly affected by, and at the mercy of, international developments they cannot control. This loss of power may not have involved legal transfers of sovereignty as has been the case within the Community, but it has had a very similar effect. The fact is that in an ever expanding range of policy and decision-making sectors states have not been able to act in isolation but have had to adjust and adapt so as to fit in with an array of external influences. The Community should not, therefore, be viewed as constituting a unique threat to the sovereignties of its member states. On the contrary, it is in some ways an attempt to meet this threat by providing a means by which the member states, if not able to regain their sovereignty, can at least reassert control over aspects of decision-making by co-operating together at levels and in ways which match post-war internationalism.

The purpose of Part One is thus to provide a base for an understanding of the Community by tracing its evolution and placing it in its historical and operational settings.

In Chapter 1 the sharp divide between pre-war and post-war West European inter-state relations is examined. The factors which explain what amounted to a post-war transformation in those relations are analysed, and the early organisational responses to that transformation are described.

Chapter 2 analyses the development of the three Communities which make up what is now usually referred to in the singular as the European Community: the European Coal and Steel Community which was founded by the Treaty of Paris in 1951, and the European Atomic Energy Community (Euratom) and the European Economic Community (EEC) both of which were established in March 1957 with the signing of the Treaties of Rome.

1

The Post-War Transformation

Historical Divisions

It has become common today, with Western European integration proceeding apace and with democratic and market-based systems being established throughout much of Eastern Europe, for commentators and observers on European affairs to emphasise the increasing unity and identity of the Continent.

It is well to remember, however, that such unity and identity as there can be said to exist – and, in truth, there is not very much if Western and Eastern Europe are lumped together – is of very recent vintage. For the fact is that throughout its history Europe has been characterised much more by divisions, tensions, and conflicts than it has by any common purpose or harmony of spirit. Even if attention is just restricted to that part of Europe which is of most interest to us in this book, which is also the part of Europe where unity has been most developed – Western Europe – the peoples and nation-states have long differed and been divided from one another in many ways.

Language has been perhaps the obvious divisive force. Linguists may identify structural similarities between European languages, but the fact is that most peoples have not been able to, and still cannot, directly converse with one another. Religion has been another source of division, with the northern countries (except Ireland) being mainly Protestant, and the southern countries (including France but excluding Orthodox Greece) being predominantly Catholic.

5

Contrasting cultural traditions and historical experiences have further served to develop distinct identifications – and feelings of 'us' and 'them' – across the map of Europe.

Such differences have helped to bind some peoples together, but they have also served to separate others from one another. Along with the legacies of power struggles and wars they help to explain why Western Europe has been divided into so many states, each with its own identity and loyalties. Some of these states – France, Spain and the United Kingdom for example – have existed in much their present geographical form for centuries. Others – including Germany, Italy and Ireland – have been constituted only comparatively recently, mostly in the nineteenth and early twentieth centuries, as nationalism flourished and as force was used to bring nation and state into closer alignment.

Until at least the Second World War, and in some cases well beyond, linguistic, religious and cultural divisions between the West European states were exacerbated by political and economic divisions.

The political divisions took the form of varying systems of government and competing ideological orientations. In the nineteenth and early twentieth centuries autocracies contrasted with emerging, and more liberal, parliamentary democracies. Between the two world wars parliamentary democracy found itself under attack and in some cases was overthrown: in Italy in 1922 by Fascism, in Germany in 1933 by Nazism, and in Spain after the 1936–9 civil war by conservative authoritarianism. It was not until the mid-1970s – following the collapse of the dictatorships of the Iberian peninsula and the overthrow of the military regime in Greece – that parliamentary democracy finally became general throughout Western Europe.

The economic divisions were no less marked. From the beginnings of the Industrial Revolution until the middle of the nineteenth century Britain was industrially and commercially dominant. Gradually it was challenged – particularly by Germany, but also by Belgium, France and others – so that by the early years of the twentieth century competition between these countries for overseas markets was fierce. At the same time, the economies of the northern countries were increasingly differentiated from those of the south, in that the former mostly had substantial industrial bases while the latter remained predominantly agricultural and underdeveloped.

Western Europe was thus long divided and many of these divisions provided sources for tensions, hostilities and wars. Finding their expression in economic and ideological competition, in drives for national power and prestige, and in territorial disputes, and compounded by dangerous mixtures of assertive/weak/incompetent leaderships, the divisions ensured that until after the Second World War rivalry and distrust governed the relationships between most of the states most of the time.

In the twentieth century alone two devastatingly destructive world wars, both of which began as European wars, have been fought. The First (1914–18) saw the countries of the Triple Entente – Britain, France and Russia – plus Italy from 1915, fighting against Germany and Austria-Hungary. The Second (1939–45) saw Germany, assisted from 1940 by Italy, attempting to impose itself by force on virtually the whole of Europe outside the Iberian peninsula.

The background to the Second World War is worth outlining briefly because it puts in perspective how dramatically different, and how suddenly found, were the more co-operative relationships between the West European states in the post-1945 era. In short, the period between the wars was characterised by particularly sharp and fluid inter-state relations. There was no stable alliance system and no clear balance of power. For the most part European states, including West European states, regarded one another with, at best, suspicion. Though multi-lateral and bi-lateral treaties, agreements and pacts abounded there was little overall pattern to them and few had any lasting effect. States came together in varying combinations on different issues in a manner which, far from indicating mutual confidence, was increasingly suggestive of fear.

From time to time in the inter-war period proposals for greater co-operation between European states were advanced but little came of them. The international climate – characterised by national rivalries and clashing interests – was not favourable, and most of the leading advocates of closer linkages were seen as having, as indeed they did have, specific national purposes in mind. Aristide Briand, for example, who was French Foreign Minister from 1925–32, supported European co-operation but clearly had as his prime aim a stable European political system which would preserve the peace settlement that had been imposed on Germany in the 1919 Versailles Treaty. Gustav Stresemann, by contrast, who was the German Foreign Minister from 1923–9, saw European co-operation as a way in which Germany could loosen the grip of Versailles and regain its position as a major power.

The lack of any real interest in European co-operation before the Second World War is revealed in the functioning of the League of Nations. Established in 1919 to provide for international collective security it was, in practice, dominated by the Europeans and had some potential as a forum for developing understandings and improving relationships between the European states. It failed, and did so for three main reasons. First, its aims were rather vague and were interpreted in different ways. Second, it was intergovernmental in its structure and therefore dependent on the agreement of all member states before any action could be taken. Third, and most importantly, the states wanted different things from it: some – notably France, most of the medium-sized central European countries which had been constituted in 1918–19 out of the collapsed Austria-Hungarian Empire, and to some extent Britain – saw it as a means of preserving the Versailles *status quo*; others – particularly Germany and Italy – wanted to use it to change the 1919 settlement and were prepared to leave or ignore it if it did not serve that purpose.

Inter-war Europe thus experienced rising tensions as national rivalries remained unharnessed and, above all, as German territorial and power ambitions could not be satisfied. When war did finally break out, the Axis Powers (Germany and Italy) gained control for a while over virtually the whole of the Continent from the Atlantic to deep inside the Soviet Union. In Western Europe only Britain and those countries which remained neutral (Ireland, Portugal, Spain, Sweden and Switzerland) were not occupied. By May 1945, when German government representatives agreed to unconditional surrender, Nazism and Fascism had been defeated, but economies and political systems throughout Europe had been severely shaken, cities and towns had been destroyed, and millions had been killed.

The Post-War Transformation

Since the Second World War the relations between the Western European states have been transformed. There are three principal aspects to this:

Over Forty Years of Peace

The states have lived peacefully with one another since 1945 and armed confrontation between any two does not now appear to be even remotely possible. As Altiero Spinelli, one of the great advocates and architects of European integration, observed in 1985 shortly before his death:

> [a] major transformation . . . has occurred in the political consciousness of Europeans, something which is completely new in their history. For centuries, neighbouring countries were seen as potential enemies against whom it was necessary to be on one's guard and ready to fight. Now, after the end of the most terrible of wars in Europe, these neighbours are perceived as friendly nations sharing a common destiny.

The belief in a common destiny is perhaps questionable, but the reality and importance of the transformation from hostile to friendly relations is not. Certainly the states continue to compete against one another in many arenas, and this does sometimes lead to strains and tensions, but these disagreements are mostly on issues where military conflict is just not relevant to the resolution of differences. In any event, such friction as there is occurs within a context in which all the states share roughly similar views as to who are basically friends and who are real or potential enemies, and within a context too where most are full or part members of the same military alliance: the North Atlantic Treaty Organisation (NATO).

A Transformed Agenda

Throughout the international system the subject matter of discussions and negotiations between states has become more varied. Whilst, as superpower relations and regional conflicts show, the case should not be overstated, international agendas have undoubtedly become less centred upon traditional or 'high policy' issues and have increasingly focused on 'low policy' issues. That is to say, policies concerned with the existence and preservation of the state, (such as defence policy and balance of power manoeuvrings), have been joined by policies concerned more with the wealth and welfare of populations (such as policies on trade, monetary stability, environmental protection, and airline safety).

This change in the content of agendas has been particularly marked throughout the Western industrialised world, and above all in the EC where a transformation can be said to have occurred. Classic 'power politics' have not, of course, disappeared, but they are just not as dominating or as prominent as they were formerly. When representatives of the twelve EC states meet it is normally to consider topics which a generation or two ago would not even have been regarded as proper subjects for international negotiations. For instance: what constitutes 'fair' economic competition, how might research information be pooled to the general advantage, should farmers be given a five or seven per cent increase in their incomes, and what should be the maximum weight of lorries permitted on roads?

New Channels and Processes

Paralleling, and partly occasioned by, the increasingly diverse international agenda, there has been a transformation in the ways in which states interrelate with one another. The traditional diplomatic means of interstate communications via Ministries of Foreign Affairs and embassies have declined in importance as new channels and processes have become established.

As with changing agendas, changing forms of interstate communications have been taken further in the Western industrialised world, and particularly in the EC, than anywhere else. There are now few significant parts of any Western state's machinery that do not have some involvement in managing external relations. Written communications, telephone conversations, telex messages, bilateral and multilateral meetings, have all become much more numerous. Contacts range from the *ad hoc* and informal to the regularised and highly structured.

In the Community, governmental representatives of different sorts meet with one another every working day. They may have as their purpose the taking of binding decisions (decisions which in some circumstances may be taken by majority vote), the explanation of possible advantageous policy co-ordination, or merely the exchanging of views and information. At the lower end of the seniority scale junior and middle-ranking officials, working often from tightly drawn negotiating briefs and with their actions subject to later approval from national capitals, convene in committees to try and hammer out detailed agreements on proposed legislation. At the other end of the scale Heads of Government regularly meet, for what are usually wide-ranging and relatively unstructured discussions, in a number of forums: in the twice yearly European Councils where all twelve Community states are represented; in bilateral meetings, which in the case of the British Prime Minister, the French President, the German Chancellor, and the Italian Prime Minister, are fixed on an at least annual basis; and in the broader setting of the annual Western Economic Summits which bring together the political leaders of Britain, France, Germany, Italy, Canada, Japan and the United States, plus the President of the European Commission and the head of government of the member state which is currently chairing the Community's Council of Ministers if he is not already present.

Explanations for the Post-War Transformation

In seeking to explain post-war co-operation and integration in Western Europe – which includes locating the foundations of, and reasons for the development of, the European Community – observers have often highlighted different factors, and sometimes indeed have looked in rather different directions. Amongst the questions that have caused difficulties are these: to what extent do the developments have deep historical roots and to what extent have they been a reaction to specifically post-1945 circumstances; what has been the balance between political and economic factors; what has been the role of general international influences as opposed to more narrowly based West European ones; and has there been a constant underlying movement in an integrationist direction or just a series of specific, and not very well co-ordinated, responses to specific problems?

In looking at the ways in which questions of this sort have been answered four broad explanatory themes can be found in the literature. For analytical purposes they will be considered here separately, but it should be recognised that, in practice, they are by no means mutually exclusive but rather complement, overlap and reinforce one another. It should be recognised, too, that their usefulness as explanations is not constant, but varies over time. So, for example, whilst political ideals and utopian visions of a united Europe may have had at least some part to play in the early post-war years, more recently they have counted for little, and it has been hard headed national calculations of economic and political advantages and disadvantages that have been the principal determinants of progress.

The Deep Roots of Integration?

Some have found the roots of post-war developments in the distant past. Supporters and advocates of European integration have been especially prominent in this regard. They have suggested that Europe is, and has long been, a unique and identifiable entity. As evidence of this it is often argued that Europe was the cradle of modern civilisation and from this developed European values and a European culture, art and literature. Walter Hallstein, the first President of the Commission of the EEC, typifies this sort of view:

> Europe is no creation. It is a rediscovery. The main difference between the formation of the United States of Europe and that of the United States of America is not that America did not have to merge a number of firmly established nation-states, but that for more than a thousand years the idea of a unified Europe was never quite forgotten . . . [The advocates of a European federation] know that Europe shares a sense of values: of what is good and bad; of what a man's rights should be and what are his duties; of how society should be ordered; of what is happiness and what disaster. Europe shares many things: its memories that we call history; achievements it can take pride in and events that are shameful; its joys and its sufferings; and not least its tomorrows (Hallstein 1972).

Clearly there is much idealism in this. People such as Hallstein are suggesting that transcending the differences, divergences and conflicts between peoples and states there has long been a certain commonality and identity of interest in Europe based on interrelationships between geography and historical, political, economic, social and cultural developments. It is a contentious view and certainly not one to which many historians would attach much importance. Division and dissension, they would contend, have been more prominent than identity of interest or shared values and experiences. Such limited commonality as has existed has largely been a consequence of geographical proximity.

But if the 'idealistic' interpretation does not now find much favour, there are still those who would wish to stress the importance of the historical dimension of Western European integration. Interstate relations in the nineteenth century are sometimes seen as foreshadowing post-1945 developments insofar as peace endured for much of the century and did so, in part at least, as a result of understandings and agreements between the major powers. The problem with this view, however, is that it rather overstates the extent to which the nineteenth century was a century of peace, and it exaggerates too, the extent to which the states did co-operate. Arguably, the so-called Concert of Nations represented an embryonic attempt to exercise strategic control through diplomacy and summitry, but that was at a time when conservative autocracies ruled much of Europe and when many of today's states did not even exist in their present forms. And in any event, the system lasted at best only from 1815 to the Crimean War. It then gave way to the wars of mid-century and later to the balance of power – which was hardly based on European trust and co-operation – as the means of seeking to preserve the peace.

It is perhaps in the field of economic history that the most fertile ground for identifying long-term influences and explanations is to be found. From about the late eighteenth century *national* economic integration began to occur, as barriers to economic activity *within* states were dismantled. This helped to promote, and in turn was encouraged by, national political integration which manifested itself in nationalism and in the elevation of the sovereign state to the status of the supreme collective unit. From about the middle of the century the achievement and successes of this internal economic and political integration, allied with an increasing interconnectedness in Europe which followed from technological changes and economic advance, resulted in increasing interstate co-operation to promote trade, competition and growth. For some economic historians an embryonic European economy was being established. Pollard, for example, has written of the mid-nineteenth century:

Europe's industrialisation proceeded relatively smoothly among other reasons precisely because it took place within what was in many essentials a single integrated economy, with a fair amount of movement for labour, a greater amount of freedom for the movement of goods, and the greatest freedom of all for the movement of technology, know-how and capital. (Pollard 1981)

But, unlike the customary pattern within nation states, there was nothing inevitable about European economic integration. Nor was there a clear and developing relationship between it and political integration. On the contrary, from the last quarter of the nineteenth century, states, for a variety of reasons, moved increasingly in the direction of economic protectionism and at the same time developed national identities and consciousness such as had not been seen before. In the first part of the twentieth century, and especially between the wars, the European free trading system virtually disappeared, as states sought to protect themselves at the expense of others and as national economies were increasingly reshaped along autarkic lines. Alongside these increasingly closed economic systems developed the ever sharper political tensions and rivalries between the states that were noted earlier.

The European historical experience thus emphasises the extremely important, but often overlooked fact, that although industrialisation and economic liberalisation provide potential bases for the further-ance of interconnections, agreements, and harmonious relations between states, they do not ensure or guarantee them. The powers of Europe went to war with their principal trading partners in 1914. Furthermore, between the wars, economic linkages did little to bring the nations together or to act as a restraint on governments when divergences developed in their aims and strategies. This must be borne in mind when, later in this chapter, attention is turned to modernisation and interdependence as explanations for post-war political and economic integration. Doubtless they have both been extremely important, but, as pre-1939 European history shows, they do not have an inevitable integrationist logic attached to them. Much depends on their relationship to the circumstances of the time and, as will now be shown, these were very different in the post-1945 world to what they had been before the war.

The Impact of the Second World War

The Second World War unquestionably marks a turning point in the West European state system. Within a few years of the war ending states were co-operating, and in some instances and in some respects were even integrating, in a manner that would have been inconceivable before the war. Fundamental to this transformation were a number of factors resultant upon the war that combined to bring about radical changes in both the climate of opinion and the perceptions of requirements. They can be grouped under two broad headings:

Political factors. These may be subdivided:

(1) The Second World War produced a greater realisation than had existed ever before that unfettered and uninhibited nationalism was a recipe for war, which in the post-1945 world was increasingly seen as meaning mass destruction. At the international level this thinking was reflected in calls for a larger and more powerful body than the pre-war League of Nations, and it played an important part in the establishment of the United Nations in 1944. But the fact that the two World Wars had begun as European wars, and that Germany was generally seen as having been the prime cause of those wars, also brought forth demands and moves for specifically European arrangements. Amongst the strongest advocates of this view were many of those who had been associated with the Resistance movements of Continental Europe which, from 1943 onwards, had come to be linked via liaising networks and from which ideas and proposals had been generated looking forward to a post-war world that would be based more on co-operation and less on confrontation.

There was thus a widely shared optimism that if the states could work together in joint schemes and organisations barriers of mistrust could be broken down. On this basis, over 750 prominent Europeans came together at the Hague in May 1948 and from their Congress issued a call to the nations of Europe to create a political and economic union. This stimulated discussions at governmental levels, and in May 1949 the Statute of the Council of Europe was signed by representatives of ten states. Article 1 of the Statute states:

> The aim of the Council of Europe is to achieve a greater unity between its Members for the purpose of safeguarding and realising the ideals and principles which are their common heritage and facilitating their economic and social progress.

> This aim shall be pursued through the organs of the Council by discussions of questions of common concern and by agreements and common action in economic, social, cultural, scientific, legal and administrative matters and in the maintenance and further realisation of human rights and fundamental freedoms.

Despite these grandiose ambitions, however, the Council of Europe was to be a disappointment to those who hoped that it might serve as the basis for a new West European state system. In part, the problem was that its aims were too vague; in part, that its decision-making structure was essentially intergovernmental and therefore weak; but mainly that some of its members, notably the UK, were not much interested in anything that went beyond limited and voluntary co-operation. (Ernest Bevin, British Foreign Secretary, commented on proposals for a really effective Council of Europe thus: 'Once you open that Pandora's box, you'll find it full of Trojan horses'.) That all said, the weaknesses of the Council should not be overstated. It was to perform, and continues to perform, certain useful functions – notably in the human rights field through its European Convention of Human Rights, and as a forum for the discussion of matters of common interest. (This latter function is valuable today not least because, with a current membership of twenty-five states, it is the largest West European regional grouping).

(2) Although it was not immediately apparent when hostilities ceased in 1945, the Second World War was to result in a fundamental redrawing of the political map of Europe. Most obviously, by the late 1940s it was clear that the legacy of war had left the Continent, and with it Germany, divided in two. In Winston Churchill's phrase an 'Iron Curtain' divided East from West.

In the West there was no question of the victorious powers – Britain and the United States – seeking or being able to impose anything like a Soviet-style straitjacket on the liberated countries. Nonetheless, if Western Europe did not quite take on the form of a bloc, liberal democratic systems were soon established, and not wholly dissimilar political ideas were soon prevailing, in most of the states. Inevitably this facilitated intergovernmental relations.

Perhaps the most important idea shared by the governments was one which stemmed directly from the East–West division: a determination to preserve Western Europe from Communism. Not only had the Soviet Union extended its influence far into the European heartland, but in France and Italy domestic communist parties were commanding considerable support and from 1947 were engaging in what looked to many like revolutionary activities. The United States shared this anti-communist concern, and the encouragement and assistance which it gave to the West European states after the war to co-operate was partly with this in mind. In March

1947 President Truman, stimulated by the events in Greece (where the Communists were trying to overthrow the government), outlined what became known as the Truman doctrine which amounted to a political guarantee of support to 'free peoples who are resisting attempted subjugation by armed minorities or by outside pressures'. This political commitment was quickly followed up in 1948 by economic assistance in the form of Marshall Aid, and in 1949 by military protection with the foundation of NATO and a guarantee to the then ten West European member states (Canada and the US brought the founding membership to twelve) of US military protection against a Soviet attack.

A role for the US in Western Europe at this time should not be seen as having been unwelcome for, contrary to the impression that is sometimes given, American aid was not unwillingly or insidiously imposed on the states but, rather, was actively sought. At the same time, the extent of the US influence should not be exaggerated. By its political, economic, and military interventions and assistance the US did exert integrationist pressures and did help to make a number of developments possible, but the US government wanted much more West European interstate integration than was to be achieved.

(3) With the post-war division of Europe, with the moving of the international power balance from European state relations to United States-Soviet relations, and with the onset of the Cold War from 1947–8 producing the possibility of Europe being the battleground between East and West, there was a sense from the late 1940s of Western Europe beginning to look like an identifiable political entity in a way in which it had not done before. Not all states or politicians shared this perspective, but amongst many of those who did it produced a desire that the voice of Western Europe should be heard on the world stage and a belief that this could be achieved only through unity and by speaking with one voice. For some of the smaller European states, which had rarely exercised much international influence and whose very existence had periodically been threatened by larger neighbours, the prospects of such co-operation were particularly attractive.

(4) The future of Germany naturally loomed large in the minds of those who had to deal with post-war reconstruction. Three times in seventy years, and twice in the twentieth century, Germany had occupied much of Europe. Rightly or wrongly it had come to be seen as innately aggressive. As a consequence, the initial inclination of

most governments after the war was to try and contain it in some way. Just how this should be done, however, divided the wartime allies, with the consequence that matters drifted until what was initially intended as an interim division of Germany into zones gave way, as the Cold War developed, into a *de jure* division: the Federal Republic of Germany (West Germany) and the German Democratic Republic (East Germany) were both formally constituted in 1949.

By this time the Soviet Union was replacing Germany as the perceived principal threat to democracy and stability in Western Europe. As this occurred those who were already arguing that a conciliatory approach towards Germany ought to be tried, (since a policy of punitive containment had demonstrably failed between the wars), saw their hands strengthened by a growing feeling that attempts must be made to avoid the development of a political vacuum in West Germany which the communists might attempt to exploit. Furthermore, and the United States government played an important role in pressing this view from the early 1950s, use of West Germany's power and wealth could help to reduce the contributions that other countries were making to the defence of Europe. The 'incorporation' of the Federal Republic into Western Europe thus had a number of political aspects to it.

Economic factors. Just as pre-war and wartime experiences helped to produce the United Nations, so did they stimulate an interest in the creation of new international economic and financial arrangements. The first fruits of this were realised at the Bretton Woods Conference in 1944 where the representatives of forty-four countries, with the UK and the USA playing the leading roles, agreed to the establishment of two new bodies. The first was the International Monetary Fund (IMF), which was to alleviate problems of currency instability by creating facilities for countries with temporary balance of payments difficulties to have access to short-term credit facilities. The second was the International Bank for Reconstruction and Development (the 'World Bank'), which was to provide long-term loans for schemes which necessitated a major investment. In 1947, at much the same time as the IMF and the World Bank became operative, international economic co-operation was taken a stage further when twenty-three countries negotiated the General Agreement on Tariffs and Trade (GATT) which had as its purpose the facilitating of trade through the lowering of international trade barriers.

Although West European governments (or, more usually, national representatives, since governments on the Continent were not properly restored until 1945–6) played their part in helping to create the new international economic arrangements, it was felt in many quarters that there should also be specifically West European based economic initiatives and organisations. In 1947–8 these feelings were given a focus, an impetus, and an urgency when the rapid post-war economic recovery that most states were able to engineer by the adoption of expansionist policies created massive balance of payments deficits and dollar shortages in particular. Governments were faced with major currency problems, with not being able to pay for their imports, and with the prospect of their economic recoveries coming to a sudden and premature end. In these circumstances, and for reasons that were not altogether altruistic – a strong Western Europe was in its political, security and economic interests too – the United States stepped in with the offer of Marshall Aid. But it was an offer that had attached to it the condition that the recipient states must endeavour to seek greater economic co-operation between themselves. As a result, the first major post-war Western European organisation, the Organisation for European Economic Co-operation (OEEC), was established, with sixteen founding member states in April 1948. Its task, in the short term, was to manage the aid, encourage joint economic policies, and discourage barriers to trade; in the longer term, its stated aim was to build 'a sound European economy through the co-operation of its members'. In the event, though the OEEC did some valuable work, the most notable perhaps being in establishing payments schemes which in the 1940s and 1950s did much to further trade between member countries, it never made much progress with its grander ambitions. Rather like the Council of Europe,its large and somewhat heterogeneous membership, coupled with the strictly intergovernmental nature of its decision-making structure, meant that ambitious proposals were always successfully opposed. Partly as a result of this, and partly in recognition of growing interdependence between all industrialised countries, the OEEC gave way, in 1961, to the Organisation for Economic Co-operation and Development (OECD) whose membership was to be open to non-European countries and which was to have broader objectives reflecting wider and changing interests.

TABLE 1.1

Membership of Western and Western European organisations

	Western Organisations		Western European Organisations				
	NATO	OECD	Council of Europe	European Community	EFTA	WEU	Nordic Council
Australia		√(1971)					
Austria		√(F)	√(1956)		√(F)		
Belgium	√(F)	√(F)	√(F)	√(F)		√(F)	
Canada	√(F)	√(F)					
Cyprus			√(1961)				
Czechoslovakia			√(1991)				
Denmark	√(F)	√(F)	√(F)	√(1973)	Withdrew in 1972 on joining EC		√(F)
Finland		√(1969)	√(1989)		√(1961)		√(F)
France	S(Since 1966)(F)	√(F)	√(F)	√(F)		√(F)	
Germany	√(1955)	√(F)	√(1951)	√(F)		√(F)	
Greece	√(1952)	√(F)	√(1949)	√(1981)			
Hungary			√(1990)				
Iceland	√(F)	√(F)	√(1950)		√(1970)		√(F)
Ireland		√(F)	√(F)	√(1973)			
Italy	√(F)	√(F)	√(F)	√(F)		√(F)	

Japan		√(1964)			
Liechtenstein					
Luxembourg	√(F)	√(F)	√(1978)	√(F)		√(F)
Malta			√(1965)	√(F)		√(F)
Netherlands	√(F)	√(F)	√(F)	√(F)		
New Zealand		√(1973)				
Norway	√(F)	√(F)	√(F)	√(F)	√(F)	√(F)
Portugal	√(F)	√(F)	√(1976)	√(1986)	Withdrew in 1985 on joining EC	√(1988)
San Marino			√(1988)			
Spain	S (1982)		√(1977)	√(1986)		√(1988)
Sweden	√(F)	√(F)	√(F)	√(F)	√(F)	
Switzerland	√(F)	√(F)	√(1962)	√(F)	√(F)	
Turkey	√(1952)	√(F)	√(1949)	√(F)		
United Kingdom	√(F)	√(F)	√(F)	√(1973)	Withdrew in 1972 on joining EC	√(F)
United States	√(F)	√(F)	√(F)	√(F)	√(F)	

Note

Dates in brackets refer to when membership of post foundation members came into effect.

Situation in February 1991.

KEY √ Full member
      S Special status or associate member
    (F) Founding member

The OEEC thus stemmed from post-war circumstances that mixed the general with the particular. That is to say, attitudes coming out of the war that favoured economic co-operation between West European states were given a direction by particular requirements that were related to the war and its immediate aftermath. Only three years later, in a way that is described in the next chapter, a similar mixture of general underlying and specific triggering factors combined to produce the first of the European Communities: the European Coal and Steel Community (ECSC).

It is, of course, true that the effect of some of the political and economic factors that have just been considered, such as the existence of Resistance leaders in governments, were essentially short-term. It might also be argued that some of the factors, such as the increased need and willingness of the states to co-operate with one another to promote economic growth, were not so much caused by the war as given a push by it. But what can hardly be disputed is that the factors taken together produced a set of circumstances associated with the war that enabled Western European co-operation and integration to get off the ground in the 1940s and 1950s.

States naturally differed in the particulars and the perceptions of their post-war situations. As a result, there was no general agreement as to just exactly what the new spirit of co-operation should attempt to achieve. Many different schemes were advanced and many different organisations were established to tackle particular issues, problems and requirements. The war did not thus produce anything remotely like a united West European movement between the states. But it did produce new realities and changed attitudes which enabled, or forced, virtually all the states to recognise at least some commonalities and shared interests. As a consequence, it became possible for new interstate European organisations to be established. Of these organisations, those that were able to offer clear advantages and benefits to members were able to act as a base for further developments. As the ECSC in particular was quickly to demonstrate, co-operation and integration can breed more of the same.

Interdependence

It has become customary to suggest that whilst both political and economic factors were crucial to Western European co-operation and integration in the formative post-war years, the former have now declined in relation to the latter. The impact of modernisation is generally agreed to be a key reason for this. It has broadened the international agenda from its traditional power and security concerns to embrace a range of economic and social issues, and at the same time it has produced an interconnectedness and interrelatedness between states, especially in the economic and monetary spheres, that amounts to an interdependence.

Economic interdependence arises particularly from three features of the post-1945 world: the enormously increased volume of world trade; the internationalisation of production – in which multi-national corporations have played a prominent part; and – especially since the early 1970s – the fluctuations and uncertainties associated with currency exchange rates and international monetary arrangements. As a result of interdependence a wide variety of economic and financial issues can no longer be limited to, and indeed in some respects do not even bear much relationship to, national boundaries. States are increasingly vulnerable to outside events and are increasingly unable to act in isolation. They must consult, co-operate and, some would argue, integrate with one another in the interests of international and national economic stability and growth.

When the nature of the problem has been seen to require a truly international economic effort most West European states have been prepared to try solutions at this level: in the IMF, in the Bank for International Settlements, in Western Economic Summits, and elsewhere. Where a regional response has seemed to be more appropriate or more practical, West European-based arrangements have been sought. The most obvious examples of such arrangements are those associated with the European Community. For instance: the Community's internal and external trading agreements are rooted in the belief that successful trade development is dependent on co-ordinated, ordered, stable, and open commercial rules and relations; the European Monetary System (EMS) stemmed from the external stimulus of the withdrawal by the US in the 1970s from its management of the international monetary system; and the gradual movement of the Community into advanced research is a response to an increasing belief that the Western European states must show a greater willingness to pool their scientific and technological resources and knowledge if they are to compete successfully in world markets against the Americans, the Japanese, and other competitors.

Economic interdependence is not the only feature of modern interdependence. Advances in communications and travel have necessarily placed on the international and European agendas issues which a generation or two ago either did not exist or were seen as being of purely domestic concern. Now it is commonly accepted that if they are to be tackled with any prospect of success they must be dealt with at an interstate level. Governments thus discuss, and in Western Europe have adopted understandings and made decisions on, matters as diverse as transfrontier television arrangements, data protection, action against drug traffickers, and football hooliganism.

But despite all the attention that is now given to modern interdependence as the motor of West European integration, and despite too the associated assertion that economic factors now far outweigh political factors in shaping the relations between the West European – and particularly the EC – states, the case should not be overstated. One reason why it should not be is that modern interdependence does not necessarily produce an inescapable and wholly unavoidable set of integrationist processes and developments: there is certainly an integrationist logic attached to modern interdependence, but for much of integration to actually proceed political choices and decisions have to be made. Another reason is that interdependence of a quite different kind – different in that it does not arise from modernisation, but rather from the diminished significance of the West European states in the age of the superpowers – has played a part in encouraging co-operation, and even a certain amount of integration, in respect of political and security considerations. In respect of political considerations, the decline in the power and weight of the individual West European states in the international system that has been apparent since at least 1945 has provided a powerful inducement for them to try and speak as one if they wish to exert a significant influence on world political events. Most of the Community states do wish to exert such an influence and so, since the early 1970s, there has been a gradual strengthening of the Community's European Political Co-operation (EPC) machinery which provides for extensive consultations, and encourages the adoption of joint positions, on foreign policy issues. In respect of security considerations, the perception, until recently at least, of the Soviet Union as Western Europe's main political enemy, allied with the inability of any single West European state to offer by itself a wholly credible defence capability, has encouraged close military co-operation in the context of both the Western Alliance and associated Western European defence groupings.

National Considerations

Whilst most Western European states since 1945 have paid at least lip service to the idea of a united Western Europe there has never been any consensus between them on what this is to mean in practice. The rhetoric has often been grand, but discussions on specific proposals have usually revealed considerable variations in ambitions, motives, intentions and perceptions. Most crucially of all, states have differed in their assessments of the consequences for them, in terms of gains and losses, of forging closer relations with their neighbours. As a result, some states have been prepared, and have been able, to go further than others, or have been prepared to do so at an earlier time. There has not, therefore, been a coherent and ordered movement towards West European unity. In the late 1940s and 1950s most states were willing to be associated with intergovernmental organisations that made few demands on them – and hence joined the newly created OEEC and the Council of Europe – but there was no similar breadth of support when organisations were proposed that went beyond intergovernmental co-operation into supranational integration. Consequently, the more ambitious post-war schemes – for the ECSC, for a European Defence Community (EDC – which in the event was never established), and for the EEC and Euratom – initially involved only a restricted membership. It was not until circumstances and attitudes in other states changed, and until an obstacle that emerged amongst the founding states themselves in the form of General de Gaulle was removed, that the Community's membership opened out in the 1970s and 1980s to include eventually most, though still not all, West European states.

So although all states have long been touched by at least some of the factors that have been examined on the last few pages, the differences between the states have been such that their interest in, and enthusiasm for, co-operation and integration processes has varied, both with regard to nature and timing. Three broad categories of states can be identified:

The six founding members of the European Community. Belgium, France, West Germany, Italy, Luxembourg and the Netherlands – the six states which, in 1951, signed the Treaty of Paris to found the ECSC and in 1957 signed the Treaties of Rome to found the EEC and Euratom – were the first to show a willingness to go beyond the essentially intergovernmental organisations which were established in Western Europe in the late 1940s. Cautiously, tentatively, and not without reservations, each took the view that the benefits of integration, as opposed to just co-operation, would outweigh what looked to be the major disadvantage – some loss of sovereignty. Some of the perceptions of the advantages of creating organisations with supranational characteristics were shared by all of the six. But there were also more nationally-based hopes and ambitions:

● For the three Benelux countries the experience of the war had re-emphasised their vulnerability to hostile and more powerful neighbours and the particular desirability of being on good terms with West Germany and France. Related to this, their size – Belgium and the Netherlands were only middle-ranking European powers whilst Luxembourg was an almost insignificant one – meant that their only real prospect of being able to exercise any sort of influence in Europe, let alone the world, was through a more unified interstate system. As for economic considerations, the idea of integration was perhaps more acceptable to them than it was to most other states since their own Benelux economic agreements and arrangements pre-dated the war, and negotiations to relaunch and deepen these were under way well before the war ended. Finally, there was the simple fact that none of the Benelux states was in a strong enough position to ignore Franco-German led initiatives for economic integration.

● Italy, too, had a number of particular reasons for welcoming close relations with other West European states. First, after over twenty years of Fascist rule followed by military defeat, European integration offered the opportunity of a new start, and from a basis of respectability. Second, in May 1947, as also occurred in France, the Communist Party left government and for some years thereafter seemed to be intent on fermenting internal revolution. The clear anti-Communist tenor of other West European governments looked comforting, and a possible basis of assistance, to Italy's nervous Christian Democratic-led governments. Third, Italy faced economic difficulties on all fronts: with unemployment, inflation, balance of payments, currency stability, and – especially in the south – poverty. Almost any scheme which offered the possibility of finding new markets and generating economic growth was to be welcomed.

● Integration helped French governments to deal with two of their key post-war policy goals: the containment of Germany, and economic growth. The ECSC was especially important in this regard in the early 1950s, offering the opportunity to break down age old barriers and hostilities on the one hand, and giving France access to vital German raw materials and markets on the other. Later in the 1950s, when 'the German problem' was seen to be no longer so pressing, but when German economic competition looked to be an increasing threat, France took steps to ensure that as part of the price of continued integration certain French interests would be given special treatment (see below).

● For Konrad Adenauer, the West German Chancellor from 1949 to 1963, it was to be primarily in and through West European unification that Germany would re-establish itself in the international mainstream and thereby regain its self-respect. Western Europe would also, along with the Atlantic Alliance, provide a much-needed buttress against the perceived threat from the East. At more specific levels the ECSC was a means by which West Germany could rid itself of Allied restrictions and interference, whilst the more open markets of the EEC offered immense opportunities for what, in the 1950s, quickly became the fastest growing economy in Western Europe.

The six post-foundation members of the European Community. Although all were to make approaches to the European Community between 1961–3 for either full or associated membership, and although all were to become full members by 1986, Denmark, Greece, Ireland, Portugal, Spain and the United Kingdom kept and/or were kept to the fringes of the integrative developments in the 1950s and did not become Community members at that time. There were a number of reasons for this:

● In the case of Spain and Portugal, political and economic circumstances were unfavourable. The political circumstances were that both countries were authoritarian dictatorships to which the democratic governments of the founding six did not wish to be too closely attached. The economic circumstances were that both were predominantly agricultural and underdeveloped, and both were pursuing essentially autarkic economic policies until the end of the 1950s: factors which hardly made them suitable candidates for the ECSC, and which had the knock-on effect of excluding them from the EEC negotiations which the founding six opened up only to the UK.

● The Greek economy was similarly unsuitable for ECSC or EEC membership, being predominantly peasant based. Additionally, Greece's history, culture and geographical position all rather put it outside the West European mainstream.

● Ireland and Denmark were also heavily dependent on agriculture and thus had little interest in the ECSC. As for the EEC, there were several reasons to doubt that it would be to their benefit, the most important of which was that both countries had strong economic and historical links elsewhere: in Denmark's case with the other Scandinavian countries and with the UK; in Ireland's case with the UK.

● Three factors were especially important in governing the UK's attitude. First, Britain saw herself as operating within what Churchill described as three overlapping and interlocking relationships: the Empire and Commonwealth; the Atlantic Alliance and the 'special relationship' with the United States; and Western Europe. Until the early 1960s Western Europe was seen as being the least important of these. Second, British governments were not prepared to accept the loss of sovereignty that integration implied. There were several reasons for this, in particular: Britain's long established parliamentary tradition; the record, in which there was considerable pride, of not having been invaded or controlled by foreign powers in modern times; a generally held view that cessation of sovereignty was neither desirable nor necessary, since Britain was still a world power of the first rank; and a certain distaste with the idea of being dependent on the not altogether highly regarded governments and countries of 'the Continent'. Third, Britain's circumstances were such that three of the four main integrationist organisations to be proposed in the 1950s had few attractions in terms of their specific areas of concern: the restrictions on national decision-making powers entailed in the ECSC looked very unappealing to a country whose coal and steel capacity far exceeded that of any of the six; the EDC would have limited governmental manoeuverability and options at a time when Britain's defences were already stretched by the attempt to maintain a world role; and Euratom looked as though it would involve sharing secrets with less advanced nuclear powers. Only the EEC seemed to have much to offer, but amongst the problems it carried with it was its proposed supranationalism. From 1955 to

1958 attempts were made to persuade the six not to be so ambitious and to direct their attention to the construction of a West European free trade area, but with no success. As a result, and with a view also to increasing her bargaining power with the six, Britain looked elsewhere: to other non-signatories of the Treaty of Rome. This led, in January 1960, to the Stockholm Convention which established the European Free Trade Association (EFTA). Its founding members were Austria, Denmark, Norway, Portugal, Sweden, Switzerland and the UK.

The reasons why the six non-founding states were later to turn to the Community are considered in Chapter 2.

Non-members of the European Community. Six significant West European states remain which are neither founding nor post-foundation members of the European Community: Austria, Finland, Iceland, Norway, Sweden and Switzerland. There are a number of reasons why these countries are not members of the Community.

● Until recently, Austrian, Swedish and Swiss neutrality was a major obstacle to Community accession. There was some doubt about the importance of the neutrality issue in the 1960s and both Austria and Sweden considered the possibility of applying for membership, but the uncertainty was seemingly removed in 1970 when the Community's Council of Ministers agreed that full membership could be granted only to those countries which accepted all of the Community's aims, obligations and rights, including the declared objectives of economic and monetary union and also political union. In the late 1980s, however, the view that neutrality was an obstacle to EC membership began to be reconsidered. The changes in the Soviet Union, the upheavals in Eastern Europe, and the end of the Cold War, were all seen as diminishing the relevance of the neutrality issue. Moreover, as the advocates of membership pointed out, Ireland claims to be a neutral country but this has scarcely weakened its ability to function as an effective Community member. Following on from this new, more flexible thinking, Austria applied for Community membership in 1989, and Sweden – following a vote in 1990 by the Swedish Parliament in favour of an application for Community membership – indicated that it would probably apply in 1991.

● Several factors have, in the past, resulted in Community membership not being seriously considered by Finland. Prominent amongst these have been: the country's relative geographical isolation; Finland's close links with other Scandinavian countries, notably Sweden; and Finland's special position in relation to the Soviet Union. None of these factors is now seen as constituting an insuperable obstacle, and a Finnish application, perhaps in conjunction with other Scandinavian applications, is quite likely in the future.

● Norway has sought Community membership on three occasions, linking its applications to those of the UK in 1962, 1967, and 1969. On the third occasion terms of entry were agreed, but were then rejected by the Norwegian people in a referendum, following a campaign in which suspicions about the implications for agriculture, fishing, and national sovereignty were all raised. Another Norwegian application is probable before too long.

● Iceland considered the possibility of Community membership at the time of the 1973 enlargement but concluded that there were too many policy difficulties in the way, especially in regard to fishing. Should a further application be considered fishing will continue to be a major problem because the Community's Common Fisheries Policy would require Iceland to allow Community vessels access to Icelandic waters.

It should not be thought that the non-membership of these six countries is an indication of a past or a present narrow nationalism or of an unwillingness to work within Western European settings. On the contrary, though each has, in the past at least, had reasons for not wishing to join the integrated structure of the Community, each has also displayed an interest in, and a willingness to be part of, West European intergovernmental organisations:

● All are members of the OECD and of the Council of Europe.

● Finland, Iceland, Norway and Sweden, plus Denmark, together constitute the Nordic Council. This organisation was established by a treaty signed in 1953 which specified the aims as being the development of co-operation in the fields of legislation, of cultural, social and economic policies, and of transport and communications. The achievements of the Nordic Council have, in practice, perhaps not wholly lived up to these rather ambitious aims but, at a minimum, the Council does provide a useful forum for joint discussions between ministers, parliamentarians and civil servants on matters of mutual interest and potential co-operation.

● Most importantly of all, the six non-Community states make up the membership of EFTA – 'Little Europe' as it is sometimes called. When it was constituted in 1960 (with Denmark, Portugal and the UK then also as members, but not, at that stage, Finland or Iceland), EFTA had two principal objectives: first, the establishment of a free trade area in industrial products between the member countries; second, making Western Europe as a whole a free trade area for industrial goods. Both of these objectives have been broadly achieved: the first with the removal of virtually all customs duties and quantitative restrictions on trade in industrial products between EFTA countries in 1966; the second with the full entry into force in 1977 of an industrial free trade area between the EC and EFTA.

Geographical proximity, shared needs and objectives, and the EC-EFTA free trade area have all helped to ensure that relations between 'the twelve' and 'the six' are close, and indeed that they have been further developed through co-operation in such areas as the environment, scientific and technical research, and transport. The relations are not, however, from EFTA's viewpoint, wholly satisfactory. One reason for this is that the EC is collectively much stronger than EFTA. A second, and related reason, is that the EC is prone to present EFTA with *de facto* situations to which EFTA countries have little option but to adjust – as, for example, is often the case when the Community lays down product specifications. This latter problem, of having to accept trading rules which they have played no part in helping to formulate, has been of increasing concern to EFTA countries as the Community's programme to complete the internal market by 1992 has gathered pace. It is a concern which has played an important part in encouraging the EFTA countries to reconsider the attraction of Community membership, and a concern too which was very much in the minds of EFTA governments when in 1990 they opened negotiations with the EC with a view to creating a European Economic Area (EEA) or European Economic Space (EES). What the projected EEA, if it is established, will look like, and what it may bring in its wake, remains to be seen, for there are an array of views on both the EC and the EFTA sides. Minimalists usually have in mind an extension of the Community's internal market to the EFTA countries coupled with perhaps some consultative EFTA input into EC decision-making. Maximalists tend to be interested in not only extending the internal market, but using the EEA as a device for something broader – to help bring the EFTA countries into the Community, or to provide a further impetus to West European, and ultimately pan-European, economic, monetary, and political union.

Concluding Remarks

Since the Second World War the way in which West European governments relate and communicate with one another has been transformed. As part of this transformation a key role has been played by new international governmental organisations. Some of these are world-wide in their composition, others are regionally based; some have sweeping but vaguely defined responsibilities, others have specific sectoral briefs; some are purely intergovernmental in structure, others are overlain with supranational powers. At a minimum all provide frameworks in which national representatives meet with one another to discuss matters of mutual interest.

At the West European level the European Community is the best known organisation. But it is far from being the only one, and its three constituent Communities were far from being the first organisations to be established. The reality is that, since the war, many proposals have been advanced, and many arrangements have been developed, involving co-operation and integration between the states. The more ambitious of these have sought to bring the whole of Western Europe together in some sort of federal union. The more cautious, and, it may be thought, the more realistic, have limited themselves to modest aims for only some of the states.

So, although the logic of circumstances and of political and economic changes have brought the states much more closely together, there can hardly be said to have been a common and coherent integrationist force at work in Western Europe in the post-war years. The states have not been bound together in a common mission. This is not to say that there have not been those who have dreamed of a United States of Europe, or that there have not been many who have participated in new interstate arrangements entertaining hopes that they would constitute a basis for further, more ambitious, developments. But it is to say that, for the most part, attitudes and actions have been governed less by the visionary and more by the many differing perceptions of the necessary.

2

The Development of the Community

The European Coal and Steel Community

Much of the early impetus behind the first of the European Communities, the ECSC, emanated from two Frenchmen. Jean Monnet, who had pioneered France's successful post-war experiment with indicative economic planning, provided much of the technical and administrative initiative and behind-the-scenes drive. Robert Schuman, the French Foreign Minister from 1948 to early 1953, acted as the political advocate. Both were ardent supporters of European unity; both believed that the OEEC and the Council of Europe – where anyone could be exempted from a decision – could not provide the impetus that was required; and both came to the conclusion that, in Monnet's words, 'A start would have to be made by doing something both more practical and more ambitious. National sovereignty would have to be tackled more boldly and on a narrower front'.

Many of those who were attracted to the ECSC saw it in very restrictive terms: as an organisation that might further certain limited and carefully defined purposes. Certainly it would not have been established had it not offered to potential member states, and in particular to its two main pillars, France and West Germany, the possibility that it might act as a means of satisfying specific and pressing national interests and needs (see previous chapter). But for some, not least Monnet and Schuman, the interest was much more ambitious and long term. When announcing the plan in May 1950,

Schuman – in what subsequently became known as the Schuman Declaration – was quite explicit that the proposals were intended to be but the first step in the realisation of a vision; a vision of a united Europe which would have Franco-German reconciliation at its heart. But, he warned: 'Europe will not be made all at once or according to a single general plan. It will be built through concrete achievements, which first create a *de facto* solidarity'. In similar vein, Monnet informed governments during the negotiations:

> The Schuman proposals provide a basis for the building of a new Europe through the concrete achievement of a supranational regime within a limited but controlling area of economic effort . . . The indispensable first principle of these proposals is the abnegation of sovereignty in a limited but decisive field.

Konrad Adenauer agreed with this. Addressing the Bundestag in June 1950 he stated:

> Let me make a point of declaring in so many words and in full agreement, not only with the French Government but also with M. Jean Monnet, that the importance of this project is above all political and not economic.

Schuman made it clear in his Declaration that whilst he hoped other countries would also participate, France and West Germany were going to proceed with the plan in any event (West Germany having already agreed privately in principle). Italy, Belgium, Luxembourg and the Netherlands took up the invitation, and in April 1951 the six countries signed the Treaty of Paris which established the ECSC. It came into operation in July 1952.

The Treaty broke new ground in two principal ways. First, its policy aims were extremely ambitious, entailing not just the creation of a free trade area, but also the laying of the foundations of a common market in some of the basic materials of any industrialised society: coal, coke, iron ore, steel and scrap. This, it was hoped, would ensure orderly supplies to all member states, would produce a rational expansion and modernisation of production, and would improve the conditions and lifestyles of those working in the industries. Second, it was the first of the European interstate organisations to display significant supranational characteristics.

These were found in the new central institutions that were established with powers, amongst other things, to: see to the abolition and prohibition of internal tariff barriers, state subsidies and special charges, and restrictive practices; fix prices under certain conditions; harmonise external commercial policy by, for example, setting minimum and maximum rates of customs duties on coal and steel imports from third countries; and impose levies on coal and steel production to finance the ECSC's activities. Four main institutions were created:

The High Authority was charged 'To ensure that the objectives set out in this Treaty are attained in accordance with the provisions thereof' (Article 8 ECSC Treaty). To enable it to perform its task the High Authority could issue, either on its own initiative or after receiving the assent of the Council of Ministers: decisions (which were to be binding in all respects in the member states); recommendations (which were to be binding in their objectives); and opinions (which were not to have binding force). Matters on which the High Authority was granted decision-making autonomy included the prohibition of subsidies and aids, decisions on whether agreements between undertakings were permissible or not, action against restrictive practices, the promotion of research, and the control of prices under certain conditions. It could impose fines on those who disregarded its decisions.

The High Authority thus had a formidable array of powers at its disposal and this, when taken in conjunction with its membership, gave it a clear supranational character. There were to be nine members, including at least one from each member state, and, crucially, all were to be 'completely independent in the performance of their duties'. In other words, none was to be, or to regard himself as being, a national delegate or representative.

In a number of respects the High Authority's powers were stronger than those which were to be given to the High Authority's equivalent, the Commission, under the Treaties of Rome. This has meant that since the institutions of the three Communities were merged in 1967, the Commission – which assumed the High Authority's powers – has had rather more room for independent manoeuvre when acting under the Treaty of Paris than it has when acting under the Treaties of Rome. In practice, however, it has not always been possible for these greater powers to be used to the full: from the earliest days of the ECSC political realities have dictated that the High Authority/Commission be sensitive to governmental opinions and policies.

The Council of Ministers was set up mainly as a result of Benelux concern that if the High Authority had too much power, and there was no forum through which the states could exercise some control, the ECSC might be too Franco-German dominated. Ministers from the national governments were to constitute the membership of the Council, each state having one representative.

'The Council shall exercise its powers in the cases provided for and in the manner set out in this Treaty, in particular in order to harmonise the actions of the High Authority and that of the Governments, which are responsible for the general economic policies of their countries' (Article 26 ECSC Treaty). More specifically, the Treaty gave the Council formal control over some, but very far from all, of the High Authority's actions: the Council had, for instance, to give its assent to the declaration of a manifest crisis which opened the door to production quotas. Decision-making procedures in the Council were to depend on the matter under consideration: sometimes a unanimous vote would be required, sometimes a qualified majority, sometimes a simple majority.

Practice has shown the Council to be not altogether consistent in the manner in which it has exercised its role under the ECSC Treaty. On the one hand, a general reluctance of the states to lose too much power over their domestic industries has normally resulted in the Council seeking to take most major decisions itself. Since decision-making in the Council has customarily proceeded on the basis of consensus, and since the states have often been unable to agree when difficult decisions have been called for, this has frequently led to no, or to very weak, decision-making. On the other hand, when practicalities and political convenience have combined to suggest a less Council-centred decision-making approach, as they did with steel from the late 1970s, then the Council has been prepared to allow the High Authority/Commission a considerable measure of independence.

The Common Assembly's role was to provide a democratic input into ECSC decision-making. In practice it can hardly be said to have done so in the early years: members were not elected but were chosen by national parliaments, and the Assembly's powers – notwithstanding an ability to pass a motion of censure on the High Authority – were essentially only advisory. However, the expansion of the remit of the Assembly under the Rome Treaties to cover all three Communities, plus developments in the 1970s and 1980s such as the introduction of direct elections and more streamlined procedures, have increasingly made for a more effective Assembly (or European Parliament as it is now called).

The Court of Justice was created to settle conflicts between the states, between the organs of the Community, and between the states and the organs. Its judgements were to be enforceable within the territory of the member states. In similar fashion to the Assembly, but not the High Authority or Council of Ministers which remained separate until 1967, the Court assumed responsibility for all three Communities in 1958.

In addition to these four main institutions a Consultative Committee, made up of producers, workers and other interested parties, was also created. Its role was to be, and has been, purely advisory.

In its early years the ECSC was judged to be an economic success. Customs tariffs and quotas were abolished, progress was made in removing non-tariff barriers to trade, the restructuring of the industries was assisted, politicians and civil servants from the member states developed the practice of working with one another, and, above all, output and interstate trade rapidly increased. (Although many economists would now query whether the increases were *because* of the ECSC.) As a result the ECSC helped to pave the way for further integration.

However, the success of the early years was soon checked. In 1958–9, when cheap oil imports and a fall in energy consumption combined to produce an overcapacity in coal production, the ECSC was faced with its first major crisis – and failed the test. The member states rejected the High Authority's proposals for a Community solution and sought their own, unco-ordinated, protective measures. The coal crisis thus revealed that the High Authority was not as powerful as many had believed and that it was not in a position to impose a general policy on the states if they were resolved to resist.

This relative weakness of the High Authority/Commission to press policies right through is one of the principal reasons why truly integrated West European coal and steel industries, in which prices and distributive decisions are a consequence of an open and free market, have not emerged. Many barriers to trade still remain. Some of these, such as restrictive practices and national subsidies, the High Authority/Commission has tried to remove, but with only limited success. Others, particularly in the steel sector (see Chapter 9), have been formulated and utilised by the Commission itself as its task has switched from encouraging expansion to managing contraction. But arguably the major problem with the ECSC has been that as coal and steel have declined in importance in relation to other energy sources, what has increasingly been required is not so much policies for coal and steel in isolation, but a co-ordinated and effective Community energy policy. National differences have prevented any such policy being possible.

From the ECSC to the EEC

In addition to the impetus that came from the ECSC there was another institutional development in the 1950s which played a particularly important role in paving the way for the creation of the two further European Communities that were to be created in 1957. This was the projected European Defence Community (EDC).

In the early 1950s, to the background of the Cold War and the outbreak of the Korean War, many Western politicians and military strategists took the view that there was a need for greater Western European co-operation in the field of defence. As part of this there was seen to be a pressing need to integrate West Germany – which was not a member of NATO – into the Western Alliance. The problem was that some European countries, especially France, were not yet ready for German rearmament, whilst West Germany itself, though willing to rearm, was not willing to do so on the basis of the tightly controlled and restricted conditions that other countries appeared to have in mind for it. In these circumstances the French Prime Minister, René Pleven, launched proposals in October 1950 which offered a possible way forward. In announcing his plan to the National Assembly he stated that the French government 'proposes the creation, for common defence, of a European Army under the authority of the political institutions of a united Europe'. By the end of 1951 the same six governments which were in the process of establishing the ECSC had agreed to establish an EDC. Its institutional structure was to be similar to the ECSC: a Joint Defence

Commission, a Council of Ministers, an advisory Assembly and a Court of Justice. In May 1952 a draft EDC Treaty was signed.

But, in the event, the EDC, and the European Political Community which increasingly came to be associated with it, were not established. Ratification problems arose in France and in Italy, and in August 1954 the French National Assembly rejected the EDC by 319 votes to 264 with 43 abstentions. There were a number of reasons why it did so: continuing unease at the thought of rearming Germany; concern that French governments would not have sole control of their military forces; doubts about the efficiency of an integrated force; disquiet that the strongest European military power (the UK) was not participating; and a feeling that, with the end of the Korean War and the death of Stalin, the EDC was not as necessary as it had seemed when it was initially proposed.

Following the collapse of the EDC, an alternative, and altogether less demanding, approach was taken to the still outstanding question of West Germany's contribution to the defence of the West. This took the form of a revival and extension of the Brussels Treaty 'for collaboration in economic, social and cultural matters and for collective defence' that had been signed in 1948 by the three Benelux countries, France and the UK. At a conference in London in the autumn of 1954 West Germany and Italy agreed to accede to the Brussels Treaty, and all seven countries agreed that the new arrangements should be incorporated into a Western European Union (WEU). The WEU came into effect in May 1955 as a loosely structured, essentially consultative, primarily defence-orientated, organisation that, amongst other things, permitted West German rearmament subject to various constraints. It also enabled West Germany to become a member of NATO.

The failure of the EDC, especially when set alongside the 'success' of the WEU, highlighted the difficulties involved in pressing ahead too quickly with integrationist proposals. In particular, it showed that quasi-federalist approaches in politically sensitive areas would meet with resistance. But, at the same time, the fact that such an ambitious scheme had come so close to adoption demonstrated that alternative initiatives, especially perhaps if they were based on the original Schuman view that political union was best achieved through economic integration, might well be successful. It was partly with this in mind that the Foreign Ministers of the ECSC six met at Messina in June 1955 to discuss proposals which had been made by the three Benelux countries for further economic integration. At their Conference the Ministers agreed on a resolution which included the following:

> The governments of Belgium, France, the Federal Republic of Germany, Italy, Luxembourg and the Netherlands consider that the moment has arrived to initiate a new phase on the path of constructing Europe. They believe that this has to be done principally in the economic sphere, and regard it as necessary to continue the creation of a united Europe through an expansion of joint institutions, the gradual fusion of national economies, the creation of a common market, and the gradual co-ordination of social policies. Such a policy seems to them indispensable if Europe is to maintain her position in the world, regain her influence, and achieve a steady increase in the living standards of her population.

To give effect to the Messina Resolution a committee of governmental representatives and experts was established under the chairmanship of the Belgian Foreign Minister, Paul-Henri Spaak. The UK was invited to participate and did so until November 1955, but then withdrew when it became apparent that UK hopes of limiting developments to the establishment of a loose free trade area were not acceptable to the six. In April 1956 the Foreign Ministers accepted the report of the Spaak Committee and used it as the basis for negotiations which, in 1957, produced the two Treaties of Rome: the more important of these Treaties established the European Economic Community (EEC), the other created the European Atomic Energy Community (Euratom).

Both before and after April 1956 negotiations between the six governments were extensive and intense. In very broad terms it can be said that clear provisions were made in the Treaties for those areas on which the governments were able to reach agreement, whilst where there were divisions matters were largely left aside for further negotiations and were either omitted from the Treaties altogether or were referred to only in a general way. So, in the EEC Treaty, the future rules on trade were set out fairly clearly, but only guiding principles were laid down for social policy and for agricultural policy.

The inclusion in the EEC Treaty of topics such as social policy and agricultural policy highlights the fact that the content of the Treaties reflected a series of compromises between the six, especially between the two strongest countries – France and West Germany. France

feared that Germany was likely to be the main beneficiary of the
more open markets of the proposed customs union and so looked for
compensation elsewhere. This took a number of forms. For instance:
insisting on special protection for agriculture – the French farmer
had historically been well protected from foreign competition and
around one fifth of the French population still earned their living
from the land; pressing the case of an atomic energy Community,
which would help guarantee France greater independence in energy
through joint use of resources; and seeking privileged relations with
the six for France's overseas dependencies.

Eventually the negotiations were completed, and, on 25 March
1957, the two Treaties were signed. Only in France and Italy were
there any problems with ratification: the French Chamber of
Deputies voted 342 for and 239 against, and the Italian Chamber
of Deputies voted 311 for and 144 against. In both countries the
largest bloc opposition came from the Communists. The Treaties
came into effect on 1 January 1958.

The Constitution of the European Community

The European Community thus has three founding treaties: the
Treaty of Paris, which was examined above; the Treaty of Rome
establishing Euratom; and the Treaty of Rome establishing the EEC.
These Treaties have been subsequently supplemented and amended
by other Treaties and Acts. Taken together, the three founding
Treaties, plus the supplementing and amending Treaties and Acts,
constitute what may be regarded as the constitution of the Community. That is to say, they provide the fundamental legal framework on which the Community is based.

Of the two Rome Treaties the EEC Treaty was, and is, by far the
most important. Article 2 of the Treaty laid down the following
broad objectives:

> The Community shall have as its task, by establishing a common
> market and progressively approximately the economic policies of
> Member States, to promote throughout the Community a harmo-
> nious development of economic activities, a continuous and
> balanced expansion, an increase in stability, an accelerated
> raising of the standard of living and closer relations between the
> states belonging to it.

DOCUMENT 2.1
Treaty establishing the European Community: contents

	Articles
Preamble	
Part One – Principles	1–8
Part Two – Foundations of the Community	
Title I – Free Movement of Goods	9–11
Chapter 1: The Customs Union	
Section 1: Elimination of Customs Duties between Member States	12–17
Section 2: Setting up of the Common Customs Tariff	18–29
Chapter 2: Elimination of Quantative Restrictions between Member States	30–37
Title II – Agriculture	38–47
Title III – Free Movement of Persons, Services and Capital	
Chapter 1: Workers	48–51
Chapter 2: Right of Establishment	52–58
Chapter 3: Services	59–66
Chapter 4: Capital	67–73
Title IV – Transport	74–84
Part Three – Policy of the Community	
Title I – Common Rules	
Chapter 1: Rules on Competition	
Section 1: Rules Applying to Undertakings	85–90
Section 2: Dumping	91
Section 3: Aids Granted by States	92–94
Chapter 2: Tax provisions	95–99
Chapter 3: Approximation of Laws	100–102
Title II – Economic Policy	
Chapter 1: Conjunctural Policy[1]	103
Chapter 2: Balance of Payments	104–109
Chapter 3: Commercial Policy	110–116
Title III – Social Policy	
Chapter 1: Social Provisions	117–122
Chapter 2: The European Social Fund	123–128
Title IV – The European Investment Bank[2]	129–130
Part Four – Association of the Overseas Countries and Territories	131–136
Part Five – Institutions of the Community	
Title I – Provisions Governing the Institutions	
Chapter 1: The Institutions	
Section 1: The Assembly	137–144
Section 2: The Council	145–154
Section 3: The Commission	155–163
Section 4: The Court of Justice	164–188
Chapter 2: Provisions Common to Several Institutions	189–192
Chapter 3: The Economic and Social Committee	193–198
Title II – Financial Provisions	199–209
Part Six – General and Final Provisions	210–240
Setting up of the Institutions	241–246
Final Provisions	247–248

---

[1] Under the Single European Act a new Chapter 1 is inserted: 'Cooperation in economic and monetary policy (Economic and Monetary Union)'. It is made up of a new Article 102a. Chapters 1, 2 and 3 above become Chapters 2, 3 and 4 respectively.

[2] Under the Single European Act three new Titles are added here:
Economic and Social Cohesion (Articles 130A to Article 130E).
Research and Technological Development (Articles 130F to 130Q).
Environmental (Articles 130R to 130T).

Many of the subsequent Treaty articles were concerned with following up these broad objectives with fuller, though still often rather general, guidelines for policy development. These policy guidelines can be grouped under two broad headings:

Policy guidelines concerned with the establishment of a common market. The common market was to be based on:

(a)   The removal of all tariffs and quantitative restrictions on internal trade. This would make the Community a free trade area.

(b)   The erection of a Common External Tariff (CET). This would mean that goods entering the Community would do so on the same basis no matter what their point of entry. No member state would therefore be in a position to gain a competitive advantage by, say, reducing the external tariffs on vital raw materials. The CET would take the Community beyond being a mere free trade area and would make it a customs union. It would also serve as the base for the development of a Common Commercial Policy (CCP).

(c)   The prohibition of a range of practices having as their effect the distortion or prevention of competition between the member states.

(d)   Measures to allow not only for the free movement of goods between the member states but also the free movement of persons, services and capital.

Policy guidelines concerned with making the Community more than just a common market. Making it exactly what, however, was left unclear, as it had to be given the uncertainties, disagreements and compromises which formed the background to the signing of the Treaty. There was certainly the implication of a movement towards some sort of general economic integration, and references were made to the 'co-ordination' of economic and monetary policies, but they were vague and implicitly long term. Such references as there were to specific sectoral policies – as, for example, the provisions for 'the adoption of a common policy in the sphere of agriculture', and the statement that the objectives of the Treaty 'shall . . . be pursued by Member States within the framework of a common transport policy' – were couched in fairly general terms.

The EEC Treaty is thus very different in character from the constitutions of nation states. Whereas the latter have little, if anything, to say about policy, the EEC Treaty has policy as its main concern. The nature of that concern is such that many have suggested that the policy framework indicated and outlined in the Treaty is guided by a clear philosophy or ideology: that of free market, liberal, non-interventionist capitalism. Unquestionably there is much in this view: on the one hand, the market mechanism and the need to prevent abuses to competition are accorded a high priority; on the other hand, there are few references to ways in which joint activities and intervention should be promoted for non-market based purposes. But the case should not be overstated. First, because competition itself is seen as requiring considerable intervention and management from the centre. Second, because there are some provisions for non-market policies: in the proposed common policy for agriculture, for example, which was given a special place in the Treaty precisely because of (mainly French) fears of what would happen should agriculture be exposed to a totally free market; in the proposed social policy which was intended to help soften unacceptable market consequences; and in the proposed common transport policy where specific allowance was to be made for aids 'if they meet the needs of co-ordination of transport or if they represent reimbursement for the discharge of certain obligations inherent in the concept of a public service'. Third, because much of the Treaty is so vague, so general, and so dependent on the future co-operation of the states for successful policy development, that there was never any question (let alone preference given the Christian Democratic and Social Democratic principles of most of the founders) of an immediate abandonment of national economic controls and a remoreseless and inevitable drive towards uninhibited free market capitalism.

The policy concerns of the Euratom Treaty are naturally confined to the atomic energy field. Chapters of the Treaty cover many vitally important areas of activity – promotion of research, dissemination of information, health and safety, supplies, a nuclear common market etc. However, and probably even more than with the EEC Treaty, differences between the states on key points resulted in the apparent force of many of the provisions of these chapters being watered down by exceptions and loopholes. For example, under Article 52 an Agency is established with 'exclusive right to conclude contracts relating to the supply of ores, scarce materials and special fissile materials coming from inside the Community or from outside'. Article 66, however, sets out circumstances in which states may buy on the world markets provided Commission approval is obtained. Similarly, Treaty provisions aimed at a pooling and sharing of technical information and knowledge are greatly weakened – and were so largely at French insistence – by provisions which allow for secrecy where national security is involved.

Where the EEC and Euratom Treaties are most similar to national constitutions is in those articles which identify the main institutions of the Communities (principally 137–98 in the EEC, 107–70 in Euratom), and those articles which specify the powers and some of the procedures of the institutions (spread throughout the Treaties). The ECSC served as the institutional model, but with certain modifications which had as their effect a tilting away from supranationalism towards intergovernmentalism. As with the ECSC, both the EEC and Euratom were to have four principal institutions:

1. An appointed Commission would assume the role exercised by the High Authority under the ECSC. That is to say, it would be the principal policy initiator, it would have some decision-making powers of its own, and it would carry certain responsibilities for policy implementation. But it would have less power than the High Authority to impose decisions on member states.

2. A Council of Ministers, with greater powers than its equivalent under the ECSC, would be the principal decision-making body. Circumstances in which it must take its decisions unanimously, and circumstances in which majority and qualified majority votes were permissible, were specified.

3. An Assembly would exercise advisory and (limited) supervisory powers. In the first instance it would be composed of delegates from national parliaments but after appropriate arrangements were made it was to be elected 'by direct universal suffrage in accordance with a uniform procedure in all Member States'.

4. A Court of Justice was charged with the duty of ensuring that 'in the interpretation and application of this Treaty the law is observed'.

A Convention, which was also signed on 25 March 1957, specified that the Assembly and the Court of Justice should be common to all three Communities.

These institutional arrangements were rather more intergovernmental in character than those who dreamed of political integration would have liked. In particular, the Council of Ministers was judged to have been given too much power and there was also disappointment that most of the key decisions in the Council would have to be made unanimously. However, there was hope for the future in that there were grounds for believing that the system could, and probably would, serve as a launching pad for a developing, a creeping, supranationalism. One of these grounds was provision in the EEC Treaty for increased use of majority voting in the Council as the Community became established. Another was the expectation that the Assembly would soon be elected by direct suffrage and that its power would thereby be increased. And a third was the seemingly reasonable assumption that if the Community proved to be a success the member states would become less concerned about their national rights and would increasingly cede greater powers to the central institutions.

Turning now to the Treaties and Acts that have supplemented and amended the three founding Treaties the most important have been:

The Treaty establishing a Single Council and a Single Commission of the European Communities. Signed in 1965, coming into force in 1967, and generally known as the Merger Treaty, this established a single Council of Ministers for all three Communities (though different individuals would attend different meetings), and merged into one Commission the High Authority of the ECSC, the Commission of Euratom, and the EEC Commission. The powers exercised by these merged bodies, were still to be based on the founding Treaties: in other words, the Treaties and the Communities themselves were not merged.

The Treaty amending Certain Budgetary Provisions of the Treaties (signed in 1970) and the *Treaty amending Certain Financial Provisions of the Treaties* (signed in 1975). Together, these two Treaties laid down a budgetary procedure and allocated budgetary powers between the Community institutions. Of particular importance, given its relative weakness in most policy areas, were the powers allocated to the Parliament. The 1975 Treaty also established a Court of Auditors to examine the accounts of all revenue and expenditure of the Community.

The Act concerning the election of the representatives of the Assembly by direct universal suffrage. Signed in 1976, but not finally ratified by all the member states until 1978, this Act provided the legal base for direct elections to the European Parliament, laid down certain rules for their conduct, but did not in any direct way increase the powers of the Parliament.

The Treaties of Accession. These have provided for the enlargement of the Community to include Denmark, Ireland and the United Kingdom (signed in 1972 and taking effect on 1 January 1973), Greece (signed in 1979 and taking effect on 1 January 1981), and Spain and Portugal (signed in 1985 and taking effect on 1 January 1986).

The Single European Act (SEA). Signed in February 1986, but not coming into force until mid-1987 because of ratification difficulties in Ireland, the SEA was something of a mixed bag, containing tidying up constitutional provisions, provisions designed to give the Community a new impetus, and provisions which altered aspects of the Community's decision-making system. The main inclusions of the SEA were:

1. A number of policy areas not specifically mentioned in the EEC Treaty, were formally incorporated and the capacity for decision-making in these areas was thereby increased. These included, most notably, environment, research and technological development, and 'economic and social cohesion' (basically regional policy).
2. The completion of the internal market by 1992 was identified as a specific goal and was incorporated into the EEC Treaty via a new Article 8A.
3. For ten EEC Treaty articles a new legislative procedure was established – the co-operation procedure. The purpose of the new procedure was to improve the efficiency of decision-making in the Council of Ministers, and to increase, though not by too much, the powers of the European Parliament. Key features of

the co-operation procedure are: the single reading of legislative proposals by the European Parliament and the Council of Ministers under the traditional consultation procedure is replaced by two readings; the Council may, subject to certain restrictions, take its decisions at both first and second readings by a qualified majority vote – this amounts to a significant increase in the Treaty base for majority voting; the European Parliament's ability to influence the content of Community legislation is increased, though it still does not enjoy full legislative powers; a strict timetable is established for the later stages of the legislative process. Legislative areas covered by the co-operation procedure include some social policy matters, implementing decisions in connection with the regional fund and research and technological development programmes, and, most crucially of all – under a new EEC Article 100A – most of the measures 'which have as their object the establishment and functioning of the internal market'.

4. The EP's role and potential influence in the Community was also increased via the establishment of a new 'assent procedure'. Under the procedure, the EP's assent, by an absolute majority of members, becomes necessary both for the accession of new members to the Community (under Article 237 EEC) and for Association Agreements between the Community and third countries (under Article 238 EEC).

5. European Political Co-operation (the official Community term for foreign policy co-operation), which had increasingly been practised since the early 1970s, but outside the Treaty framework, was put on a legal basis. (But not by Treaty incorporation).

6. Meetings of the twelve Heads of Government in the framework of the European Council, which had been taking place since 1975, were, for the first time, given legal recognition. (But not by Treaty incorporation).

7. The capacity of the Court of Justice, which had been becoming very overstretched, was extended by the provision for the establishment of a new Court of First Instance.

Since it began functioning in 1958 the Community has naturally developed in many ways. The most important of those can be grouped under the three headings which now follow.

Enlargement

The most obvious change since the Community's foundation has been the doubling of the size of membership from six states to twelve.

The first enlargement could have occurred much earlier than it did had the French President, General de Gaulle, not opposed UK applications to join the Community which were made in 1961 and 1967 – applications to which separate applications from Denmark, Ireland and Norway were, in practice, attached. There has been much speculation about the reasons for the General's veto: he feared that the UK would rival and would attempt to thwart his desire to place France at the centre of the European stage; he believed UK membership would unsettle the developing Franco-German alliance – an alliance that was given symbolic force with the signing in 1963 of a Friendship Treaty beteween the two countries; he was suspicious of the UK's close links with the US and thought they would pave the way for American penetration and domination of Europe if the UK joined the Community. Whatever the explanation, the fact is the UK was barred from membership until after the resignation of de Gaulle in 1969 and the election as President of Georges Pompidou. A different view was then taken in Paris: the UK might serve as a useful counterweight to the increasingly strong and self-confident Germany; UK governments would lend support to the French opposition to pressures within the Community for increased supra-nationalism; and France would probably gain economically by virtue of having better access to UK markets and as a result of the UK being a net contributor to the Community budget.

The reasons for the UK's changed position on Europe were a mixture of the political and the economic. Politically, it was increasingly clear that the UK was no longer a world power of the first rank. The Suez debâcle underlined the decline, and the increasing tendency from 1960 for key world issues to be discussed between the USA and the USSR on a purely bilateral basis further confirmed it. Paralleling this decline the nature and status of the 'special relationship' with the USA weakened and became increasingly questionable. Further to all this the Empire was giving way to the Commonwealth, a very loose organisation and not one that was capable of providing the UK with much international political support.

On all the usual economic indicators, such as growth in trade, in investment, in gross national product, and in income, the member states of the EC were outperforming the UK. For example, between 1958–69 real earnings in Britain increased by about 38 per cent, whereas in the EC they increased on average by about 75 per cent. Quite simply the figures appeared to show that the Community was a success; all this at a time when the UK's pattern of trade, even when not a Community member, was turning away from the Commonwealth and towards Europe. Moreover, the growing economic strength of the EC seemed to be linked with a growing political status.

When Pompidou opened the door the Heath government thus willingly took the UK in. It was joined by Denmark and Ireland, both of which had traditional economic and cultural links with the UK and which had consciously tied their applications to the Community with those from the UK since the early 1960s.

The accession of Greece was also delayed longer than Greek governments would have liked, but for very different reasons. The initial problem, recognised on both sides when Greece made its first approaches to Brussels soon after the EEC came into being, was the underdeveloped nature of the Greek economy. A transition period prior to membership was deemed to be necessary and this was negotiated in the form of an Association Agreement that came into force in 1962. The object of the Association was the 'continuous and balanced strengthening of trade and economic relations between the contracting parties, having particular regard to the need to secure an accelerated development of the Greek economy'. Full incorporation into the Community would follow when the Greek economy was capable of sustaining the obligations imposed by membership. However, from April 1967, when there was a military coup in Greece, until June 1974, when civilian government was re-established, the Association Agreement was virtually suspended. It might be thought that the effect of this would have been to further delay full membership. In fact, it had the opposite effect. After elections in Greece in November 1974 the new government immediately made clear its wish to become a full member of the Community. The Commission issued a formal Opinion that Greece was still not economically ready and proposed a pre-accession period of unlimited duration during which economic reforms could be implemented. In response the Greek government restated its wish for full membership and, in so doing, particularly emphasised how Community membership could help both to underpin Greek democracy and to consolidate Greece's West European and Western Alliance bonds. The Council of Ministers was sympathetic to these arguments, rejected the Commission's Opinion, and membership negotiations were opened in July 1976.

As with Greece, political considerations were also extremely important in influencing the relations between the two Iberian states and the Community prior to their accession. Initially the influence was a negative one: had not both Spain and Portugal been governed by dictatorial political systems until the mid-1970s they would in all probability have been members of the Community long before they were. Not that there is anything in the Treaties specifying that Community members must be liberal democracies: Article 237 of the EEC Treaty simply says 'Any European State may apply to become a member of the Community'. To date, however, the assumption has been that a democratic political system is a necessary qualification for entry. (Quite what the Community would do should democracy be overthrown in a member state is uncertain).

So, although both Spain and Portugal requested negotiations on an association with the Community as early as 1962, and Spain made it quite clear that its request was with a view to full membership at some future date, both countries were treated with caution by the Community. Eventually they were granted preferential trade agreements – that for Spain coming into force in 1970, and for Portugal in 1973 as part of an agreement between the Community and all EFTA countries – but it was only with the overthrow of the Caetano regime in Portugal in 1974 and the death of General Franco in 1975 that full membership became a real possibility. Portugal applied in March 1977 and Spain in July 1977. The negotiations were protracted and difficult, covering, amongst many problems, the threat posed to other Mediterranean countries by Spanish agriculture, the size of the Spanish fishing fleet, and the implications of cheap Spanish and Portuguese labour moving north. As in the Greek negotiations political factors helped to overcome difficulties: member states wished to encourage political stability in southern Europe; there was the opportunity to widen and strengthen the political and economic base of the Community; and, by helping to link southern Europe to the north, there were seen to be strategic advantages for both Western Europe and NATO.

All three enlargements have inevitably affected and changed the Community in important ways. First, and most obviously, the Community has, simply by becoming bigger, become a more important international organisation. It now contains a population of over 340 million; its membership includes all the larger, and traditionally more influential, West European states; and it is the world's principal commercial power, accounting for around 22 per cent of world imports and 21 per cent of world exports (not counting commerce between the member states themselves).

Second, internal decision-making has become more complex, with twelve representatives sitting around the Council of Ministers' table rather than six, and with a much wider range of national and political interests wishing to be satisfied.

Third, and this is linked to the previous point, the Franco-German axis, which did so much to set the pace in the 1960s and early 1970s has been, if not undermined in its influence, less central and less dominating. More generally, as the number of smaller states have increased, it has not been quite so easy for the larger states to push their preferences through.

Fourth, the policy debates, concerns, and priorities of the Community have been affected as the new members have brought with them their own requirements and problems. So, for example, and of considerable importance for the future development of the Community, the growing influence, as a result of the second and third enlargements, of southern, less industrialised and poorer countries has produced pressures both for a reorientation of the Common Agricultural Policy away from northern temperate products towards Mediterranean products, and also for more redistributive policies which will directly assist economic development in the south. (The North–South divide does not, of course, coincide completely with industrial/non-industrial or rich/poor divides: much of northern Spain is industrialised, most of Ireland is not; most of the UK outside southern England is relatively poor, much of northern Italy is relatively rich).

Before leaving the history of the Community's enlargements it is worth making the point, because there has been some misunderstanding on the matter, that the incorporation of the territory of the former German Democratic Republic (GDR) into the Community in 1990 did not constitute an enlargement. German unification took the form of the GDR integrating into the Federal Republic of Germany, so there was no question of a new state joining the Community, nor, therefore, any need for an Accession Treaty.

The full implications of German unification for the Community remains to be seen. In the short term there are difficulties, and transitional arrangements are playing an important part in giving the territory of the former GDR time to adjust to the rigour of Community laws and policies in areas such as the internal market and the environment. In the medium to long term the power of Germany – which was already by far the strongest Community state in economic and financial terms, and which now also becomes by far the largest state in population terms (a population of 80 million, as compared to 55–58 million in France, Italy, and the UK) – is likely to be increased still further.

Developments in Community Policy and Decision-making Processes

In general terms, it may be said that the Rome Treaties indicated a pattern of policy and decision-making in which the Commission would propose, the Parliament would advise, the Council would decide, and the Court would interpret. In many respects this is indeed how Community relationships and processes have worked in practice. But there have also been important additions and amendments to the projected pattern. The nature of these additions and amendments is examined in some detail in later chapters, but three are particularly worth noting at this stage.

First, the relationships between the four institutions themselves have altered in a number of ways. As the Community has evolved, all of the institutions have extended their interests and responsibilities and as this has happened they have increasingly become less compartmentalised and less self-contained within the Community system. A certain blurring has occurred as some of the lines of division over who does what have become less clear. The best example of this is the way in which the Council, by becoming progressively much more involved in initiating and setting the Community's policy agenda, has usurped some of the Commission's proposing responsibilities.

Second, an increasing range and number of participants not associated with the four main institutions have become involved in Community policy and decision-making. The most important of these participants are the Heads of Government who, in the European Council, have come to assume a number of important responsibilities, some of which have had the effect of reducing the power and manoeuvrability of both the Council of Ministers and the Commission. Prominent amongst other actors who have inserted, or have attempted to insert, themselves into the Community's decision-making processes are the many national and transnational sectoral interests and pressures that have come to cluster around the Community institutions in order to monitor developments and, where possible, to advise or pressurise the formal decision-makers.

Third, Community processes have simply become more varied and more complex over the years as they have come to function in many different ways at many different levels. In addition to what occurs in the structured settings of Council and Commission meetings, Parliamentary plenaries and committees, and Court sittings, there is a mosaic of less formal channels in which representatives of the institutions, the states, and interests, meet and interact to discuss and produce policies and decisions. Which processes and channels operate in particular cases, and what types of interactions occur therein, varies considerably from sector to sector, and can even do so from decision to decision.

Development of Policies

Along with its institutional structure and its decision-making processes the Community is most distinguished from other international organisations by the range and weight of its policy responsibilities and commitments. These have expanded steadily over the years, stimulated and encouraged by factors such as the provisions of the Treaties, the increasing internationalisation of economic forces, stiffening international economic competition, a growing recognition of the benefits of working together, integrationist pressures emanating from Community institutions, and the stimulus that policy development in one sphere often gives to developments in others.

The best known of the Community's policies is the Common Agricultural Policy (CAP). Consuming well over half of the Community's budget it has been the focus of frequent disagreements and clashes, most of them centring on whether and how to deal with the related problems of guaranteed prices and overproduction. Since the early 1980s a series of measures have been adopted which have had the effect of bringing at least some aspects of the CAP's problems under control.

Though not, until recently at least, receiving as much publicity as the CAP, the policies which lie at the heart of the Community's policy framework are those which are aimed at creating what is variously referred to as 'the Common Market', 'the internal market', and 'the Single European Market'. In essence, these are policies which are designed, on the one hand, to promote the free movement of goods, people, services and capital between the member states, and, on the other hand, are designed to enable the Community to act jointly and present a common front in its economic and trading relations with third countries. Since the mid-1980s the Community's '1992' momentum has given a considerable boost to these market-based policies, and has also stimulated developments in related policy areas. Most notable of these related areas are policies designed to move the Community towards becoming an economic and monetary union, and initiatives aimed at giving to the market 'a social dimension'.

In addition to its increasing involvement in market and market-related policies, the Community has, over the years, moved into other policy areas too. Amongst the many 'non-market' and 'non-economic' areas in which it is now involved to at least some degree are foreign policy, internal security policy, environmental policy, and cultural policy.

So extensive and diverse has the Community's policy framework become that it now incorporates initiatives and developments in virtually every sphere of public policy. No other combination of states has arrangements even remotely like those which apply in the Community where co-operation and integration are consciously practised across such a wide range of policy sectors, and where so many policy-making and policy-implementation responsibilities have been removed from the hands of individual states and given over to collective institutions.

The nature of the Community's policy interests and responsibilities are examined at length in Part Three.

PART TWO

The Institutions and Political Actors of the Community

Introduction

As was indicated in Chapter 2 there are four main Community institutions: the Commission, the Council of Ministers, the European Parliament, and the Court of Justice. Chapters 3–6 consider each of these institutions, and the political actors that are associated with them. Chapter 6 has also been taken as the most appropriate place to examine the nature and status of Community law.

In Chapter 7 the European Council is examined. As will be shown, these summits of Heads of Government, although given no place in the founding Treaties, have come to play an extremely significant role in the life of the Community.

Finally, Chapter 8 looks at those institutions and actors which, though not given a chapter in their own right because of pressures of space, nonetheless also exercise an important influence in the Community: the Economic and Social Committee, the European Investment Bank, the Court of Auditors, and Interests.

3

The Commission

Frequently portrayed as the civil service of the Community, the Commission is in reality both rather more, and rather less, than that: rather more in the sense that the Treaties, and political practice, have assigned to it much greater policy initiating and decision-making powers than national civil services, in theory at least, enjoy; rather less in that its role regarding policy implementation is greatly limited by virtue of the fact that it is the member states themselves which are charged with most of the Community's day-to-day administrative responsibilities.

The Commission is centrally involved in Community decision-making at all levels and on all fronts. With an array of power resources and policy instruments at its disposal – and strengthened by the frequent unwillingness or inability of the Council of Ministers to provide clear leadership – the Commission is at the very heart of the Community system.

Appointment and Composition

Seated at the summit of the Commission are the individual Commissioners who are each in charge of particular policy areas and who meet collectively as the College of Commissioners. Originally, they numbered nine, but with the three Community enlargements their size has grown: to 13, to 14, and now to 17. Each of the five larger countries have two Commissioners (France, Germany, Italy, Spain, and the UK), and the remaining seven smaller countries each have one.

A new Commission is appointed every four years, with individual terms of office being renewable. According to Article 158 of the EEC Treaty, the method of appointment must be 'by common accord of the Governments of the Member States'. The thinking behind this procedure is that a collective appointment emphasises the Community, rather than the national, base of the Commission: Commissioners are not supposed to be national representatives. It is much the same sentiment that requires Commissioners, on taking up their appointment, to give a 'solemn undertaking' that they will serve the Community alone and will 'neither seek nor take instructions from any government or any other body'.

In practice, such a full and impartial 'Community consciousness' is neither achieved nor attempted. Although in theory the Commissioners are collectively appointed they are, in fact, national nominees. It would, therefore, be quite unrealistic to expect them, on assuming office, suddenly to detach themselves from previous loyalties and develop a concern solely for 'the wider European interest' – not least since a factor in their appointment is likely to have been an expectation that they would keep an eye on the national interest. (A particularly graphic illustration of this latter point was seen in the way that the UK Commissioner, Lord Cockfield, was not reappointed by Mrs. Thatcher to the Commission which took up office in January 1989. She believed he had been over zealous in his support for aspects of the internal market programme for which he was responsible, and rather than looking to British interests had 'gone native'.)

The Treaty insistence on complete independence of Commissioners is therefore interpreted flexibly. Indeed, total neutrality is not even desirable since the work of the Commission is likely to be facilitated by Commissioners maintaining links with sources of influence throughout the Community and this they can most easily do in their own member states. But the requirements of the system and the necessities of the Community's institutional make-up are such that real problems arise if Commissioners try and force their own state's interests too hard. It is both legitimate and helpful to bring favoured national interests onto the agenda, to help clear national obstacles from the path, to explain to other Commissioners what is likely to be acceptable in 'my' national capital. But to go further and act consistently and blatantly as a national spokesman is to risk losing credibility with other Commissioners. It also makes it difficult for the Commission to function properly since clearly it cannot fulfil its set tasks if its divisions match those of the Council of Ministers. The Commission which was appointed to office in January 1985 under the Presidency of Jacques Delors soon ran into difficulties of this kind: the chauvinism of some of its members played an important part in limiting the ability of the Commission to act efficiently as a coherent team. Open criticisms by members of the German government of its two Commissioners for allegedly failing to defend their country's interests in Brussels created further problems.

There are no rules or understandings as to what sort of people, with what sort of experience and background, member governments should nominate. In general, it would be fair to say that Commissioners tend to be former national politicians just short of the top rank. However, there are many who do not fully fit such a description. So a significant – and increasing – number have held senior ministerial posts in their own countries, whilst others – now constituting a declining number – are best described as 'experts', 'technicians', or 'prominent national figures' of one kind or another.

Given the diverse political compositions of the Community's national governments there is naturally a range of political opinion represented in the Commission. The smaller countries tend to put forward somebody from, or associated with, their largest party. The five larger countries vary in what they do, but 'split representations' are common practice. Crucially, all governments have made it their custom to nominate people who are broadly pro-European and who have not been associated with any extremist party or any extreme of a mainstream party. So whilst Commissions have certainly contained party political differences, these have usually been within a range that has permitted at least reasonable working relationships.

The most prestigious and potentially influential Commission post is that of the Presidency. The President is the principal representative of the Commission; he must try to encourage a sense of direction and a co-ordination of effort amongst his Commission colleagues; and he may take on specific policy portfolios of his own if he chooses. Inevitably, therefore, the states take care over the appointment. According to the EEC Treaty the President 'shall be appointed from amongst its members . . . in accordance with the same procedure as that laid down for the appointment of members of the Commission (Article 161 EEC). In practice what happens is that the second of these conditions, requiring that the appointment be 'by common accord of the Governments of the Market States', is met – the European Council making the appointment, after taking extensive informal soundings and consulting with the European Parliament's Enlarged Bureau; the first condition, however, requiring that the appointment be from amongst the members of the Commission, is not strictly adhered to in that the appointment is usually confirmed by the European Council at its June meeting in the year before the post is taken up – which is well before most of the other members of the incoming Commission have been announced. Reflecting the importance of the office, the appointee has tended to be someone with senior ministerial experience and considerable political weight in his own country. Although formally appointed for only a two-year term it has become customary to allow Presidents to remain in office for at least the full term of a Commission, that is four years.

The distribution of the policy portfolios between the Commissioners is largely a matter of negotiation and political balance. The President's will is the most important single factor, but he cannot allocate posts simply in accordance with his own preferences. He is intensively lobbied – by the incoming Commissioners themselves, and sometimes too by governments trying to get 'their' Commissioners into positions which are especially important from the national point of view. Furthermore, the President is made aware that re-nominated Commissioners – of which there are likely to be nine or ten – may well be looking for advancement to more important portfolios, and that the five states which have two Commissioners expect at least one of 'their' nominees to be allocated a senior post. Bearing in mind all of these difficulties it is not surprising that unless a resignation, a death, or an enlargement enforces it, reshuffles do not usually occur during the four year lifetime of a Commission.

To assist them in the performance of their duties – by, for example, keeping them informed of developments within and outside their allocated policy areas, and by liaising with other parts of the Commission and outside institutions and interests – Commissioners have personal *cabinets*. These consist of small teams of officials, normally numbering six. Mostly they are fellow nationals of the Commissioner, although at least one is supposed to be drawn from another member state. They are usually recruited either from national political parties or are seconded from domestic civil services or from some part of the Community's administration.

Below the Commissioners lies the Commission bureaucracy. This constitutes by far the biggest element of the whole Community administrative framework. Of a total Community administrative staff of around 23500 just over 16000 are employed by the Commission. Of these about 10000 are concerned with policy and executive tasks, about 3200 with scientific research (most of these being employed at the Joint Research Centre's establishment at Ispra in Italy), and about 2700 are engaged in the translation and interpretation work which arises from the Community's nine working languages. (There are 72 possible language combinations, although most of the Commission's internal business is conducted in French or English.) The majority of the Commission's non-research staff are based in and around the Commission's headquarters in the Berlaymont Building in Brussels.

Most of the Commission employees are engaged on a permanent basis following open examinations, which, for the administrative grades in particular, are highly competitive. An internal career structure exists and most of the top jobs are filled by internal promotion. However, pure meritocratic principles are disturbed by a policy that tries to provide for a reasonable national balance amongst staff. All governments have watched this closely and have sought to ensure that their own nationals are well represented throughout the Community's administrative framework, especially in the policy-making 'A' grades. For the most senior posts something akin to an informal national quota system operates.

This multi-national staffing policy of the Commission, and indeed of the other Community institutions, has both advantages and disadvantages. The main advantages are:

1. Staff have a wide range of experience and knowledge drawn from across all the member states.
2. The confidence of national governments and administrations in Community decision-making is helped by the knowledge that compatriots are involved in policy preparation and administration.
3. Those who have to deal with the Community, whether they be senior national civil servants or paid lobbyists, can often more easily do so by using their fellow nationals as access points. A two way flow of information between the Community and the member states is thus facilitated.

The main disadvantages are:

1. Some senior personnel decisions are not made on the basis of objective organisational needs but result from national claims to posts and from lobbying activities which often become associated with this. The parachuting of outsiders into key jobs is less easy than it was – partly because staff and unions have pressed for a better internal career structure – but in the Commission's upper reaches promotion is still not based on pure meritocratic principles.

2. Senior officials can sometimes be less than wholly and completely Community-minded. For however impartial and even-handed they are supposed to be, they cannot, and usually do not wish to, completely divest themselves of their national identifications and loyalties.

Organisation

The Directorates General

The work of the Commission is divided into separate policy areas in much the same way as at national level governmental responsibilities are divided between ministries. Apart from specialised agencies and services – such as the Statistical Office and the Joint Research Centre – the Commission's basic units of organisation are its twenty-three Directorates General. Somewhat confusingly for those who do not know their way around the system these are customarily referred to by their number rather than by their policy responsibility. So, for example, External Relations is DGI, Agriculture is DGVI, and Energy is DGXVII (see Table 3.1).

The size and internal organisation of DGs varies. Most commonly, they have a staff of between 150 and 450, divided into three or four directorates, which in turn are each divided into three or four divisions. However, policy importance, workloads, and specialisations within DGs, produce many departures from this norm. Thus, to take size, DGs range from DGIX which employs just over 2500 people and DGVI which employs around 850, to the relatively recently created DGXXII and DGXXIII which each employ around 60. As for organisational structure, DGI has nine director-

TABLE 3.1

Directorates General and Special Units of the Commission

Directorates General

DGI	External Relations
DGII	Economic and Financial Affairs
DGIII	Internal Market and Industrial Affairs
DGIV	Competition
DGV	Employment, Industrial Relationships and Social Affairs
DGVI	Agriculture
DGVII	Transport
DGVIII	Development
DGIX	Personnel and Administration
DGX	Information, Communication and Culture
DGXI	Environment, Nuclear Safety and Civil Protection
DGXII	Science, Research and Development
DGXIII	Telecommunications, Information Industry and Innovation
DGXIV	Fisheries
DGXV	Financial Institutions and Company Law
DGXVI	Regional Policies
DGXVII	Energy
DGXVIII	Credit and Investments
DGXIX	Budgets
DGXX	Financial Control
DGXXI	Customs Union and Indirect Taxation
DGXXII	Co-ordination of Structural Policies
DGXXIII	Enterprises' Policy, Distributive Trades, Tourism and Social Economy

Special Units and Services
Secretariat General of the Commission
Legal Service
Spokesman's Service
Translation Service
Joint Interpretation and Conference Service
Statistical Office
Consumer Policy Service
Joint Research Centre
Task Force 'Human resources, education, training and Youth'
Euratom Supply Agency
Security Office
Office for Official Publications of the European Communities

ates and twenty-four divisions, and DGVI has eight directorates (two of which are themselves subdivided) and thirty-two divisions; by contrast DGXXIII has only two directorates and no divisions, while DGXXII has no directorates and only three divisions.

The Hierarchical Structure

The hierarchical structure within the Commission is as follows:

● All important matters are channelled through the weekly meetings of the College of Commissioners. At these meetings decisions are taken unanimously if possible, but by majority vote if need be.

● In particular policy areas the Commissioner who is assigned the portfolio carries the main leadership responsibility.

● DGs are formally headed by directors general who are responsible to the appropriate Commissioner.

● Directorates are headed by directors who report to the director general or, in the case of large DGs, to an assistant director general.

● Divisions are headed by heads of division who report to the director responsible.

The structure thus appears to be quite clear. In practice, it is not completely so. At the topmost echelons, in particular, lines of authority and accountability are sometimes blurred. One reason for this is that a poor match often exists between Commissioners' portfolios and the policy responsibilities of the DGs. Community enlargements and the consequent increasing size of the Commission over the years have allowed for greater policy specialisation on the part of individual Commissioners, and a better alignment with the responsibilities of individual DGs, but, even now, most Commissioners carry several portfolios, each of which may touch on the work of a number of DGs. Moreover, the content of portfolio responsibilities is changed from Commission to Commission. Some, such as Budget, Agriculture, or Regional Policy, are more or less fixed, but others, of a broader and less specific kind, can be varied, or even created, depending on how a new President sees the role and tasks of the Commission and what pressures the Commissioners themselves exert.

Another structural problem that arises in relation to Commissioners is the curious halfway position in which they are placed. To use the British parallel, they are more than permanent secretaries but less than ministers. For whilst they are, on the one hand, the principal Commission spokesmen in their assigned policy areas, they are not members of the Council of Ministers – the body which takes the final policy decisions on important matters.

These structural arrangements mean that any notion of individual responsibility, such as exists in most member states in relation to ministers – albeit usually only weakly and subject to the prevailing political currents – is difficult to apply to Commissioners. It might even be questioned whether it is reasonable that the Commission should be subject to collective responsibility – as it is by virtue of the Treaties which oblige it to resign if a motion of censure on its activities is passed in the EP by a two-thirds majority of the votes cast, representing a majority of all members. (No motion of censure has ever been passed.) Collective responsibility may be thought to be fair insofar as all Commission proposals and decisions are made collectively and not in the name of individual Commissioners, but, at the same time, it may be thought to be unfair insofar as much of the Commission's activity and the fortunes of its attempts to develop policy are dependent on the Council. Indeed, the Commission is at a theoretical risk of being dismissed by a Parliament frustrated by its inability to censure the Council.

Decision-Making Mechanisms

The hierarchical structure that has just been described produces a 'model' route via which proposals for decisions make their way through the Commission machinery:

● An initial draft is drawn up at middle-ranking A-grade level in the appropriate DG. The parameters of the draft are likely to be determined by existing Community policy, or by guidelines that have been laid down at senior Commission and/or Council levels.

● The draft is passed upwards through superiors until the College of Commissioners is reached. During its passage the draft may be extensively revised.

● The College of Commissioners can do virtually what they like with the proposal. They may accept it, reject it, refer it back to the DG for re-drafting, or defer taking a decision.

From this 'model' route all sorts of variations are possible, and in practice are commonplace. For example, where draft proposals are relatively uncontroversial, or where there is some urgency involved, procedures and devices can be employed which have as their purpose the prevention of logjams at the top and the expediting of business. One such procedure enables the College of Commissioners to authorise the most appropriate amongst their number to take decisions on their behalf. Another procedure is the so-called 'written procedure' by which proposals which seem to be straightforward are circulated amongst all Commissioners and are officially adopted if no objection is lodged within a specified time, usually a week. Urgent proposals can be adopted even more quickly by 'accelerated written procedure'.

Another set of circumstances producing departures from the 'model' route is where policy issues cut across the Community's administrative divisions – a common occurrence given the sectoral specialisations of the DGs. For example, a draft directive aimed at providing a framework in which alternative sources of energy might be researched and developed would probably originate in DGXVII (Energy), but would have direct implications too for DGXII (Science, Research and Development), DGXIX (Budgets), and perhaps DGIII (Internal Market and Industrial Affairs). Provision for liaison and co-ordination is thus essential if the Commission is to be effective and efficient. There are various procedures and mechanisms which attempt to provide this necessary co-ordination. Four of these are particularly worth noting.

First, the President of the Commission has an ill-defined, but generally expected, co-ordinating responsibility. A forceful personality may be able to achieve a great deal in forging a measure of collective identity out of the varied collection of people, from quite different national and political backgrounds, who sit around the Commission table. But it can only be done tactfully and with adroit use of social skills. Jacques Delors, who first became President in January 1985, and who began a second term of office in January 1989, unquestionably has the requirement of a forceful personality, but he has also displayed traits and acted in ways which, many observers have suggested, have had the effect of undermining the team spirit of his Commissions: he has indicated clear policy preferences and interests of his own; he has made important policy pronouncements before fully consulting with his colleagues in the Commission; he has criticised Commissioners in Commission meetings and in public; and he has sometimes appeared to give more weight to the counsel of personal advisers than to that of Commissioners.

Second, the College of Commissioners is, in theory at least, in a strong position to co-ordinate activity and take a broad view of Commission affairs. Everything of importance is referred to the Commissioners' weekly meeting. At that meeting the whole sweep of Commission interests is represented by the portfolios of those gathered around the table.

Commissioners' meetings are always preceded by other meetings designed to ease the way to decision-making. Informal and *ad hoc* consultations may occur between those Commissioners particularly affected by a proposal. The Commissioners' agenda is always considered at the weekly meeting of the *chefs des cabinets* who try to resolve as many differences as possible. On a less formal basis, officials from the different *cabinets*, who are generally well known to one another and whose offices are grouped together on the upper floors of the Berlaymont Building, might exchange views on a proposal if it seems that problems might arise. (Normally *cabinets* do not become involved until a proposal has been formally launched by a DG, but earlier consultation sometimes occurs).

Third, an increasing awareness of the co-ordination problem has resulted in the emergence of a number of practices and forums which have brought together people from different parts of the Commission below the level of the Commissioners themselves. So, in many policy areas, important co-ordinating functions are performed by a host of standing and *ad hoc* committees, task forces and project groups, and formal and informal meetings from Director General level downwards.

Fourth, the main institutional agency for promoting co-ordination is the Secretariat General of the Commission, which is specifically charged with ensuring that proper co-ordination and communication takes place across the Commission. In exercising this duty the Secretariat satisfies itself that all Commission interests have been consulted before a proposal is submitted to the College of Commissioners.

However, despite these various co-ordinating arrangements a feeling persists in many quarters that the Commission continues to function in too compartmentalised a manner, with insufficient attention paid to overall Community policy coherence. Amongst the problems are these:

1. The Commission has a rather rigid organisational framework. Despite the development of horizontal links of the kind that have just been noted, structural relationships, both between and within DGs, remain too vertical. Some encouragement has been given, principally via the President's office, to the creation of agencies and teams which can plan on a broad front, but these are not sufficiently developed, and in any event they have had difficulties in asserting their authority in relation to the DGs – especially the larger and traditionally more independent ones. As for the President himself, he has no formal powers to direct the actions of DGs, let alone the authority to dismiss or reassign the duties of those in the DGs whom he judges to be incompetent or unco-operative.

2. Departmental and policy loyalties tend to discourage new and integrated approaches to problems and the pooling of ideas. Demarcation lines between spheres of responsibility are too tightly drawn, and policy competences are too jealously guarded.

3. Sheer workload has made it difficult for many Commissioners and senior officials to look much beyond their own immediate tasks. One of the duties of a Commissioner's *cabinet* is supposedly to keep him abreast of general policy developments, but it remains the case that the Commissioner holding the portfolio on, say, energy, can hardly be blamed if he has little to contribute to a Commission discussion on the milk market regime.

Responsibilities and Powers

Some of the Commission's responsibilities and powers are prescribed in the three founding Treaties and in Community legislation. Others have not been formally laid down but have developed from practical necessities and the requirements of the Community system.

Whilst recognising that there is, in practice, some overlap between the categories, the responsibilities and associated powers of the Commission may be grouped under six major headings: initiator and proposer of policies, executive functions, guardian of the legal framework, external representative and negotiator, mediator and conciliator, and the conscience of the Community.

Initiator and Proposer of Policies

The Commission is charged with the responsibility of proposing to the Council of Ministers measures which are likely to advance the development of Community policies. Article 155 of the EEC Treaty states this quite clearly: the Commission 'shall formulate recommendations or deliver opinions on matters dealt with in this Treaty, if it expressly so provides or if the Commission considers it necessary'.

What this means, in practice, is that the Council's legislative capacity is heavily dependent on the willingness and ability of the Commission to put proposals before it. The Council cannot initiate and draft legislation itself. Furthermore, if the Council wishes to amend a Commission proposal, Article 149 of the EEC Treaty states that it can only do so either with the Commission's agreement or by acting unanimously if the Commission disagrees. If neither of these two routes are open, the Council must accept the Commission's proposal as it stands, reject it, or refer it back to the Commission for reconsideration and resubmission at a later date.

In addition to these formal powers, political realities arising from the institutional structure of the Community also dictate that the Commission should have a major policy initiating role. The most important of these realities is that there is nothing like a Community Prime Minister, a Community Cabinet, or Community ministers capable of providing the Commission with clear and consistent policy direction. Senior Commission officials who have transferred from national civil services are often greatly surprised at the lack of political direction from above and at the amount of room for policy initiation that is available to them. Their duties are often only broadly defined and there can be considerable potential, especially for the more senior A- grade officials, to stimulate development in specific and, if they wish, new and innovative policy areas. An indication of the scale of this activity is seen in the fact that in an average year the Commission is likely to send the Council 700–800 proposals, recommendations, and drafts for Council instruments, and over 200 communications, memoranda and reports.

To give an example of this initiating and proposing role of the Commission, the task of translating the 1992 internal market drive into specific legislative proposals has been its responsibility. This it has done with the production of draft legislative proposals – totalling 282 in mid-1990 – covering fields of activity as varied as the simplification of customs checks and formalities, the technical harmonisation of industrial products, the harmonisation of animal health and plant health rules, and the opening up of public procurement.

But, important though its role is, it must be emphasised that the Commission does not have a complete monopoly over policy initiation in the Community, nor does it have a totally free hand in what it does. As will be shown in later chapters all sorts of other institutions and actors – including member states, the Council of Ministers, the European Parliament, sectional groups, local authorities, and private firms – attempt to play a part too, by bringing policy options onto the political agenda and by exerting pressure directly on the Commission when that is possible. From its earliest deliberations the Commission is obliged to take note of many of these outside voices if its proposals are to produce legislation, and legislation that can be successfully implemented. It must concern itself not only with what is desirable but also with what is possible. The policy preferences of others must be recognised.

The Commission's advisory committee network.   Extensive sounding and listening processes therefore precede and accompany Commission policy development. An important part in these processes, especially at the pre-proposal stage (that is, before the Commission has formally presented a proposal to the Council), is played by a vast network of advisory committees that have been established over the years. The committees are of two main types:

(a)   *The expert committees.*   These consist of national officials, experts and specialists of various sorts. Although nominated by national governments the members are not normally viewed as official governmental spokesmen – in the way that members of Council working parties are (see Chapter 4) – so it is usually possible for the committees to conduct their affairs on a very informal basis. Many of these committees are well established, meet on a fairly regular basis, and have a more or less fixed membership; others are *ad hoc* – set up, very frequently, to discuss an early draft of a Commission legislative proposal – and can hardly be even described as committees in that they may only ever meet once or twice. As for their interests and concerns, some of the committees are broad and wide ranging, such as the committees advising on aspects of competition policy, whilst others are more specialised and technical, such as the Pharmaceuticals Committee or some of the committees advising on programme management.

(b) *The consultative committees.* These are composed of representatives of sectional interests and are organised and funded by the Commission without reference to the national governments. Members are normally appointed by the Commission from nominations made by representative Community level organisations: either umbrella groups such as the Union of Industries in the European Community (UNICE), the European Trade Union Confederation (ETUC), and the Committee of Professional Agricultural Organisations of the European Community (COPA), or more specialised sectoral organisations and liaison groups such as the Common Market Group of the International Union of Railways (IUR), or the Committee of Transport Unions in the Community (ITF-ICFTU). The effect of this appointments policy is that the consultative committees are made up overwhelmingly of full-time employees of associations and groups. The largest number of consultative committees are to be found in the agriculture sector, where there are some twenty committees for products covered by a Community market regime, plus half a dozen or so more general committees. Most of the agricultural advisory committees have a membership of between thirty and fifty, but there are a few exceptions: the largest are those on cereals, pigmeat, and agricultural structure policy, all of which have fifty-four members; the smallest are the vetinary committee and the committee on hops, each of which have fourteen members.

In addition to these two types of committees there are many hybrids with mixed forms of membership.

Most of the advisory committees are chaired and serviced by the Commission. A few are serviced by the Council and are, technically, Council committees, but the Commission is entitled to observer status on these so the distinction between the two types of committees is of little significance in terms of their ability to advise the Commission.

The extent to which policy sectors are covered by advisory committees varies. One factor making for variation is the importance of the policy within the Community's policy framework – it is hardly surprising, for example, that there should be many more agricultural advisory committees than there are educational advisory committees. Another factor is the dependence of the Commission in particular policy areas on outside expertise and technical knowledge. And a third factor is the preferences of DGs – some incline towards the establishment of committees to provide them with advice, others prefer to do their listening in less structured ways.

The influence exercised by the advisory committees varies enormously. In general, the committees of national experts are better placed than the consultative committees because they can often go beyond offering the Commission much needed technical advice, to alerting it to probable governmental reactions to a proposal and, therefore, to possible problems that may arise at a future decision-making stage if certain views are not incorporated. Expert committees also have the advantage over consultative committees of tending to meet more regularly – often convening as necessary when something important is in the offing, whereas consultative committees gather on average no more than two or three times a year. Usually, consultative committees are at their most influential when they have high-ranking figures amongst their membership, when they are given the opportunity to discuss policy at an early stage of development, when the timetable for the enactment of a proposal is flexible, and when the matter under consideration is not too constrained by existing legislation.

Of the many pressures and influences to which the Commission is subject in the exercise of its policy initiation functions, the most important are those which emanate from the Council of Ministers. When the Council indicates that it wishes to see certain sorts of proposals laid before it, the Commission is obliged to respond. However, important though the Council has become as a policy initiating body, (see Chapter 4), the extent to which this has produced a decline in the initiating responsibilities and powers of the Commission ought not to be exaggerated. For the Council often finds it difficult to be bold and imaginative, and tends to be better at responding than at originating and proposing. Further to this, there has been an increasing tendency since the early 1980s for major policy initiatives to be sanctioned at European Council rather than Council of Ministers level, and the Commission has adjusted itself quite well to this shift. Three examples, covering issues of great importance, illustrate this. First, the Commission's 1985 White Paper *Completing the Internal Market*, (often referred to as the Cockfield White Paper after the Commissioner who pioneered it), which spelt out a rationale, a programme, and a timetable for completing the internal market by 1992, was approved at the June 1985 Milan summit. Six months later, at the Luxembourg summit, it was agreed that the institutional reforms that were necessary if the 1992 objective was to be achieved, would constitute part of the Single European Act. Second, the Communication from the Commission to the Council entitled *The Single Act: A New Frontier for Europe*, which was launched amidst considerable publicity early in 1987 – and which came generally to be referred to as 'the Delors package' – was central to the 1987–8 reform negotiations that culminated in major budgetary, agricultural and structural fund changes that were agreed at the February 1988 Brussels summit. Third, at the Strasbourg European Council in December 1989, the Commission's *Community Charter of the Fundamental Social Rights of Workers* (commonly referred to as 'the Social Charter') was adopted. The *Charter* did not contain specific legislative proposals for the application of the *Charter* – they were left to an accompanying action programme – but the adoption of the *Charter* has since acted as an important reference point, and a crucial political legitimiser, for the development of a social dimension to the internal market.

Executive Functions

The Commission exercises wide executive responsibilities. That is to say, it is closely involved in the management, supervision and implementation of Community policies. Just how involved varies considerably across the policy spectrum but, as a general rule, it can be said that the Commission's executive functions tend to be more concerned with monitoring and co-ordinating developments, laying down the ground rules, carrying out investigations and giving rulings on significant matters (such as proposed company mergers, state aids, and applications for derogations from Community law), than they are with detailed 'ground level' policy implementation.

Three aspects of the Commission's executive functions are worth special emphasis.

(1) *Rule-making powers.* It is not possible for the Treaties or for Council legislation to cover every possible area and eventuality in which a rule may be required. In circumstances and under conditions that are defined by the Treaties and/or Council legislation the

Commission is, therefore, delegated rule-making powers. In this the Commission is in a similar position to national executives: because of the frequent need for quick decisions in that grey area where policy overlaps with administration, and because too of the need to relieve the normal legislative process of over-involvement with highly detailed and specialised matters, it is desirable to have truncated and special rule-making arrangements for 'administrative' and 'technical' law.

The Commission normally issues between 4000 and 5000 legislative instruments per year. These are in the form of directives, regulations, and decisions. (The Commission also issues a large number of other instruments – in particular recommendations and opinions – but these do not usually have legislative force.) Most of this Commission legislation is confined to the filling in of details, or the taking of decisions, that follow automatically from Council legislation. So the greatest proportion of Commission legislation is made up of regulations dealing with price adjustments and market support measures under the Common Agricultural Policy. Exhibit 6.1 provides an example of such legislation. (See Chapter 6 for an examination of the differing nature of Community legislative instruments.)

But although most of the Commission's rule-making powers are confined to the routine and the straightforward, not quite all are. In at least three areas opportunities exist to make not just 'administrative' law, but what verges on 'policy' law. First, under the ECSC Treaty, the Commission is granted extensive rule-making powers, subject, in many instances, only to 'consultations' with the Consultative Committee of the ECSC and with the Council of Ministers. Article 60, for example, gives the Commission powers to define what constitutes 'unfair competitive practices' and 'discrimination practices', and under Article 61 it may set maximum prices. If a state of 'manifest crisis' is declared, as it was in October 1980 because of the Community's chronic over-production of steel, the Commission's powers are increased further: it may then set minimum prices (Article 61) and also, with the 'assent' of the Council of Ministers, establish a system of production quotas (Article 58). Second, the management of the Community's Common External Tariff gives the Commission considerable manoeuvrability. It is, for example, empowered to introduce preventive measures for a limited period in order to protect the Community market from dumping by third countries. Third, in furtherance of the Community's competition policy, the Commission, supported by decisions of the Court of Justice, has taken advantage of the rather generally phrased Article 85 of the EEC Treaty to clarify and develop the position on restrictive practices through the issuing of regulations and decisions.

(2) *Management of Community finances.* On the revenue side of the budget Community income is subject to tight constraints determined by the Council (see Chapter 11 for an explanation of budgetary revenue). In overseeing the collection of this income the Commission has two main duties. First, to see that the correct rates are applied within certain categories of revenue. Second, to ensure that the proper payments are made to the Community by the national authorities which act as the Community's collecting agents.

On the expenditure side, the administrative arrangements vary according to the type of expenditure concerned. The Commission must, however, always operate within the approved annual budget (the Community is not legally permitted to run a budget deficit) and on the basis of the guidelines for expenditure headings that are laid down in Community law. Of the various ways in which the Community spends its money two are especially important in that, together, they account for around 80 per cent of total budgetary expenditure.

First, there is the Guarantee section of the European Agricultural Guidance and Guarantee Fund (EAGGF). This takes up around 55 per cent of the annual budget and is used for agricultural price support purposes. General management decisions concerning the EAGGF – such as whether, and on what conditions, to dispose of product surpluses – are taken by the Commission, usually via an appropriate management committee (see below). The practical application of agricultural policy and management decisions occurs at national levels through appropriate agencies (see Chapter 12).

Second, there are the structural funds, which consist of the European Regional Development Fund (ERDF), the European Social Fund (ESF), and the Guidance Section of the EAGGF. Following the inclusion, via the SEA, of a new Title V in the EEC Treaty on 'Economic and Social Cohesion', and, in particular, of a new Article 130A under Title V which states 'the Community shall aim at reducing disparities between the various regions and the backwardness of the least-favoured regions', it was decided in 1988 to double the size of the structural funds over a five year period so that they would account for 25 per cent of the budget by 1993. It was also decided in 1988, again following the SEA and Treaty amendment provisions, to reform the funds so that instead of each having its own rules and objectives they would combine and concentrate their attention, through strategic multi-annual programmes, on five shared objectives: developing the backward regions, converting or adjusting the declining industrial regions, combatting long-term unemployment, integrating young people into the job market, and adjusting agricultural structures and developing the rural areas. As part of the reform the decision-making mechanisms of the funds were changed so as to create a more genuine partnership between the Community, national governments, and regional and local authorities. The partnership is based on a four stage process, in which the Commission plays a key role at each stage. The stages are as follows:

1. National governments, in consultation with both the Commission and with the competent regional and local authorities, submit to the Commission three to five year plans. The plans – which can be national, regional, or local in their scope – identify strategies and priorities for achieving the five objectives and indicate how Community financial assistance is to be used.

2. On the basis of the plans submitted by the member states, in dialogue with the partners, and after consulting the appropriate advisory committee – either the Advisory Committee on the Development and Conversion of Regions, the Committee of the European Social Fund, or the Committee on Agricultural Structures and Rural Development – the Commission draws up what are known as Community Support Frameworks (CSFs). By setting out a statement of the priorities for action, outlining the forms of assistance that are to be made available, and indicating the financial allocations that are envisaged, CSFs provide a reference framework for the applications for assistance which are made to the funds.

3. Procedures for operationalising CSFs vary. The three main forms of implementation are through operational programmes (there may be several types of programme in a particular region), individual applications for large-scale projects, and global grants (whereby the Commission entrusts the administration of a budget to a national or regional intermediary).

4. Monitoring and assessment of CSFs and individual operations is undertaken by monitoring committees on which sit representatives both of the Commission and of national, regional, and local partners.

Moving beyond the different parts of the Commission's financial management functions to look at the overall financial picture, it is clear that the Commission's ability to manage Community finances effectively is greatly weakened by its reliance on the Council. For the Council controls the upper limits of the revenue base, and framework spending decisions are taken by different groups of ministers. In the past this sometimes caused considerable difficulties because it meant that if it became obvious during the course of a financial year that expenditure was exceeding income the Commission could not step in at an early stage and take appropriate action by, for example, increasing the Value Added Tax ceiling on revenue or reducing agricultural price guarantees. All the Commission could, and regularly did do, was to make out a case to the Council as to what should be done. This dependence on the Council still remains, but the general situation is not so fraught as it was, because, following decisions that were taken at the February 1988 European Council meeting, there are now planned and clearer controls on the growth of both income and expenditure, and there are provisions for the Commission to act quickly if expenditure expands beyond targets in the main 'problem' area of agriculture – notably by imposing financial penalties on farmers if production thresholds are exceeded. The Commission is thus now more capable of effective financial management than formerly it was.

Before leaving the Commission's responsibilities for financial management it should also be noted that the Commission has some responsibilities for co-ordinating and managing finances which are not drawn exclusively from Community sources. These responsibilities mostly cover environmental programmes and scientific and technological research programmes in which the member states are joined by non-member European states – mainly from the EFTA countries.

A particularly important programme area in which the Commission has assumed co-ordination and management responsibilities is not even exclusively European based. The seven-nation Western

Economic Summit of July 1989 called on the Commission to co-ordinate a programme of assistance from the twenty-four OECD countries to Poland and Hungary. This resulted in the PHARE programme (Poland and Hungary: Aid for the Restructuring of Economies) which, in 1990, was extended to Bulgaria, Czechoslovakia, Yugoslavia, Romania and, since it was still independent at the time, East Germany. The PHARE programme is by no means the only channel via which Western aid is being made available to the fledgling democracies of Central and Eastern Europe but it is an extremely important one with billions of Ecu being made available for purposes such as increasing investment, expanding vocational training, and improving environmental standards.

(3)   *Supervision of 'front line' policy implementation.* The Commission's role with regard to the implementation of Community policies is primarily that of supervisor and overseer. It does undertake a limited amount of direct policy implementation – in connection with competition policy for example – but the bulk of the practical/routine/day-by-day/front line implementation of Community policies is delegated to appropriate agencies within the member states. Examples of such national agencies are: Customs and Excise Authorities (which deal with most matters in relation to movements across the Community's external and internal borders); veterinary inspection teams (which check quality standards on foodstuffs); and Ministries of Agriculture and Agricultural Intervention Boards (which are responsible for controlling the volume of agricultural produce on domestic markets and which deal directly with farmers and traders about payments and charges).

To ensure policies are applied in a reasonably uniform manner throughout the twelve states the Commission attempts to supervise, or at least hold a watching brief on, the national agencies and the way they perform their Community duties. It is a task that carries with it many difficulties. Four of these are especially important.

First, the Commission is not, in general, well enough resourced for the job. It is, therefore, heavily dependent on the good faith and willing co-operation of the states. Even in those policy spheres where it is in almost constant communication with national officials the Commission cannot know everything that is going on. And with respect to those areas where contacts and flows of communication between Brussels and national agencies are irregular and not well ordered, it is almost impossible for Commission officials to have any very accurate idea as to what is happening 'at the front'. Even if the Commission comes to suspect that something is amiss with an aspect of policy implementation, lack of resources can mean that it is not possible for the matter to be fully investigated: for example, the unit responsible for the co-ordination of fraud prevention is tiny in relation to the size of the problem – it had a staff of only twenty-seven officials in 1990.

The second difficulty is that even where they are willing to co-operate fully, national agencies are not always capable of implementing policies as the Commission would ideally wish. One reason for this is that some Community policies are, by their very nature, extremely difficult to administer. For example, the CAP requires that virtually all cross-border movement of produce must be checked – a task that even greatly enlarged national customs authorities could not possibly fully implement. Similarly, the Common Fisheries Policy is extremely difficult to police, with the provisions on fishing zones, total allowable catches, and conservation measures requiring surveillance measures such as obligatory and properly entered logbooks, port inspections, and aerial patrols. Another reason why national agencies are not always capable of effective policy implementation is that national officials are often poorly trained and/or are over-burdened by the complexities of Community rules. The maze of rules which officials have to apply is illustrated by the import levy on biscuits which varies according to cereal, milk, fat and sugar content, while the export refund varies also according to egg content. Another example of rule complexity is seen in respect of the export of beef which, at the beginning of 1988, was subject to forty-three separate regulations, which were themselves subject to eighty-two permanent and 145 temporary amendments.

The third difficulty is that agencies in the member states do not always wish to see Community law applied. Competition policy, for example, is rich in such examples, but there is often little the Commission can do against a deliberately recalcitrant state given the range of policy instruments available to governments which wish to assist domestic industries, and given too the secretiveness with which these can often be arranged.

The fourth, and final, difficulty is that Community law can be genuinely open to different interpretations. Sometimes indeed it is deliberately flexible so as to allow for adjustments to national circumstances.

The role of management and regulatory committees. As is clear from the above discussion, a number of different procedures apply with regard to how the Commission exercises its executive functions. An important dimension of these differences concerns the role of management and regulatory committees. These committees have some role to play with regard to each of the three aspects of the Commission's executive powers that have just been outlined, but particularly the first two. This is because the committees are very important with regard to how the Commission may act when it wishes to adopt appropriate implementing/adaptive measures in respect of Council legislation.

Aware that the arrangements regarding the Commission's implementing powers were becoming ever more confusing and complex, and aware, too, that the projected completion of the internal market by 1992 would entail a host of implementing decisions, the Single European Act provided for a clarification of the procedures. On the basis of the SEA, and of a Council decision of 13 July 1987, the Commission's management and implementing powers in respect of Council decisions were clarified and streamlined. While no new procedures were introduced, it was established what the possible procedures were, and some guidelines were laid down for which should apply in particular cases.

As can be seen from Table 3.2 there are significant differences between the powers of the different types of committee: advisory committees can only *advise*; management committees can *block* Commission decisions by a qualified majority; regulatory committees must give their *approval* for Commission decisions by a qualified majority. These differences have led to disputes between the Council on the one hand and the Commission and the EP on the other. Indeed, when the 1987 reforms were being discussed, the EP only wanted Procedures I and II, and the Commission did not want IIIb or Safeguard Measure b, so, almost inevitably, there have been disagreements since 1987 as to which procedure should apply – with both the Commission and the EP claiming that the Council has not used the advisory committee procedure as much as was anticipated by the Single European Act.

TABLE 3.2

Procedures to be used in respect of the Commission's implementing powers[1]

Procedure I (Advisory Committees)	The Commission submits a draft of the measures to be taken to the committee. The committee delivers an opinion on the draft, by a simple majority if necessary. The Commission takes 'the utmost account' of the opinion delivered by the committee.
Procedure II (Management Committees)	The Commission submits a draft of the measures to be taken to the committee. If the Commission's measures are *opposed* by a qualified majority in the committee then either: Variant (a) The Commission *may* defer application of its decision for up to one month; Variant (b) The Commission *shall* defer application of its decision for up to three months. Within the one month and three month deadlines the Council may take a different decision by a qualified majority vote.
Procedure III (Regulatory Committees)	The Commission submits a draft of the measures to be taken by the committee. If the Commission's measures are not *supported* by a qualified majority in the committee, or if no opinion is delivered, the matter is referred to the Council. The Council may, within a period not exceeding three months, take a decision on the Commission's proposal by a qualified majority. If the Council does not act within the three month period then either: Variant (a) The proposal shall be adopted by the Commission; Variant (b) The proposal shall be adopted by the Commission except where a *simple* majority in the Council votes against adoption.
Safeguard Measures (Mainly trade)	No committee is appointed, but the Commission must notify, and in some cases must consult with, the member states in respect of a measure to be taken. If any member state asks for the Commission's measures to be referred to the Council, within a time limit to be determined, then either: Variant (a) The Council may take a different decision by a qualified majority within a time limit to be determined; Variant (b) The Council must confirm, amend, or revoke the Commission's decision. If the Council takes no decision within a time limit to be determined the Commission's decision is revoked.

[1] Which procedure applies is specified in the enabling Council legislation.

Concentrating attention now just on management committees and regulatory committees – advisory committees having been discussed earlier – both types of committee are chaired and serviced by the Commission. The committee members are governmental representatives, with, in an average-sized committee, two or three middle-ranking officials from appropriate ministries attending on behalf of each state. There is no hard and fast distinction of either principle or policy responsibility between the two types of committee. Management committees in the past were mostly concerned with agriculture – there are currently over twenty of these, most of them having a specific sectoral responsibility for the CAP's product regimes – but there are now an increasing number of management committees in other areas too. The regulatory committees tend to be concerned with harmonisation and vary greatly in their sectoral interests. Some, such as the Standing Committee on Feedingstuffs and the Committee on General Customs Rules, have fairly broad briefs. Others, notably the numerous Committees for the Adaptation to Technical (and Scientific) Progress of Directives, are highly specialised: they include commmittees on Dangerous Substances and Preparations, Quality of Water Intended for Human Consumption, and Fertilisers. All of these committees, management and regulatory, meet as appropriate, which means almost weekly in the case of agricultural products requiring frequent market adjustments such as cereals, sugar, and wines, and in other cases means hardly at all.

Both types of committees do similar things, with variations occurring not so much between management and regulatory committees as such, but rather between individual committees according to their terms of reference, the nature of the subject matter with which they are concerned, and how they are regarded by the Commission. In addition to considering proposed Commission decisions, agenda items for committee meetings could include analysing the significance of data of various kinds, looking at how existing legislation is working, considering how existing legislation may be modified to take account of technical developments (the particular responsibility of the Technical Progress Committees), and assessing market situations (a prime task for the agricultural committees).

Those who criticise the Community on the grounds that it is undermining national sovereignties sometimes cite regulatory and management committees as part of their case. They point to the rarity of adverse opinions, the low number of no opinions, the frequency with which measures go through without unanimous support, and the ability of the Commission – especially under the management procedure – to ignore or circumvent unfavourable votes. There is, however, another side to this; a side which suggests that the power of the Commission to control the committees and impose its will on the states ought not to be exaggerated. Four points in particular ought to be noted. First, although some of the committees do exercise important powers, they tend, for the most part, to work within fairly narrowly defined limits. Anything very controversial is almost invariably referred to a Council meeting. Second, many negative votes by states are cast tactically rather than as part of a real attempt to stop a proposal. That is to say, a national delegation might well recognise that a measure is going to be approved but will vote against it or will abstain to satisfy a political interest at home. Third, as with all aspects of its activity, it is just not in the Commission's long-term interests to abuse its powers by forcing unwelcome or unpopular measures through a committee. It wants and needs co-operation, and if a proposal meets serious opposition in a committee a good chairman will, unless special circumstances prevail, suggest revisions rather than press a vote which may have divisive consequences. Finally, the Council tends to be jealous of its powers and would move quickly against the Commission if it thought committees of any sort were being used to undermine Council power. Indeed, the watchfulness of the Council in this regard is no more clearly seen than in the way it has been very reluctant, since the 1987 reforms, to honour the agreement that it would give priority to advisory committees – over which its control is very limited – for internal market proposals: up to the end of 1988 the Council had accepted this procedure only seven times out of the twenty-four times it had been proposed by the Commission.

The Guardian of the Legal Framework

In association with the Court of Justice, the Commission is charged with ensuring that the Treaties and Community legislation are respected. This role links closely with the Commission's supervisory and implementing responsibilities. Indeed, the lack of a full Community-wide policy implementing framework means that a legal watchdog role acts, to some extent, as a substitute for that detailed day-to-day application of policies that at national levels involves, as a matter of routine, such activities as inspecting premises, checking employee lists, and auditing returns. It is a role that is extremely difficult to exercise: transgressors of Community law do not normally wish to advertise their illegal actions, and they are often protected by, or themselves may even be, national governments.

The Commission may become aware of possible illegalities in one of a number of ways. In the case of non-incorporation or incorrect incorporation of a directive into national law that is obvious enough, since directives normally specify a time by which the Commission must be supplied with full details of national incorporation measures. A second way is through self-notification. States, for example, are obliged to notify the Commission about all national draft regulations and standards concerning technical specifications so that the Commission may satisfy itself that they will not cause barriers to trade. Similarly, under Article 93 of the EEC Treaty, state aids must be referred to the Commission for its inspection. Self-notifications also come forward under Article 85 of the EEC Treaty, because although parties are not obliged to notify the Commission of possible restrictive business practices, they frequently do, either because they wish for clarification as to whether or not a practice is in legal violation, or because they wish to seek an exemption. (If notifications are not made within specified time limits exemptions are not permissible.) A third way in which illegalities may come to the Commission's attention is from the many representations that are made by individuals, organisations, firms or member states who believe their interests are being damaged by the alleged illegal actions of another party. For example, Germany has complained about the amount of subsidisation given by many national governments to their steel industries. A fourth way is through the Commission's own efforts. Such efforts may take one of several forms: investigations by one of the small monitoring/investigatory/fraud teams that the Commission has in a few policy areas; careful analysis of the information that is supplied by outside agencies; or simply a Commission official reading a newspaper report that suggests a government or a firm is doing, or is not doing, something that looks suspicious under Community law.

Infringement proceedings are initiated against member states for not notifying the Commission of measures taken to incorporate directives into national law, for non-incorporation or incorrect incorporation of directives, and for non-application or incorrect application of Community law – most commonly in connection with internal market and industrial affairs, indirect taxation, agriculture, and environmental and consumer protection. Before any formal action is taken against a state it is informed by the Commission that it is in possible breach of its legal obligations. If, after the Commission has carried out an investigation, the breach is confirmed and continued, a procedure comes into force, under Article 169 of the EEC Treaty, whereby the Commission

> shall deliver a reasoned opinion on the matter after giving the state concerned the opportunity to submit its declarations. If the state concerned does not comply with the opinion within the period laid down by the Commission, the latter may bring the matter before the Court of Justice.

Since most infringements have implications for the functioning of the market, the Commission usually seeks to ensure that these procedures operate according to a tight timetable: normally about two months for the state to present its observations and a similar period for it to comply with the reasoned opinion.

Most cases, it must be emphasised, are settled at an early stage. So, in an average year, the Commission might issue around 600 letters of formal notice, deliver 200 reasoned opinions, and make 100 references to the Court of Justice. Italy, France, and Greece consistently figure high in these lists (see Table 10.2). One reason for so many early settlements is that most infringements occur not as a result of wilful avoidance of Community law but rather from genuine differences over interpretation or from national administrative and legislative procedures which have occasioned delay. Although there are differences between member states in their enthusiasm for aspects of Community law they do not usually wish to engage in open confrontation with Community institutions.

If states do not wish to submit to a Community law it is, therefore, more customary for them to drag their feet rather than be openly obstructive. Delay can, however, be a form of obstruction, in that states know it could be years before the Commission, and even more the Court of Justice, brings them to heel. Environmental legislation illustrates this, with most states not having fully incorporated and/or implemented only parts of long-standing Community legislation – on matters such as air pollution, bathing water, and drinking water. When the Commission launched an offensive on the environmental front in 1989–90 – with the issuing of warning letters, reasoned opinions, and the launching of Court proceedings – Spain faced possible prosecution on 57 of the 160 directives in force, Belgium on 46, Greece on 45, France on 41, Italy on 40, and the UK on 31.

The Commission has no power to impose penalties on member states which it holds to be in breach of Community law. Respect for its decisions is dependent on the goodwill and political judgement of the states themselves, backed up by the ability of the Commission to make a referral to the Court of Justice. However, in certain circumstances the Commission can fine individuals, firms and organisations, subject to their right to appeal to the Court of Justice. Article 85 of the EEC Treaty, which prohibits restrictive practices of various kinds, Article 86 which prohibits abuse of a dominant trading position, and a number of regulations and Court judgements, provide the principal bases for this stronger Commission position *vis-à-vis* undertakings. Three examples of these regulations and Court judgements are worth citing – partly because of their intrinsic importance, and partly because they illustrate the different ways in which the Commission attains effective operating power:

1. Council Regulation 17/62, which gives effect to the principles set out in Articles 85 and 86, is especially important because it specifies the Commission's investigative and punitive powers. Under 17/62 the Commission can call for information, require that parties submit to an investigation, send in its own officials to examine a company's books, and issue fines.

2. In September 1989 the Court issued an important judgement in Joined Cases 46/87 and 227/88 *Hoechst* v. *Commission*. The legal proceedings arose from incidents in February 1987 when officials from DGIV's investigative division attempted to enter the premises of the German chemical firm Hoechst in order to investigate reports of a cartel for polyethylene and PVC. Hoechst obtained a local court order enabling them to keep the officials out, and subsequently initiated action in the Court for the annulment of three Commission decisions against Hoechst. The Court rejected the proceedings for annulment and in its judgement confirmed the Commission's responsibility as regards applying the Community's competition rules and clearly defined the responsibilities of the Commission and the national authorities in the conduct of investigations.

3. In the important area of company mergers, Council Regulation 4064/89, which came into effect in September 1990, specifies the Commission's powers in some detail: specified information regarding proposed mergers and takeovers above certain limits have to be notified to the Commission; on receipt of the information the Commission must decide within one month whether it proposes to either let the deal go ahead on the grounds that competition would not be harmed, or whether it wishes to 'open proceedings'; if it wishes to 'open proceedings' it has four months to carry out an investigation, during which it is entitled to enter the premises of firms and seize documents; any firm that supplies false information during the course of a Commission inquiry, or implements a merger/takeover without gaining clearance from the Commission, is liable to be fined up to 10 per cent of its annual sales.

If at all possible the Commission avoids taking formal action against firms. This is partly because of the ill-feeling that can be generated by open confrontations, and partly because formal action necessitates the use of cumbersome and protracted bureaucratic procedures within the Commission itself. Offending parties are, therefore, encouraged to fall into line or to reach an agreement with the Commission during the extensive informal processes that always precede formal action. If this fails, however, fines can result. Thus, in April 1986 a price-fixing cartel of petrochemical companies led by Montedison, ICI, Shell, and Hoechst, was fined a total of 55 million Ecu (£35m). It was deemed to be in breach of Community competition rules by fixing quotas for polypropylene (a plastic) which kept the price well above its real market level. Less punitively, in December 1986, the Commission issued a token fine of 50000 Ecu (£36000) on three major acid manufacturers – Unilever, Henkel, and Oleofina – for exchanging confidential information between 1979 and 1982 about their sales of certain products. This was the first occasion the Commission had imposed fines for a pure exchange of information agreement. In explaining its action the Commission stated: 'This exchange of information, normally regarded as business secrets, provided each of them with a means to monitor the activities of its major competitors and to adjust its own behaviour accordingly'.

In exercising the role of guardian of the legal framework the Commission thus attempts to operate in a flexible and politically sensitive manner. It would not be in its, or the Community's interests, to use an overly heavy hand. A good example of the way in which political calculation, as well as legal interpretation, is employed by the Commission in the exercise of this role was seen in the much publicised Renault case: in March 1988 the Commission approved French government aid to Renault subject to certain conditions; in November 1989 the approval was revoked, on the grounds that Renault had not kept its part of the bargain; in the deliberations which followed the Commission initially leant towards ordering Renault to pay back most of the aid, but following protracted negotiations at the highest levels – involving, at times, the Commissioner responsible (Sir Leon Brittan) and the French Prime Minister (Michel Rocard) a deal was struck under which Renault would pay back half of the FFr 12 billion (£1.26b) it had received.

As with most of its other activities, the Commission's ability to exercise its legal guardianship role is blunted by a number of constraints and restrictions. Three are especially important:

● The problem of limited resources means that choices have to be made about which cases are worth pursuing, and with what vigour. For example, only fifty officials – in a specially created task force located in DGIV – were appointed to undertake the detailed and highly complex work that is necessary to give effect to the 1989 company merger regulation. And as one Community official told *The Financial Times* in 1989 in connection with state aids: 'It is depressing to think that there are 30 of us here trying to control state aid, while in the Walloon region of Belgium alone there are 150 doling it out'.

● Relevant and sufficiently detailed information can be difficult to obtain – either because it is deliberately hidden from prying Commission officials, or because, as is the case with many aspects of market conditions, reliable figures are just not available. An example of a Community law which is difficult to apply because of lack of information is the *Council Directive of 2 April 1979 on the conservation of wild birds* (79/409/EEC). Amongst other things, the Directive provides protection for most species of migrant birds and forbids killing for trade and by indiscriminate methods. Because the shooting of birds is popular in some countries, several governments have been slow to transpose the Directive into national law, and then reluctant to do much about applying the law once it has been transposed. On the first of these implementing problems – transposition – the Commission can acquire the information it needs since states are obliged to inform it of the measures they have taken. Dissatisfaction with the slowness of transposition has led the Commission to initiate action in the Court against Belgium, France, Germany, Greece, Italy and the Netherlands. On the second of the implementation problems however – application of the law by national authorities against transgressors – the Commission has been much less able to make judgements about whether states are exercising their responsibilities: it is very difficult to know what efforts are really being made by national authorities to catch shooters and hunters.

● Political considerations can inhibit the Commission from acting as vigorously as it could in certain problem areas and in particular cases. This is largely because it does not normally wish to upset or politically embarrass member states if it is at all avoidable: the Commission does, after all, have to work closely and continously with the states both on an individual and – in the Council of Ministers – on a collective basis. An example of political pressures inhibiting the Commission is seen in the above cited conservation of wild birds Directive: in addition to the practical problems it has in acquiring information about the killing of birds, the Commission's sensitive political antennae also serve to hold it in check in that it is well aware of the unpopularity and political difficulties that would be created for some governments if action was to be taken against the thousands who break this law. Another example of the inhibiting role of political pressures is seen in the cautious line that the Commission has traditionally adopted towards multinational corporations which appear to be in breach of Community competition law: to take action against a multinational is to risk generating political opposition from member states in which the company is based, and also risks being self-defeating in that it may cause the company to transfer its activities outside the Community. (There are also, of course, practical problems of the sort noted in the previous point when seeking to act against multinationals: it is very difficult to follow investigations through when dealing with organisations which are located in several countries, some of which may be outside Europe.)

External Representative and Negotiator

Of the different aspects of the Community's external relations there are five in which the Commission plays a particularly prominent role.

First, acting under the authority of Articles 228–231 of the EEC Treaty, the Commission represents the Community and participates in the work of a number of important international organisations. Four of these are specifically mentioned in the Treaty: the United Nations and its specialised agencies, the General Agreement on Tariffs and Trade (GATT), the Council of Europe, and the Organisation of European Economic Co-operation (now OECD). A specific example of how the Commission links up with other organisations may be seen in its relations with the International Energy Agency (IEA). The IEA was established in 1974 as an autonomous agency within the OECD. Its main aim was to reduce members' dependence on oil imports. Almost inevitably, the IEA overlaps at many points in its work and its programmes with the Community and hence a liaising framework, and if possible a co-ordinating one, is highly desirable between the two organisations. This is attempted principally by Commission participation in the Standing Groups which act as the IEA's main policy formulators and which bring together on a regular basis senior energy specialists from the IEA member states. In a less structured manner, mutual awareness and liaison between the Community and the IEA is also assisted by the fact that many of those who represent their countries in IEA forums are the very same people who appear in Community forums in Brussels.

Second, the Commission has responsibilities for acting as a key point of contact between the Community and non-member states. Over 130 countries have diplomatic missions accredited to the Community and the Commission is expected to keep them informed about Community affairs, either through the circulation of documents or by making its officials available for information briefings and lobbying. The Community, for its part, maintains an extensive network of diplomatic missions abroad, numbering over eighty delegations and offices, and these are staffed by Commission employees.

Third, the Commission is entrusted with important responsibilities in regard to applications for Community membership. On receipt of an application the Council normally asks the Commission to carry out a detailed investigation of the implications and to submit an opinion (an opinion that the Council need not, of course, accept – as it did not in 1976 when it rejected the Commission's proposal that Greece be offered a pre-accession period of unlimited duration and instead authorised negotiations for full membership). If and when negotiations begin, the Commission, operating within Council approved guidelines, acts as the Community's main negotiator except on show-piece ministerial occasions or when particularly sensitive or difficult matters call for an inter-ministerial resolution of differences. The whole process – from the lodging of an application to accession – can take years. Portugal, for example, applied in March 1977; the Commission forwarded a favourable opinion to the Council in May 1978; negotiations opened in October 1978 and were not concluded until March 1985; and Portugal eventually joined in January 1986 – eight years and ten months after applying.

Fourth, the Commission is centrally involved in determining and conducting the Community's external trade relations. It represents the Community both in formal negotiations, such as those conducted under the auspices of GATT, and in the more informal and exploratory exchanges such as are common between, for example, the Community and the USA over world agricultural trade, or between the Community and Japan over access to each other's markets.

The constitutional base for the Commission's external trade role is found in Article 113 of the EEC Treaty:

> The Commission shall submit proposals to the Council for implementing the common commercial policy. Where agreements [on trading matters] with third countries need to be negotiated, the Commission shall make recommendations to the Council, which shall authorise the Commission to open necessary negotiations. The Commission shall conduct these negotiations in consultation with a special committee appointed by the Council to assist the Commission in this task and within the framework of such directives as the Council may issue to it.

So, on the basis of a brief determined by the Council, with the outcome of negotiations subject to Council approval, and with national officials in the Article 113 Committee carefully monitoring its actions, the Commission acts as the Community's external trade negotiator. How much room for manoeuvre it has in undertaking this task varies according to circumstances. Usually, differences of both principle and special interest between the member states result in the negotiating brief being fairly tightly drawn – reflecting, often, a compromise between those countries which tend towards protectionism and those which favour free trade. While Commission officials acknowledge privately that the Council mandate is usually less of a dead weight than is often supposed, there is no doubt that the Commission's flexibility in negotiations is often constrained by the necessity of not disturbing compromises that have been agreed only with difficulty in the Council. (Although it should also be said that it is not unknown for the Commission to use Council reins to the Community's advantage: during negotiations it can be helpful to say, in response to an unwanted proposal 'the Council would never agree to that'.) In particularly difficult negotiations adjournments may be sought to allow the Commission to return to the Council in order to seek approval for an amended brief which might break a deadlock. The use of a tandem arrangement, in which the Commission and the Council jointly represent the Community, is sometimes used to increase flexibility.

Fifth, the Commission has important negotiating and managing responsibilities in respect of the various special external agreements which the Community has with many countries and groups of countries. These agreements take various forms but the more 'advanced' – the economic co-operation agreements and the association agreements – go beyond the 'privileged' trading conditions which are invariably at their heart, to include provisions for such things as European Investment Bank loans, financial aid, and political dialogue.

Mediator and Conciliator

Much of Community decision-making, especially in the Council of Ministers, is based on searches for agreements between competing interests. The Commission is very much involved in trying to bring these agreements about and a great deal of its time is taken up looking for common ground which can create compromises that are somewhat more than the lowest common denominator. As a consequence, the Commission is often obliged to be guarded and cautious with its proposals. Radical initiatives, involving perhaps what it really believes needs to be done, are almost certain to meet with fierce opposition. More moderate proposals on the other hand, perhaps taking the form of adjustments and extensions to existing policy, and presented preferably in a technocratic rather than an ideological manner, are more likely to be acceptable. In other words, the Commission is often subject to an enforced incrementalism.

The Commission is not the only Community body that consciously seeks to oil the wheels of decision-making. As is shown in the next chapter, the Council itself has taken steps to improve its own machinery. But the Commission is particularly well placed to act as mediator and conciliator. One reason for this is that it is normally seen as being non-partisan: its proposals may, therefore, be viewed less suspiciously than any which come from, say, the chairman of a Council working party. Another reason is that in many instances the Commission is simply in the best position to judge what proposals are likely to command support, both inside and outside the Council. This is because of the continuous and extensive discussions which the Commission has with interested parties from the earliest considerations of a policy proposal through to its enactment. Unlike the other institutions, the Commission is represented at virtually every stage and in virtually every forum of the Community's decision-making system.

Although there are naturally limitations on what can be achieved, the effectiveness with which the Commission exercises this mediating role can be considerably influenced by the competence of its officials. While, for example, one Commission official may play a crucial role in driving a proposal through a Council working party, another may be so incompetent as not only to prejudice the Commission's own position but to threaten the progress of the whole proposal. Many questions must be handled with care and political sensitivity: when should a proposal be brought forward and in what form?; at what point will an adjustment in the Commission's position open the way to progress in the Council?; is there anything to be gained from informal discussions with 'awkward delegations'? These, and questions such as these, call for highly developed political skills.

The Conscience of the Community

In performing each of the above tasks the Commission is supposed to stand above and beyond sectional and national interests. While others might look to the particular, it should look to the general;

while others might look to the benefits to be gained from the next deal, it should keep at least one eye on the horizon. As many have described it, the Commission should be the 'conscience' of the Community.

Christopher Tugendhat, a former Commissioner, has commented on this role. Among other things, he states, the Commission exists 'to represent the general interest in the welter of national ones and to point the way ahead, but also drawing the attention of member states to new and more daring possibilities' (Tugendhat, 1986). Ideally this may be so. But, in practice, it is very difficult to operationalise. One reason for this is that it is highly questionable whether such a thing as the 'general interest' exists: there are few initiatives which do not threaten the interests of at least some – were this not the case there would not be so many disagreements in the Council. Another reason is that many in the Commission doubt whether it is worth pursuing 'daring possibilities' if it is clear that they will be rejected and may even generate anti-Commission feelings.

In practice, therefore, the Commission tends not to be so detached, so far-seeing, or so enthusiastic in pressing the *esprit communautaire*, as some would like. This is not to say that it does not attempt to map out the future or attempt to press for developments that it believes will be generally beneficial. Nor is it to deny that the Commission is sometimes ambitious in its approach and long term in its perspective – as, for example, is demonstrated with its internal market pro-gramme and the Social Charter. But the fact is that the Commission does operate in the real Community world, and often that necessi-tates looking to the short rather than to the long-term, and to what is possible rather than what is desirable.

Concluding Remarks

It is frequently stated that there has been a decline in the powers of the Commission since the mid-1960s. Commentators have particu-larly stressed a diminution in the Commission's initiating role and a corresponding weakening in its ability to offer real vision and leadership to the Community. It has become, it is claimed, too reactive in exercising its responsibilities: reactive to the pressures of the many interests to which it is subject; reactive to the immediacy of events; and above all, reactive to the increasing 'instructions' which are given to it by the Council of Ministers and the European Council. Unquestionably, there is something in this view. The explanation for why it has happened is to be sought in a combination of factors. The rather rigid vertical lines within the Commission's own organisational structure make it difficult for a broad vision to emerge. The tensions which are seemingly present between the politically creative elements of the Commission's responsibilities and the bureaucratic roles of administering and implementing have perhaps never been properly resolved, or even tackled. Beyond such internal considerations, factors as varied as the accession of states which are anxious to protect their independence, the frequent appearance on the Community agenda of politically sensitive matters, and the desire of politicians not to cede too much power to others if it can be avoided, have resulted in the states being reluctant to grant too much autonomy to the Commission.

But the extent to which there has been a decline should not be exaggerated. In some respects, indeed, there has been an increase in influence as the Commission has adapted itself to the ever-changing nature of, and demands upon, the Community. As has been shown, the Commission exercises, either by itself or in association with other bodies, a number of crucially important functions. It may not be quite the motor force that some of the founding fathers had hoped for, but in many ways it is both central and vital to the whole Community system.

4

The Council of Ministers

The Council of Ministers is the principal meeting place of the national governments and is the EC's main decision-making institution.

When the Community was founded in the 1950s many expected that in time, as joint policies were seen to work and as the states came to trust one another more, the role of the Council would gradually decline, especially in relation to the Commission. This has not happened. On the contrary, by jealously guarding the responsibilities that are accorded to it in the Treaties, by exercising influence in areas that are properly the responsibility of the Commission, and by adapting and extending its internal mechanisms to enable it more easily to cope with the EC's ever increasing policy commitments, the Council has greatly enhanced its position in the Community. This has naturally produced some frustration in the Commission, and in the European Parliament. It has also ensured that national governments are centrally placed to influence most aspects of Community business.

There was also a general expectation when the Community was founded that governments would gradually come to be less concerned about national sovereignty considerations and that this would be reflected in an increasing use of majority voting in the Council. Until the 1980s, however, there was little movement in this direction: even where the Treaties permitted majority votes the Council normally preferred to proceed on the basis of consensual agreements. This preference for unanimity naturally bolstered the intergovernmental, as opposed to supranational, side of the Community's nature and resulted in Council decision-making processes tending to be slow and protracted. As will be shown, this situation has changed considerably in recent years.

Responsibilities and Functions

The principal responsibility of the Council is to take decisions which become Community law. As was shown in the previous chapter, the Commission also has law-making powers but these are usually limited, tightly drawn, and based on enabling Council legislation. Virtually all proposals for politically important and/or sensitive legislation have to receive Council approval in order to be adopted. Normally, the Council has to act on the basis of proposals which are made to it by the Commission, and after receiving advice from the EP and the Economic and Social Committee (ESC), but, crucially, it alone decides. The Council is, therefore, in effect the Community's legislature. In 1989 it adopted 70 directives, 394 regulations and 161 decisions.

But, if the Council is the Community's legislature in the sense that it converts proposals into legal acts, its legislative capacity is significantly restricted by the requirement of the Treaties that it can usually act only on the basis of Commission proposals. This means that it does not have the constitutional power to initiate or draft proposals itself. In practice, ways have been found, if not to completely circumvent the Commission, at least to allow the Council a significant policy initiating role. Article 152 of the EEC Treaty has been especially useful: 'The Council may request the Commission to undertake any studies the Council considers desirable for the attainment of the common objectives, and to submit to it any appropriate proposals'. In the view of many observers, the use that has been made of Article 152, and the very specific instructions which have sometimes been issued to the Commission under its aegis, is against its intended spirit. Be that as it may, the political weight of the Council is such that the Commission is bound to pay close attention to what the ministers want.

In addition to Article 152, four other factors have also enhanced the Council's policy initiating role:

1. The increasing adoption by the Council of opinions, resolutions, agreements and recommendations. These are not legal texts but they carry political weight and it is difficult for the

Commission to ignore them. Sometimes they are explicitly designed to pressurise the Commission to come up with proposals for legislation.

2. The movement of the Community into policy spheres which are not covered, or are not covered clearly, in the Treaties. This sometimes produces uncertainty regarding the exact responsibilities of Community bodies, and hence grey areas which the Council can exploit.

3. The increasingly developed Council machinery. There are now many places in the Council's network where ideas can be generated. The emergence of the Council Presidency as a key Community actor has played a particularly important role in enabling the Council to influence policy directions and prior ities.

4. The increasing willingness of the states to found aspects of their co-operation not on Community law but on non-binding agreements and understandings. This is most obviously seen in European Political Co-operation and issues such as terrorism and drug control, but it does sometimes also happen in other, more conventional, Community spheres where national differences make it very difficult for law to be agreed. Such non-legal arrangements do not have to be Commission initiated.

Not only has the Council encroached on the Commission's policy initiating function but it has also joined it in exercising important responsibilities in the key activities of mediation and consensus building. Of course, as the forum in which the national representatives meet, the Council has always served the function of developing mutual understanding between the states. Moreover, a necessary prerequisite for successful policy development has always been that Council participants display an ability to compromise in negotiations. But, as the Community has grown in size, as more difficult policy areas have come onto the agenda, and as political and economic change has broken down some of the pioneering spirit of the early days, so has positive and active mediation come to be ever more necessary: mediation primarily between the different national and ideological interests represented in the Council, but also between the Council and the Commission, the Council and the Parliament, and the Council and non-institutional interests. The Commission has taken on much of this task but, so too, has the Council.

Composition

The Ministers

Ministerial meetings are at the apex of the Council machinery. Under the Merger Treaty there is only one Council of Ministers but, in practice, there are many in the sense that the work of the Council is divided into policy areas. The General Council, which is composed of Foreign Ministers, has the widest brief: it deals with general issues relating to policy initiation and co-ordination, with external political relations, and often too with matters which, for whatever reason, are particularly politically sensitive. More sectoral matters are dealt with in the so-called 'Technical Councils', which are made up of Ministers of Agriculture, of Energy, of Environment and so on.

Often, the national representatives who attend Council of Ministers meetings differ in terms of their status and/or their policy responsibilities. This can inhibit efficient decision-making. The problem arises because the states themselves to decide by whom they wish to be represented, and their decisions may vary in one of two ways:

The level of seniority. Normally, by prior arrangement, Council meetings are attended by ministers of a similar standing, but circumstances do arise when delegations are headed at different levels of seniority. This may be because a relevant minister has pressing domestic business or because it is judged that an agenda does not warrant his attendance. Occasionally, he may be 'unavoidably delayed' because he does not wish to attend an unwanted or a politically awkward meeting. Whatever the reason, a reduction in the status and political weight of a delegation may make it difficult for binding decisions to be agreed.

The sectoral responsibility. Usually it is obvious which government departments should be represented at Council of Ministers meetings, but not always. Doubts may arise because agenda items may straddle policy divisions, or because member states organise their central government departments in different ways. As a result, it is possible for ministers from rather different national ministries, with different responsibilities and interests, to be present. The difficulties which this creates are sometimes compounded, especially in broad policy areas, by the minister attending not feeling able to speak on behalf of other ministries with a direct interest and therefore insisting on a reference back to national capitals.

States are not, therefore, always comparably represented at Council of Ministers meetings. But whether a country's principal spokesman is a senior minister, a junior minister, or, as occasionally is the case, the Permanent Representative or even a senior diplomat, care is always taken to ensure that national interests are defended. The main way in which this is done is by the attendance, at all Council of Ministers meetings, not only of the national spokesmen, but of small national delegations. The task of the supporting teams – which are comprised of appropriate national officials and experts – is to ensure that the head of the delegation is properly briefed, fully understands the implications of what is being discussed, and does not make negotiating mistakes. Sometimes, when very confidential matters are being discussed, or when a meeting is deadlocked, the size of delegations may, on a proposal from the President, be reduced to 'Ministers plus two', 'Ministers plus one', or, exceptionally, 'Ministers and Commission'.

Council of Ministers meetings are normally convened by their President, but it is possible for the Commission or a member state to take the initiative. The Presidency rotates between the states on a six monthly basis: January until June, July until December (see Figure 4.1 for the order of rotation). The main tasks of the Presidency are as follows:

1. Arranging (in close association with the Council Secretariat), and chairing all Council meetings from ministerial level downwards (apart from a few committees and working parties which have a permanent chairman). These responsibilities give to the Presidency a considerable control over how often particular Councils and Council committees and working parties meet, over agendas, and over what happens during the course of meetings.
2. Launching and building a consensus for initiatives. A successful Presidency is normally regarded as one which gets things done.

This can usually only be achieved by extensive negotiating, persuading, manoeuvring, cajoling, mediating and bargaining with and between the member states, and with the Commission and the European Parliament.

3. Ensuring some continuity and consistency of policy development. An important way in which this is achieved is via the so-called 'troika' arrangements which provide for co-operation between the preceding, the incumbent, and the succeeding Presidencies.

4. Representing the Council in dealings with outside bodies. This task is exercised most frequently with regard to other Community institutions (such as regular appearances before the European Parliament), and with non-member countries in connection with certain external Community policies.

Holding the Presidency has advantages and disadvantages. One advantage is the prestige and status that is associated with the office: during the six month term of office the Presidential state is at the very heart of Community affairs; its ministers – especially its Head of Government and its Foreign Minister – meet with prominent international statesmen and dignatories on behalf of the Community; and media focus and interest is considerable. Another advantage is that during its term of office a Presidency can do more than it can as an ordinary member state to help shape, and set the pace of, Community policy priorities. The extent of the potential of the Presidency in terms of policy development should not, however, be exaggerated: a Presidency does not start with a clean sheet but has to be much concerned with uncompleted business from previous Presidencies; related to this last point, an increasingly important part of the 'troika' arrangement is 'rolling work programmes' in which measures to be taken by the Council are co-ordinated between the three participating states, rather than being left solely to the preferences of the incumbent state; and, finally, six months just does not provide sufficient time for the full working through of policy initiatives – especially if legislation is required. As for the disadvantages of holding the Presidency, one is the blows to esteem and standing that are incurred when a state is judged to have had a poor Presidency, and another is the heavy administrative burdens that are attached to the job – burdens which some of the smaller states find difficult to carry.

Altogether there are around 90 Council of Ministers meetings in an average year (87, for example, in 1989) with a certain bunching occurring in relation to key features of the Community timetable: the budgetary cycle, the annual agricultural price-fixing exercise, and the ending of a country's six month Presidency. So, for example, in the closing week of the Dutch Presidency, in June 1986, six different sets of national ministers were brought together in an attempt to make progress on items as diverse as co-ordinated action against South Africa (Foreign Ministers) to liberalising the European aviation industry (Transport Ministers).

The regularity of meetings of individual Councils reflects their importance in the Council system and the extent to which there is Community interest and activity in their policy area. So Foreign Ministers, Agriculture Ministers, and Economic and Finance Ministers (in what is customarily referred to as the Ecofin Council) meet most regularly: usually about once a month, but more frequently if events require it; Internal Market Ministers, Budget Ministers, and Fisheries Ministers follow next, with around four or five meetings per year; other Councils – such as Research, Energy, Industry, and Environment – meet only two or three times a year, or even just once or twice a year in fringe areas such as Health and Cultural Affairs.

Unless there are particularly difficult matters to be resolved meetings do not normally last more than a day. A typical meeting would begin about 10.00 a.m. and finish around 6.00 p.m. or 7.00 p.m. Foreign Ministers, Agriculture Ministers, and Budget Ministers are the most likely to meet over two days, and when they do it is common to start with lunch on Day 1 and finish sometime before lunch on Day 2.

Outside the formal Council framework some groups of ministers, particularly Foreign Ministers and Ecofin Ministers, have periodic weekend gatherings, usually in the country of the Presidency, which are used for the purpose of discussing matters on an informal basis without the pressure of having to take decisions.

The Committee of Permanent Representatives

Each of the states has a national delegation, or Permanent Representation as they are more usually known, in Brussels which acts as a kind of Embassy to the Community. These are headed by a

Permanent Representative, who is normally a diplomat of very senior rank, and are staffed, in the case of the larger states, by thirty to forty officials, plus back-up support. Some of the officials are drawn from the Diplomatic Services of the member states, others are seconded from appropriate national Ministries such as Agriculture, Trade, and Finance.

Of the many forums in which governments meet 'in Council' below ministerial level the most important is the Committee of Permanent Representatives (COREPER). Although no provision was made for such a body under the Treaty of Paris, ministers established a co-ordinating committee of senior officials as early as 1953, and under the Treaties of Rome the Council was permitted to create a similar committee under its Rule of Procedure. Under Article 4 of the Merger Treaty these committees were merged and were formally incorporated into the Community system: 'A committee consisting of the Permanent Representatives of the Member States shall be responsible for preparing the work of the Council and for carrying out the tasks assigned to it by the Council'.

There are, in fact, two COREPERs. Each normally meets once a week. COREPER 2 is the more important and is made up of the Permanent Representatives. Because of its seniority it is the more 'political' of the two COREPERs and works mainly for the Foreign Ministers (and through them for the European Council) and Ecofin. It also usually deals with issues for other Council meetings that are particularly sensitive or controversial. COREPER 1 consists of the Deputy Permanent Representatives. Amongst the policy areas it normally deals with are environment, social affairs, transport and the internal market. Agriculture, because of the complexity and volume of its business, is not normally dealt with by COREPER at all but separately by the Special Committee on Agriculture (SCA). On agricultural matters the SCA is of comparable significance and status to COREPER and is staffed by senior officials, either from the Permanent Representations or from national Ministries of Agriculture. Like the two COREPERs it meets weekly.

Committees and Working Parties

A complicated network of committees and working parties assists and prepares the work of the Council of Ministers, COREPER and the SCA.

The *committees* are of different types. They include:

● Council committees in the strict sense of the term are those standing committees which are serviced by Council administrators. There are only a handful of these, of which the Energy Committee and the Committee on Education are examples. Council committees are composed of national officials and their role is essentially to advise the Council and the Commission as appropriate and, in some instances, as directed. A particularly important and rather special Council committee is the Article 113 Committee which deals with commercial policy. Any significant action undertaken by the Community in international trade negotiations is preceded by Community co-ordination via this Committee. It normally meets once a week: the full members – who are very senior officials in national Ministries of Trade or the equivalent – meet monthly, and the deputies – who are middle-ranking officials from the Ministries, or sometimes from the Permanent Representations – meet three times a month. The Committee performs two main functions: it drafts the briefs on which the Commission negotiates on behalf of the Community with third countries (the Committee's draft being referred, via COREPER, to the Ministers for their approval); and it acts as a consultative committee to the Council and the Commission – by, for example, indicating to the Commission what it should do when problems arise during the course of a set of trade negotiations.

● The Standing Committee on Employment is also a Council serviced committee, but its membership is unusual in two respects: first, it is composed not only of governmental representatives but also of sectional interest representatives – the latter being drawn from both sides of industry; and, second, the governmental representations are headed by the Ministers themselves – or, if they are unable to attend, by their personal representatives. The Committee meets twice a year to discuss matters of interest and, where possible, to make recommendations to the Social Affairs and Employment Council. The nature of the membership of the Committee, with ministerial representation, means that where general agreement can be found, the matter is likely to be taken up by the Council.

● Various committees which are, technically, Commission committees, report to, or feed into, the Council, as well as the Commission, in an advisory capacity. Their access to the Council usually stems either from their founding mandates, the importance of their policy competences, the eminence of their memberships, or from some combination of all three. The most important of these committees is the Monetary Committee which was established under Article 105 of the EEC Treaty: 'In order to promote co-ordination of the policies of Member States in the monetary field to the full extent needed for the functioning of the common market, a Monetary Committee with advisory status is hereby set up'. The Committee's prestige and power is explained by four main factors. First, it is given a broad brief in very important policy areas. The main focus of its work covers the European Monetary System, (it is crucial when realignments of currencies in the EMS are being considered), capital movements, international monetary relations, and, more recently, the various issues that arise in connection with Economic and Monetary Union. (On most of these matters the Committee works closely with another very important committee, the Committee of Governors of Central Banks.) Second, the Committee enjoys unusually privileged access to both the Commission and the Council. Indeed, in relation to the latter, the Committee's chairman normally reports several times a year directly to the Ecofin Council on the Committee's work. Third, the Committee meets regularly – including, normally, before Ecofin Council meetings – and is supported in most aspects of its work by an Alternates Committee and a small number of working parties. Finally, the members of the Committee – of which there are two from each member state, plus two from the Commission – are mostly senior and influential figures from Finance Ministries and Central Banks: people, in other words, who can normally communicate directly with whomsoever they wish, and people who are customarily listened to.

● In addition to the 'formally constituted' committees that have just been described – formally constituted in the sense that they were established by the Treaties or by Community legislation – many other committees also assist the work of the Council. Not always referred to as committees, but sometimes as groups or simply meetings, these are most often found in policy areas which are not fully part of Community structures and processes. Such committees perform a variety of tasks: within the context of European Political Co-operation there is a now well established committee structure – made up of the Political Committee, the Correspondents Group, and about twenty specialised working groups – which seeks to facilitate the exchange of information, co-ordinate positions, and prepare the work of the Foreign Ministers; within the context of the Trevi Group, officials meet to perform similar functions in connection with internal security matters – reporting in their case to Interior Ministers; and there has been an increasing tendency in recent years for *ad hoc* committees of senior national officials to be established for the purpose of developing initiatives and policies (though not, of course, for the purpose of drafting legislation) in new, and sometimes sensitive areas – monetary union, for example, and drugs.

The role of the *working parties* (or working groups) is more specific than that of most of the committees in that they are responsible for carrying out a detailed analysis of formally tabled Commission proposals for Council legislation. The number of working parties in existence at any one time varies according to the overall nature of the Community's workload and the preferences of the Presidency in office, but in recent years there have usually been between 120–140. Members of the working parties, of whom there may be up to three or four per member state, are almost invariably national officials and experts based either in the Permanent Representations or in appropriate national ministries. Occasionally governments appoint non-civil servants to a working party delegation when highly technical or complex issues are under consideration.

Working parties meet as and when they are required, usually with an interval of at least three weeks between meetings so as to allow the General Secretariat time to circulate minutes and agendas – all in the languages of the member states. For working parties with a heavy workload meetings may be regular, for others, where nothing much comes up within their terms of reference, there may be very few meetings at all. Up to ten or eleven different working parties can be in session in Brussels on some days. On completion of their analyses of the Commission proposals, groups report to COREPER or to the SCA.

The Council Secretariat

The main administrative support for the work of the Council is provided by the General Secretariat. This has a staff of just over 2000, of whom around 200 are at 'A' grade, that is, diplomatic level. The Secretariat's base is in the Charlemagne Building which is next door to the Commission in Brussels.

The Secretariat's main responsibility is to service the Council machinery – from ministerial to working party levels. This it does by activities such as preparing draft agendas, keeping records, providing legal advice, processing and circulating decisions and documentation, translating, and generally monitoring policy developments so as to provide an element of continuity and co-ordination in Council proceedings. This last task includes seeking to ensure a smooth transition between Presidencies by performing a liaising role with officials from the preceding, the incumbent, and the incoming Presidential states.

In exercising many of its responsibilities, the Secretariat works closely with representatives from the member state of the President-in-office. This is essential because key decisions about such matters as priorities, meetings and agendas are primarily in the hands of the Presidency. Before all Council meetings at all levels Secretariat officials give the Presidency a full briefing about subject content, about the current state of play on agenda items, and about possible tactics – 'the Danes can be isolated', 'there is strong resistance to this in Spain and Portugal so caution is advised', 'a possible vote has been signalled in the agenda papers and, if taken, will find the necessary majority' and so on.

In addition to making use of the Council's Secretariat there is also a natural tendency for Presidents to rely heavily on their own national officials as they seek to achieve a successful six-month period of office by getting measures through. It is largely for this reason that the staff of a state's Permanent Representation increases in size during a Presidential tenureship. Something approaching a dual servicing of the Presidency is apparent in the way at Council meetings, at all levels, the President sits with officials from the Council's General Secretariat on his one side and national advisers on the other.

The Operation of the Council

The Hierarchical Structure

As indicated above, a hierarchy exists in the Council consisting of the General Council, the Technical Councils, COREPER and the SCA, and the committees and working parties. The European Council is also sometimes thought of as being part of this hierarchy but, in fact, it is not properly part of the Council system, even though it does have the political capability of issuing what amount to instructions to the ministers (see Chapter 7).

The Council's hierarchical structure is neither tight nor rigidly applied. The General Council's seniority over the Technical Councils is, for example, very ill-defined, whilst important committees and working parties can sometimes communicate directly with Technical Councils. Nonetheless, the hierarchy does, for the most part, work. This is best illustrated by looking at the Council's procedures for dealing with a Commission proposal for Council legislation.

The first stage is initial examination of the Commission's text. This is normally undertaken by a working party, or if it is of very broad application, several working parties. Since most working parties are permanent it is usually clear to which party the proposal should go. If necessary, a new working party can be established.

Progress, as at all Council levels, depends largely on the factors outlined in Table 4.1. Unless there is known to be provision for majority voting by ministers (votes are not taken below ministerial level), or special circumstances apply and an issue is forced, the general rule is that a working party may take as long as is necessary to reach an agreement. The General Secretariat of the Council, however, is always pressing for progress and tries to ensure that a working party does not need to meet more than three times to discuss any one proposal.

The first working party meeting on a proposal normally consists of a general discussion of key points. Subsequent meetings are then taken up with a line by line examination of the Commission's text. If all goes well, a document is eventually produced indicating points of agreement and disagreement, and quite possibly having attached to it reservations that states have entered to indicate that they are not yet in a position formally to commit themselves to the text or a part of it. (States may enter reservations at any stage of the Council process. These can vary from an indication that a particular clause of a draft text is not yet in an acceptable form, to general witholdings of approval until the text has been cleared by appropriate national authorities.)

The second stage is the reference of the working party's document to COREPER, or, in the case of agriculture, to the SCA. In being placed between the working parties and the Council of Ministers

TABLE 4.1

Principal factors determining the progress of a proposal through the Council

- The urgency of the proposal.
- The controversiality of the proposal and support/opposition amongst the states.
- The extent to which the Commission has tailored its text to accomodate national objections/reservations voiced at the pre-proposal stage.
- The complexity of the proposal's provisions.
- The ability of the Commission to allay doubts by the way it gives clarifications and answers questions.
- The judgements made by the Commission on whether, or when, it should accept modifications to its proposals.
- The competence of the Presidency.
- The agility and flexibility of the participants to devise (usually through the Presidency and the Commission) and accept compromise formulae.
- The ability and willingness of the states to use majority voting.

COREPER acts as a sort of filtering agency for ministerial meetings. It attempts to clear as much of the ground as possible so as to ensure that only the most difficult and sensitive of matters will detain the ministers in discussion. So, where the conditions for the adoption of a measure have been met in a working party, COREPER is likely to confirm the working party's opinion and advance it to the ministers for formal enactment. Where, however, agreement has not been possible in a working party COREPER can do one of three things: try to resolve the issue itself (which its greater political status might permit); refer it back to the working party, perhaps with accompanying indications of where an agreement might be found; or pass it upwards to the ministers.

Whatever progress proposals have made at working party and COREPER levels, formal adoption is only possible at ministerial level. Ministerial meetings thus constitute *the third stage* of the Council's legislative procedure.

Items on ministerial meeting agendas are grouped under two headings. Matters which have been agreed at COREPER level, and on which it is thought Council approval will be given without discussion, are listed as 'A points'. These do not necessarily fall within the policy competence of the Council that is meeting but may have been placed on the agenda because the appropriate Technical

Council is not due to meet for some while. Ministers retain the right to raise objections on 'A points', and if any do the proposal may have to be withdrawn and referred back to COREPER. Normally, however, 'A points' are quickly approved without debate. Such is the thoroughness of the Council system that ministers can assume they have been thoroughly checked in both Brussels and national capitals to ensure they are politically acceptable, legally sound, and not subject to outstanding scrutiny reservations. Ministers then proceed to consider the 'B points', which may include items left over from previous meetings, matters which it has not been possible to resolve at COREPER or working party levels, or proposals which COREPER judges to be politically sensitive and must be decided by the politicians. All 'B points' will have been extensively discussed by national officials at lower Council levels, and on most of them a formula for an agreement will have been prepared for the ministers to consider.

As can be seen from Exhibit 4.1 ministerial meetings – in this case a meeting of Agriculture Ministers – can have very wide and mixed agendas. Four observations are particularly worth making about the sorts of agenda items which arise:

● There are variations regarding what ministers are expected to do. The range of possibilities includes the taking of final decisions, the adoption of common positions (see below and Chapter 10), the approval of negotiating mandates for the Commission, the resolution of problems that have caused difficulties at lower levels of the Council hierarchy, and – simply – the noting of progress reports.

● Some items concern very general policy matters, whilst others are highly specialised and technical in nature.

● Most items fall within the sectoral competence of the ministers who have been convened, but a few – such as those on the environment and the ECSC in the Exhibit – do not.

● As well as policy issues, agenda items can also include administrative matters – such as appointments to advisory committees.

The position of the General Council rather suggests that there would, in certain circumstances – such as when a policy matter cuts across sectoral divisions, or when Technical Councils cannot resolve key issues – be a fourth legislative stage involving the Foreign Ministers. In practice, though recourse to such a stage would frequently be desirable, it is by no means customary. A principal reason for this is that the theoretical seniority enjoyed by the General Council over other Councils has no legal basis. Rather it stems only from a rather ill-formulated understanding that the General Council has special responsibility for dealing with disputes which cannot be resolved in the Technical Councils, for tackling politically sensitive matters, and for acting as a general co-ordinating body at ministerial level. Another factor limiting the role of the General Council is that often the Foreign Ministers are not able, or willing, to act any more decisively in breaking a deadlock than is a divided Technical Council. Members of the General Council may, indeed, have no greater seniority in rank, and may even be junior, to their national colleagues in, say, the Budget or the Agriculture Councils. In any case, Technical Councils are often not willing to refer their disputes 'upwards': Ministers of Agriculture, Trade, Environment etc., have as much authority to make Community law as do Foreign Ministers and they normally prefer to take their own decisions – unless something which is likely to be very unpopular can be passed on elsewhere. The General Council is thus of only limited effectiveness in resolving issues that have created blockages in the Technical Councils and in counteracting the fragmentation and sectoralism to which the Council of Ministers is unquestionably prone. The same is true of joined or 'jumbo' Councils, which bring together, but only on an occasional basis, different groups of ministers.

This absence of clear Council leadership and of an authoritative co-ordinating mechanism has had the consequence of virtually forcing the European Council to assume responsibilities in relation to the Council of Ministers, even though it is not formally part of the Council hierarchy. Increasingly at their meetings the Heads of Government have gone beyond issuing general guidelines to the Council of Ministers, which was intended to be the normal limit of European Council/Council of Ministers relationships when the former was established in 1974. Summits have often been obliged to try and resolve thorny issues that have been referred to them by the Council of Ministers, and have also had to seek to ensure – principally via policy package agreements of the sort that were agreed at Fontainebleau in 1984, Luxembourg in 1985, and Brussels in 1988 – that there is some overall policy direction and coherence in the work of the Council of Ministers. The European Council can only go so far, however, in performing such problem solving, leadership,

EXHIBIT 4.1

A Council of Ministers meeting: items considered and decisions taken

1430th meeting of the Council – Agriculture –
Luxembourg, 15, 16 and 19 October 1990

MULTILATERAL TRADE NEGOTIATIONS WITHIN GATT (AGRICULTURE)

Following a lengthy debate on the Community offer concerning the agriculture part for the Uruguay Round negotiations, the Council found that it was not possible to reach an agreement on this proposal, which would therefore be submitted to the General Affairs Council in Luxembourg on 22 October 1990 . . .

ADJUSTMENTS TO THE ARRANGEMENTS FOR OILS AND FATS

Pending receipt of the Opinion of the European Parliament, the Council held an initial exchange of views on the proposals for measures

- designed to take into account the expiry, at the end of 1990, of the standstill period during which the Spanish and Portuguese national arrangements prior to accession have been allowed to remain in force with regard to the control of prices and quantities of vegetable oils other than olive oil;
- concerning the aid scheme for the production of olive oil.

Following its debate, the Council invited the Special Committee on Agriculture to continue its work on the subject to enable it to reach a speedy conclusion, as soon as it had received the Opinion of the European Parliament . . .

VETERINARY AND PLANT PROTECTION PRODUCTS SECTORS

Plant protection products containing certain active substances

The Council adopted the Directive amending the Annex to Directive 79/117/EEC prohibiting the placing on the market and use of plant protection products containing certain active substances . . .

Council Resolution on measures to be taken in the veterinary field

The Council adopted a Resolution on measures to be taken in the veterinary field with a view to the completion of the internal market.

This Resolution clarifies the guidelines which emerged from examination of a memorandum submitted to the Council by the Italian government in 1989 on the measures to be taken at both Community and Member-State-level, in order to reach completion of the internal market in the veterinary sector. It established the commitments that the Council and the Commission should make in order to have the appropriate means to reach this objective.

Prevention of pathogens

The Council examined the Commission proposal laying down the veterinary rules for the disposal and processing of animal waste, for its placing on the market and for the prevention of pathogens in feedingstuffs. This proposal is designed to harmonize the conditions for treating animal waste and in particular certain waste considered as high-risk materials for the transmission of certain diseases.

In the course of this examination it appeared that the text submitted to the Council might, taking into account various technical amendments and certain assurances given by the Commission, constitute the basis for a compromise for the majority of the delegations.

The Council therefore agreed to instruct the Permanent Representatives Committee to continue examining this matter with a view to submitting it to the Council again for adoption at its next meeting . . .

Animal health conditions for fresh poultry meat

Pending receipt of the Opinion of the European Parliament, the Council held an initial exchange of views on the Commission proposal designed to harmonize the animal health rules governing intra-Community trade and imports from third countries of poultry meat and to fix certain requirements aimed at preventing the spread of the main contagious diseases.

As the text submitted was still the subject of some reservations, the Council asked the Permanent Representatives Committee to continue examining it.

It will resume examination of this item as soon as it has received the Opinion of the European Parliament . . .

MISCELLANEOUS DECISIONS

Other decisions in the agricultural sector

The Council adopted:

– the Directive on animal health conditions governing intra-Community trade in, and imports from third countries of, poultry and hatching eggs. This Directive aims to harmonize the animal health rules at Community level and to promote the completion of the internal market.

– the Regulations:
  • amending Regulation No. 804/68 on the common organization of the market in milk and milk products;
  • amending Regulation No. 2658/87 on the tariff and statistical nomenclature and on the Common Customs Tariff and Regulation (EEC) No. 2915/79 determining the groups of products and the special provisions for calculating levies on milk and milk products.

These amendments are designed to treat identically powdered unflavoured yoghurts in the same way as flavoured yoghurts, to abolish certain requirements for products which have received aid for private storage and to add a new product (crispbread) which may benefit – in respect of its milk ingredient – from export refunds.

Fisheries

The Council adopted the decision on the temporary extension of the Agreement between the European Economic Community and Mauritania on fishing off the coast of Mauritania for the period from 1 July 1990 to 31 July 1990.

Environment

The Council authorized the Commission to take part, on the Community's behalf, in the negotiations to draft a Co-operating Agreement for the protection of the North East Atlantic from accidental pollution. The Council also decided, subject to certain conditions, that the Community should sign this Agreement.

The purpose of the Agreement will be to establish a system of co-operation enabling prompt and effective action to be taken in the event of a pollution accident at sea which threatened the marine environment in general and the interests of the coastal states in particular.

The Convention would be signed by the Community, France, Spain, Portugal and Morocco.

ECSC

The Council gave two assents:

– concerning a memorandum on the establishment of a sixth ECSC programme of ergonomics research for the steel and coal industries;

– on the draft decision establishing the delivery levels of ECSC steel products of Portuguese origin onto the rest of the Community market, excluding Spain.

Appointments

The Council decided on:

– the replacement of
  • four full members and two alternate members of the Administrative Board of the European Foundation for the Improvement of Living and Working Conditions;
  • an alternate member of the Advisory Committee on the Training of Midwives;
  • a full member of the Advisory Committee on Pharmaceutical Training;
  • a full member and an alternate member of the Advisory Committee on Training and Nursing.

– the appointment of two full members and two alternate members of Greek nationality of the Advisory Committee on Training in Nursing.

Source: General Secretariat of the European Communities, Press Release 9141/90 (152) (Extracts) and co-ordinating roles: partly because it is timetabled to meet only twice a year, but also because many national leaders prefer to avoid getting too involved in detailed policy discussions.

Decision-Making Procedures

The Treaties provide for three basic ways in which the Council can take a decision: unanimously; by a qualified majority vote; or by a simple majority vote.

● *Unanimity* is normally required where a new policy is to be initiated or an existing policy framework is to be modified or further developed. It is also required when the Council wishes to amend a Commission proposal against the Commission's wishes. Abstentions do not constitute an impediment to the adoption of Council decisions that require unanimity.

● *Qualified majority voting* usually applies where proposals are designed to implement, clarify or are otherwise within established policy guidelines. Additionally, and crucially, where proposals fall under the co-operation procedure (see Chapter 10), qualified majority voting rules apply at the Council first reading stage, and, under specified circumstances, at the second reading stage. Under the qualified majority voting rules France, Germany, Italy and the UK have 10 votes each; Spain has 8; Belgium, Greece, the Netherlands and Portugal have 5; Denmark and Ireland have 3; and Luxembourg has 2. Of this total of 76 votes, 54 votes (that is 70 per cent of the total) constitutes a qualified majority vote. This means that the five larger states cannot outvote the smaller seven, and also that two large states cannot by themselves constitute a blocking minority. Under the qualified majority voting rules an abstention has the same effect as a negative vote, since the total vote required to achieve a majority is not reduced as a result of an abstention.

● *Simple majority voting*, in which all states have one vote each, is used mainly for procedural purposes.

Until recently, proposals were not usually pushed to a vote in the Council when disagreements between the states existed, even when majority voting was perfectly constitutional under the Treaties. To appreciate the reasons for this it is necessary to go back to the institutional crisis of 1965.

In brief, events unfolded in the following way. The Commission, in an attempt to move progress in areas which had almost ground to a halt, put forward a package deal which had important policy and institutional implications. The most important aspects of its proposals were the completion of the Common Agricultural Policy, changing the basis of Community income from national contributions to own resources, and the granting of greater powers of control to the European Parliament over the use of those resources. The French government objected to the supranational implications of these proposals. It also used the occasion to register its opposition to what it saw as the increasing political role of the Commission and to the imminent prospect of the Community moving into a stage of its development in which there was to be more majority voting in the Council. When no agreement could be reached on these matters in the Council France withdrew its representatives from the Community's decision-making institutions in July 1965, though it continued to apply Community law. This so-called 'policy of the empty chair' continued for six months and was ended only after the French government, under strong domestic pressure, agreed to attend a special Council meeting in Luxembourg in January 1966. The outcome of that meeting is usually referred to as the *Accords de Luxembourg* or the Luxembourg Compromise. In fact, there was little agreement or genuine compromise but rather a registering of differences. This is apparent from the official communiqué:

I   Where, in the case of decisions which may be taken by majority vote on a proposal of the Commission, very important interests of one or more partners are at stake, the Members of the Council will endeavour, within a reasonable time, to reach solutions which can be adopted by all the Members of the Council while respecting their mutual interests and those of the Community, in accordance with Article 2 of the Treaty.

II   With regard to the preceding paragraph, the French delegation considers that where very important interests are at stake the discussion must be continued until unanimous agreement is reached.

III   The six delegations note that there is a divergence of views on what should be done in the event of a failure to reach complete agreement.

IV   The six delegations nevertheless consider that this divergence does not prevent the Community's work being resumed in accordance with the normal procedure.

Although it had no constitutional status, the Luxembourg Compromise came to profoundly affect decision-making in the Council at all levels. It did so because point II of the communiqué came to be interpreted as meaning that any state had the right to exercise a veto on questions which affected its vital national interests – and the states themselves determined when such interests were at stake. On only one occasion has the Compromise been openly breached. This was in May 1982 when the British government attempted to veto the annual agricultural prices settlement by proclaiming a vital national interest. The other states did not believe that such an interest was at stake, (and with some reason given that the UK had already approved the constituent parts of the package). The view was taken (correctly) that the British were trying to use agricultural prices to force a more favourable outcome in concurrent negotiations over UK budgetary contributions. Agricultural ministers regarded this attempted linkage as quite invalid. They also thought it was over-demanding, since the dispute was played out to the background of the Falklands crisis in which the UK government was being supported by her Community partners even though some were unenthusiastic. Prompted by the Commission, the Belgian Presidency proceeded to a vote on the regulations for increasing agricultural prices and they were approved by seven (of the then ten) states. Denmark and Greece abstained, not because of any sympathy for Britain but because of reservations about the possible supranational implications of the majority vote.

The Luxembourg Compromise did not, it should be emphasised, replace a system of majority voting by one of unanimous voting. On the contrary, before 1966 majority voting was rare and, indeed, it was its proposed phasing-in that the French were most concerned about. From 1966, the norm became one not of unanimous voting but one of no voting at all. Decisions came to be made by letting issues run until an agreement finally emerged. As a result, the veto has been formally invoked only occasionally, and then usually only for very short periods. Germany, for example, has only formally used a veto once: in 1985 it vetoed a modest cereals price cut which had been agreed by its nine partners (with the interesting consequence that the Commission, acting under Articles 5 and 155 of the EEC Treaty, stated that the Council was not fulfilling its obligations and introduced Commission regulations on grain prices. No state challenged this course of action and the prices came into effect).

The Single European Act, with its provisions for greater use of majority voting (see below), was seen by many observers as heralding the demise of the Luxembourg Compromise. In the event it has not quite done so because the Compromise has been invoked on one occasion since the SEA came into force in mid-1987: in June 1988, at an Agriculture Council meeting which was near to finalising the 1988–9 agricultural price review, the Greek Minister invoked the Compromise because of dissatisfaction with the 'green drachma' realignment which the other eleven states were offering to Greece – with the consequence that the meeting broke up and had to be reconvened at a later date. The Compromise is perhaps, therefore, now best thought of as usually in a deep sleep, but subject to very occasional awakening.

Clearly, the most visible aspect of the Luxembourg Compromise was the national veto – a veto to which some still make reference when they wish to claim that Community membership has not fundamentally undermined national sovereignty. A less visible, but in practice much more significant effect, was in the stimulus it gave to the Council of Ministers to take virtually all of its decisions unanimously. But the preference for unanimity, which still exists despite the increasing use of majority voting, was not, and is not, just a consequence of an unofficial agreement made over twenty-five years ago. There are strong positive reasons for acting only on the basis of unanimity. In many ways the functioning and development of the Community is likely to be enhanced if policy-making processes are consensual rather than conflictual. Thus, national authorities (which may be governments or parliaments) are unlikely to undertake with much enthusiasm the necessary task of transposing Council directives into national law if the directives are perceived as domestically damaging, or if they are being unwillingly imposed following a majority vote in the Council. Nor is it likely that national bureaucracies will adopt helpful attitudes towards the implementation of unwanted legislation. More generally, the use of majority votes on important and sensitive matters could well create grievances that could have disruptive implications right across the Community's policy spectrum.

For good reasons, as well as perhaps some bad, decision-making in the Council thus usually proceeds on the understanding that difficult and controversial issues are not imposed. Where it is clear that a state or states have serious difficulties with a proposal they are normally allowed time. They may well be put on the defensive, asked to fully explain their position, pressed even to give way or at least to compromise, but the possibility of resolving an impasse by a vote tends to be avoided if possible. Usually, the item is held over for a further meeting, with the hope that in the meantime informal meetings or perhaps COREPER will find the basis of a solution. All states, and not just the foremost advocates of the retention of the veto (initially France, more latterly Denmark, the UK, and, to a more limited extent, Greece and Ireland) accept that this is the only way Council business can be done without risking major divisions.

But though there are good reasons for preferring unanimity, if the principle were to be applied too universally and too rigidly it could be as damaging as Council divisions since the pace would be determined by the slowest and many much needed decisions would never be made at all. Such has often been the reality of the Community. However, majority voting has never been completely excluded. On internal staffing matters, and, more importantly, during the annual budgetary procedure where decisions cannot be indefinitely delayed and postponed, majority voting has long been common practice. Since the mid-1980s majority voting has come to be used in certain policy sectors too. Four main factors explain its increased use:

● Attitudes have slowly changed. There has been an increasing recognition, even amongst the most rigid defenders of national rights and interests, that decision-making by unanimity is a recipe not only for procrastination and delay, but often for no decision-making at all. The situation whereby consensus is the rule, even on issues where countries would not object too strongly to being voted down, has increasingly been seen as unsatisfactory in the face of the manifest need for the Community to become efficient and dynamic in order, for example, to assist its industries to be able to compete successfully on European and world markets.

● The 1981 and 1986 enlargements of the Community, which brought the membership to twelve, clearly made unanimity on policy

issues all the more difficult to achieve and hence increased the
necessity for majority voting.

● The Single European Act extended the number of policy
areas in which majority voting was constitutionally permissible.
Crucially, under the new co-operation procedure, the extension included most of those matters that were covered by the priority
programme of completing the internal market by 1992: harmonisation of technical norms, opening up public procurement, removing
restrictions in banking, insurance, capital controls and so forth.
Moreover, the discussions which accompanied the SEA were based
on the assumption that the new voting procedures would be used.

● In July 1987, the General Council, in accordance with an
agreement it had reached in December 1986, formally amended
the Council's Rules of Procedure. Among the changes was a relaxa-
tion of the circumstances by which votes could be initiated: whereas
previously only the President could call for a vote, under the new
Rules any national representative and the Commission also have the
right, and a vote must be taken if a simple majority agrees.

In 1986, the last full year before the SEA came into force, over one
hundred decisions were taken by majority vote, most of them in the
three main areas provided for in the EEC Treaty: budget, agriculture, and external trade. Since 1986 the number has increased to well
beyond one hundred, though to exactly what figure is impossible to
say. It is impossible to say for two main reasons. First, the Council
meets in secret and does not release minutes of its proceedings –
though much of what happens does, in fact, usually leak out in one
way or another. Second, what really amounts to majority voting
often occurs without a formal vote being taken. This may take the
form of a state which is opposed to a proposal that otherwise
commands general support preferring to try and extract concessions
in negotiations rather than run the risk of pressing for a vote and
then finding itself being outvoted. Or it may take the form of the
Presidency simply announcing 'we appear to have the necessary
majority here', and that being left unchallenged, and not therefore
formally voted on, by a dissenting state. Unless an important point of
principle or a damaging political consequence is at stake a country in
a minority thus often chooses not to create too much of a fuss when,
as is the case, for example, in agreeing external trade negotiating

briefs for the Commission, qualified majority voting rules apply and a decision cannot be forever delayed.

Important, however, though this development of majority voting is, consensual decision-making remains, and can be expected to remain, a key feature of Council processes. Certainly, on what are judged to be 'important', 'sensitive', and 'political' matters, as opposed to 'technical' matters, many proposals will continue to lie on the table until agreement is found. This may involve delay, but the duty of the national representatives at all Council levels is not only to reach decisions but is also to defend national interests (see Chapter 12 for further discussion of this point.) As long as governments are concerned not to cede too much of their national sovereignties to the Community, it can be anticipated that the unanimity principle will be retained for certain types of decisions.

The formal processes by which Council meetings are conducted and business is transacted are broadly similar at ministerial, COREPER, and working party levels. As can be seen from Figure 4.1, at one end or one side of the table sits the Presidency – whose delegation is led by the most senior figure present from the country currently holding the Presidency; at the other end or side sit the Commission representatives; and ranged between the Presidency and the Commission are the representatives of the twelve member states – with the delegation from the country holding the Presidency sitting to the right of, but separate from, the President.

As indicated earlier, the Presidency plays a key role in fixing the agenda of Council meetings, both in terms of content and the order in which items are considered. The room for manoeuvre available to the Presidency should not, however, be exaggerated for, quite apart from time constraints, there are several factors which serve to limit options and actions: it is difficult to exclude from the agenda of Council meetings items which are clearly of central interest or which need resolution; the development of rolling programmes means that much of the agenda of many meetings is largely fixed; and anyone in a COREPER or a ministerial meeting can insist a matter is discussed provided the required notice is given. A Presidency cannot, therefore, afford to be too ambitious or the six month tenureship will probably be seen to have been a failure. With this in mind the normal pattern for an incoming President of a reasonably important Technical Council is to take the view that of, say, forty proposed directives in

FIGURE 4.1
Rotation of Council Presidency between the states and seating arrangements in Council meetings

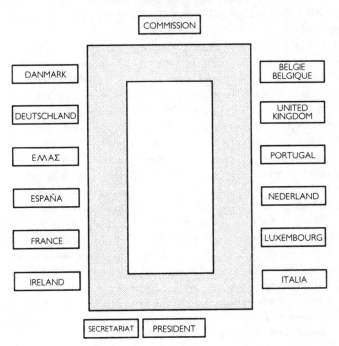

Notes:
1. This figure shows the seating arrangements when Italy holds the Presidency (which it last did July–December 1990). National delegations sit in strict alphabetical order according to how their country's name is spelt in their own language.
2. The arrangements apply to all Council meeting at all levels. (So, if a round table is used, the Commission still sits opposite the Presidency.)
3. With each change of Presidency all states move round one place in a clockwise direction.
4. In the round of Presidencies which began with Belgium in the first half of 1987 and which will end with the United Kingdom in the second half of 1992, the Presidency rotates in alphabetical order, that is in an anti-clockwise direction on the diagram. Because of variations in the responsibilities of Presidencies between the first half and second half of the year – most of the work on agricultural prices is done in the first half and most of the work on the budget in the second half – the next round of Presidencies will see pairs of countries reversing their alphabetical order: so Denmark will assume the Presidency for the first half of 1993 and Belgium for the second half.

his policy area, he is going to try and get eight particular ones through. This will then be reflected in the organisation of Council business, so that by the end of the Presidency four may have been adopted by the Council, while another three may be at an advanced stage.

At ministerial level Council meetings can often appear to be chaotic affairs: not counting interpreters there can be around one hundred people in the room – with each national delegation putting out a team of perhaps six or seven, the Commission a similar number, and the Presidency being made up of both General Secretariat and national representatives; participants frequently change – with ministers often arriving late or leaving early, and some of the officials coming and going in relation to items on the agenda; ministers are constantly being briefed by officials as new points are raised; there are huddles of delegations during breaks; requests for adjournments and postponements are made to enable further information to be sought and more consideration to be given; and telephone calls may be made to national capitals for clarifications or even, occasionally, for authorisation to adopt revised negotiating positions. Not surprisingly, delegations which are headed by ministers with domestic political weight, which are well versed in the Community's ways, which have mastered the intricacies of the issues under consideration, and which can think quickly on their feet, are particularly well placed to exercise influence.

A device which is sometimes employed at Council meetings, especially when negotiations are making little progress, is the *tour de table* procedure. By this, the President invites each delegation to give a summary of its thinking on the matter under consideration. This ensures that discussion is not totally dominated by a few, and, more importantly, establishes the position of each member state. It can thus help to clarify the possible grounds of an agreement and provide useful guidance to the President as to whether a compromise is possible or whether indeed he can attempt to move to a decision. As well as advantages there are, however, also drawbacks with the procedure: in particular, states can find it more difficult to alter their position once they have 'gone public', and it is very time-consuming – even if each state restricts itself to just five minutes a *tour* takes an hour. Presidencies do then tend, and are normally advised by the General Secretariat, to be cautious about using the procedure unless there seems to be no other way forward: better usually to use another approach, such as inviting the Commission to amend its proposal, or seeking to isolate the most 'hard line' state in the hope that it will back down.

This last point highlights how important the Presidency can be, not only at the agenda setting stage but also during meetings themselves. An astute and sensitive chairman is often able to judge when a delegation that is making difficulties is not terribly serious: when, perhaps, it is being awkward for domestic political reasons and will not ultimately stand in the way of a decision being made. A poor chairman, on the other hand, may allow a proposal to drag on, or may rush it to the point that a state which, given time, would have agreed to a compromise may feel obliged to dig in its heels.

An extremely important feature of the whole Council network is the role of informal processes and relationships. Three examples demonstrate this. First, many understandings and agreements are reached at the lunches that are very much a part of ministerial meetings. These lunches are attended only by ministers and the minimum number of translators. (Most ministers can converse directly with one another – usually in French or English – although the entry of Greece, Spain, and Portugal has reduced this capacity.)

Second, where difficulties arise in ministerial negotiations a good chairman can make advantageous use of scheduled and requested breaks in proceedings to explore possibilities for a settlement. This may involve holding off-the-record discussions with a delegation that is holding up an agreement, or it may take the form of a tour of all delegations – perhaps in the company of the relevant Commissioner and a couple of officials – to ascertain 'real' views and fall-back positions.

Third, many of the national officials based in Brussels come to know their counterparts in other Permanent Representations extremely well: better, sometimes, than their colleagues in their own national capitals or Permanent Representations. This enables them to make judgements about when a country is posturing and when it is serious, and when and how a deal may be possible. A sort of code language may even be used between officials to signal positions on proposals. So, for example, a veto under the Luxembourg Compromise would never be invoked in a working party or in COREPER for that would be to prejudge the 'political' discussion in the Council of Ministers. But if a representative was to state 'this is very important for my minister', or 'my minister is very strongly pressurised on this', other participants would recognise that signals were being given to them that further deliberations were necessary at their level if more serious difficulties were to be avoided when the ministers gathered.

Concluding Comments

The structure and functioning of the Council is generally recognised as being unsatisfactory in a number of important respects. In particular: power is too dispersed; there is insufficient cohesion between, or sometimes even within, the sectoral Councils; and decision-making processes are often too cumbersome and too slow.

It seems unlikely that anything very radical will be done to tackle these problems in the foreseeable future, even though the number of policy issues and policy problems coming before the Council continues to increase. The obvious solutions can all be ruled out on the grounds of impracticability or political unacceptability. For example, the Council will not permit any significant reduction of its powers in relation to those of the Commission. An extension of majority voting is highly likely, but any movement to make it the norm for all decision-making will be fiercely resisted by some. And the idea which has sometimes been floated of creating a 'super' Council, with authority to impose an overall policy pattern on subsidiary Technical Councils, does not convince many: it may be useful for knocking a few heads together, but, as the experience of the European Council shows (see Chapter 7), the dream of authoritative national leaders rationally formulating policy frameworks in the 'Community interest' does not accord with political realities.

However, if radical reform is unlikely, smaller, more gradual, but by no means insignificant, shifts are possible and are indeed happening. The increasing use of majority voting is the most obvious case in point. Another development is the increasing co-operation between succeeding Presidencies and the development of rolling policy programmes. Changes of this sort may not perhaps be producing the dynamic and streamlined institutional structure that many would like to see, but they are nonetheless playing an important part in helping to bring about a more efficient Council of Ministers.

5

The European Parliament

Powers and Influence

Since it was first constituted, as the Assembly of the European Coal and Steel Community, the European Parliament – the title it adopted for itself in 1962 – has generally been regarded as a somewhat ineffective institution. It is a reputation which, today at least, is not entirely justified. For whilst it is true that the EP's constitutional powers are not comparable with those of national legislatures, developments over the years have come to give it, in practice, a not inconsiderable influence in the Community system. As with national parliaments this influence is exercised in three main ways: through the legislative process, through the budgetary process, and through control and supervision of the executive.

Parliament and Community Legislation

The EP has a number of opportunities to influence Community legislation.

First, it sometimes participates in policy discussions with the Commission at the pre-proposal legislative stage. The Commission may, for example, float a policy idea before an EP committee, or committee members themselves may suggest policy initiatives to the Commission.

Second, the EP can formally adopt its own ideas for suggested legislation and then attempt to persuade the Commission to take them up. The most usual way of doing this is via own initiative reports, which are reports that the Parliament itself initiates. Over one hundred own initiative reports are usually approved by the EP each year.

Third, the annual budgetary cycle provides some opportunities for exercising legislative influence. In large measure this is due to the *Joint Declaration of 30 June 1982 by the European Parliament, the Council and the Commission on various measures to improve the budgetary procedure.* Amongst the 'various measures' it was agreed that if the EP puts appropriations into the budget for items for which there is no legal base – in other words, the EP opens new budget lines – the Commission and the Council will seek to provide the necessary base by drafting new legislation. It was further agreed that expenditure limits in respect of legislation should not be set in the legislative process, but in the budgetary process – where the EP has more power.

Fourth, the Commission has, in recent years, displayed an increased willingness to discuss its legislation programme and timetable with the EP. This has come about both as a result of pressure from the Parliament, and the desirability, from the Commission's viewpoint, of having a good working relationship with the Parliament. Principal stages in the exchanges between the two on the programme and the timetable are as follows: the Commission adopts its work programme for the year in early January; the programme is formally presented to the EP as soon as possible after its adoption – usually in an address by the President of the Commission to the January plenary session; the programme is debated by the EP – at either the January or February plenaries, or at both – and resolutions may be adopted; the Commission and the EP's Enlarged Bureau (see below) agree – in March or April – on the programme and on an indicative timetable.

The Commission, it must be said, is very much the leading party in these exchanges, for not only is debate and discussion based on its proposals but it is under no obligation to accept views which are advanced by the EP. Accommodations to EP's views have, however, been made. The 1990 annual legislative programme and indicative timetable provided something of a breakthrough in this regard for they were adopted by the Enlarged Bureau and the Commission – during the April plenary session – only after undertakings were made on either side: for its part the Commission agreed to give a higher priority to social legislation (for which the EP was pressuring), and also agreed to a new code of conduct governing relations between the two institutions on aspects of certain legislative procedures; for its part the EP agreed to lift the obstructionist attitude which, as a bargaining lever, it was employing in respect of 1992 internal market proposals.

Fifth, and most importantly, the EP must be consulted on, though its approval is not necessary for, most significant Council legislation. If the Council acts prematurely, and does not wait for Parliament to declare an Opinion, the 'law' will be ruled invalid by the Court of Justice. Any uncertainty on this point was removed by the isoglucose case ruling in 1980 when the Court annulled a Council regulation on the grounds that it had been issued before Parliament's Opinion was known. The isoglucose case ruling does not give the EP an indefinite veto over Council legislation, for it is obliged by Treaty to issue Opinions and the Court in some of its judgements has referred to the duty of loyal co-operation among Community institutions, but it does give it a very useful delaying power.

Since July 1987, and the entry into force of the Single European Act, the nature of the EP's consultative powers has varied according to the Treaty articles under which the proposed legislation falls. For most articles, the traditional system of one reading, or consultation, remains. That is to say, Parliament is asked for an Opinion on Commission proposals for Council legislation on only one occasion. Once that Opinion is given the Council may take a decision. What use the EP is able to make of this single referral depends, in part at least, on its own subject competence and its tactical skills. The standard way of proceeding is to take advantage of Article 149 of the EEC Treaty which states: 'As long as the Council has not acted, the Commission may alter its original proposals, in particular where the Assembly has been consulted on that proposal'. If the Commission can be persuaded to alter a proposal so as to incorporate the EP's views, the prospects of those views becoming part of the text that is finally approved by the Council are greatly enhanced. With this in mind, the EP attempts to convince and to pressurise the Commission. Normally, pressurising takes the form of voting on amendments to proposals, but not voting on the resolution which formally constitutes the Opinion until after the Commission has stated – as it is obliged to do – whether or not it accepts the amendments. If the Commission does accept the amendments the

EP votes for the legislative resolution and the amendments are incorporated into the Commission's proposal. If the Commission does not accept the amendments, or at least not all of them, the EP may judge the Commission position to be unsatisfactory and, as a result, may seek to delay the progress of the proposal by referring it back to the appropriate Parliamentary committee for further consideration.

For ten EEC Treaty articles, the SEA extended the EP's consultative rights by creating a new co-operation procedure. In essence, what this does is to add extra legislative stages: whereas, under the consultation or single reading procedure, the Council can take final decisions after the EP has issued Opinions, under the co-operation procedure the Council is confined to adopting 'common positions' which must then be referred back to the EP for a second reading. At second readings the EP continues to lack full legislative powers – final decisions on legislative texts are still taken by the Council when, at its second readings, it considers EP responses to common positions – but the procedure does encourage the Commission, and even more importantly the Council, to take the EP's views seriously and to engage in inter-institutional bargaining. The most important Treaty article covered by the co-operation procedure is Article 100A, which was incorporated into the EEC Treaty under the SEA, and which deals with harmonisation measures that have as their purpose the establishment and functioning of the internal market (see Chapter 10 for a fuller explanation of the co-operation procedure).

Clearly the EP's rights and obligations to issue Opinions on legislative proposals fall a long way short of giving it full legislative powers. Nonetheless they are rights and obligations which are not to be underestimated in their significance. Moreover, the Parliament's ability to follow up on its Opinions has, in several respects, improved considerably in recent years:

● It is now established that if the Council under the consultation procedure, or at first reading under the co-operation procedure, amends a legislative proposal in such a way that it becomes significantly different from the text that was considered by the EP, then the proposal is referred back to the EP for a further consultation or for another first reading. (There is, of course, room for dispute here as to when the text adopted by the Council does depart significantly from the earlier Commission text.)

● New procedures charge relevant EP committee officers to monitor the progress of proposals on which Opinions have been given. Furthermore, the Commission and the Council now report back to the EP and its committees on the course of proposals (although the Council is often accused by MEPs of providing insufficient information).

● There is some evidence that at conciliation meetings – which are meetings where delegations from the Council and the EP try to resolve differences between them in respect of certain categories of Community legislation – the position of ministers are not always as fixed or as rigid as formerly they were.

● Under the co-operation procedure, where there is statutory provision for a second reading, Parliament can follow-up on the Council during the course of the legislative process itself. The Council is obliged to provide the EP with an explanation for the common position – including giving reasons for any EP amendments that have been rejected – and if the EP is dissatisfied it can exert further pressure at its second reading by amending or rejecting the common position by a vote that includes an absolute majority of its members.

It is very difficult to estimate the precise effect of EP deliberations on the final form of legislative acts. One reason for this is that a great deal of EP persuading and lobbying is impossible to monitor because it is carried out via informal contacts with Commission and Council representatives. Another reason is that the Commission and the Council often go halfway in agreeing to the sense of EP amendments, but object to the way in which they are phrased or to specific parts of them. In general, however, it is clear that the Commission is more sympathetic than is the Council: so, whereas the Commission, on average, accepts between about 65–80 per cent of EP amendments at the first or the single reading stage, with much of the remaining 20–30 per cent being rejected for technical rather than political reasons, the Council's acceptance rate is considerably lower, especially where there is only a single reading. Sometimes less than 20 per cent of EP amendments appear in the final legislative text (see Chapter 10 for further discussion of the EP's influence on the content of legislation).

Over 200 resolutions embodying Opinions on legislative proposals are normally passed each year. As can be seen from Table 5.1 rather more proposals are subject to the consultation procedure than are subject to the co-operation procedure. (Some of the 55 proposals listed in the first reading column of the co-operation procedure, also, of course, appear in the 71 listed in the second reading column.)

Having established that the EP does have a genuine legislative role, the weaknesses to which it is subject will now be outlined.

The first, and most obvious weakness, is that the voice of the EP does not carry full legislative authority. Unlike national parliaments, the EP does not have the final say over what is, and what is not, to become law. Under both the consultation and co-operation procedures the Council has the power – in some cases on the basis of a qualified majority vote, in other cases on the basis of unanimity – to overturn EP amendments which have and have not been accepted by the Commission, and to ignore EP rejections of legislative proposals (see Chapter 10 for a more detailed explanation of the Council's powers in this regard). The Council can also choose not to act at all on legislative proposals it does not like – at any one time there are usually around 400–500 proposals on which the Parliament has given an Opinion that still await a Council decision. (Proposals subject to the co-operation procedure are not exempt from such Council inaction, since the restricted timetable that is attached to the procedure only comes into play once the Council has adopted its common position.)

The second weakness is that although the EP usually attempts to deliver Opinions as soon as possible, so as to ensure they are available to the Council at an early stage of its deliberations, it is by no means unusual for the Council, before the Opinion of the EP has been delivered, to take decisions 'in principle' or 'pending the Opinion of the European Parliament'. This is especially common where the initial referral to the EP was delayed, where there is some urgency about the matter, or where a Council Presidency is anxious to push the proposal through. Whatever the reason, it is hardly likely that in such circumstances the EP's Opinion will count for much.

The third weakness is that the EP is not consulted on all Council legislation. The greatest weakness in this regard is its lack of any right to be consulted on the range of external trade agreements which the Council concludes with third countries on behalf of the twelve under Article 113 (EEC). The Council and the Commission (which conducts the actual trade negotiations) may choose to discuss trade matters with the EP on an informal basis, but there is little evidence

TABLE 5.1

The year in Parliament: 1989

Part-session	Normal consultations (single reading)	Cooperation procedure I¹	Cooperation procedure II¹	Assents (Articles 237 and 238 EEC)	EP Rules 56 and 58 EP Rules 63 and 121 (own-initiative reports)	(resolutions following statements and oral questions)	EP Rule 64 (resolutions on urgent subjects)	Budget questions	Miscellaneous decisions and resolutions
January	4	4	4	–	15	3	16	3	1
February	17	5	7	2	17	–	18	–	1
March	16	8	3	–	24	2	17	–	1
April	18	6	11	1	21	5	10	6	2
May	26	19	11	–	45	–	18	2	–
July	–	–	–	–	–	1	–	–	2
September	7	–	13	–	3	16	21	–	2
October I	12	5	13	–	1	5	10	–	–
October II	4	3	7	–	–	5	–	2	–
November	12	2	2	–	2	9	11	1	1
December	12	3	–	–	1	13	10	5	2
Total	128²	55³	71⁴	3	129	59	131	19⁵	10

¹ I: first reading; II: second reading.
² Including 72 where Parliament proposed amendments to and 4 where it rejected Commission proposals.
³ Including 45 where Parliament proposed amendments to Commission proposals.
⁴ Including 48 where Parliament proposed amendments to Commission proposals.
⁵ Including 7 consultations.

Source: XXIIIrd General Report on the Activities of the European Communities, 1989.

of Parliament bringing much influence to bear. In only two sets of circumstances does the EP have formal responsibilities for matters which have external trade implications: the SEA established that Parliament's assent, by an absolute majority of its component members, must be given before the Council can either (a) accept applications for Community membership, or (b) conclude association agreements with third countries under Article 238 of the EEC Treaty. The first of these circumstances is obviously only for very occasional use. The second, however, has a more recurring application and has been used to some effect. Indeed on four occasions within the first twelve months of the SEA coming into force the EP witheld its assent from additional financial protocols to the Community's agreement with Israel. The main reason for this was that Israel had allegedly done nothing about earlier Community complaints concerning the treatment of West Bank Palestinian farmers.

The fourth and final weakness is that the EP does not have to be consulted on – although, in practice, it is notified of – Commission legislation. This is despite the fact that, numerically, Commission legislation makes up most of Community legislation (see Chapter 6). There are different views on the significance of this. Pointing to the political and expenditure implications of some Commission legislation, critics argue that this is another example of executive power and of legislative and democratic weakness. Others, however, emphasise that Commission legislation is usually highly technical and of a kind that needs quick decisions; as such, it is similar to the decrees, ordinances and other minor legislative acts that national administrations issue and which are commonly accepted as an inevitable aspect of decision-making in the modern world.

Parliament and the Community Budget

Thanks mainly to the 1970 *Treaty amending Certain Budgetary Provisions of the Treaties* and the 1975 *Treaty amending Certain Financial Provisions of the Treaties* the EP enjoys considerable Treaty powers in relation to the Community's budget. These include:

1. The right to propose 'modifications' to compulsory expenditure. (This principally means agriculture – which comprises around three-fifths of the total budget.) Modifications that entail increases in total expenditure require qualified majority

support in the Council to be accepted. Where increases are not involved, owing perhaps to a proposed increase being offset by a proposed decrease, a qualified majority vote is required for rejection – a negative majority as it is called.

2. The right to propose 'amendments' to non-compulsory expenditure (which means most things apart from agriculture) subject to a pre-determined 'maximum rate of increase'. Acting by a qualified majority the Council may modify these amendments, but Parliament can reinsert and insist on them at its second reading of the budget.

3. Under Article 203(8) of the EEC Treaty as revised in 1975, Parliament 'acting by a majority of its members and two thirds of the votes cast may, if there are important reasons, reject the draft budget and ask for a new draft to be submitted to it'. In other words the EP may reject the whole budget if it does not like the Council's final draft.

Following the introduction of direct elections for MEPs in 1979, extensive use was made of the powers just listed in the 1980s. Virtually every aspect of the rules, including the power of rejection, were tested to see how far they could be taken. Major confrontations with the Council, far from being avoided, seemed at times almost to be sought as the EP attempted to assert itself. For most of the 1980s, however, this assertion was limited in its effect. It was so because although the EP enjoyed joint decision-making powers with the Council on the budget, the powers of the two bodies were not equally balanced. Parliament was still very much restricted in what it could do: restricted by the Treaty which gave it very little room for manoeuvre in the major budgetary sector, compulsory expenditure; restricted by the Council's attitude, which tended to be one of wishing to limit Parliament's influence as much as possible; and restricted by its own inability – because of conflicting loyalties and pressures – to be wholly consistent and resolved in its approach.

For the most part, these restrictions still apply. However, developments occurred in 1988 which have increased the EP's influence on the Community budget. Following decisions taken by the European Council in February 1988 on budgetary matters, the EP, together with the Commission and the Council of Ministers, put its name, in June 1988, to *The Interinstitutional Agreement on Budgetary Discipline and*

Improvement of the Budgetary Procedure (see Document 11.1). This commits all three institutions to a financial perspective for the years 1988 to 1992. Key features of the perspective are provisions for a significant increase in non-compulsory expenditure and a significant decrease in compulsory expenditure, (thus realising aims for which the EP had been pressing for years), and the setting of clear ceilings for both types of expenditure. The main benefits of the *Interinstitutional Agreement*, in power terms, for the EP were twofold. First, its influence over compulsory expenditure, which in the past had been very limited, was potentially increased. It was so because Parliament's approval was now required for any upward movement of the ceiling. Second, the very act of the Council agreeing to sign a financial perspective with the EP, gave to the latter an extra element of leverage in budgetary discussions. (The EP's role in relation to budgetary decision-making is discussed further in Chapter 11.)

Control and Supervision of the Executive

Virtually all parliaments have difficulties in attempting to exercise controlling and supervisory powers over executives. On the one hand, they are usually hampered by the executives themselves, which do not welcome the prospect of being investigated and which therefore seek to protect themselves behind whatever constitutional, institutional and party political defences are available. On the other hand, parliamentarians themselves tend not to have the requisite information, the specialist knowledge, or the necessary resources that are required effectively to monitor, and if necessary to challenge, executive activity.

The EP shares these problems but additionally has two particular ones of its own. First, a key aspect of control and supervision of executives is with regard to policy implementation: is policy being implemented efficiently and for the purposes intended by relevant law? The Commission is the most obvious body to be called to account on these questions. But in many policy spheres the Commission's executive role is very limited and consists essentially of attempting to co-ordinate the work of outside agencies operating at different administrative levels. Such agencies, of which national governments are the most important, are often reluctant to open the books or to adopt co-operative attitudes towards EP investigators.

Certainly there is little question of government ministers allowing themselves to be grilled by the EP on the competency and honesty of their national bureaucracies.

The second problem specific to the EP is that on broad controlling and supervisory issues – such as whether the Community executive is acting responsibly in the execution of its duties, and whether it is fulfilling its Treaty obligations – problems arise from the blurring of roles between the Commission and the Council. In theory, the former proposes and implements whilst the latter decides, but as has been shown in Chapters 3 and 4 this distinction is not rigidly adhered to in practice. Insofar as the Council has assumed an increasing importance in what are theoretically Commission functions, the EP's supervisory powers have been weakened. This is because Parliament is not so constitutionally strong in relation to the Council as it is to the Commission, nor does it have the access to the former that it does to the latter.

The EP's ability to control and supervise the Commission and the Council will now be considered separately.

In relation to the Commission, the EP can use five main powers and channels. First, by carrying a motion of censure by a two-thirds majority of the votes cast, including a majority of all MEPs, it can dismiss the College of Commissioners. In practice it has never done so. The main reason why it has not is that the power of dismissal is really too blunt a controlling instrument for most purposes. In all normal circumstances the EP has no wish to dismiss the Commission. Rather it just wishes to find out what the Commission is up to, what its plans are, and how effectively it is managing Community policies. In any event, even if the Commission were to be dismissed, the EP would have no formal say in the appointment of the new Commissioners. An aggrieved Council could re-appoint the very same people (though it is unlikely that all would accept re-appointment in such circumstances).

Second, under Article 143 of the EEC Treaty, the Parliament 'shall discuss in open session the annual general report submitted to it by the Commission'. This debate used to be one of the highlights of the Parliamentary year, but there is not much evidence of it ever having produced any concrete results. In recent years it has come to be superseded in importance by the debate on the annual programme of the Commission.

Third, under Article 205 of the EEC Treaty (which was added by the 1975 Treaty) 'The Commission shall submit annually to the Council and to the Assembly the accounts of the preceding financial year relating to the implementation of the budget. The Commission shall also forward to them a financial statement of the assets and liabilities of the Community'. On the basis of an examination of the accounts and the financial statement, and having examined also the annual report of the Court of Auditors, Parliament 'acting on a recommendation from the Council which shall act by a qualified majority, shall give a discharge to the Commission in respect of the implementation of the budget' (Article 206b EEC). Under its discharge powers the EP can require the Commission and other institutions to take appropriate steps so as to ensure action on the comments appearing in the decision giving discharge.

Fourth, Parliament's standing committees have remits that are broad enough to allow them to attempt to exercise supervisory functions if they choose to do so. However, the Commission is not anxious to encourage investigations of itself, and the committees are not sufficiently well resourced to be able to probe very far. The Committee on Budgetary Control, which is specifically charged with monitoring policy implementation, is in a typically weak position: with only a handful of grade-A officers employed to assist it, it cannot hope to do anything other than cover a small fraction of the Commission's work.

Finally, questions can be asked of the Commission. These take different forms: written questions – of which 1711 were tabled in 1989; oral questions in question time – 581 in 1989; and oral questions with or without debate – 127 in 1989.

If the EP is not able to call the Commission fully to account it is even more restricted in its ability to exercise control over the Council. There are three main reasons for this.

The first reason arises from the role of the Council as the meeting place of the member states. To make it, or any of its members, directly responsible to the EP would be to introduce a measure of supranationalism into the Community that has been, and is, unacceptable to most governments. The view has been taken that insofar as Council members are to be responsible it should be principally to their national parliaments. In other words, the Council as a collective body is not to be responsible to anyone, whilst individual members are not to be responsible to another Community institution. (It might be added that this does not always stop ministers, if they find themselves being pressed too hard in their national legislatures, from hiding behind the closed doors of Council meetings and 'immovable' Community partners.)

Second, some important Council developments and activities have occurred outside the formal Community framework, with consequent difficulties for the EP in asserting a supervisory role for itself. European Political Co-operation (foreign policy) and economic and monetary liaison/consultation between governments are examples of this. (Although on EPC in particular, the case should not be overstated: ministerial appearances before EP plenaries and committees have become institutionalised, and the SEA stated that member states 'shall ensure that the European Parliament is closely associated with European Political Co-operation. To that end the Presidency . . . shall ensure that the views of the European Parliament are duly taken into consideration').

Third, the very nature of the Council – with its ever-changing composition, its specialist Councils, and its rotating Presidency – makes continuity of relations between it and the EP difficult to establish.

The amount of access the EP gets to the Council depends in large part on the attitude of the country holding the Presidency. There are, however, certain set points of contact which, if they do not enable the EP to exercise an overall control on the Council, at least provide it with opportunities to challenge the Council on its general conduct of affairs. Thus, ministers from the Presidency usually attend the EP committees that deal with their spheres of responsibility at least twice during their country's Presidency. MEPs can seek to use these occasions for informal discussions with the Council, or to have wide-ranging question and answer sessions on the Council's priorities and performance. Ministers from the Presidency also regularly attend EP plenary sessions and participate in important debates. And the EP can, through the Presidency, ask questions of the Council and the Council of Foreign Ministers on EPC matters (the two are distinct because of their different constitutional positions). The procedures used for asking questions are similar to those used for questions to the Commission. In 1989, 144 written questions, 172 oral questions in question time, and 52 oral questions with or without debate were asked of the Council, and 114 written questions, 130 oral questions in question time, and 17 oral questions with or without debate were asked of the Council of Foreign Ministers.

Elections

Until 1979 MEPs were nominated by national parliaments from amongst their members. Various consequences followed from this: parties not represented in their national legislature could not be represented in the EP; virtually all MEPs were pro-integrationists, since sceptics and opponents in national parliaments were generally unwilling to allow their name to be considered for nomination; and MEPs were limited in the time they could give to their European responsibilities.

However, Article 138 of the EEC Treaty included the following provision: 'The Assembly shall draw up proposals for elections by direct universal suffrage in accordance with a uniform procedure in all Member States'. The Assembly approved such proposals as early as 1960, but found itself frustrated by another Article 138 requirement which stated: 'The Council shall, acting unanimously, lay down the appropriate provisions, which it shall recommend to Member States for adoption in accordance with their respective constitutional requirements'. That the first set of direct elections were not held until 1979 is witness to the feeling of some member governments – initially mainly the French, later the Danes and the British – that direct elections were rather unwelcome: unwelcome because they had supranational overtones, and unwelcome because they might be followed by pressures for institutional reform in the EP's favour. Even after the principle of direct elections was eventually won and it was agreed they would be held on a fixed five-year basis, no uniform electoral system could be agreed, nor has been agreed since. Consequently, the three sets of direct elections to have been held to date – in 1979, 1984 and 1989 – were all contested on the basis of different national electoral arrangements (see Table 5.2). Eleven of the twelve states use one of several different forms of proportional representation; the UK uses its traditional single member constituency 'first past the post' system, apart from in Northern Ireland where proportional representation is used to ensure that the nationalist minority wins a seat. It seems likely that if the UK were to concede on the principle of proportional

TABLE 5.2

**National arrangements for the 1989 elections
to the European Parliament**

	Number of MEPs	Entitle- ment to vote	Eligibi- lity for election	Electoral system	Number of constitu- encies
Belgium	24	18	21	PR with PV[1]	3
Denmark	16	18	18	PR with PV	1
FRG	81	18	18	PR without PV[2]	10 + 1 (Berlin)
Greece	24	18	21	PR without PV	1
Spain	60	18	18	PR without PV	1
France	81	18	23	PR without PV	1
Ireland	15	18	21	PR with STV[3]	4
Italy	81	18	25	PR with PV	5
Luxembourg	6	18	21	PR with vote splitting	1
Netherlands	25	18	25	PR with PV	1
Portugal	24	18	18	PR without PV	1
United Kingdom	81	18	21	Majority vote system (Northern Ireland – PR with STV)	78 + 1 (Northern Ireland: 3 seats)
Total	518				

Notes:
[1] Proportional representation with preferential vote.
[2] Proportional representation without preferential vote.
[3] Proportional representation with single transferrable vote.
Source: Directorate General for Research, European Parliament (adapted).

representation, a common form of proportional representation could be agreed between the states.

In addition to the differences between their electoral systems, there are also other differences between the states regarding their EP electoral arrangements. The most significant are these: candidate eligibility ranges from 18 years to 25 years; there is an array of different rules concerning the right to vote of people not living in the country of which they are a citizen; Italy is the only country to permit non-nationals to contest elections (and one was elected in 1989); and voting takes place not on one day but on two – with, in 1989, Denmark, Ireland, the Netherlands, Spain and the UK voting on Thursday, 15 June and the other seven countries voting on Sunday, 18 June.

One other feature of EP electoral arrangements that merits comment is that there is an enormous variation in size of population per MEP: in 1989 it ranged from 1:747000 voters in Germany to 1:62000 voters in Luxembourg. The reason for this is that the seats are distributed among the states on grounds of political balance as well as democratic equitability: so, the 'big four' each have 81 despite their different sized populations, and the smaller countries are, in strict arithmetical terms, overrepresented in an attempt to ensure that they are not totally swamped in EP decision-making processes.

A subject that has been much discussed in the context of EP elections is voter turnout. Many have argued that a high turnout would serve to enhance the EP's legitimacy and democratic base and, partly in consequence of this, would also place the EP in a strong position to press for increased powers.

In the event, turnout in each of the first three direct elections has been relatively low (see Table 5.3). In 1979 only 62 per cent of those eligible to vote did so, in 1984 the figure was 61 per cent, and in 1989 58.4 per cent.

TABLE 5.3

Elections to the European Parliament: voter turnout

	1979	1984	1989
	%	%	%
Belgium[1]	91.4	92.2	90.7
Denmark	47.8	52.3	46.1
France	60.7	56.7	48.7
Germany	65.7	56.8	62.4
Greece[1]	78.6[2]	77.2	79.8[5]
Ireland	63.6	47.6	68.3[5]
Italy	85.5	83.9	81.5
Luxembourg[1]	88.9	87.0	87.8[5]
Netherlands	58.1	50.5	47.2
Portugal	—	72.2[4]	51.3
Spain	—	68.9[3]	54.8
United Kingdom	32.6	32.6	36.2
Total	62	61	58.4

Notes:
[1]Voting compulsory
[2]Elections of October 1981
[3]Elections of June 1987
[4]Elections of July 1987
[5]General election held on the same day

Various factors have been put forward to explain the low turnouts. It is, for example, generally agreed that because EP elections do not offer any prospect of a change of government, of switches in policy, or of the making or unmaking of political reputations, they do not provide much of a base for the generation of popular interest or political excitement. It is further accepted by most observers that the election campaigns have had little overall coherence or co-ordination. They have essentially been national contests, but of a secondary sort. In 1989, for example, there was little sense of the 1984–9 Centre-Right EP majority defending its record, or of the Left seeking to gain control. Nor did 'European' issues have much of an impact. Finally, observers have noted that many of the forces which do much to focus attention and generate interest in national electoral campaigns have approached the EP elections in, at best, a half-hearted manner: media interest has been limited; national political parties have been generally reluctant to commit resources to their Euro-campaigns; party activists have tended to be disinterested; and a conscious attempt has been made by some governments to play down the importance of the elections because they are frequently interpreted as being, in part at least, 'mid-term' national elections, or unofficial referenda on the government's performance in office.

Political Parties and the European Parliament

Party political activity is seen at three main levels in relation to the EP: the transnational, the political groups in the EP, and the national.

The Transnational Federations

Very loosely organised transnational federations, grouped around general principles, exist for co-ordinating, propagandist, and electioneering purposes. The three main federations were created in similar circumstances in the mid-1970s: out of existing, but extremely weakly based, liaising and information exchanging bodies, and as a specific response to the continuing development of the EC and the anticipated future use of direct elections for the EP. These three federations are: the European People's Party – Federation of Christian Democratic Parties of the European Community (EPP); the

Federation of Liberal and Democratic Parties of the European Community (LDP); and the Confederation of the Socialist Parties of the European Community (CSP).

Some supporters of European integration have hoped that the federations might develop into organisations providing leadership, vision and co-ordination at European level, and perhaps might even serve as agents of unification to their heterogeneous memberships. They have failed to do so. Their principal weakness is that, unlike national parties or the EP political groups, they are not involved in day-to-day political activity in an institutional setting. They have, therefore, no very clear focus and cannot develop attachments and loyalties. From this, other weaknesses flow: low status; limited resources – they are heavily dependent on the EP political groups for administrative and financial support; and loose organisational structures based on periodic Congresses and bureaux meetings.

The federations have not, therefore, been able to do very much, even though there certainly are tasks that Community-wide transnational parties could usefully perform, such as long-term policy planning, the harmonisation of national party differences, and educating the electorate about Europe. Such influence as they have exercised has been largely confined to the EP elections, when manifestos have been produced and a few joint activities have been arranged. Even the manifestos, however, have reinforced the general picture of weakness for they have usually been somewhat vague in content (necessarily so given the need to reconcile differences), and have been utilised by only a few of the constituent member parties (because EP elections are contested, for the most part, along national lines).

Beyond the three main federations, other groupings of an even looser nature have surfaced from time to time, usually to try and co-ordinate election activities. They have included Green, Regional, Communist, and Extreme Right alliances. All have been internally divided and have been hard pressed to put together even minimalist common statements.

The Political Groups in the European Parliament

Partisan political activity in the EP is mainly channelled via the political groups. Under the current Rule of Procedure (4th edition, 1987) a minimum of twenty-three MEPs is required for a group to be formed if all the members come from a single state. If they come from two member states eighteen is sufficient, and if they come from three or more states the minimum is twelve.

Groups have been formed and developed for a number of reasons. The principal basis and unifying element of most of the groups is ideological identification. Despite the many differences which exist between them, MEPs from similar political families and traditions are naturally drawn to one another. All the more so when co-operation serves to maximise their influence, as it does in the EP in all sorts of ways – from electing the President to voting on amendments.

Organisational benefits provide another inducement to political group formation. For example, funds for administrative and research purposes are distributed to groups on the basis of a fixed amount per group (the non-attached being regarded as a group for these purposes) plus an additional sum per member. No-one is, there-fore, unsupported, but clearly the larger the group the more easily it can afford a good back-up service.

There are also advantages in the conduct of Parliamentary business that stem from group status, since the EP arranges much of what it does around the groups. Although non-attached members are not formally excluded from anything by this – indeed they are guaranteed many rights under the Rules of Procedure – they can, in practice, be disadvantaged: in the distribution of committee chair-manships for example, or in the preparation of the agendas of plenary sessions.

Between 1984 and 1989 there were eight political groups in the Parliament. Following the 1989 elections this number was increased to ten. The reason there have been, and are, so many groups is simply that the 518 MEPs reflect the wide range of political opinion that exists across the Community, both as regards ideological and national identification. In both the 1984 and 1989 elections candi-dates from no less than around sixty different national political parties were elected.

Since the 1989 elections the political groups, in declining order of size, have been as follows:

Socialist Group. The Socialists are the largest single group in the EP. They include amongst their membership at least one MEP from each member state. Reflecting the breadth of European socialism the

TABLE 5.4

Political Groups in the European Parliament after the 1989 elections

Groups	Belgium	Denmark	France	Germany	Greece	Ireland	Italy	Luxem-bourg	Nether-lands	Portugal	Spain	UK	Total
Socialists	8	4	22	31	9	1	14	2	8	8	27	46	180
European People's Party	7	2	6	32	10	4	27	3	10	3	17	1	122
Liberal and Democratic Reformists	4	3	13	4	–	2	3	1	4	9	6	–	49
European Democrats	–	2	–	–	–	–	–	–	–	–	–	32	34
Greens	3	–	8	7	–	–	7	–	2	1	1	–	29
European Unitarian Left	–	1	–	–	1	–	22	–	–	–	4	–	28
European Democratic Alliance	–	–	13	–	1	6	–	–	–	–	2	–	22
European Right	1	–	10	6	–	–	–	–	–	–	–	–	17
Left Unity	–	–	7	–	3	1	–	–	–	3	–	–	14
Rainbow Group	1	4	1	1	–	1	3	–	–	–	2	1	14
Independents	–	–	1	–	–	–	5	–	1	–	1	1	9
Totals	24	16	81	81	24	15	81	6	25	24	60	81	518

members of the group have sometimes found co-operation difficult. In part this has been because of ideological diversity within the group, with opinions ranging from 'far left' state interventionists to 'moderate' social democrats. In part it has been caused by national party groups being reluctant to concede national interests to wider European interests. And in part it has stemmed from differences within the group on the very bases and direction of European integration.

Group of European People's Party (EPP). The EPP is basically the Christian Democratic group. It used to be dominated by the German CDU/CSU and the Italian DC, but since 1989 it has had a broader base and, like the Socialist group, has included in its ranks at least one MEP from every Community country. The group is broadly Centre-Right in its political orientation but internal differences do exist, notably on social issues.

Liberal Democratic and Reformist Group (LDR). In some respects this is the most divided group of all, and the most difficult to pinpoint in terms of its ideas. It contains certain Leftist elements, but it is basically a combination of parties of the Centre and the Right.

European Democratic Group (ED). This is by far the most nationally homogeneous group, being made up of thirty-two British Conservatives and two Danish Conservatives. The group's base was broadened for a while after Spain's entry into the Community in 1986, when the Spanish Popular Party joined the group, but after the 1989 EP elections they left to join the EPP. A problem for the ED group has long been divisions amongst British Conservative MEPs: between those who might broadly be described as Euro-sceptic Thatcherites, and those who are sympathetic to further integration. This division has resulted in other Centre-Right groups being unwilling to accept ED overtures of a possible merger. However, with Mrs. Thatcher now gone, some sort of merger – probably with the EPP – is likely in the future.

Group of the Greens in the European Parliament. In the 1984–9 Parliament, Environmentalists and Ecologists sat with 'non-Green' MEPs of various sorts as part of an extremely heterogeneous Rainbow Group. In the 1989 elections the Green representation was considerably increased, to such an extent indeed that the Greens were not only able to constitute their own group, but they became the fifth largest group. (They would have been the fourth largest group had some form of proportional representation been used in the UK where the Greens, with 15 per cent of the vote, secured a much higher percentage of the vote than any of the Green parties which did achieve representation.) Beyond their common concern with 'green issues', the Greens are not very homogeneous, with some of their MEPs coming from a clear Left background and others thinking of themselves as neither Left nor Right. The diffuseness of the Green group is encapsulated by the seven Italian Green MEPs: they were elected from four different party lists, including two separate Green lists.

Group for the European Unitarian Left (EUL). Between 1979 and 1989 the Communists sat in the Parliament as part of one group. There was, however, always a great gulf between the two main constituent parties of the group, with the Italian PCI being virtually social democratic in its orientation and the French PCF being much more traditional and orthodox in character. After the 1989 elections this gulf was formalised and two separate groups were formed, with the PCI becoming the dominating component of the newly constituted EUL. In early 1991 the PCI changed its name to the Democratic Party of the Left – a symbolic recognition of its essentially moderate Left character. In the EP the EUL is in many respects close to the Socialist group in its ideological perspective and its policy preferences.

Group of the European Democratic Alliance (EDA). The two main component parties of the EDA – the French Gaullists and the Irish Fianna Fail – share a general Centre-Right political outlook and a firm commitment to the CAP. Neither has been large enough to constitute a group on its own, but both, for different reasons, have been reluctant to link up with one of the more established Centre-Right groups. The EDA has, therefore, served as a useful marriage of convenience for both of them.

Technical Group of the European Right (ER). An Extreme Right group was formed in the 1984–9 Parliament based on the French National Front (FN) and the Italian Social Movement (MSI). In 1989, when newly elected German MEPs from the Republican Party joined the group, the MSI MEPs decided to sit as Independents. The main disagreement with the Republicans was over the South Tyrol issue, where the MSI have been fierce defenders of the Italian-speaking minority. The ER group is highly nationalistic in its attitudes, and has focused particularly on what it sees as unacceptably liberal attitudes to ethnic and immigration issues. The group is virtually completely ostracised by the other groups in the EP.

Left Unity (LU). The LU group consists of MEPs from the more hard-line Communist parties of France, Greece, and Portugal, plus one MEP from the Irish Workers Party. The group's rigid stance on many issues, coupled with its generally hostile attitude to further European integration, results in it being somewhat distanced from the other groups on the Left.

Rainbow Group (RBW). In the 1984–9 Parliament the RBW group brought together, on a very loose basis, Greens, Anti-EEC Danes, and Regionalists. Following the departure of the Greens after the 1989 elections to constitute their own group, the RBW group became the smallest of the EP's political groups – with just thirteen MEPs. Insofar as the group has any coherence it is in its attempts to protect regional and minority interests.

The political groups thus all contain significant internal divisions, usually of both an ideological and a national character. Inevitably this has a weakening effect. So, for example, it is difficult, whatever their ideological principles might suggest to them, for French MEPs to vote for a cut in agricultural prices or for Portuguese MEPs not to support increases in the Regional Fund.

Three other factors also make for looseness and a limited ability on the part of the groups to control and direct their members. The first of these factors arises from the political powers of the EP and the institutional setting in which it is placed. With no government to sustain or attack, no government-sponsored legislation to pass or reject, MEPs do not have the same semi-automatic 'for' or 'against' reaction that is so typical of much national parliamentary behaviour. The second factor is structural. Unlike parties in national legislatures, the political groups are not part of a wider organisational framework from which emanate expectations of co-operative and united behaviour and generally recognised notions of responsibility and accountability. Rather most of them are quasi-federal bodies functioning in a multicultural environment. This is seen in a number of ways: the constituent member parties of the larger groups hold their own separate meetings and have their own leaderships; in seeking to encourage group unity, group leaders can invoke no effective sanctions against, and can withold few rewards from, MEPs who do not fall into line; and, in looking to their political futures, it is not only their political group or its leadership that MEPs must cultivate but also their national parties at home. The third factor is that MEPs can have claims on their loyalties and their votes which compete with the claims of the political groups. One source of such claims are the numerous interest groups with which many MEPs are closely associated. Another source is the EP's fifty or so intergroups which bring together, usually on a relatively informal basis, MEPs from different political groups who have similar views on particular issues. (The intergroups come in many different forms and vary considerably in the nature and range of their policy focus. Amongst their number are the Federalist Intergroup for European Union, the Friends of Israel Intergroup, the Central American Intergroup, the Media Intergroup, the Rural Areas Intergroup, the Animal Welfare Intergroup, and the Elderly People Intergroup.)

However, despite the many weaknesses of the groups, it is important to emphasise that they are still of central importance in determining how the EP works.

Some of the functions and tasks they fulfil and the privileges they enjoy are specifically allocated to them under the Rules of Procedure or by decisions of Parliament. These include guaranteed representation on key EP bodies and committees and speaking rights in plenary sessions.

Other functions have not been formally laid down, but have developed more out of political necessity, advantage, and convenience. This is most obviously seen in the way the groups are the prime determiners of tactics and voting patterns in the EP. The week prior to plenary sessions is set aside for political group meetings. At these meetings efforts are made to agree a common group position on matters of current importance. Should a deal be attempted with another political group on the election of the President? What is the group's attitude to a Commission proposal for a Council directive? What tactics can the group employ to present an unwelcome own initiative report being approved by a committee? In dealing with such questions internal group differences may have to be tackled, and sometimes they may not be resolved. But, of the many influences bearing down on MEPs, political group membership is normally the single most important factor correlating with how they vote.

Before leaving the political groups a few comments about the overall political balance of the EP are required.

From 1979 to 1989 a nominal Centre-Right majority existed, based on the EPP, the LDR, the ED, and the EDA. Since 1989 there has been a nominal Left-Green, or Red-Green, majority. This post-1989 majority is based on the Socialists, the Greens, the EUL, the LU, and the RBW.

The nature of the nominal majority existing at any one time unquestionably affects the interests and priorities of the EP, as is demonstrated by the greater attention that has been given to social and environmental issues since 1989. But the word 'nominal' has to be attached to 'majority' because majorities have not existed at all in any formal sense, and majorities have not, in practice, displayed much political coherence or consistency. There are three main reasons for this. The first is the many and varied divisions between, and sometimes within, the political groups. Various liaising channels and mechanisms exist via which groups attempt to reach agreements and strike deals, but these are of limited effectiveness where fundamental policy differences exist. On some issues it is by no means unusual for the views of political groups on the Centre-Left and Centre-Right, or at least of some MEPs within these groups, to be closer to each other than to the views of other Left and Right groups: the ED, for example, is usually closer to the Socialists on agricultural issues than it is to any group on the Right. The second reason is that a number of issues which have taken up much of the EP's time have cut across the majorities and have attracted support from virtually all of the political groups. Examples of such issues are action on combatting racism in Europe, the provision of assistance to the countries of the developing world, and the need for the further development of European integration. And the third reason is that the EP frequently and consciously attempts to avoid being divided along Left–Right lines when it votes, especially on important issues. If it can present itself as united, it is in a stronger position to pressurise the Commission and the Council to accept its views.

National Parties

National political parties are involved in EP related activities in three
main ways. First, most candidates in the European elections are
chosen by the national parties. This means that MEPs inevitably
reflect national party concerns and are normally obliged, if they wish
to be reselected, to continue to display an awareness of these
concerns.

Second, European election campaigns are essentially national
election campaigns conducted by national parties. Use may be
made of the transnational manifestos, but voters are directed by
the parties primarily to national issues and the results are assessed
primarily in terms of their domestic implications. That the European
dimension is limited is no more clearly seen than in the lack of any
consistent Left–Right movement in voting patterns across the
member states in European elections.

Finally, in the EP itself, national party groups exist within the
political groups. This is an obvious potential source of political group
disharmony and sometimes does create strains. Problems do not arise
so much from the national groups having to act on specific domestic
instructions. This does sometimes occur, but, generally, organisational links between the national groups and national party leaderships are weak and the former have a reasonably free hand within
general party guidelines. The problem is simply that each national
party group inevitably tends to have its own priorities and loyalties.

Composition

In addition to party political attachments there are other aspects of
the composition of the EP which are also of interest and importance.
Three are particularly worthy of comment.

The Dual Mandate

After the 1979 elections some 30 per cent of MEPs were also members
of their national legislature. This figure was inflated however,
because many MEPs had contested the election primarily for
domestic political reasons and had no firm commitment to completing their terms of office. By the end of the Parliament the number of

dual mandates had been more than halved. What, therefore, seemed to be a big drop after the 1984 elections, to around 12 per cent of MEPs holding a dual mandate, in fact reflected a trend that was already well under way; a trend that was assisted in 1984 and 1989 by some parties actively trying to discourage dual mandates and by Belgium forbidding it altogether under national law.

Among the consequences of this decline in the dual mandate has been a weakening of links between the EP and national parliaments. Most parties have procedures of some kind for maintaining contact between the two levels but they tend to be weak, and frequently the EP group is seen as something of a poor relation. A more positive outcome of the decline of dual mandates has been that MEPs with one mandate rather than two have more time and energy for their EP duties. This has been reflected in more days spent in plenaries and committees, more Parliamentary questions, and more reports.

Continuity

The degree of change and turnover in personnel affects the way most organisations work. The EP is no exception to this: the more effective MEPs tend to be those who have developed policy interests and expertise in European affairs over time, and who have come to know their way around the Community system.

Lack of continuity in membership was a problem *during* the 1979–84 Parliament, with nearly one quarter of MEPs being replaced before the 1984 elections. However, as was noted above, that was always likely to be an inflated figure, with many prominent politicians standing in 1979 who had no intention of making a political career in the EP. Events since have, indeed, shown the anticipated settling down, with only a relatively small proportion of MEPs now resigning before they end their term of office.

As for turnover of MEPs *between* elections, it is certainly higher than is common in national parliaments, but not alarmingly so: around half of the MEPs who were elected in 1984 had sat in the 1979–84 Parliament, and over half of those who were elected in 1989 were returning. Of the 1989 intake, 110 first took their seats between 1979 and 1984, 96 first sat in 1984, 2 in 1985, 38 in 1986, 28 in 1987, 4 in 1988, and 240 in 1989. (1986 was exceptional because of Spanish and Portuguese accession, and 1987 because Spain and Portugal held their first direct elections to the EP.)

Competence and Experience

It is sometimes suggested that MEPs are not of the same calibre and do not carry the same political weight as their counterparts in national legislatures. Because the EP is weak, the argument runs, it attracts mostly weak members, or members who regard it merely as a stepping stone to national transfer or advancement.

There is something in this view. Major national figures have tended either not to contest EP elections or not to have completed their terms of office. (The provision in the 1976 'Direct Elections Act' making national governmental office incompatible with EP membership has not helped in this regard.) Additionally, a few MEPs have transferred from the EP to national legislatures.

But the situation should not be exaggerated. Competition to be an MEP is normally fierce, requiring all the customary political skills. Most MEPs do have considerable public experience, either in national or regional politics, or in an executive capacity with a major sectional interest. Amongst the MEPs who were elected in 1989 there were thirty-five former ministers from national governments.

Perhaps the key point to be emphasised is that it should not be assumed that those who choose to stand for, and work in, the EP are necessarily settling for second best. Many are firmly committed to their responsibilities and have developed a competence and an experience which is different from, but which is not necessarily inferior to, that of national parliamentarians.

Organisation and Operation

The Multi-site Problem

The work of the EP is carried out on three sites in three different countries. Plenaries are held in Strasbourg at the Palais de L'Europe. Committees usually meet in Brussels, where the Parliament has office and meeting room facilities close to the Council and the Commission. Most of the 3000 staff who work in the Secretariat of the Parliament are based in Luxembourg (this figure does not include the 450 who work in the Secretariats of the political groups).

This situation is clearly unsatisfactory, and it is a source of grievance and annoyance amongst most MEPs. A reasonably conscientious MEP may well have to change his working location half a dozen times in an average month. His work diary is likely to look something like this: one week attending the monthly plenary at Strasbourg; from two to five days in committee(s), probably in Brussels but sometimes elsewhere; two to four days in political group meetings and group working parties, probably in Brussels; whatever time remains in his constituency (if he has one), visiting somewhere as part of an EP delegation, in Luxembourg consulting with officials on a report, or at home.

If the EP had one base, and especially if that was Brussels, it is likely that Parliament's efficiency, influence and visibility would all be increased. However, the Council has the power of decision on the matter, and hard lobbying from the Luxembourg and French governments has ensured that arguments for 'sense to prevail' and a single site to be agreed have not been acted upon.

Arranging Parliamentary Business

Compared with most national parliaments the EP enjoys a considerable independence in the arrangement of its affairs. That is not to say it can do whatever it likes. The Treaties oblige it to do some things – such as deliver Opinions on Commission proposals for Council legislation – and prevent it from doing others – such as censuring the Council. But, on many agenda, timetable and other organisational matters it remains, to a considerable degree, its own master.

A major reason for this independence is, once again, the special institutional setting in which the EP operates. The Community executive does not have to be as concerned to control what the EP does as do national governments with their legislatures. This is because although EP pronouncements and activities can be unwelcome to the Council and the Commission, they do not normally have politically damaging or unmanageable consequences.

A second, and closely related, reason is the lack of any clear and consistent identification, of either a positive or negative kind, between the EP and the Community executive. In national parliaments business is shaped to a considerable degree by political attachments. But the Commission is made up of officials who are nominally non-partisan, whilst the Council is multi-party, multi-ideological, and multi-national in its membership. As for the 'persuasive devices' that national executives have at their disposal to further encourage loyalty, neither the Commission nor the Council has patronage to dispense.

A third reason is that the EP is entitled to adopt its own Rules of Procedure. This it has done, amending and streamlining the Rules in such ways as to make the Parliament both more efficient and more influential.

Most decisions by the EP about its operation and functioning are not taken in plenary session but are delegated to either the President, the Bureau, or the Enlarged Bureau.

The President of the EP is elected to office for a two and a half year term. According to Rule 18 of the Rules of Procedure the President 'shall direct all the activities of Parliament and of its bodies under the conditions laid down in these Rules'. In practice, this means that the President has many functions, such as presiding over debates in the chamber, referring matters to committees as appropriate, and representing the EP in dealings with other Community institutions and outside bodies. An effective President must be an administrator and a politician, skilled in organising and also in liaising and bargaining.

The Bureau consists of the President and Parliament's fourteen Vice-Presidents. Like the President, the Vice-Presidents are elected for a two and a half year period of office, though by tradition the posts are distributed amongst the member states. Various organisational matters are dealt with by the Bureau, such as making recommendations on the composition of committees and deciding on the composition and structure of the Parliament's Secretariat. To assist it in the performance of its duties, and in particular to take responsibility for financial and administrative matters concerning members, five quaestors, who are also elected, sit in the Bureau in an advisory capacity.

For certain key purposes the members of the Bureau are joined by the chairmen of the political groups or their representatives and two non-voting delegates from the non-attached groups. This constitutes the Enlarged Bureau. Its functions include: deciding on the seating arrangements in the Chamber – a potentially sensitive and highly symbolic issue when groups do not wish to be seated too far to the left or to the right of the hemicycle; drawing up the draft agenda of plenary sessions; and ruling on the permissibility and order of questions addressed to the Council and the Commission.

The Committees of Parliament

Much of the EP's work is carried out by committees. These are of two types. The first, and by far the most important, are standing or permanent committees. There are 18 of these (see Table 5.5). The second are *ad hoc* committees which are established to investigate special topics.

Assignment of MEPs to the permanent committees occurs at the beginning and half way through each five year term. Assignment to the *ad hoc* committees is as required. According to the Rules of Procedure, all committee members are elected to their positions on the basis of proposals made by the Bureau to Parliament which are 'designed to ensure fair representation of Member States and of political views'. What this means, in practice, is that the political groups negotiate the share-out of committee memberships on a basis proportionate to their size. Most MEPs become a member of one

TABLE 5.5

Standing committees of the European Parliament

Title	Number of Members
1. Political Affairs	56
2. Agriculture Fisheries and Rural Development	47
3. Budgets	32
4. Economic and Monetary Affairs and Industrial Policy	52
5. Energy, Research and Technology	34
6. External Economic Relations	29
7. Legal Affairs and Citizen's Rights	34
8. Social Affairs, Employment and the Working Environment	41
9. Regional Policy and Regional Planning	38
10. Transport and Tourism	30
11. Environment, Public Health and Consumer Protection	51
12. Youth, Culture, Education, the Media and Sport	31
13. Development and Co-operation	43
14. Budgetary Control	28
15. Institutional Affairs	38
16. Rules of Procedure, the Verification of Credentials and Immunities	27
17. Women's Rights	33
18. Petitions	25

standing committee – though a few are on as many as three – and a substitute member of another.

The permanent committees perform various duties, such as explore ideas with the Commission, foster own initiative reports, and discuss developments with the President-in-Office of the Council. Their most important task, however, is to examine legislative proposals on which an EP Opinion is required. The standard way of proceeding (other than where a proposal is completely straightforward and uncontroversial, which may result in it being dealt with by special procedures allowing for rapid approval) is as follows:

(1) Each proposal is referred to an appropriate committee. Should a proposal overlap the competency and interest of several committees up to three may be asked for their views, but one is named as the committee responsible and only it reports to the plenary session.

(2) The responsibility for drawing up the committee's report is entrusted to a *rapporteur*. Though formally chosen by their fellow committee members, *rapporteurs* are, in practice, like committee chairman and many others in the EP who hold nominally elected positions, appointed as a result of negotiations between the political groups: negotiations that, in this case, are carried out by group 'co-ordinators' from the different committees. In drawing up the report the *rapporteur* can call on assistance from various places: primarily from Parliament's Secretariat, but also from his personal research assistant (the EP provides funds to enable each MEP to have at least one such assistant), from the Secretariat of his political group, from research institutes, and even from the Commission. Some *rapporteurs* hardly use these facilities and do most of the work themselves; others do little more than present what has been done on their behalf.

(3) A first draft is produced for consideration by the committee according to an agreed timetable. Following changes that were introduced as part of the 1987 EP Rules of Procedure, drafts are normally presented in four main parts: Amendments to the Commission Proposal (if there are any); a Draft Legislative Resolution; an Explanatory Statement; and Annexes (if there are any), including Opinions of other committees. How much discussion the draft provokes, and how many committee meetings are required before a text is adopted that can be recommended to the plenary, depends on the complexity and controversiality of the subject matter. Factors likely to shape the reactions of committee members include national

and ideological perspectives, lobbying by outside interests, and views expressed by the Commission. (See Exhibit 5.1 for extracts from a committee report.)

(4) The *rapporteur* acts as the committee's principal spokesman when the report is considered in the plenary. In this capacity he may have to explain the committee's view on amendments put forward by non-committee members, or he may be called upon to use his judgement in making recommendations to Parliament on what it should do when the Commission goes some, but not all, of the way in accepting committee-approved amendments. Occasionally – when, for example, the Commission offers a mixed package – committee meetings may be hurriedly convened during plenary sessions.

(5) Where the co-operation procedure applies, the role and activity of committees at the second reading stage is similar to that at the first reading. That is to say, they examine a proposal – which is now in the form of the Council's common position – and make recommendations to the plenary. The responsibility for drawing up reports is conferred automatically on the committees involved in the first reading and the *rapporteur* remains the same. The reports normally have two main sections: Recommendations for the Second Reading (which may provide for approval of, rejection of, or amendments to, the common position – amendments often having the intention of reestablishing the EP's position as defined at the first reading, or to produce a compromise with the Council); and Justifications or Explanatory Statements.

A number of factors help to determine how the EP committees work, and how much influence they exercise. The most important of these factors are:

● *The significance of the policy area within the Community system.* The Committee on Agriculture, for example, deals with matters which loom much larger in the Community scale of things than the Committee on Youth, Culture, Education, The Media and Sport.

● *The power of Parliament within the policy area.* The influence of the Committee on Budgets is enormously enhanced by the real budgetary decision-making powers that the Treaties give to Parliament. Similarly, the Committee on Budgetary Control would be much weaker if the EP did not have the statutory responsibility to grant, postpone, or refuse a discharge to the Commission in respect of the implementation of the Community's budget.

EXHIBIT 5.1

Extracts from a European Parliament Committee Report

9 December 1987   SERIES A   DOCUMENT A 2-251/87

[*]   REPORT

drawn up on behalf of the Committee on the Environment, Public Health and Consumer Protection

on the proposal from the Commission of the European Communities to the Council (COM(87) 120 final – Doc. C 2-34/87) for a decision amending Decision 86/85/EEC establishing a Community information system for the control and reduction of pollution of the sea caused by oil and other harmful substances

The Committee on the Environment, Public Health and Consumer Protection hereby submits to the European Parliament the following draft legislative resolution together with explanatory statement:

A

DRAFT LEGISLATIVE RESOLUTION

embodying the opinion of the European Parliament on the proposal from the Commission of the European Communities to the Council for a decision amending Decision 86/85/EEC establishing a Community information system for the control and reduction of pollution caused by spillage of hydrocarbons and other harmful substances at sea

The European Parliament

– having regard to the proposal from the Commission to the Council (COM(87) 120 final),
– having been consulted by the Council pursuant to Article 130s of the EEC Treaty (Doc. C 2-34/87),
– having regard to, and approving, the legal basis proposed,
– having regard to the report of the Committee on the Environment, Public Health and Consumer Protection (Doc. A 2-251/87),
– having regard to the result of the vote on the Commission's proposal,
1.   Approves the Commission's proposal;
2.   Calls on the Council to notify Parliament should it propose to depart from the text approved by Parliament;
3.   Calls on the Council to consult Parliament again should it propose to make substantial modifications to the Commission's proposal;
4.   Instructs its President to forward to the Council and Commission, as Parliament's opinion, the text of the Commission's proposal as voted by Parliament and the corresponding legislative resolution.

B

EXPLANATORY STATEMENT

Although prevention of pollution should be the key element in environmental policy there will always be incidents involving the threat of pollution of the environment. Consequently, a preventive policy will always require the back-up of measures to control the effects of accidents.

The first stage in establishing adequate resources is to inventorize the resources already available for the control of accidents. To some extent existing Community information systems already meet this requirement. The expansion of the Community information system proposed by the Commission is a useful step towards controlling pollution of inland waterways and pollution of the sea into which such waterways discharge . . .

We therefore recommend that the Commission should, without delay, devise a programme capable of supporting the development of resources for controlling environmental accidents at sea and on inland waterways involving harmful substances other than oil.

* = Consultation procedure requiring a single reading

● *Committee expertise.* Many committee members just do not have the requisite specialised skills or knowledge to be able to explore relevant issues in depth or to question the Commission on the basis of a fully informed understanding of policy. For example, few members of the Committee on Energy, Research and Technology have an appropriate technical background. The Committee on Legal Affairs and Citizen's Rights, on the other hand, is composed mainly of lawyers or legal experts.

● *Secretariat support.* In terms of numbers, all committees are thinly resourced in their administrative back-up. Each has, on average, only about five or six senior officials and these, because of the EP's recruitment policy, usually have a generalist rather than a specialist background. However, amongst these small teams there do appear to be variations in competence and enthusiasm.

● *Committee chairmanship.* The role of committee chairmen can be vital in guiding the work of committees. They can help to push business through; they can assist *rapporteurs* in rallying support for reports that are to be debated in plenaries; they can help to create committee harmony and a constructive working atmosphere; and they can do much to ensure that a committee broadens its horizons beyond simply reacting to initiatives that others present to it.

● *Committee cohesiveness.* One of the reasons why, for example, the Committee on Development and Co-operation is rather more influential than a number of other committees is that it tends to display a high degree of cohesiveness. With members of the committee being united on the desirability of improving conditions in the developing countries, discussions tend to revolve around questions of feasibility rather than ideological desirability. The Agriculture Committee, on the other hand, attracts MEPs who are both supportive and critical of the CAP and hence it tends often to be sharply internally divided.

Plenary Meetings

There are usually eleven plenary meetings, or part-sessions as they are properly known, per year: one each month apart from August. Part-sessions last from Monday afternoon to Friday midday.

The agenda for plenaries is drafted by the President and the Enlarged Bureau in consultation with the committees, the political groups, and the EP's Secretariat. Their recommendations have to be approved by the plenary itself. With time so tight, items which many

MEPs consider to be important inevitably do not get onto the agenda, whilst those that do make it normally have to be taken at pace. Strict rules govern who can speak, when, and for how long: the effect of the rules is often to restrict speakers to committee and political group spokesmen.

Plenaries have three standard elements. First, the bread and butter business is the consideration of reports from committees. As indicated earlier these reports now produce over 200 resolutions embodying Opinions and over 100 resolutions embodying own initiatives per year. Second, time is set aside for debates on topical and urgent matters. These usually result in about 150–200 resolutions being adopted every year. Finally, there is a 1½ hour Commission Question Time and a 1½ hour Council Question Time. Who answers on behalf of the Commission and the Council depends on the policy content of the questions (which are known in advance), preferences expressed by the Parliament, and who is available.

In addition to these three standard activities, there are a number of other possible agenda items. For example, statements by the Commission and the Council, addresses by distinguished foreign guests, and – at least twice a year – a report on European Council meetings by the Head of Government of the incumbent Presidency.

The EP in plenary does not, it should be said, give the impression of being the most dynamic of places. Attendance in the chamber is poor, the translation problem limits spontaneity, and much immediacy is lost by the practice of taking most votes in clusters at allocated voting times rather than at the end of debates. (These times are often not even on the same day as the debate.) Nonetheless, working procedures have been gradually improved over the years, most notably by the removal of much minor business from the floor of the chamber.

Concluding Remarks: Is the EP Becoming a 'Proper' Parliament?

The EP has clearly assumed an increased role in the Community in recent years. Several factors account for this, not least the Parliament's own efforts to increase its powers.

In attempting to enhance its role and influence the Parliament has pursued a dual strategy. On the one hand there has been a *maximalist* approach, which has been directed towards achieving fundamental reform of inter-institutional relations, and especially increasing the powers of the Parliament *vis-à-vis* the Council of Ministers. In 1984 this approach led to the EP approving the *Draft Treaty establishing the European Union*, which played a part – though not perhaps as important a part as its supporters have claimed – in helping to bring about the SEA. In 1990, in the context of the increasingly heard debate about the Community's 'democratic deficit', and as part of the lead-up to the Intergovernmental Conference on Political Union, the approach led to the EP approving reports which called, amongst other things, for co-decision-making legislative powers with the Council, for the ability to initiative legislation, and for the right to elect the President of the Commission on a proposal from the European Council. On the other hand there has been a *minimalist* approach which has seen the EP using its existing powers to the full and doing whatever it can to see how far these powers can be pressed. As part of this approach the EP has made use of the enhanced status and increased vigour that has stemmed from direct elections, has taken advantage whenever it can of favourable Court judgements, and has contracted a number of formal and informal understandings with other Community institutions which have brought it certain benefits.

But notwithstanding all its efforts and the increased influence for itself that it has achieved, the EP is still commonly regarded as being a rather special sort of advisory body rather than a proper parliament. The main reason for this is that its constitutional powers remain considerably weaker than those of national parliaments. It does not have full legislative powers, its budgetary powers are circumscribed, and it cannot overthrow a government.

However, in assessing the importance of the EP, attention should not be restricted to its constitutional capabilities. For when the comparison with national parliaments is extended to encompass what actually happens in practice, the powers exercised by the EP are in several key respects comparable with the powers exercised by many national parliaments. Indeed, it is not difficult to make out a case that in exercising some of its functions – scrutinising legislative proposals, for example, and contributing to the debate about future developments – the EP exerts a greater influence over affairs than do some of the more executive-dominated parliaments in some of the member states.

6

Community Law and the Court of Justice

The Need for Community Law

An enforceable legal framework is the essential basis of decision-making and decision application in all democratic states. Although not itself a state this also applies to the EC. It does so because the Community is more than merely another international organisation in which countries co-operate with one another on a voluntary basis for reasons of mutual benefit. Rather it is an organisation in which states have voluntarily surrendered their right, across a broad range of important sectors, to be independent in the determination and application of public policy.

If there was no body of law setting out the powers and responsibilities of the institutions and the member states of the Community, and if there was no authority to give independent rulings on what that law is and how it should be interpreted, effective Community decision-making would not be possible. Of course, law is not the only factor shaping the Community's decision-making processes. As in any organisation, practice evolves in the light of experience of what is possible and what works best. The tendency to often not press for a vote in the Council even when it is legally permissible is an obvious example of this. But the law does provide the basic setting in which decisions are made. It lays down that some things must be done, that some cannot, and that some may be. So, for example, it is by virtue of Community law that agricultural prices can no longer be fixed in national capitals but must be agreed at Community level, that the

Commission is entitled to take certain types of decisions without reference to other institutions, and that the European Parliament is permitted to increase the annual budget within specified limits.

The existence of Community law is also crucial with regard to policy implementation. For if decisions took the form only of vague intergovernmental agreements, and if those agreements could be interpreted by member states in whatever way was most beneficial and convenient for them, common policies would not, in practice, exist and the whole rationale of the Community would be undermined. The likes of the *common* agricultural policy, the *common* competition policy, the *common* commercial policy, and the harmonisation of matters as diverse as maximum axle weights of lorries and minimum safety standards at work, can be fully effective only if they are based on *common laws* that are capable of *uniform* interpretation in *all* member states.

The Sources of Community Law

A Community legal order is thus an essential condition of the Community's existence. The sources of that order are to be found in a number of places: the Treaties, Community legislation, international law, the general principles of law, and judicial interpretation.

The Treaties

The three founding Treaties, plus the Treaties and Acts supplementing and amending the founding Treaties, constitute the so-called primary legislation of the Community. They may also be regarded as making up the Community's written constitution.

National constitutions in liberal democracies normally do two main things: they establish an institutional structure for decision-making, and they set out – often in a bill of rights – freedoms of the individual and restrictions on the power of decision-makers over the citizenry. The Treaties of the Community exercise the first of these tasks, but only in a very restricted way the second. The establishment of the institutional structure is seen, most obviously, in the identification of the Commission, the Council, the Court and the Parliament as the major institutions of the Community, and by the laying down of rules governing relations between them and also between them and the member states. As for the establishment of individual rights, the scope is largely restricted to certain economic freedoms – a reflection of the concerns of the Community and of the fact that it does not carry the comprehensive responsibilities of nation states.

But if the Treaties and Acts which make up the constitution of the Community do not fulfil all the tasks of national constitutions, they are much concerned with something that is normally not considered to be appropriate subject matter for constitutions: policy. This takes the form of enunciation of general principles on the one hand and the identification of policy sectors that are to be developed on the other. The main general principles are those of the EEC Treaty that are designed to promote competition and the free movement of goods, persons, services, and capital, all behind a common external tariff and a common commercial policy. The policy sectors that are identified, with varying degrees of precision regarding how they are to be developed, include: coal and steel (ECSC); atomic energy (Euratom); agriculture, social, and transport (EEC); and regional, environmental, and research and technological development (SEA).

Community Legislation

Laws adopted by the Community institutions constitute secondary legislation. They are concerned with translating the general principles of the Treaties into specific rules and are adopted by the Council or the Commission according to procedures that are described in other chapters of this book. While there is no hard and fast distinction between Council and Commission legislation, the former tends to be broader in scope and concerned with more important or more controversial matters. Commission legislation, which numerically is by far the most voluminous of the two, is largely administrative/technical in nature, and is usually subject to tight guidelines laid down in enabling Council legislation.

The Treaties distinguish between different types of Community legislation (Article 14 ECSC, Article 189 EEC, Article 161 Euratom): regulations, directives, decisions, and recommendations and opinions.

Regulations (called general decisions under the ECSC). A regulation is:

1. Of 'general application'; that is, it contains general and abstract provisions which may be applied to particular persons and circumstances.
2. 'Binding in its entirety'; that is, it bestows rights and obligations upon those to whom it is addressed, and member states must observe it in full and as written.
3. 'Directly applicable in all Member States'; that is, without the need for national implementing measures, it takes immediate legal effect right across the Community on the date specified in the regulation. (Normally this is the same day as, or very shortly after, the regulation is published in the *Official Journal of the European Communities*. This, in turn, is usually only a day or two after the regulation has been adopted).

Most regulations are adopted by the Commission and concern highly specific and technical adjustments to existing Community law. The majority relate to the CAP. Exhibit 6.1 is a typical regulation.

Directives (recommendations under the ECSC). 'A directive shall be binding, as to the result to be achieved, upon each Member State to which it is addressed, but shall leave to the national authorities the choice of form and method' (Article 189 EEC).

In theory, a directive is thus very different from a regulation: it is not binding in its entirety but only in 'the result to be achieved'; it is addressed to member states and does not claim general applicability; it is not necessarily addressed to all member states; and appropriate national measures need to be taken to give the directive effect. As a consequence directives tend to be rather more general in nature than regulations. They are not quite so much concerned with the detailed and uniform application of policy, as with the laying down of policy principles which member states must seek to achieve but which they can pursue by the appropriate means under their respective national constitutional and legal systems. (Such appropriate means can vary from administrative circulars to new laws approved by national legislatures.)

The distinction between regulations and directives should not, however, be exaggerated because, in practice, a number of factors often result in a blurring. First, directives are almost invariably addressed to all states and are so because they are usually concerned with the harmonisation of laws and practices in fields of Community

EXHIBIT 6.1

COMMISSION REGULATION (EEC) NO 2755/87

OF 15 SEPTEMBER 1987

FIXING THE AID FOR SOYA BEANS

THE COMMISSION OF THE EURO-
PEAN COMMUNITIES,

Having regard to the Treaty establishing
the European Economic Community,

Having regard to the Act of Accession of
Spain and Portugal,

Having regard to Council Regulation
(EEC) No 1491/85 of 23 May 1985 laying
down special measures in respect of soya
beans([1]), as amended by Regulation
(EEC) No 1921/87([2]); and in particular
Article 2(7) thereof,

Whereas the amount of the aid referred to
in Article 2(1) of Regulation (EEC) No
1491/85 was fixed by Commission Regulation (EEC) No 2638/87([3]);

Whereas it follows from applying the rules
and other provisions contained in Regulation (EEC) No 2638/87 to the information
at present available to the Commission
that the amount of the aid present in force
should be altered as set out in this
Regulation,

HAS ADOPTED THIS REGULATION:

Article 1

1. The aid referred to in Article 2 of
amended Regulation (EEC) No 1491/85
is hereby fixed in the Annex.

2. In cases of advance fixing of the aid
the amount shall however be confirmed
or altered with effect from 16 September
1987 to take account, where appropriate,
of the effects of application of the system of
maximum guaranteed quantities for soya
seed.

Article 2

This Regulation shall enter into force on
16 September 1987.

This Regulation shall be binding in its entirety and directly applicable in
all Member States.

Done at Brussels, 15 September 1987.

For the Commission
Frans ANDRIESSEN
Vice-President

([1]) OJ No L 151, 10.6.1985, p. 15.

([2]) OJ No L 183, 3.7.1987, p. 19.

([3]) OJ No L 248, 1.9.1987, p. 50.

ANNEX

Aid for soya beans([1])

(ECU/100 kg)

	Seed harvested in		
	Spain	Portugal	another Member State
Seed processed in:			
— Spain	0,000	33,910	33,910
— Portugal	22,084	0,000	33,910
— another Member State	22,084	33,910	33,910

([1]) Subject to confirmation of the amount to be deducted in accordance
with the system of guaranteed maximum quantities.

activity. Exhibit 6.2 is a typical harmonising directive. Second, some directives are drafted so tightly that there is very little room for national authorities to incorporate adjustments. Third, directives contain a date by which the national procedures to give the directive effect must have been complied with. The Commission has to be notified of national implementing measures, and states which do not comply by the due date are liable to have proceedings initiated against them which can, ultimately, result in a case before the Court of Justice. Fourth, the Court has ruled that in some instances directives are directly applicable; for example, where national implementing legislation has been unduly delayed or where it has departed from the intent of the original directive.

Decisions (called individual decisions under the ECSC). 'A decision shall be binding in its entirety upon those to whom it is addressed' (Article 189 EEC). It may be addressed to any or to all member states, to undertakings, or to individuals. Many decisions are highly specific and are, in effect, administrative rather than legislative acts. Others are of a more general character and can be akin to regulations or even, occasionally, directives.

Decisions are adopted in a whole range of circumstances. For example: to institute a pilot action programme; to authorise grants from one of the Community's funds; to allow an exemption from an existing measure; or to counter dumping from a third country.

Recommendations and Opinions (opinions only under the ECSC). Recommendations and opinions have no binding force and so, strictly speaking, do not formally constitute part of Community law. However, the Court of Justice has on occasions referred to them, so their legal status is not always completely clear. The same applies to some of the other non-binding devices which the Community institutions use for such purposes as floating ideas, starting a legislative process, promoting co-ordination, and encouraging harmonisation. These include memoranda, communications, conventions, programmes, guidelines, agreements, declarations, resolutions, and decisions not made under Article 189.

In order to accommodate the mosaic of different national circumstances and interests which exist on many policy issues the Community's legislative framework needs to be creative, flexible, and capable

EXHIBIT 6.2

COUNCIL DIRECTIVE

of 16 February 1987

fixing guidelines for the assessment of additives in animal nutrition

(87/153/EEC)

THE COUNCIL OF THE EUROPEAN COMMUNITIES,

Having regard to the Treaty establishing the European Economic Community,

Having regard to Council Directive 70/524/EEC of 23 November 1970 concerning additives in feedingstuffs([1]), as last amended by Commission Directive 86/525/EEC([2]), and in particular Article 9 thereof,

Having regard to the proposal from the Commission,

Whereas Directive 70/524/EEC provides that the examination of additives must be performed on the bases of a dossier forwarded officially to the Member States and to the Commission;

Whereas such dossiers must make it possible to verify that additives comply, in respect of their proposed use, with the general principles laid down in the Directive for their inclusion in the Annexes thereto;

Whereas it has been found necessary to provide for the dossiers to be compiled in accordance with common guidelines defining the scientific data which make it possible to identify and characterize the product concerned and the studies necessary in order to evaluate, in particular, their efficacy and their safety for man, animals and the environment;

Whereas the guidelines are intended primarily as a general guide; whereas, depending on the nature of the additive or its conditions to use, the extent of the studies necessary in order to evaluate its properties or its effects may vary;

([1]) OJ No L 270, 14.12.1970, p. 1.

([2]) OJ No L 310, 5.11.1986, p. 19.

Whereas it is indispensable to apply the principles of good laboratory practice when developing additives intended for use in feedingstuffs to ensure that the results of laboratory tests are not disputed; whereas recourse to procedures involving the use of laboratory animals for experimental or other scientific purposes should be kept to a minimum;

Whereas the guidelines have been drawn up on the basis of present scientific and technical knowledge and they may be adapted if necessary to any developments in this sphere,

HAS ADOPTED THIS DIRECTIVE,

Article 1

Member States shall prescribe that the dossiers which must accompany every request for the inclusion of an additive or a new use of an additive in the Annexes to Directive 70/524/EEC are to be compiled in accordance with the guidelines set out in the Annex to this Directive.

Article 2

This Directive shall apply without prejudice to provisions on:

(a) good laboratory practice for the purposes of mutual acceptance of data for the evaluation of chemical products; and

(b) the protection of animals used for experimental or other scientific purposes.

Article 3

Member States shall bring into force the laws, regulations or administrative provisions necessary in order to comply with this Directive by 31 December 1987 at the latest. They shall forthwith inform the Commission thereof.

Article 4

This Directive is addressed to the Member States.

Done at Brussels, 16 February 1987.

For the Council
The President
L. TINDEMANS

of permitting differentiation. There are four main ways in which it is so:

● As has just been shown the Community makes use of a variety of formal and quasi-formal legislative instruments.

● There are considerable variations between directives regarding the time periods permitted for incorporation into national law. So, for example, amending directives may have to be incorporated almost immediately, whereas innovative or controversial directives, or directives which involve substantial capital expenditure in order to be properly applied, may not be required to be incorporated for some years.

● Devices which allow for adaptation to local conditions and needs are often either attached to legal texts or are authorised by the Commission after an act has come into force. Examples of such devices include exemptions, derogations, and safety clauses.

● Provided the Commission is satisfied that the relevant provisions 'are not a means of arbitrary discrimination or a disguised restriction on trade between Member States' (Article 100A EEC), states are permitted to apply national legislation which is 'tougher' than EC legislation in respect of certain matters – notably protection of the environment and of the working environment.

The complexity of Community legislation is closely linked with its considerable volume. In an average year as many as 13000 instruments of all types may be adopted. Most of these are administrative measures of a routine, non-political, recurring kind such as price adjustments. With regard to the major, or clear, categories of legislation, around 4000 regulations are usually produced, about 500 decisions, and around 100 directives. Of these, the Council issues approximately 400 of the regulations, 170 of the decisions, and 80 of the directives.

International Law

International law is notoriously vague and weak, but the Court of Justice has had occasional recourse to it when developing principles embodied in Community law. Judgements have also established that insofar as the Community is increasingly developing an international personality of its own and taking over powers from the states the same rules of international law apply to it as apply to them:

regarding treaty law, for example, and the privileges and immunities of international organisations.

The many international agreements to which the Community is a party are sometimes viewed as another dimension of international law. However, since they are implemented by legislative acts they are probably better viewed as constituting part of Community legislation.

The General Principles of Law

All three Treaties charge the Court of Justice with the task of ensuring 'that in the interpretation and application of this Treaty the law is observed' (Article 164 EEC, Article 136 Euratom, Article 31 ECSC). The implication of this, and of certain other Treaty articles, (notably 173 and 215 EEC) is that the Court need not regard written Community law as the only source of law to which it may refer.

In practice, this has meant that the Court, in making its judgements, has had regard to the general principles of law when they have been deemed to be relevant and to apply. Now, exactly what the general principles of law are, gives rise to controversy. Suffice to note here that principles which have been cited by the Court include proportionality (the means used to achieve a given end should be no more than is appropriate and necessary to achieve the end), non-discrimination (whether between nations, product sectors, firms, or individuals), adherence to legality, and respect for procedural rights. As for fundamental human rights the Court has referred to them on several occasions: so, for example, in *Hauer* v. *Land Rheinland-Pfalz* (Case 44/79) the Court ruled that fundamental rights are an integral part of the general principles of law and the Court must ensure their observance.

Judicial Interpretation

Although case law has traditionally not played a major role as a source of law in most of the member states of the Community (the United Kingdom and Ireland are the main exceptions), the rulings of the Court of Justice have played an important part in shaping and making Community law. This stems partly from the Court's duty of ensuring that Community law is interpreted and applied correctly. It stems also from the fact that much of Community statute law is far from clear or complete.

The lack of precision in much of the Community's statute law arises from a number of factors: the relative newness of the Community; the problems of the decision-making processes that so often lead to weak compromises and to avoidance of necessary secondary legislation; and the speed of change in some spheres of Community activity which makes it very difficult for the written law to keep abreast of developments. In many fields of apparent Community competence the Court thus has to issue judgements from a less than detailed statutory base. In the different types of cases that come before it – cases of first and only instance, cases of appeal, cases involving rulings on points of Community law that have been referred by national courts – the Court, therefore, inevitably and frequently goes well beyond merely giving a technical and grammatical interpretation of the written rules. It fills in the gaps in the law and, in so doing, it not only clarifies the law, but it creates new law. This is seen both in the way national courts are expected to – and generally do – respect its judgements, and in the way the Court has increasingly come to cite its own case law.

In short, the Court is, in effect, extending Community law through its interpretations and judgements.

The Content of Community Law

The content of Community law is described at some length in Chapter 9, in the context of the examination that is presented there of Community policies. Attention here will, therefore, be confined to briefly noting some points of general significance.

The first point is that Community law does not range as widely as national law. It is not, for instance, directly concerned with criminal law or family law. Nor does it have much to do with policy areas such as education or health. What Community law is primarily concerned with – and, in this, it reflects the aims and the provisions of the Treaties – is economic activity. More particularly, Community law is strongly focused in the direction of, to quote Article 2 of the EEC Treaty, 'establishing a common market and progressively approximating the economic policies of the Member states'. To these ends, much of Community law is to be found in the overping, and often highly technical, areas of commercial law, competition law, business law, and law relating to the free movement of goods, services, capital and labour within the Community market.

The second point is that no policy area contains a comprehensive code of Community law. Even in areas where there is a high degree of Community regulation, such as external commercial relations and the functioning of agricultural markets, national laws covering various matters still exist. Community law thus sits side-by-side with national law, constituting an important part of the overall legal framework of member states in some policy spheres, being of only marginal significance in others.

The third point is that the range of Community law has broadened out considerably over the years. Certainly, as noted above, Community law is primarily economic in character, but less dominantly so than it was. A good illustration of this is seen in the considerable volume of Community environmental law that now exists, dealing with matters as diverse as air and water pollution, disposal of toxic wastes, and protection of endangered bird species. This expansion of Community law into an increasing number of policy areas has occurred, and is still occurring, for several reasons. Prominent amongst these reasons are: sectional pressures; increasing recognition of the benefits which can accrue in many fields of activity from joint action; and growing feelings that the Community market can only function smoothly, efficiently, and equitably, if there are common rules covering matters such as health and safety at work, entitlements to social welfare benefits, and mutual recognition of educational and professional qualifications.

The Status of Community Law

In Case 6/64 *Costa* v. *ENEL* the Court of Justice stated:

> By creating a Community of unlimited duration, having its own institutions, its own personality, its own legal capacity of representation on the international plane and, more particularly, real powers stemming from limitation of sovereignty or a transfer of powers from the states to the Community, the Member States have limited their sovereign rights, albeit within limited fields, and have

thus created a body of law which binds both their individuals and themselves'.

Community law thus constitutes an autonomous legal system imposing obligations and rights on both individuals and member states, and limiting the sovereignty of member states. There are three main pillars to this legal system: direct applicability, direct effect, and primacy.

Direct Applicability

Community law is directly applicable where there is no need for any national measures to be taken in order for the law to have binding force within member states. Of the different statutory sources of Community law only regulations are always directly applicable. However, it has been established, principally via Court of Justice judgements, that other legal acts may also be directly applicable when their structure and content so allow and certain conditions are satisfied.

Direct Effect

This term refers to the principle whereby certain provisions of Community law may confer rights or impose obligations on individuals which national courts are bound to recognise and enforce. Having initially established the principle in 1963 in the case of *Van Gend en Loos* (Case 26/62) the Court, in a series of judgements, has gradually strengthened and extended the scope of direct effect so that it now applies to most secondary legislation except where discretion is explicitly granted to the addressee. Many of the provisions of the Treaties have also been established as having direct effect, although the Court has ruled that it does not apply in some important spheres, for example, free movement of capital.

(Although the details of what is an extremely complicated legal debate cannot be rehearsed here, it should be noted that the distinction that has just been drawn between direct applicability and direct effect is not one that all lawyers accept. A consequence of this is that the terms have given rise to considerable confusion and much debate. Even official Community sources, including the Court itself, have not used the terms consistently or with precision.)

Primacy

Somewhat surprisingly, there is no explicit reference in the Treaties to the primacy or supremacy of Community law over national law. Clearly the principle is vital if the Community is to function properly, since if member states had the power to annul Community law by adopting, or giving precedence to, national law then there could be no uniform or consistent Community legal order: states could apply national law when Community law was distasteful or inconvenient to them. The Court, therefore, from an early stage, took an active part in establishing the primacy of Community law. National courts, it has consistently asserted, must apply Community law in the event of any conflict, even if the domestic law is part of the national constitution. An example of Court statements on primacy may be taken from *Simmenthal* v. *Commission* (Case 92/78) where the Court concluded:

> Every national court must, in a case within its jurisdiction, apply Community law in its entirety and protect rights which the latter confers on individuals and must accordingly set aside any provision of national law which may conflict with it, whether prior or subsequent to the Community rule.

In general, national courts have accepted this view of the Court and have given precedence to Community law. A few problems do still remain – notably in relation to fundamental rights guaranteed by national constitutions – but for the most part the authority and binding nature of Community law is fully established.

Powers and Responsibilities of the Court of Justice

The Court of Justice – which is based in Luxembourg and which must not be, though it often is, confused with the Strasbourg-based European Court of Human Rights – has two main functions. First, it is responsible for directly applying the law in certain types of cases. Second, it has a general responsibility for interpreting the provisions of Community law, and, in so doing, it must attempt to ensure that the application of the law, which on a day-to-day basis is primarily the responsibility of national courts, is consistent and uniform.

Inevitably, for the reasons that were explained earlier, these duties result in the Court making what is, in effect, judicial law. This is most clearly seen in three respects.

First, Community competence has been strengthened and extended by Court judgements. Social security entitlements illustrate this. Most governments have not wished to do much more about entitlements than co-ordinate certain aspects of their social security systems. The Court, however, through a number of judgements, has played an important part in pushing the states in the direction of harmonising some of their practices – with regard to the rights of migrant workers for example. It has also extended the provisions of certain laws in ways the states did not envisage when they gave them their approval in the Council. Interestingly, in issuing judgements in social security cases, the Court has often used the EEC Treaty and not Community legislation as its legal base – because the Council can change legislation much more easily than it can the Treaty.

Another example of the Court strengthening and extending Community competence is seen in a judgement it gave in May 1990 in a preliminary ruling case. The case – *Barber* v. *Guardian Royal Exchange Assurance Group* – had been referred by the UK's Court of Appeal. The Court of Justice ruled that occupational pensions are part of an employee's pay and must therefore comply with Article 119 of the EEC Treaty which deals with equal pay for men and women. Regarding the particular issue that gave rise to the case, the Court stated that it was contrary to Article 119 to impose different age requirements for men and women as conditions for obtaining pensions on compulsory redundancy under a private pension scheme.

The area where the Court has exercised the greatest influence in strengthening and extending Community competence is in regard to internal market matters. In some cases this has been a result of practices being ruled to be illegal by the Court, and in others it has been a consequence of Court judgements pressurising/enabling/forcing the Commission and the Council to act – as, for example, in de-regulating transport services.

Second, and of crucial importance in respect of the internal market, Court judgements have saved the Community the need to make law in existing areas of competence. A particularly influential judgement was issued in February 1979 in the *Cassis de Dijon* case (Case 120/78) which concerned the free circulation of the French blackcurrant liqueur. The Court ruled that national food standards legislation cannot be invoked to prevent trade between member states unless it is related to 'public health, fiscal supervision and the defence of the consumer'. The principle of 'mutual recognition' – whereby a product lawfully produced and marketed in one member state must be accepted in another member state – was thus established, with the result that the need for legislation to harmonise standards so as to facilitate trade was much reduced. Of course, the *Cassis de Dijon* judgement does not rule out challenges to the principle of 'mutual recognition' or to its application. For example, in the much publicised case *Commission* v. *Germany* (Case 178/84), the German government attempted to protect its brewers by arguing that whereas their product was pure, most so-called foreign beers contained additives and needed to be excluded from the German market on health grounds. In March 1987 the Court upheld the 'mutual recognition' principle and ruled that a blanket ban on additives to beer was quite disproportionate to the health risk involved; the German insistence on its own definition of beer amounted to a barrier to trade. In a similar ruling in July 1988 (Case 407/85) the Court ruled against an Italian prohibition on the sale of pasta products which are not made (as all Italian pasta is) from durum (hard) wheat; the Court stated that the importation of German pasta – which is made from a mixture of hard and soft wheat – was not prejudicial to consumers' health nor was it misleading.

Third, the powers of the institutions have been clarified, and in important respects have been significantly affected, by the Court. Three judgements will be cited to illustrate this. (1) In October 1980, in the isoglucose case (Case 138/79), the Court ruled that the Council could not adopt legislation until it had received Parliament's Opinion (see Chapter 5 for further consideration of this case). (2) In July 1986, in a case brought by the Council and supported by Germany, France and the United Kingdom against the Parliament (Case 34/86), the Court specified limitations on the EP's budgetary powers. (3) In October 1988, in the 'Wood Pulp' cases (joined Cases 89, 104, 114–117, 125–129/85), the Court upheld and strengthened the power of Community institutions to take legal action against non-EC companies. (In this case the Commission had imposed fines on a number of American, Canadian and Finnish producers of wood pulp in respect of concerted practices which had affected selling prices in the Community. The Court ruled that the key factor in determining the Community's jurisdiction was not where companies were based, nor where any illegal agreements or practices were devised, but where illegalities were implemented.)

In fulfilling its responsibilities the Court cannot itself initiate actions. It must wait for cases to be referred to it. This can happen in one of a number of ways:

Failure to Fulfil an Obligation

Under Articles 169 and 170 (all subsequent Treaty references in this Chapter are to the EEC Treaty except where otherwise stated) the Court rules on whether member states have failed to fulfil obligations under the Treaty. Actions may be brought either by the Commission or by other member states. In either case, the Commission must give the state(s) concerned an opportunity to submit observations and must then itself deliver a reasoned opinion. Only if this fails to produce proper compliance with Community law can the case be referred to the Court of Justice.

In practice – as Table 10.2 shows – failures to fulfil obligations are usually settled well before they are brought before the Court. When an action is brought the Commission is almost always the initiator. It is so partly because if a member state is behind the action it is obliged to refer the matter to the Commission in the first instance, and partly because member states are extremely reluctant to engage in direct public confrontations with one another (though they do sometimes try to encourage the Commission to, in effect, act on their behalf). Such cases in recent years have led to rulings against Italy that its duties on imported gin and sparkling wine were discriminatory, against the UK that it had taken insufficient national measures to give full effect to the 1976 directive on sexual discrimination, and against Belgium for failing to implement three directives which harmonise certain stock exchange rules.

Application for Annulment

Under Article 173, the Court may be called upon by a member state, the Council, or the Commission, to review the legality of Council or Commission acts that have binding force. The Court itself has also ruled, most notably in its July 1986 judgement on the powers of the Parliament under the budgetary procedure, that 'an action for annulment may be brought against the acts of the European Parliament which are intended to have legal effects *vis-à-vis* third parties'. In the words of the Treaty, grounds for annulment are 'lack of competence, infringement of an essential procedural requirement, infringement of this Treaty, or of any rule of law relating to its application, or misuse of powers'.

An increasingly important aspect of Court activity under this heading arises in connection with the greater use of majority voting in the Council of Ministers since the mid-1980s. Governments which find themselves outvoted on legislative proposals to which they are opposed can, if they think they have a case, appeal to the Court for the annulment of the legislative act on the grounds that the Commission should have used a legal base where unanimity was required. The Greek government, for example, made such an application to the Court in respect of a regulation which was adopted in December 1987 which set the standards for maximum levels of radioactive contamination for agricultural goods imported into the Community. The Greek case rested on the claim that the regulation should not have been treated as falling under trade policy (where qualified majority voting rules apply), but as falling under environmental policy (where unanimity is required for adoption). The Court did not agree with the Greek government. In giving its judgement in May 1990 the Court ruled that the regulation concerned trade in goods and was therefore a trade policy regulation even if it did contain elements of environmental protection.

Article 173 also allows any 'natural or legal person' (that is to say, private individuals or companies) to institute proceedings for annulment, although only on a restricted basis. Rulings under this provision have tended to serve as useful underpinnings to some Community policies, notably competition policy, commercial policy and the highly controlled and directed policies for steel that were pursued in the 1980s.

Unlimited Jurisdiction With Regard to Penalties

In certain limited spheres of activity, notably competition policy, the Commission is empowered to impose penalties to ensure compliance with Council regulations. Under Article 172, the Council regulations may grant unlimited jurisdiction to the Court regarding the penalties provided for in the regulations. In practice, this means that aggrieved parties may appeal against Commission decisions and the penalties it has imposed. As such, this is another form of action for annulment. The Court may annul or confirm the decision and increase or decrease the fine. In the great majority of judgements the Commission's decisions are upheld. There has been no example of a fine being increased.

Failure to Act

Should the Council or the Commission fail to act on a matter provided for by the Treaty, the member states, the institutions of the Community, and, in restricted conditions, 'natural or legal persons', may initiate an action before the Court under Article 175 to have the infringement established. Such actions are rare, but one that attracted much attention was initiated by the Parliament, with the support of the Commission, against the Council in 1983. The case concerned the alleged failure of the Council to take action to establish a Common Transport Policy, despite the provision for such a policy in the EEC Treaty. The judgement, which was delivered in May 1985, was not what the Parliament or the Commission had hoped for. The Court ruled that whilst there was a duty for legislation to be produced, it had no power of enforcement because the Treaty did not set out a detailed timetable or an inventory for completion; it was incumbent upon the national governments to decide how best to proceed.

Actions to Establish Liability

'In the case of non-contractual liability, the Community shall, in accordance with the general principles common to the laws of the Member States, make good any damage caused by its institutions or by its servants in the performance of their duties' (Article 215). Under Article 178, the Court has exclusive jurisdiction to decide whether the Community is liable, and if so, whether it is bound to provide compensation.

This means that the Community may have actions brought against it on the grounds of it having committed an illegal act. The complex mechanisms of the Common Agricultural Policy have produced by far the most number of such cases, threatening indeed to overwhelm

TABLE 6.1

Cases brought before the European Court of Justice since 1953
(situation at 31 December 1989)

	ECSC				Free movement of goods and customs union	Right of establishment and freedom to supply services	Taxation
	Scrap compensation	Transport	Competition	Other²			
Actions brought	167	35	66	265⁴	745	133	259
				(3)	(72)	(19)	(19)
Cases not resulting in a judgement	25	6	24	123	153	30	56
				(11)	(19)	(2)	(4)
Cases decided	142	29	42	138	468	79	166
				(6)	(39)	(5)	(27)
Cases pending	–	–	–	4	124	24	37

Notes:

The figures in brackets represent the cases dealt with by the Court in 1989.

[1] Cases concerning more than one subject are classified under the most important heading.

[2] Levies, investment declarations, tax charges, miners' bonuses, production quotas.

[3] Contentious proceedings, Staff Regulations, community terminology, Lomé Convention, short-term economic policy, commercial policy, relations between Community law and national law and environment.

[4] Including 2 cases transferred to the Court of First Instance.

[5] Including 73 cases transferred to the Court of First Instance.

[6] Including 78 cases transferred to the Court of First Instance.

[7] Including 153 cases transferred to the Court of First Instance.

[8] Including 1 case decided by the Court of First Instance.

Source: XXIIIrd General Report on the Activities of the European Communities, 1989.

	EEC								
Com-pet-tion	Social security and free move-ment of workers	Agri-culture	Trans-port	Article 220 Conv-entions	Other[3]	Eur-atom	Privi-leges and imm-unities	Proceed-ings by staff of instit-utions	Total
462[5]	461	1 155	55	71	363	14	14	2 388[6]	6 653[7]
(69)	(40)	(63)	(4)	(3)	(52)	–	(1)	(40)	(385)
48	41	107	11	5	93	1	3	1 361	2 087
(4)	(6)	(7)	–	–	(9)	–	–	(13)	(75)
319	357	917	35	59	203	12	10	941[8]	3 917[8]
(16)	(26)	(54)	(2)	(1)	(26)	(1)	–	(50)	(253)
95	63	131	9	7	67	1	1	86	649

the Court in the early 1970s. As a consequence the Court became increasingly unwilling to accept non-contractual liability cases, at least on the basis of first instance, and made it clear that they should be brought before national courts.

In the 1970s the Court also ruled that the circumstances in which the Community could incur non-contractual liability and be liable for damages were strictly limited. Of particular importance in this context were judgements in 1978 on two joined cases concerning skimmed milk (Cases 83 and 94/76 and 4, 15 and 40/77). Community legislation obliged the food industry to add skimmed milk to animal feed as part of an effort to reduce the surplus on powdered milk. A number of users challenged the legality of this, on the grounds that the Community's solution to dealing with the problem was discriminatory. In its first judgement, the Court ruled that the powdered milk regulations were, indeed, invalid because they did not spread the burden fairly across the agricultural sector. In its second judgement, however, it ruled that it was only exceptionally and in special circumstances, notably when a relevant body had manifestly and seriously exceeded its powers, that the Community should be liable to pay damages by virtue of a legislative measure of a political and economic character being found to be invalid.

References for Preliminary Rulings

The types of cases referred to above are known as direct actions. That is to say, the Court is called upon to give a judgement in a dispute between two or more parties who bring their case directly before the Court. References for preliminary rulings are quite different, in that they do not involve the Court itself giving judgements in cases, but rather require it to give interpretations on points of Community law to enable national courts to give judgement in cases which they are hearing.

References are made under Article 177 which states that national courts may, and in some circumstances must, ask the Court to give a preliminary ruling where questions arise concerning the interpretation of the Treaty or the validity and interpretation of acts of the institutions of the Community. The Court cannot make a pronouncement on a case which happens to have come to its attention unless a reference has been made to it by the appropriate national court, and parties to a dispute have no power to insist on a reference or to object to one being made. It is the exclusive prerogative of the national court to apply for a preliminary ruling. Once a reference has been made, the Court is obliged to respond but it can only do so on questions which have been put to it and it may not pronounce on, or even directly attempt to influence the outcome of, the principal action. Interpretations made by the Court during the course of preliminary rulings must be accepted and applied by the national court that has made the referral.

Preliminary rulings now constitute the largest category of cases that come before the Court. With only occasional dips, references have progressively increased: from one in 1961, to 32 in 1970, to 106 in 1979, to 138 in 1989. Preliminary rulings serve three principal functions. First, they help to ensure that national courts make legally 'correct' judgements. Second, because they are generally accepted by all national courts as setting a precedent, they promote the uniform interpretation and application of Community law in the twelve member states. Third, they provide a valuable source of access to the Court for private individuals and undertakings who cannot directly appeal to it, either because there is no legal provision or because of inadequacy of funds.

Membership and Organisation of the Court

The Court consists of thirteen judges, each of whom is appointed for a six year term of office which may be, and frequently is, renewed. To ensure continuity turnover is staggered in three yearly cycles.

According to the Treaties, judges are to be appointed 'by common accord of the Governments of the Member States' from amongst persons 'whose independence is beyond doubt and who possess the qualifications required for appointment to the highest judicial offices in their respective countries or who are juriconsults of recognised competence'. In practice, there is something of a gap, in spirit at least, between these Treaty provisions and reality. First, because each state is permitted one nomination that is automatically accepted, leaving only the thirteenth judge to be appointed by a common accord. Second, because in making their choices governments have tended not to worry too much about the judicial qualifications or experience of their nominations, but have looked rather for a good background in professional activities and public service. There is no evidence of 'political' appointments being made, in the way in which they are to the United States Supreme Court, but the fact is that soundness and safeness seem to be as important as judicial ability. At the time of his initial appointment the typical judge is a legally qualified 'man of affairs' who has been involved with government in his native country in some way, but who has, at best, served in a judicial capacity for only a limited period.

The judges elect one of their number to be President of the Court for a term of three years. His principal function is to see to the overall direction of the work of the Court by, for example, assigning cases to the Court's Chambers, appointing judge-rapporteurs to cases, and setting schedules for cases. He is also empowered, on application from a party, to order the suspension of Community measures and to order such interim measures as he deems to be appropriate.

Assisting the judges in the exercise of their tasks are six advocates-general. The duty of advocates-general is 'acting with complete impartiality and independence, to make, in open court, reasoned submissions on cases brought before the Court of Justice...' (Article 166 EEC). This means that an advocate-general, on being assigned to a case, must make a thorough examination of all the issues involved in the case, take account of all relevant law, and then present his conclusions to the Court. The conclusions are likely to include observations on the key points in the case, an assessment of Community law touching on the case, and a proposed legal solution.

In principle, advocates-general are appointed on the same Treaty terms and according to the same Treaty criteria as the judges. In practice, since not all states can claim an advocate-general, appointments are more genuinely collective than is the case with judges – but only up to a point, since the larger states have usually been able to ensure that they have one post each. At the same time, however, the judicial experience of advocates-general tends to be even more questionable than is that of the judges; certainly few have ever served in a judicial capacity in their own states.

In addition to the judges and the advocates-general, each of whom is assisted by two legal secretaries, the Court employs a staff of around 650. Most of these are engaged either in administrative duties – such as registering and transmitting case documents – or in providing language services.

The increasing number of cases coming before the Court – in the 1960s there were around 50 in an average year, today there are between 300 and 400 (385 in 1989) – has made it impossible for everything to be dealt with in plenary session. There has, therefore, been an increasing tendency for cases to be assigned to Chambers. However, cases brought by a member state or by one of the Community institutions, cases deemed to be especially important, and cases where a member state so requests, must be heard by the Court sitting in plenary session. (A quorum for the plenary Court is seven judges.) In general, a matter is referred to a Chamber of three judges if it is based upon relatively straightforward facts, raises no substantial points of principle, or where the circumstances are covered by existing case law. Cases involving complex findings of fact, or novel or important points of law, which do not require to be heard by the full Court, are assigned to a Chamber of five judges.

Under the Single European Act the Court was given an additional means of enabling it to deal more expeditiously and more effectively with its constantly expanding workload: the Council was empowered to establish, at the request of the Court, a Court of First Instance. Such a request was quickly made and in 1988 the Court of First Instance was established by Council Decision 88/591. The Court began to function in November 1989.

The Court of First Instance has jurisdiction in three areas: disputes between the Community and its staff; actions brought against the Commission under the ECSC Treaty; certain aspects of the competition rules. The Court cannot hear actions brought by member states or by one Community institution against another, nor can it deal with references for preliminary rulings. All decisions of the Court are subject to appeal to the Court of Justice on points of law.

The Court has twelve judges. Their conditions of appointment and terms of office are similar to those of the judges of the Court of Justice. Most of the work of the Court of First Instance is undertaken in one of the Court's five chambers: these have a membership of between three and five judges. Unlike in the Court of Justice, no advocates-general are appointed to the Court of First Instance. Where the exercise of the function of advocate-general is seen as being necessary – which it is not in all cases – the task is undertaken by one of the judges; the judge so designated cannot take part in the judgement of the case.

The Procedure of the Court

The procedure of the Court of Justice involves both written and oral stages. The former are more important, with cases being conducted largely away from the public eye via the communication of documents between interested parties and Court officials. Not much happens in open court.

Without going into all the details and possible variations, direct action cases proceed broadly along the following lines:

● Relevant documentation and evidence is assembled. The Court, under the direction of a duly appointed judge-rapporteur, may have to take a very pro-active role in gathering the information that it needs and in soliciting the views of interested parties. This may involve holding a preparatory enquiry at which oral and documentary evidence is presented. (In preliminary ruling cases the procedure is very different: the national court making the reference should have provided with its submission a summary of the case and of all relevant facts, a statement of the legal problem, and the [abstract] question it wishes the Court to answer.)

● A public hearing is held at which the essentials of the case are outlined, at which the various parties are permitted to present their views orally, and at which the judges and advocates-general may question the parties' lawyers.

● Following the public hearing, the advocate-general appointed to the case examines it in detail. He and his staff look at all relevant Community law and then come to a decision that appears to them to be correct in legal terms. A few weeks after the public hearing the advocate-general presents his submission to an open session of the Court.

● Acting on the advocate-general's submission, and on the basis of a draft drawn up by the judge-rapporteur, the Court prepares its decision. Deliberations are in secret and decisions are made, where there is a disagreement, by majority vote (hence the need for an odd number of judges). Judgements must be signed by all the judges who have taken part in the proceedings and no dissenting opinions may be published. (In their oath of office members swear to preserve the secrecy of the deliberation of the Court.)

Three problems associated with the Court's proceedings ought to be mentioned. First, there is a lengthy gap between cases being lodged at the Court and final decisions: on average, about twelve to fiftec months for preliminary rulings and nearly two years for direc actions. In special cases, however, interim judgements are issued and accelerated procedures are used. Second, lawyers' fees usually mean that going before the Court can be an expensive business, even though there is no charge for the actual proceedings in the Court itself. This does not, of course, place much of a restriction on the ability of member states or Community institutions to use the Court, but it can be a problem for individuals and small firms. There is a small legal aid fund, but it cannot remotely finance all potential applicants. Third, the use of majority voting, coupled with the lack of opportunity for dissenting opinions, has encouraged a tendency, which perhaps is inevitable given the different legal backgrounds of the judges, for judgements sometimes to be less than concise; occasionally even to be fudged.

Community Law and the Court of Justice: Concluding Observations

The legal framework described in the previous pages constitutes the single most important feature distinguishing the Community from other international organisations. The member states do not just co-operate with one another on an intergovernmental basis but have developed common laws designed to promote uniformity. The claim to legal supremacy in the interpretation, application and adjudica-tion of these laws constitutes a central element of the supranational character of the Community.

This has necessarily involved the states in surrendering some of their sovereignty. They are obliged to submit to a legal system over which they have only partial control. As a corollary, their govern-ments are also sometimes prevented from introducing national laws they themselves desire.

The Court of Justice has played an extremely important part in establishing the Community's legal order. Whether it is acting as an international court, a court of review, a court of appeal, or a court of referral (roles which, in practice, greatly overlap) it is frequently as much a maker as an interpreter of law. Of course, judges everywhere help to shape the law, but this is especially so in the Community where the Court has had much more manoeuvrability available to it than is customary within states. It has used this potential to considerable effect: to help clarify relations between the institutions and between the institutions and the member states; to help determine, clarify and extend policy content in many different spheres; and to help develop and foster the *esprit communautaire*.

7

The European Council

Origins

Although no provision was made in the founding Treaties for summit meetings of Heads of Government a few such gatherings did occur in the 1960s and early 1970s. In 1974, at the Paris summit, it was decided to institutionalise these meetings with the establishment of what soon became known as the European Council.

The main reason for the creation of the European Council was a growing feeling that the Community was failing to respond adequately or quickly enough to new and increasingly difficult challenges. Neither the Commission, whose position had been weakened by the intergovernmental emphasis on decision-making that was signalled by the Luxembourg Compromise, nor the Council of Ministers, which was handicapped both by sectoralism and by its practice of proceeding only on the basis of unanimous agreements, were providing the necessary leadership. A new focus of authority was seen as being required to try and make the Community more effective, both domestically and internationally. What was needed, argued France's President Giscard d'Estaing, who, with West Germany's Chancellor Schmidt, was instrumental in establishing the European Council, was a body which would bring the Heads of Government together on a relatively informal basis to exchange ideas, to give direction to policy development, and perhaps sometimes to break deadlocks and clear logjams. It was not anticipated that the leaders would concern themselves with the details of policy.

Rather, the intention was that they would operate at a very general level. In a similar manner to the Western Economic Summits, which were also established at this time, it was hoped the European Council would promote the co-ordination and clarification of interstate relations and would serve to further understanding at the highest political level.

The formal creation of the European Council was very simple: a few paragraphs were issued as part of the Paris communiqué. The two key paragraphs were these:

> Recognising the need for an overall approach to the internal problems involved in achieving European unity and the external problems facing Europe, the Heads of Government consider it essential to ensure progress and overall consistency in the activities of the Communities and in the work on political co-operation.
>
> The Heads of Government have therefore decided to meet, accompanied by the Ministers of Foreign Affairs, three times a year and, whenever necessary, in the Council of the Communities and in the context of political co-operation. The administrative secretariat will be provided for in an appropriate manner with due regard for existing practices and procedures.

Two points about this communiqué are particularly worth emphasising. First, it was vague and left a number of questions largely unanswered, especially as regards the precise role and functioning of the European Council. Subsequent summit declarations (notably London 1977 and Stuttgart 1983) have done something, but not a great deal, to clarify matters. As a result, the evolution and operation of the European Council have owed much more to the preferences of participants and practical necessities than they have to agreed rules and requirements.

Second, the communiqué had no constitutional or legal standing. It announced a political agreement between the national leaders but it did not formally or legally integrate the European Council into the Community framework. In a somewhat similar fashion to the Luxembourg Compromise and European Political Co-operation, the European Council was thus to be part of the 'unofficial' approach to integration rather than the 'official' Treaty-based approach. Even when, in the Single European Act, the European Council was eventually accorded legal recognition, it was so only in two short paragraphs that were confined to clarifying membership, and reducing the minimum number of meetings per year from three to two. The paragraphs, moreover, were not incorporated into the Treaties.

Membership

The Single European Act states:

> The European Council shall bring together the Heads of State or of Government of the Member States and the President of the Commission of the European Communities. They shall be assisted by the Ministers for Foreign Affairs and by a Member of the Commission.

This means that there are twenty-six negotiating participants at European Council meetings: two from each member state (the Head of Government and Foreign Minister – apart from France whose delegation is always led by the President, who is Head of State, accompanied by either the Prime Minister or the Foreign Minister), plus two from the Commission. Apart from these twenty-six, only a very restricted number of other people are permitted to be present at the formal sessions of the European Council: interpreters; six officials – two from the country holding the Presidency, one from the Council Secretariat (a major job of these three officials is to make an accurate record of proceedings), and three from the Commission – including the Secretary General of the Commission; and national civil servants, but only on the basis of one adviser per country being allowed entrance at any one time.

Each state has a suite in the vicinity of the meeting room which is available to its official delegation and from which officials may be summoned as required. Official delegations are restricted to seventeen in number, but states always supplement their official delegations with numerous other officials who make up what are customarily described as the non-official or technical delegations.

The membership of the European Council is thus based on the Council of Ministers model in the sense that it is made up of national delegations, plus the Commission. Unlike in the Council of Ministers, however, the participants in European Council sessions are not physically accompanied by teams of national officials.

Organisation

Preparing European Council meetings

Much of the responsibility for preparing European Council meetings rests with the Presidency – a post that is held concurrently with the Presidency of the Council of Ministers. How closely the Head of Government of the incumbent Presidency becomes involved in these preparations depends very much on circumstances, style and personal preference. Some act in a low-key manner and do little more than circulate their eleven colleagues with a letter indicating topics to be discussed and ways in which it is proposd to try and deal with them; others, especially those who are faced with a difficult meeting or who are looking for media attention, may well play a very active and public role – including making a tour of some or all of the national capitals.

Whatever the preparatory work that Heads of Government themselves choose to do, national officials and Foreign Ministers are invariably extensively engaged in pre-European Council preparations. The 'standard' procedure is for senior officials from the Presidency, working with the Secretariat of the Council of Ministers (the European Council does not have its own Secretariat) and in liaison with the Commission, to identify topics that can be, ought to be, or need to be discussed. These are then channelled through COREPER, or, in the case of EPC matters, through the Political Committee (which is made up of Political Directors from Foreign Offices). Finally, about ten days before the European Council meeting, Foreign Ministers meet to finalise the general shape of the agenda and, usually, to engage in exploratory pre-summit negotiations. To this 'standard' procedure may well be added – especially when it looks as though a European Council meeting will be difficult – numerous preparatory meetings of officials and the convening of extra meetings of the Council of Foreign Ministers and of appropriate Technical Councils.

Setting the Agenda

The subject matter of European Council meetings, depends on many factors:

● Some issues are almost always on the agenda. So, time is usually allowed for a discussion of the general economic situation in the Community, and in recent years time has usually also been set aside for some consideration of progress towards the completion of the internal market.

● The Commission may be pressing an initiative which the Presidency and at least some of the states are sympathetic to. This was the background to the discussion on the Social Charter at the 1989 Strasbourg summit.

● The Presidency, perhaps supported by, or even pressed by, the Commission and all or some of the other eleven states, may wish to use a European Council meeting to make or to formalise an important policy or institutional breakthrough. The events leading up to the two Intergovernmental Conferences (IGCs) which opened at the end of 1990 illustrate this: the decision to call an IGC on Economic and Monetary Union was taken at the 1989 Strasbourg summit; the decision to call a parallel IGC on Political Union was taken at the special April 1990 Dublin summit; the setting of dates for the opening of the two IGCs was taken at the June 1990 Dublin summit; the IGCs were formally opened at the December 1990 Rome summit.

● Decisions may be urgently needed on matters which the Council of Ministers has been unable to resolve. This is the reason why there were so many summit discussions in the 1980s on budgetary and agricultural reform.

● Business may be left over from, or have been referred from, a previous summit. Such was the case with the decision taken at the June 1985 Milan summit to establish an IGC and to require it to report to the December 1985 Luxembourg summit.

● International circumstances may require discussions, declarations, and decisions. So, the December 1990 Rome summit decided to send emergency food aid to the Soviet Union, lifted the voluntary ban on EC investments in South Africa, urged the negotiating parties in the suspended GATT world trade talks to reach a balanced agreement as soon as possible, and re-affirmed Community support for the UN-US stance on the Gulf crisis.

The regular, twice-yearly, European Council meetings contain on their agendas a mixture of most of the factors that have just been itemised. When special summits are held, however, the situation is rather different for they are usually convened for a specific purpose and therefore they have a much narrower agenda. So, the February 1988 Brussels summit was called to try and resolve pressing budgetary, and budgetary related, problems. The special Dublin summit of April 1990 was called to discuss German unification – though in the event the much broader question of political unification in the Community also featured prominently on the agenda. And the special Rome summit of October 1990 – which many thought was not really required and suspected had been called because the Italians wanted the prestige and status of an extra summit during their Presidency – focused mainly on Economic and Monetary Union.

Location and Timing of Meetings

The six-monthly meetings of the European Council that are specifically provided for in the SEA are held in the country of the Presidency. It had been anticipated that extra meetings would be held in Brussels, but when both Ireland and Italy arranged for an extra meeting during their Presidencies in 1990 they held them not in Brussels but in their national capitals. (The four 1990 summits have come to be referred to as Dublin 1 and Dublin 2, and Rome 1 and Rome 2.)

The regular meetings of the European Council take place towards the end of a Presidency – in June and December. They are held over a two-day period, normally – though by no means always – beginning with a working lunch on day one and ending in the late afternoon of day two. The timing and length of special summits depends largely on the reasons for which they have been called – Dublin 1, for example, was held on a Saturday in April.

The Conduct of Business

The customary, though by no means rigidly adhered to, format for the regular European Council meetings is as follows:

● Participants gather over lunch. Informal discussions begin immediately.

● On the basis of the (normally loose) agenda that has been agreed in advance, a full plenary session is held in the afternoon.

Since 1987 this opening session has included an address from the President of the European Parliament.

● In the evening two dinners – one for Heads of Government and the President of the Commission, one for Foreign Ministers and the other representative of the Commission – provide an opportunity for further informal discussions.

● The dinners drift into informal sessions. The Heads have what has come to be referred to as their 'fireside chat', the Foreign Ministers often discuss EPC matters.

● During the night Presidency and Council Secretariat officials prepare a draft of conclusions on the first day's business and/or work on a form of words that can serve as a basis for further negotiations the next day.

● Another plenary session is held in the morning, and perhaps afternoon, of day two. This usually picks up from the previous day's discussions, but with the draft that has been worked on during the night now tabled. With the leaders now trying to move towards conclusions, breaks in proceedings may be called for, most usually by the Presidency, so as to permit delegations to carefully study the implications of proposals or so as to allow for informal discussions.

● The summit normally ends some time in the afternoon with the publication of a statement which is issued in the form of a 'Conclusions of the Presidency'. The statement is customarily agreed to by all, but there are two sets of circumstances in which unanimity may be lacking. First, since 1985 there has been some limited use of voting in European Council meetings. This has largely been because of growing irritation with UK opposition to integrationist developments. It is no coincidence that on each occasion a vote has been taken the UK has been in the minority: at Milan in 1985 when Denmark, Greece and the UK were outvoted on the establishment of the Intergovernmental Conference which led to the SEA; at Strasbourg in 1989 when the UK was in a minority of one on both the adoption of the Social Charter and on the calling of the Inter-governmental Conference on Economic and Monetary Union; and at the special Rome summit in 1990 when the UK was again in a minority of one on the setting of a date for Stage 2 of Economic and Monetary Union. Second, some states may attach reservations to the statement: thus, the preamble to the conclusions of the 1985 Luxembourg summit which, in effect, agreed the SEA, included the following – 'Denmark has stated that it was unable to take a position

on these texts. A blanket reservation on the part of Denmark therefore remains. Italy has made its final acceptance conditional upon
examination by the Italian Parliament. There are also a few reservations on specific points'.

● Press conferences are held for the hundreds of journalists who
attend European Councils, and who do so much to turn the summits
into major media events. The President of the European Council and
the President of the Commission normally hold a joint press conference, and each delegation holds one of its own. Different versions of
what has happened are often given on these occasions.

The negotiating, the bargaining, and the compromising which can
be such a part of European Council meetings is worth illustrating
with an example. The specially convened February 1988 Brussels
summit will be taken because it illustrates these politicking processes
in a particularly dramatic way. The summit was called after summits
at Brussels and Copenhagen in 1987 had failed to resolve a number of
pressing interrelated issues – notably on controlling the CAP,
increasing non-agricultural expenditure, and expanding the Community's resource base. The depth of differences between the
delegations at the special summit prevented the German Presidency
from being able, on the morning of day two, to formally table a text
which would serve as a basis for further discussions. (The Dutch and
the UK were the most isolated because of their strong line on the
need for CAP controls.) This led to the summit breaking up into a
series of smaller groups with which the President – Chancellor Kohl –
and advisers held 'confessionals' i.e. informal discussions designed to
identify 'ideal' and 'acceptable' solutions. One of the key 'confessionals' involved the President meeting the Dutch and UK Prime
Ministers and the President of the Commission. When the plenary
eventually recommenced it continued until after midnight. At midnight, the President informed the participants that UK resistance to
a compromise that the other eleven (including the Dutch) were
prepared to accept left him with no option but to close the meeting.
At this point, the Spanish Prime Minister called for a few minutes
adjournment so as to allow for a final reconsideration by all parties,
and when the leaders returned Mrs. Thatcher announced that,
subject to Foreign Ministers later agreeing to certain still unresolved
matters on CAP controls, the UK would accept the package. (Her
principal reasons for agreeing to the deal were, in all probability, a

desire not to allow another summit breakdown to endanger the proposed completion of the internal market, and also advice from her officials that postponement of the issues until the next summit would not improve the UK's negotiating position or produce further concessions from the other states.) Eventually, at 2.00 a.m., the agreement was announced and press conferences were held.

Activities

The European Council has a relatively free hand with regard to what it may, and may not, do. This is, as noted above, partly because there are no constitutional or other legal provisions setting out its responsibilities, and it is partly because the political status of the participants is such as to put them generally beyond much challenge.

As a result, the activities undertaken by the European Council have tended to vary, according both to the preferences of the personalities involved and changing circumstances and requirements. So, in the second half of the 1970s, when President Giscard d'Estaing and Chancellor Schmidt determined much of the direction and pace, considerable time was given over to general discussions of major economic and monetary problems. For much of the 1980s, by contrast, when some participants – notably Mrs. Thatcher and the Commission – began to press particular distributional questions, and when policy issues were increasingly referred 'upwards' from the Council of Ministers for resolution, the summits came to be much concerned with quite detailed decision-making. Towards the end of the 1980s another shift began to occur and much of the European Council's time and attention came to be taken up with the general direction and development of the Community, and in particular to the questions of Economic and Monetary Union and Political Union.

Borrowing (with a couple of adaptations) the categories suggested by Bulmer and Wessels (1987) the main areas of European Council activity can be grouped under six broad headings:

The Economic and Social Situation Within the Community

Summits usually review both the overall economic and social situation within the Community, and also often look at particular questions relating to economic growth, trade patterns, inflation, monetary instability, and unemployment. However, differences between the states on what should be done, coupled with, until recently at least, a widely-shared determination to ensure that national hands remain firmly placed on key economic controls, has meant that these discussions have not usually been able to produce very much beyond general exhortations on topics such as controlling inflation, tackling unemployment, and encouraging investment.

International Economic and Monetary Issues

Economic growth, inflation, trade and similar issues, are not, of course, purely internal Community matters. They have vitally important international dimensions, and the summits have often explicitly looked to these: usually either with a view to co-ordinating the Community's position in international negotiations (notably the Western Economic Summits), or with a view to putting pressure on other economic powers (especially the USA and Japan) to revise their economic, monetary, or trading policies.

Economic and Monetary Integration

Summits have been extremely important in regard to moves and decisions designed to further economic and monetary integration in the Community. They have been so in three particular respects. First, the European Monetary System (EMS) was created over four summits (supplemented by numerous meetings outside the summits) in 1978–9. Second, the prioritisation of the programme to complete the internal market was agreed at Milan in June 1985 and was confirmed later the same year at Luxembourg. Since the programme began to unfold its progress has been regularly reviewed at summits. Third, the momentum for Economic and Monetary Union (EMU), which gathered considerable force from the late 1980s, stemmed very much from European Council decisions: the Hanover summit in June 1988 recalled that the SEA had confirmed the objective of pro-gressive realisation of EMU and entrusted to a committee, chaired by Jacques Delors, the task of studying and proposing concrete stages leading to EMU; the June 1989 Madrid summit agreed that the 'Delors Report' (which had been presented in April 1989) repre-sented a basis for further work, agreed that stage one of EMU would begin on 1 July 1990, and also agreed that an Intergovernmental

Conference (IGC) would be needed to lay down developments beyond stage one; the Strasbourg 1989 summit formally agreed to the convening of the IGC; the June 1990 Dublin summit decided that the IGC would be opened at the December 1990 Rome summit and instructed the relevant Councils of Ministers and other competent bodies to undertake all appropriate preparations; the special October 1990 Rome summit agreed that stage two of EMU would begin on 1 January 1994; and the December 1990 Rome summit was used to give a ceremonial opening to the IGC.

International Political Issues

The European Council has issued many declarations on important aspects of international affairs: for example, on East–West relations, South Africa, Afghanistan, Poland, and the Middle East. There is not, it has to be said, much evidence of these having had any effect – except perhaps in respect of the Arab–Israeli conflict where the Community's leaders' attempts (which were signalled in their 1980 Venice Declaration) to steer a middle way between the two sides and to encourage a dialogue in which the Palestine Liberation Organisation is a participant, has at least made an important contribution to the debate as to how the dispute might eventually be resolved.

Specific Community Policy Issues

Despite the original intention that the European Council should operate at a fairly general level it has, in practice, often concerned itself with quite specific policy issues. There are three main reasons for this: some Heads of Government are not averse to being involved in sectoral policy deliberations; some issues are so sensitive and/or so intractable that it has required the authority of national leaders to deal with them; and the European Council is, because of its non-sectoral nature, often the best placed institution to put together the package deals that are frequently required to reach agreements on issues that cut across policy sectors, or which can only be resolved by linking up issues in one sector with issues in another. Sometimes this involvement with specific policy issues has taken the form of playing a significant role in policy initiation. This was the case with the creation of the New Community Instrument at the Brussels 1977 summit, the establishment of the Integrated Mediterranean Programmes at Dublin in 1984, and the adoption of the Social Charter at Strasbourg in 1989. At other times it has involved tackling issues that the Council of Ministers have been unable to resolve. For example, at summits in the early 1980s, CAP reform, UK budgetary rebates, and budgetary resources were constantly on European Council agendas until a package deal was eventually agreed at the Fontainebleau summit in 1984. Within a couple of years of Fontainebleau all these issues had reappeared as problems and, along with demands for expanding the size of the social and regional funds, dominated two unsuccessful summits in 1987 and the ultimately successful special summit at Brussels in 1988.

Constitutional and Institutional Matters

These have come up in the European Council in three main forms. First, the summits have discussed, and have agreed the general arrangements for, the three Community enlargements. (The approval for the first enlargement was given at the 1969 Hague summit, that is before the European Council was formally established.) Second, the summits have considered, and have sometimes taken action on, a range of specific institutional matters. For example: direct elections to the EP; the location of the EP; the administrative support for European Political Co-operation; and the efficiency of the Commission. Third, the European Council has stimulated debate on, and has taken certain decisions within the context of, what is commonly referred to as 'European Union' – by which is normally meant a more integrated Community with stronger, more federal, institutional structures. The stimulation of debate has primarily been through the issuing of declarations (notably the Solemn Declaration on European Union which was issued at the 1983 Stuttgart summit), and the commissioning of reports (such as the Report of the Three Wise Men commissioned at the 1978 Brussels summit and the Dooge Committee Report commissioned at the 1984 Fontainebleau summit). The taking of decisions has occurred in connection with two developments: (a) The 1985 Luxembourg summit agreed to the SEA which provided for some constitutional revisions. On the whole, it must be said, the SEA package was rather modest, reflecting the unwillingness of most governments at the time to commit themselves firmly to political integration: commissioning reports and agreeing to general declarations does not, after all, demand very much; ceding sovereignty – by, for example, agreeing to proposals for a stronger Commission, more majority voting in the Council of Ministers, and real legislative powers for the EP – does. (It might be added that the SEA appears as particularly timid and cautious when set alongside the EP's 1984 Draft Treaty on European Union, which included proposals for Council-EP joint decision-making: proposals which, despite EP hopes and intense lobbying, the European Council did not seriously consider.) (b) The special April 1990 summit at Dublin confirmed the European Council's commitment to Political Union and instructed the Foreign Ministers to carry out a quick and detailed study of the need for possible Treaty changes with a view to the convening of an IGC on the matter; the June 1990 Dublin summit formally agreed to the convening of an IGC and decided that it would be opened at the December 1990 Rome summit; the Rome summit presided over the formal opening of the IGC on Political Union (as well as the aforementioned IGC on EMU).

The European Council thus exercises a number of functions, the relative importance of which can vary from summit to summit. Three functions are particularly important. First, it is a forum, at the highest political level, for identifying and pronouncing on medium and long-term Community goals, for exchanging ideas, and for building mutual understanding and confidence. Second, it is a policy initiator and dispenser of policy guidelines. Third, it is a decision-maker – both on matters which it has come to be commonly accepted fall within its sphere of responsibility (such as constitutional and major institutional issues), and matters where it acts as a sort of court of appeal for problems unresolved by the Council of Ministers.

Other functions tend to be of secondary importance. In some cases this is not because of their intrinsic nature, but rather because, in practice, they do not add up to very much. So foreign policy declarations rarely have much noticeable effect on their intended targets – partly because the declarations are often couched in language that is extremely vague, and partly because they are not usually supported by effective policy instruments. As for the potentially extremely important function of co-ordination of policy sectors, that can hardly be said to be seriously attempted at all, except, perhaps, and almost indirectly, via periodic package deals where some attempts have been made to link developments in different sectors. (The already quoted 1988 Brussels summit provides such an example: the different parts of the agreement – covering improved budgetary discipline measures, tighter CAP controls, expansion of the structural funds, and an increase in the Community's budgetary resources – were seen, by at least some of the participants, as being interdependent.)

One function, it must be emphasised, that the European Council does not exercise is that of legislator. It does have the potential to make Community law – by transforming itself into a special Council of Ministers – but it has never done so. Its decisions are thus political decisions. Where it is intended that its decisions should be given legal effect, the customary Community legislative procedures have to be applied. (There is no guarantee that an agreement in the European Council will automatically produce ease of passage through these procedures. One reason for this is that the guidelines laid down by the European Council are sometimes insufficiently precise to clear all political obstacles. Another reason is that governments occasionally decide after a summit that their delegation gave too much away and that ground must be recovered by taking a tough line in the Council of Ministers.)

The European Council and the Community System

Institutionalised summitry in the form of the European Council has inevitably increased the influence of the states in the Community system. It has also added an extra intergovernmental element to the nature of the Community: by virtue of the fact that the leaders usually act on the basis of unanimous agreements – either because they prefer to or, where subsequent Council legislation is required to give their decisions effect, because they may in effect be required to.

However, although the European Council has unquestionably become an important Community institution, its role is still by no means clear. Certainly, the original idea that it would provide overall strategic direction, but would not get involved with policy detail, has not been rigorously followed. What happens at individual summits is not part of any regularised or consistent pattern. So some summits have been relatively low key affairs and have done little more than pronounce on some aspect or aspects of current international developments, indicate one or two policy initiatives in fringe policy areas, and cobble together a concluding statement exuding general goodwill. Other summits, by contrast – and this type was common in the 1980s – have been surrounded by atmospheres of crisis and by prophecies of catastrophe should they fail to produce firm decisions on key and pressing issues: frequently they have failed, but the catastrophes have never quite happened, and the next summit, or next but one, has usually been able to find an agreement via the customary Community method of compromise.

The creation and development of the European Council has inevitably had implications for the roles and functioning of the other principal Community institutions:

● The Commission has seen some further undermining of its special position regarding policy initiation. 'Further' because, as was shown in Chapters 3 and 4, the Council of Ministers has also increasingly exercised policy initiating and mediating responsibilities. However, the Commission has, to some extent, been compensated for this slippage by being permitted to enter into political discussions with national leaders at the summits, and also by being able – and sometimes being required – to submit reports and documents to the summits. (See Chapter 3 for examples of very influential Commission submissions to summits.)

● The Council of Ministers has lost power to the European Council by virtue of the increasing tendency of most major issues to go through the summits in some form. However, the extent of the loss should not be exaggerated. First, because there is certainly no clear hierarchical relationship between the two bodies in the sense that the Council of Ministers feels obliged to refer all significant matters 'upwards'. Second, there is no consistent line of division between the two regarding who does what, other than the Council of Ministers alone being responsible for making legislation. Certainly, there is no question of the European Council taking 'first order' decisions and the Council of Ministers being confined to 'second order' decisions. And, third, since the European Council only meets for four, or perhaps six, days a year, it cannot normally hope to do anything more than sketch outlines in a restricted number of areas.

● The EP has been largely by-passed by the European Council and so must be regarded as having experienced some net loss of power. It is true that, since 1981, the President of the European Council has given a verbal report on each summit meeting to the next EP part-session, and it is also the case that, more recently, the practice has begun to develop of the EP President being permitted to address summits so as to be able to inform the national leaders of the Parliament's thinking on key issues. However, there is no evidence of either of these procedures producing much in the way of influence. Far more important is the almost complete lack of influence of the EP on European Council agendas or deliberations, and the tendency of the Council of Ministers to take the view that legislation which stems from European Council decisions is non-negotiable.

● Since the European Council operates largely on an extra constitutional basis, and since its decisions are political rather than legal in character, its existence has had few implications for the Court of Justice. Or, rather, it has had few direct implications. It can, however, be argued that any increase in a non-constitutional approach to integration necessarily constitutes a corresponding decrease in the influence of the Court of Justice given its attachment to, indeed its restriction to, questions that have a legal base.

Concluding Comments

The record of the European Council is mixed. On the one hand there have been failures, or at least the non-fulfilment of hopes. This was particularly so in the period from about 1980–8: summits became rather routinised and bureaucraticised; too often time was devoted to policy detail rather than to mapping out the future; disputes about distributional issues were seemingly always in the air; and the decisions that were taken on institutional reforms were hardly pioneering or wide-ranging. On the other hand there have been positive achievements: understandings between national leaders have been furthered; important goals have been identified and/or given an impetus (such as on the internal market, the social dimension, and EMU); and agreements have been worked out on matters that were either unsuitable for, or could not be resolved by, the Council of Ministers.

That there should be pluses or minuses in the record is not altogether surprising. The summits were, after all, established on a very loose and ill-defined basis and it was thus perhaps inevitable, given the status of the participants, that they would be drawn into attempting to do a host of different things. It was also perhaps inevitable, given the composition and mode of functioning of the summits, that they would experience some of the problems of intergovernmental conflict that are so characteristic of the Council of Ministers.

8

Other Institutions and Actors

The Economic and Social Committee

Origins

In the negotiations which led to the Rome Treaties it was decided to establish a consultative body comprised of representatives of socio-economic interests.

There were four principal reasons for this decision. First, five of the six founding states – Germany was the exception – had such bodies in their own national systems. The main role of these bodies was to provide a forum in which sectional interests could express their views, and in so doing could supplement the popular will as expressed via parliaments. Second, the essentially economic nature of the Community meant that sectional interests would be directly affected by policy developments and would be key participants in, and determiners of, the development of integration. Third, it was not thought that the Assembly (as the EP was then called) would be an effective forum for the expression of sectional views. Fourth, the institutional framework of the Rome Treaties was based on the Treaty of Paris model, and that had provided for a socio-economic advisory body in the ECSC Consultative Committee.

Accordingly, the EEC and Euratom Treaties provided for a common Economic and Social Committee (ESC). It was to have an advisory role and it was to be made up of representatives of various types of economic and social activity.

Membership

Since the 1986 Community enlargement the ESC has had 189 members. These are drawn from the member states as follows:

Belgium	12	Italy	24
Denmark	9	Luxembourg	6
France	24	Netherlands	12
Germany	24	Portugal	12
Greece	12	Spain	21
Ireland	9	United Kingdom	24

Members of the Committee are proposed by national governments and are formally appointed by the Council of Ministers. The term of office lasts for four years, which may be renewed.

To ensure that a broad spectrum of interests and views are represented the membership is divided into three, more or less equally sized, groups. Each national complement of members is supposed to reflect this tripartite division. The three groups are:

Group I – Employers. Just less than half of this group are drawn from industry. The rest are mostly from public enterprises, commercial organisations, banks, insurance and so forth.

Group II – Workers. The great majority in this group are members of national trade unions.

Group III – Various interests. About half of this group are associated either with agriculture, small and medium-sized businesses, or the professions. The rest are mostly involved with public agencies and local authorities, consumer groups, environmental protection organisations etc.

All members are appointed in a personal capacity and not as delegates of organisations. However, since most members are closely associated with, or are employees of, national interest organisations (organisations that are, in many cases, affiliated to Euro-organisations) it is inevitable that they do tend to act as representatives of, and spokesmen for, a cause.

The administrative support for the Committee is provided by a Secretariat which employs a staff of around 500.

Organisation

The Committee elects a Chairman and a Bureau from amongst its members, each for a term of two years. The main responsibility of the Chairman is to act as the ESC's principal representative in relations with other Community institutions, member states, and non-EC organisations and states. The Bureau, which has 30 members – the President, two Vice-Presidents, and nine members from each group – assists with outside relations and is also responsible for the general organisation of the Committee's work.

The groups operate in a somewhat similar fashion to the political groups in the EP. That is to say, they meet on a regular basis – there was a total of 96 group meetings in 1989 – to review matters of common concern, to discuss their work, and (particularly in the more cohesive groups I and II) to attempt to agree voting positions on proposals and issues that are due to be considered in plenary sessions. Group representatives in sections and study groups (see below) also sometimes meet together to co-ordinate their activities.

Most of the work of the ESC consists of giving Opinions on Community related matters. In a manner similar to the way in which the detailed work on Opinions in the EP is undertaken by committees, so in the ESC it is undertaken by sections, each of which draws its membership from the groups. There are nine sections:

Agriculture
Industry, Commerce, Crafts and Services
Economic, Financial and Monetary Questions
Social, Family, Educational and Cultural Affairs
Transport and Communications
External Relations
Energy, Nuclear Questions, and Research
Regional Development
Environment, Public Health and Consumer Affairs

The sections appoint *rapporteurs* to prepare draft Opinions on their behalf. How *rapporteurs* go about this depends on circumstances and preferences. Usually use is made of a sub-committee or a study group; assistance may be called for from the ESC Secretariat – though resources for this purpose are thin; and – a common occurrence – help may be sought, or be offered from, Euro or national sectional interests. In the sections an attempt is usually made to develop a common position on Opinions, though on controversial issues this is not always possible to achieve. In an average year there are usually around 70–80 section meetings and some 300 meetings of sub-committees and study groups. (In addition, there are 300–400 miscellaneous meetings and meetings sponsored by the three groups. Many of these are concerned in some way with the preparation of Opinions.)

Plenary meetings are held in Brussels, over a two-day period, usually ten or eleven times a year. Agendas are dominated by consideration of reports from the sections. The standard procedure for dealing with reports is for each to be introduced by its *rapporteur*, for a debate to be held, and for a vote to be taken. On uncontroversial items the vote may be taken without discussion or debate.

Functions

The ESC engages in a number of activities:

1. It issues information reports on matters of contemporary interest and concern.
2. It liaises, via delegations, with a host of other international bodies and groupings.
3. It seeks to promote understanding between sectional interests by, for example, organising conferences, convening meetings, and being represented at congresses and symposia.
4. It seeks to take advantage of various contacts it has with other Community institutions to press its views. The most regularised of these contacts is with the Commission: Commission officials, and sometimes Commissioners themselves, attend plenaries and meetings of sections. Occasionally ministers address plenaries.
5. Above all, as noted above, it issues Opinions on a range of Community matters. Opinions are issues in one of three sets of circumstances:

Mandatory referral.   Under Article 198 (EEC) and Article 170 (Euratom) 'The Committee must be consulted by the Council or by the Commission where this Treaty so provides'. Compared with the EP there are not so many policy areas where the Treaties do so provide, but many important areas are nonetheless included. So, under the EEC Treaty the ESC must be consulted on matters pertaining to agriculture, freedom of movement for workers, the right of establishment, transport, approximation of laws, social policy, the European Social Fund, and vocational training. Under the Euratom Treaty the Committee has to be consulted on such matters as research and training programmes, health and safety, and investment. Under the SEA these areas of mandatory consultation were further extended to include internal market issues, economic and social cohesion, environment, and research and technology.

Optional consultation.   The Committee may be consulted by the Council or the Commission 'in all cases in which they consider it appropriate' (Article 198 [EEC], and Article 170 [Euratom]). Until the entry into force of the SEA some 80 per cent of ESC Opinions were based on optional consultation. With the widening of the scope of mandatory referral this figure has fallen markedly.

Own initiatives.   Following pressure over a long period, the 1972 summit of Community leaders granted the ESC the right to issue Opinions on its own initiative. It can thus pronounce on almost any Community matter it wishes other than those which fall under the European Coal and Steel Community. The reason for this exclusion is, as noted above, that the ECSC has a separate Consultative Committee. With 96 members – who are divided into three equal groups of producers, workers, consumers and dealers – the Consultative Committee performs similar functions for the ECSC as does the ESC for the EEC and Euratom. The Consultative Committee normally meets about six times a year.

The ESC normally issues 150–180 consultative documents per year. In 1989 the figure was 171, this being made up of 154 Opinions requested by the Council or the Commission, 13 own-initiative

Opinions, and 4 information reports. Amongst the 1989 Opinions issued on Council/Commission referrals were ones on the Commission's proposed Social Charter, a Council directive approximating the laws of the member states in respect of certain trace metals, and a Council decision aimed at improving the business environment for small and medium-sized enterprises. (Exhibit 8.1 is a typical Opinion given on referral.) Own initiative Opinions given in 1989 included ones on poverty, environmental policy, and relations between the Community and the newly industrialising countries of South-East Asia.

A point of contrast worth noting between ESC and EP Opinions is that the ESC is not as concerned as the EP to reach a single position which excludes all minority views. It is quite possible for minority positions to be attached as annexes to ESC Opinions which have received majority support in the plenary. So, for example, in April 1987 the plenary rejected the Opinion proposed by the Section on Agriculture on the 1987–8 agricultural price proposals; to the Opinion that was approved, an annex was attached in the form of a 'Statement by the Farmers'.

Influence

The influence exercised by the ESC on Community policy and decision-making is limited. Evidence of this is seen, for example, in the follow-up reports to ESC Opinions which the Commission produces: these tend to include relatively few unambiguous acceptances of ESC recommendations, but include many evasive comments along the lines 'The Commission has taken note of the ESC Opinion' or 'The Opinion will be useful to the Commission staff in their exchanges of views with the Council'. Such ESC recommendations as are taken up usually cover relatively minor points and, in any event, are often as much a consequence of pressure that is exerted by other institutions and interests as by ESC pronouncements (this point is further discussed in Chapter 10).

There are a number of reasons why the ESC is in a relatively weak position to exercise power. First, the Council and the Commission are not obliged to act upon its views. This also, of course, applies to the EP on most non-budget matters but at least in its case it *has* to be consulted on *most* important proposals, its Opinion *must* be delivered

EXHIBIT 8.1

An Opinion of the Economic and Social Committee

No C 328/8 ·   Official Journal of the European Communities   22.12.86

Opinion on the proposal for a Council Directive on the approximation of the laws of the Member States relating to materials and articles intended to come into contact with foodstuffs([1])

(86/C/328/03)

On 29 April 1986 the Council decided to consult the Economic and Social Committee, under Article 198 of the Treaty establishing the European Economic Community, on the abovementioned proposal.

The preparatory work was referred to the Section for Protection of the Environment, Public Health and Consumer Affairs. This appointed Mr Poul Antonsen as rapporteur.

The Section adopted its opinion on 1 and 2 September 1986.

At its 239th plenary session (meeting of 17 September 1986) the Economic and Social Committee adopted the following opinion unanimously:

1. General comments

1.1 The Committee approves the Commission's proposal subject to the following comments.

1.2 The Committee has reservations regarding the proposed 'Advisory Committee Procedure', but this subject is dealt with in its opinion on 'Completion of the Internal Market: Community Legislation on Foodstuffs'.

2. Specific Comments

2.1   *Article 2*

The Committee welcomes the emphasis put by the Commission on public health, and stresses the need to treat public health as a matter of the utmost importance.

2.2   *Article 2*

There seems to be a discrepancy between the English (bring about an unacceptable change in the composition of the foodstuffs or a deterioration in the organoleptic characteristics thereof) and German versions of the second indent. The discrepancy is also found in the present Directive 76/893/EEC.

2.3   *Article 2*

The word 'unacceptable' is imprecise, its meaning should be specified.

([1]) OJ No C 124, 23.5.1986, p. 10.

Done at Brussels, 17 September 1986.

2.4   *Article 3*

The Committee feels it should be made clear that rules on composition can be applied, as well as rules on migration. Care should be taken to ensure that Article 3 is not administered in such a way as to constitute a trade barrier.

2.5   *Article 5*

The Committee draws attention to the need for labelling to take account of the requirements of the blind and weak-sighted.

2.6   *Article 9*

The Committee feels that this article should specify a time limit, consistent with those set in Article 10, for repeal of Directive 76/893/EEC.

2.7   *Annex 1*

The Committee proposes that the Commission add 'covering materials made of paraffin or microcrystalline wax' as these are not considered to be plastics for the purposes of Article I of Directive 82/711/EEC.

2.8   *Annex II.2*

The Committee finds that the expression 'suitable' is not clear and does not give any indication of what toxicological testing would be needed in a given case. (The Commission has, however, at the Section meeting referred to reports of the Scientific Committee for Food, Third series, 1977: Toxicological evaluation of a substance for materials and articles intended to come into contact with foodstuffs.)

The Chairman
of the Economic and Social Committee
Gerd MUHR

before proposals can be given legislative effect, and delaying powers are available to strengthen its bargaining position. The ESC is not so well placed: the range of issues on which consultation is mandatory is more restricted; the deliverance of its Opinion is often therefore not necessary for further progress; and even when its Opinion is required it can be made subject to a timetable that is so tight as not to allow sufficient time for a considered response – the Council and the Commission can, if they consider it necessary, set a time limit as short as ten days for the submission of an ESC Opinion.

The second weakness follows on from this last point: it is by no means uncommon for proposals to be referred to the ESC at a stage of advancement when agreements between the key decision-makers have already been made in principle and are difficult to unscramble.

Third, the ESC is not the only, and in many circumstances is not even the most important, channel available to sectional interests wishing to exert pressure on Community decision-makers. Direct access to Council representatives and to Commission officials, and representation in advisory committees, is seen by many as being more useful than activity in the ESC – not least because these other channels often offer greater opportunities than does the ESC for influencing policy proposals at the pre-proposal stage.

Finally, members of the ESC serve only in a part-time capacity and are, therefore, very limited in what they can do. In addition, the fact that they serve – in theory at least – in a personal rather than a representational capacity means that there are rarely any very strong reasons why the Commission or the Council should listen to them if they do not wish to do so.

The ESC is sometimes described as the Community's 'alternative' or 'additional' assembly. As is evident from the above discussion, this description does not stand up – especially since the introduction of direct elections in 1979 which have had the effect of further enhancing the standing, capacity, and influence of the EP in relation to the ESC.

What the ESC basically does is two things. First, it provides a useful forum in which representatives of sectional interests can come together on a largely co-operative basis to exchange views and ideas. Second, it is a consultative organ that gives some limited – but in most cases only very limited – opportunities for interests to influence Community policy and decision-making.

The European Investment Bank

Functions

The European Investment Bank (EIB) was established under Articles 129 and 130 of the EEC Treaty. Its members are the member states of the Community. The Bank is located in Luxembourg.

According to Article 130 the task of the EIB is to contribute, on a non-profit making basis, via the granting of loans and the giving of guarantees, to the 'balanced and steady development of the Community'. What this means, in practice, is that the Bank's main job is to act as a source of investment finance for projects which further certain Community goals. In so doing, it is by far the largest provider of Community loan finance. In 1989 Bank lending totalled 12.3 billion Ecu, the bulk of which was drawn from the Bank's own resources, and the balance of which (200 million Ecu) came from New Community Instrument (NCI) and budgetary sources. Over 90 per cent of EIB loans are for projects within the member states and the remainder for projects outside.

In respect of the loans made within the Community, two main conditions have to be satisfied for the Bank to consider providing finance. First, the project must comply with the economic policy objectives laid down in Article 130 of the EEC Treaty. These objectives are interpreted fairly broadly but at least one of the following criteria normally has to be met:

1. The project must further the economic development of the Community's less prosperous regions. Well over 50 per cent of loans in recent years have gone to the more underdeveloped areas – with Italy being the largest national beneficiary. The finance has been used primarily to assist with communications and other infrastructure, the productive sector, and capital spending on energy installations.
2. The project must involve modernisation and must generally improve the competitiveness of Community industry. Under this heading, particular support has been given to the introduction of, and further development of, advanced technology.
3. The project must be of common interest to several member states or to the Community as a whole. In this connection, the Community's energy objectives have been given a high

priority – notably by financing projects designed to reduce dependency on oil imports through encouraging energy saving, developing indigenous resources, diversifying imports etc. The Community's environmental policies have also received support – with half of the 'environmental loans' being made available to the water sector (catchment, treatment and supply), and with the rest going to projects dealing with such problems as atmospheric pollution, waste management, land conservation, and urban improvement.

Second, the project must be economically viable, and the loan must be guaranteed by adequate security. This is because although the EIB is not a profit-making body it is not a loss-making one either: apart from in certain specified and strictly limited circumstances, the Bank's loans are not subsidised from the Community budget but must be financed from the Bank's own capital. This capital comes from two sources: subscriptions by the member states, and borrowing – in the EIB's own name and on its own credit – on capital markets inside and outside the Community. Of these two sources, borrowing is by far the largest element and since the sums raised must be repaid from the Bank's own financial operations the Bank must take appropriate steps to protect itself.

A major attraction for potential EIB borrowers is that loans are offered at very competitive rates. They are so because the Bank enjoys a first class international credit-rating and is thus itself able to borrow at favourable rates. Other advantages of EIB loans are that they are generally made available at fixed interest rates, and repayments can often be deferred for the first two or three years.

Two other features of EIB loans are also worth noting. First, the Bank does not usually lend more than 50 per cent of the investment cost of a project. Borrowers need to find additional sources of loan finance, with the consequence that the Bank very frequently operates on a co-financing basis with national banks. Second, the Bank generally only deals directly with large loans – of more than about 10m Ecu. This does not, however, mean that only large-scale investment is supported because, mainly via its global loan facility, the Bank opens lines of credit to intermediary institutions – such as regional development agencies and, more commonly, national financial institutions – which then lend the money on in smaller amounts. Global loans account for around 25 per cent of total EIB lending and are directed principally towards small and medium-sized enterprises. An administrative problem with global loans is that the intermediary agencies which act on the EIB's behalf and which are delegated responsibility for appraising applications and negotiating with the potential borrowers tend to make their decisions according to traditional banking criteria and not with much of an eye to Community objectives.

In addition to the activities which have just been described, certain other EIB responsibilities should also be mentioned:

● Under the New Community Instrument the Commission is empowered to borrow money on the capital markets. It does so under conditions and for purposes that are specified in guidelines laid down by the Council of Ministers. Once the Commission has decided upon the eligibility of projects the Bank decides whether to grant loans and administers those which are approved.

● The Commission may also borrow funds on capital markets in connection with certain ECSC (300m Ecu in 1989) and Euratom (none in 1989) activities. The Commission decides on the granting of loans, and the Bank is responsible for financial appraisal and management.

● Many projects are eligible for both EIB loan finance and for Community grant aid. Where this is the case – and it applies mainly in connection with the European Regional Development Fund and the Integrated Mediterranean Programmes – the Bank works closely with other interested parties, especially the Commission, to work out appropriate financial arrangements.

Organisation

The Bank is not legally or formally linked in with 'mainstream' Community policy and decision-making processes. It liaises with other Community institutions and actors as appropriate, but it is not subject to the usual pattern of Commission initiation, EP scrutiny, Council approval, and Court of Justice interpretation. The Bank's decision-making bodies are, thus, fairly autonomous. They consist of the following:

1. The *Board of Governors* decides on total funding and lays down general directives on the Bank's activities. It is also responsible for formally appointing members of the Board of Directors and the Management Committee. The Board of Governors is composed of one minister per member state – usually the Minister of Finance – and normally meets once a year. Certain major decisions of the Board have to be made unanimously, others can be made by a majority of members representing at least 45 per cent of subscribed capital.

2. The *Board of Directors* has a general responsibility for ensuring that the Bank is managed according to the provisions of the Treaty, the Bank's Statute, and directives issued by the Governors. More specifically the Board has sole responsibility for deciding on loans and guarantees, raising funds and fixing interest rates. There are 22 Directors: 21 are nominated by the member states and are senior figures in national financial institutions or national Ministries of Finance/Economics/Industry; one is nominated by the Commission. The Board of Directors normally meets every four to six weeks.

3. The *Management Committee* controls current operations, makes recommendations to the Board of Directors and is responsible for implementing decisions made by the Directors. The Committee is a full-time body consisting of the Bank's President and six Vice-Presidents. It meets every working day.

Supporting, and operating under, these decision-making bodies is the EIB's administration. This is divided into seven Directorates: General Administration; Operations in the Community 1; Operations in the Community 2; Operations Outside the Community; Finance and Treasury; Research; and Legal. There is also a Technical Advisory Service. In all, the EIB employs around 700 staff.

Concluding Comments

The EIB is a bank, not a grant-dispensing body. This means that it must observe certain basic banking principles. At the same time, however, it is a Community institution charged with furthering a number of policy objectives. These two roles – of banker and Community institution – do not always sit easily together.

The scale of EIB borrowing and lending is small when compared with the total operations of commercial banks across the member states. The role of the Bank should not, however, be underestimated. After the World Bank it is the second largest institutional borrower on the international capital markets, and though the impact of its lending activities may be slight across the Community as a whole, it is by no means insignificant in targeted spheres and regions. What the Bank basically does is to act as a useful complement to the private sector by financing Community-oriented projects which commercial institutions do not wish to finance, do not wish to finance wholly, or do not wish to finance on terms that are sufficiently attractive to potential borrowers.

The Court of Auditors

The 1975 *Treaty amending Certain Financial Provisions of the Treaties...*, which entered into force in 1977, replaced the then two existing Community audit bodies – the Audit Board of the EEC and Euratom and the ECSC Auditor – with a single Court of Auditors. The Court is based in Luxembourg.

Membership and Organisation

There are twelve members of the Court: one from each member state. They are appointed by a unanimous vote of the Council of Ministers on the basis of nominations made by national governments and after there have been consultations with the EP. At its November 1989 part-session the EP, for the first time, voted to reject nominations – one made by France and one by Greece. The EP vote was not binding on the Council, but France nonetheless submitted a new name. Greece claimed it had difficulties in finding a suitable alternative candidate so the EP decided, at the December part-session, to accept both appointments in order to enable both posts to be filled by the new year.

At the time of their appointment, members of the Court must belong to, or have belonged to, an external audit body in their own country, or be persons who are appropriately qualified in some other capacity. Appointment is for a six year period, which may be renewed. As with other 'non-political' Community bodies, a condition of appointment is that the members will act in the general interest of the Community and will be completely independent in the performance of their duties.

The members elect one of their number to be the President of the Court. His term of office is for three years and is renewable. The President sees to the general efficient running of the Court and also represents it in its external relations.

Members are assigned a specific sector of activity for which they hold a particular responsibility regarding the preparation and implementation of the decisions of the Court. Each sector falls under one of three audit groups which act primarily as co-ordinating agencies and filters for plenary sessions of the whole Court. All important decisions are taken in plenaries, by majority vote if need be.

As with several other Community institutions, the administration supporting the Court is rather small in size given the potential importance of the work to be done. At the beginning of 1989 there were 239 people engaged in audit duties, 62 in the language service, and 78 in administrative departments. Inevitably such modest staffing resources greatly restricts the number of things the Court can attempt to do.

Activities of the Court

Under the 1975 Treaty the Court is required to examine 'the accounts of all revenue and expenditure of the Communities'. In exercising this responsibility the Court engages in two main types of activity.

The first is to carry out annual audits to see whether revenue has been received and expenditure has been incurred in a lawful and regular manner, and also to examine whether the financial management of Community authorities has been sound. The auditing powers of the Court cover the general budget of the Community, plus certain financial operations that are not included in the budget such as borrowing and lending facilities of the ECSC and aid to developing countries that is financed by national contributions.

The auditing of the general budget, which is the Court's most important single task, and the related process of granting a discharge to the Commission on its implementation of the budget, proceed as follows:

● The Commission is required to draw up, for each financial year, accounts relating to the implementation of the budget, a financial statement of the assets and liabilities of the Community, and an analysis of the financial year. The main responsibility for collecting and presenting this information (the internal audit) lies with DGXX (Financial Control). The documentation must be forwarded to the Council, the EP, and the Court of Auditors by no later than 1 June of the following financial year.

● The Court undertakes its audit (the external audit) partly on the basis of an examination of the Commission documentation and partly on the basis of its own independent investigations. The latter, which begin before the Commission documentation arrives, involves examining records supplied by, and requested from, Community institutions and member states (which in the latter case means liaising closely with national audit bodies and appropriate national agencies) and also, where necessary, carrying out on-the-spot investigations. The purpose of this Court audit is not to replicate what has already been covered by the internal audit, but rather to add an extra dimension to the Community's overall auditory control by examining the adequacy of internal procedures – particularly with regard to their ability to identify significant irregular and unlawful transactions and to properly evaluate the extent to which correct financial management (in terms of economy, efficiency and effectiveness) is being practiced. By 15 July, the Court transmits to all relevant institutions any comments which it proposes to include in its annual report to which it believes there should be, or there may wish to be, a reply. After the receipt of replies, which must be submitted by 31 October, the Court adopts the final version of its annual report. This has to be communicated to the Community's other institutions by 30 November.

● The EP, acting on a recommendation of the Council, is supposed to give discharge to the Commission in respect of the implementation of the budget by 30 April of the following year. To this end, the EP's Budgetary Control Committee examines all relevant documentation, particularly that produced by the Court of Auditors. Normally, discharge is given by the due date, but not always. In 1987, for example, dissatisfaction with several matters resulted in the discharge for the 1985 financial year being deferred and it was only after the Commission had taken remedying measures that discharge was eventually given in January 1988.

The second main activity of the Court is to submit observations and deliver Opinions on a range of subjects. This it does in three sets of circumstances: special reports on specific aspects of the audit are prepared, either on the Court's own initiative or at the request of another institution; a Community institution may ask the Court to submit an Opinion on a matter, usually concerning financial aspects of draft legislation; and when the Council enacts a financial regulation it is obliged to seek an Opinion from the Court on the draft text. From its establishment in 1977 to the end of 1989 the Court adopted sixty-three special reports and delivered sixty-seven Opinions.

The Effectiveness of Financial Controls

Unquestionably, controls over Community revenue and expenditure could be improved were there the political will to do so. For example, procedures could be tightened so as to prevent member states from imposing the limitations they occasionally apply to the audit enquiries considered necessary by the Court of Auditors. The Court's own attempts to extend its influence beyond questions of financial rectitude into considerations of policy efficiency could be encouraged, and even formalised. And the particular problem of fraud – which is generally thought to account for at least ten per cent of the Community budget, most of it in connection with agriculture payments – could be tackled more effectively if resources at both Community and member state levels were expanded and if proposals that have long been advocated by the Court for streamlining administrative practices were adopted. (Regarding this latter point, it has long been the case that those responsible for implementing Community policies are inclined to react in a defensive manner to criticisms from the Court. An example of this was seen in 1990 when the Commission rejected many of the findings of the Court's highly critical *Special report No.2/90 on the management and control of export refunds*. Amongst its criticisms the report noted: (a) that in many cases the Commission fails to fully document, monitor or evaluate decisions; (b) Commission decisions fixing the levels and scale of export farm subsidies are often based on a lack of documentation and other material; (c) customs facilities and controls are frequently inadequate.)

But though the Community's financial control mechanisms are far from being perfect, especially in relation to the complexities of the Common Agricultural Policy, their deficiencies should not be over-stated. The fact that total Community expenditure is still very modest, especially as compared with total public expenditure in the Community (see Chapter 11 for details), means that Community decision-makers, far from being able to be financially profligate are, for the most part, obliged to work to tight budgets and within limited resources. Moreover, Community operations and programmes are subject to reasonably rigorous, if not as extensive as is ideally desirable, investigations via the internal and external audits.

Interests

Different Types

A vast range of non-governmental interests cluster around Community processes. These interests are of four main types.

Regional and local authorities. Many sub-governmental decision-making bodies in the member states seek to have a direct role in Community processes. How extensive a role depends partly on the amount of autonomy and manoeuvrability they enjoy at national level. The German *Lander* (states), for example, which enjoy a considerable measure of independence within Germany's quasi-federal system, have opened up several lines of – primarily informal – contact with the Commission, and some have established their own economic promotion offices in Brussels. This is not usual, however, and a more common practice is for regional and local authorities to work with the Community through *ad hoc* delegations and/or via the locally-based Community liaison officers which many have appointed with the brief to attract funds from the various sources of Community finance.

Private and public companies and corporations. In addition to any involvement they may have via interest group organisations (see below) some economic undertakings seek to have direct dealings with Community authorities. Ford, for example, have taken worries about the competitiveness of the motor industry to the Commission, and electronics manufacturers such as Philips and Thomson have lobbied for higher and more uniform tariff levels on products from Japan.

National interest groups. Many circumstances result in nationally-based interest groups attempting to involve themselves in Community processes. For example, an association representing beer producers may wish to press for the removal of discriminating excise duties that have the effect of preventing its members competing in the market of another member state. Or an environmental interest group may want to see more effective implementation of existing Community legislation on disposal of sewage into the sea. In seeking to play a part in Community processes, most national interest groups are confined to working from their national offices or via a European interest group, but a few of the larger industrial and agricultural groups have, in addition to a domestic and a European group base, their own representatives and agents permanently based in Brussels.

Euro-groups. There are somewhere in the region of 700 Euro-groups. These are groups which draw their membership from several countries and which operate at, and in so doing seek to represent the interests of their sector or cause at, the Community level. Given their particular Community orientation it is worth looking at the Euro-groups in a little detail.

Their *policy interests* naturally reflect the policy priorities and policy concerns of the Community. This is most obviously seen in the variety of the agriculture lobby where over 150 Euro-groups are to be found. These range in nature from the broadly-based Committee of Professional Agricultural Organisations (COPA), which seeks to represent most types of farmers on most issues, to highly specialised groups representing the likes of yeast producers and pasta manufacturers. Pressure groups usually go where power goes, and what has happened in agriculture, quite simply, is that as considerable policy responsibilities have been transferred from national capitals to the Community then so has a Euro-lobby developed to supplement – not replace – the domestic lobbies.

In addition to agriculture, other areas of activity prominently represented amongst the Euro-groups are industrial and trade interests, commerce, service industries (banking, insurance, transport and the liberal professions are all well represented), trade unions, consumers, and environmentalists.

The *membership* of Euro groups also varies considerably. It does so in four main respects. First, there are variations in the breadth of the membership base. Some groups – the so-called umbrella groups – have a broad membership base and seek to represent a whole sector or area of activity. Examples of umbrella groups are COPA, the Union of Industries of the European Community (UNICE), the European Trade Union Confederation (ETUC), the European Environmental Bureau (EEB), and the European Bureau of Consumers' Associations (BEUC). Because of the breadth of their membership some of these umbrella groups have considerable difficulty in maintaining internal cohesion and presenting a common front: ETUC, for example, has traditionally had to try and reconcile differences between socialist, communist, and Christian trade unions, whilst COPA has had problems in recent years in managing the differential agricultural sectoral implications of reforms in the CAP. Most groups, however, are more narrowly focused than the umbrella groups and seek to speak on behalf of a specific industry, process, service, or product. Examples of such groups are the European Union of Fruit and Vegetable Wholesalers, Shippers, Importers and Exporters (EUCOFIL), the European Association of Manufacturers of Business Machines and Data Processing Equipment (EUROBIT), and the Federation of European Explosive Manufacturers (FEEM).

Second, there are variations in terms of whether membership is via affiliation or is direct. In most cases membership is based on affiliation by national sectoral or, in the case of a few of the larger Euro-groups, national peak (cross-sectoral) organisations. Since the mid-1980s, however, there has been a growth in direct membership groupings and organisations. The most important development in this regard has seen major industrial, often multinational, companies coming together, frequently as a supplement to, rather than as an alternative to, their involvement in affiliation-based sectoral groups. In some instances these link-ups between companies is highly informal and they are perhaps best thought of as gatherings rather than as Euro-groups. Examples of such direct membership groupings/linkages are the Association of Petrochemical Producers in Europe (APPE), the Round Table of European Industrialists (comprised of forty or so heads of major European industrial companies), and the European I.T. Industry Round Table (comprised of heads of Western Europe's twelve main information technology companies).

Third, there are variations in the representativeness of groups. Since most Euro-groups are based on national affiliates the number of people they can claim to represent naturally reflects the factors determining group membership at national levels. So, sectional interests are usually better placed than promotional interests. Similarly, amongst sectional interests, Euro-groups representing interests which are well mobilised at national levels, such as dairy farmers and textile manufacturers, naturally tend to be much more genuinely representative than groups acting on behalf of poorly mobilised sections of populations such as agricultural labourers or consumers.

Fourth, there are variations in the width of the Community base of groups. At one end of the spectrum, many Euro-groups draw their members from only a few states – which, in the case of activities which are carried on throughout the Community, can weaken a group's representational claims. At the other end of the spectrum, some groups are not EC specific and draw members from most European states: ETUC for example has thirty affiliates from twenty countries, whilst UNICE represents thirty-two business federations from twenty-two European countries. Membership of this latter sort, which goes beyond the geographical borders of the Community, has advantages and disadvantages: on the one hand, it can help to promote international co-operation and increase group resources; on the other hand, and this is a charge that has frequently been laid against ETUC, it can serve to dilute group concentration on, and therefore influence within, the Community.

In terms of *resources*, only a few large umbrella groups have well appointed offices with a full-time staff that is numbered in double figures. Amongst these are COPA (by far the best resourced, with a full-time staff of around 45), UNICE, ETUC, CEA (European Insurance Committee), and GCECEE (Savings Banks Group of the EEC). More commonly, groups rely heavily on the resources of national affiliates and themselves employ only one or two full-time officials – who often do not have their own separate offices but work either from home or from accommodation that is made available to them by an affiliate (usually the Belgian) or an appropriate umbrella group. Many groups do not even stretch to one permanent employee and work purely through affiliates or through part-time and temporary representatives and agents whose services are called upon as and when the need arises.

The *organisational structure* of most Euro-groups is extremely loose. The central group organs usually enjoy only a very limited independence from the national affiliates, whilst the affiliates themselves are autonomous in most respects and are not subject to central discipline. In addition, key decisions made at central level are usually taken only on the basis of unanimous votes, though some groups – including COPA – do have provisions for weighted majorities on some issues. These loose structures can weaken the effectiveness of Euro-groups, by making it difficult for them to put forward collective views which are anything more than rather vague lowest common denominators. At the same time, however, moves to create stronger structures risks groups not affiliating, or national affiliates concentrating almost exclusively on their national level activities.

Just how extensive and complex a group's organisational structure is depends largely on its size. The more specialised and poorly resourced groups usually operate on a fairly rudimentary basis, often merely via an annual meeting and an executive committee which meets as required. The large umbrella groups, by contrast, usually have an extensive structure, typically made up of a general meeting which meets at least once a year, an executive committee which meets once every four to six weeks, specialist policy committees whose frequency of meetings depends on the business in hand, a President, and a full-time Secretariat which is headed by a Secretary General. COPA has the most developed structure (see Figure 8.1).

Finally, with regard to their *functions*, Euro-groups normally attempt to do two main things. First, they seek to gather and exchange information – both in a two-way process with Community organs and with and between national affiliates. Second, they seek to have their interests and views incorporated into Community policy, by persuading and pressurising those who make and implement policy. Not all Euro-groups, of course, attempt or are able to exercise these functions in equal measure: for example, in those sectors where Community policy is little developed they often choose to give a higher priority to the first than to the second function.

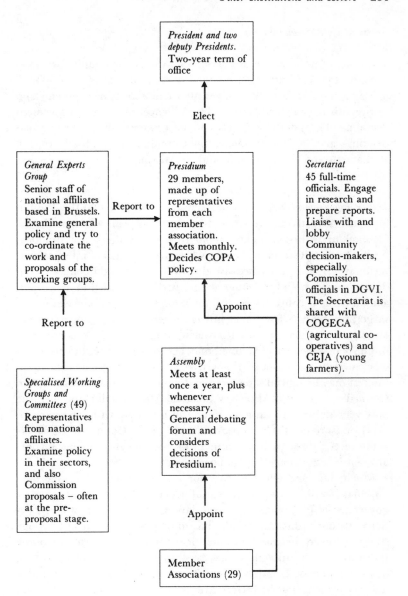

President and two
deputy Presidents.
Two-year term of
office

Elect

General Experts Group
Senior staff of national affiliates based in Brussels. Examine general policy and try to co-ordinate the work and proposals of the working groups.

Report to

Presidium
29 members, made up of representatives from each member association. Meets monthly. Decides COPA policy.

Secretariat
45 full-time officials. Engage in research and prepare reports. Liaise with and lobby Community decision-makers, especially Commission officials in DGVI. The Secretariat is shared with COGECA (agricultural co-operatives) and CEJA (young farmers).

Report to

Appoint

Specialised Working Groups and Committees (49)
Representatives from national affiliates. Examine policy in their sectors, and also Commission proposals – often at the pre-proposal stage.

Assembly
Meets at least once a year, plus whenever necessary. General debating forum and considers decisions of Presidium.

Appoint

Member Associations (29)

Figures are as of late 1990

FIGURE 8.1
Organisational structure of COPA

Access to Decision-makers

The long, complex and multi-layered nature of Community processes provides many points of access for interests, and so many opportunities for them to keep themselves informed about developments and to press their cases with those who influence, make, and implement decisions. The points of access can be grouped under three broad headings: national governments, the Commission, and the European Parliament and the Economic and Social Committee.

National governments. A major problem for interests is that they cannot normally directly approach either the European Council or the Council of Ministers. This is partly because there are practical problems involved in lobbying what are, in effect, international negotiations, it is partly because the meetings are held behind closed doors, but it is mainly because neither body has wished to make itself available, as a collective entity, for regularised or intensive interest targetting. Only a few direct linkages therefore exist, and these are largely restricted to the most powerful of interests. So, the President in Office of a Technical Council may occasionally meet the president of a powerful Euro-group, or a written submission from an influential interest may be officially received and circulated prior to a European Council or Council of Ministers' meeting. More usually, however, the only way an interest can hope to establish contact with, and perhaps exert pressure on, the European Council or the Council of Ministers is indirectly: through a government or governments looking favourably on its cause or feeling obliged to act on its behalf.

Much time and effort is, therefore, spent by interests, especially national interests, attempting to influence the positions adopted by governments in Community negotiations. In the case of the European Council, this task usually has to be undertaken at at least one stage removed because national leaders do not normally allow themselves to be directly lobbied. With the Council of Ministers, however, one of a number of factors may result in doors being opened. Amongst such factors are: some interests, such as most of the major national agricultural groups, enjoy – for a mixture of political, economic, technical, and other reasons – an insider status with relevant government departments, which means that they are consulted as a matter of course on proposals and developments

within their sphere of interest; when a technically complicated matter is under consideration, governments usually seek the advice of relevant interests at an early stage of the Council process – with perhaps Council working party or management committee members communicating directly with interest representatives; and when the co-operation of an interest is important for the effective implementation of a Community proposal, its views may well be actively sought, or received and listened to if an approach is made.

This last point touches on another reason, in addition to trying to influence Council decision-making, why interests may approach national governments: they may wish to influence the way Community decisions are implemented. One way in which they can attempt to do this is by making their views known to governments when measures are being devised to incorporate Community directives into national law. And if relevant ministries can be persuaded to delay, or not to monitor too closely, the implementation of directives on, say, disposal of pollutants, or safety standards in the workplace, some interests may well have much to gain financially.

The Commission.   The Commission is the main target for most interests. It is so, primarily, because of its central importance in so many different respects: in policy initiation and formulation; in taking many final decisions; in following proposals through their legislative cycle; in managing the Community's spending programmes; and in policy implementation. An important contributory reason why the Commission attracts so much interest attention is simply that it is known to be approachable.

The Commission makes itself available to interests because several advantages accrue to it from so doing. First, interests often have access to specialised information and to knowledge of how things are 'at the front' which the Commission needs if it is to be able to exercise its own responsibilities efficiently. Second, the Commission's negotiating hand with the Council of Ministers is strengthened if it can demonstrate that its proposals are supported by influential interests. Third, and this is in some ways the other side of the coin of the previous point, if the Commission does not consult with and try to satisfy interests, and comes forward with proposals to which influential interests are strongly opposed, the proposals are likely to meet with strong resistance at Council of Ministers level. Fourth,

with regard specifically to Euro-groups, where groups come forward
with broadly united and coherent positions they can greatly assist the
Commission by allowing it to deal with already aggregated views and
by enabling it to avoid becoming entangled in national and ideological differences between sectional interests. For this reason almost
500 of the 700 or so Euro-groups are on a register which the
Commission keeps of officially recognised groups. Recognition
means that the relevant DGs keep the groups informed on matters
which will be of interest to them, and are prepared usually to consult
with them too. The main reasons for non-recognition are either that
the Commission does not regard the group as a proper Euro-group –
perhaps because it consists just of two or three large companies – or it
may not be seen as very effective in 'delivering' aggregated and co-
ordinated views to the Commission.

Until about the mid-1970s the Commission displayed a strong
preference for talking to Euro-groups rather than national groups,
and to governments rather than sub-governmental national authorities. In more recent years, however, this attitude has been relaxed
and most interests of significance have been able to have their views
at least considered by the Commission. The procedures by which the
contacts and communications occur are many and are of both a
formal and informal nature. They include:

1. The extensive advisory committee system. This primarily exists
   for the precise purpose of allowing interests to make their views
   known to Community authorities, and in particular to the
   Commission (see Chapter 3).
2. The Social Dialogue – or, as it is also known, the Val Duchesse
   Dialogue – provides for an exchange of views between the
   Commission and the two sides of industry. It has, since 1985,
   regularly brought together, at the most senior and at working
   group levels, representatives from the Commission, trade union
   representatives from ETUC, and representatives from the two
   main employers' and industrial organisations – UNICE and
   the European Centre of Public Enterprises (CEEP).
3. Commissioners and DG officials receive numerous delegations
   from interests.
4. Representatives of the Commission travel to member states to
   meet interests and to attend conferences and seminars where
   interests are represented.

5. A few of the larger Euro-groups invite Commission representatives to attend some of their working parties and committee meetings.
6. Informal meetings and telephone conversations between Commission and interest representatives occur constantly.
7. Interests present the Commission with a mass of written documentation in the form of information, briefing and policy documents of different sorts.

Naturally, the extent and nature of the communications between any one interest and the Commission vary considerably according to a number of factors. A small national interest in a specialised area may only require occasional contact at middle ranking official level with one particular Directorate General. By contrast, an active umbrella group may wish to be permanently plugged into the Commission at many different points. As an indication of how extensive the links can be, some of the access channels available to COPA are worth noting: about every four to six weeks the Presidium of COPA meets the Commissioner for Agriculture; the Secretary General of COPA and the Director General of DGVI (Agriculture) meet regularly and often speak to each other several times a week on the telephone; at all levels, the staff of COPA are in almost constant touch with staff in DGVI and, less frequently, are in close contact with staff in other DGs – notably DGXIX (Budgets); and COPA is strongly represented, both in its own right and via affiliates, on all the agricultural advisory committees and also on certain other leading advisory committees such as the Standing Committee on Employment and the Harmonisation of Legislation Committee.

The European Parliament and the Economic and Social Committee. The special advisory positions held by the EP and the ESC in the Community makes them natural, albeit generally second-ranking, targets for interests.

In the case of the ESC there are, of course, factors which put it in a special position *vis-à-vis* interests: its membership is largely made up of interest representatives and its very *raison d'être* is to act as the Community's principal forum for interest representation and expression. The ways and the extent to which the ESC exercises these representative and expressive roles were examined earlier in the chapter.

With regard to the EP, it has been very noticeable, not least in the swelling ranks of lobbyists who attend the Strasbourg plenaries, that as the role and influence of the Parliament in the Community system has grown, so has it increasingly attracted the attention of interests. Among the lobbying possibilities available to interests in respect of the EP are the following:

1. A general circulation of literature amongst MEPs may have the effect of improving the image of an interest or changing the climate of opinion in the interest's area of concern.
2. MEPs can be directly approached with a view to persuading them to vote in a particular way on a particular issue (which may well be possible given the lack of voting discipline in the EP), or with a view to persuading them to support the interest's view in a committee or a political group.
3. Interests have some opportunities for direct contacts with EP committees and political groups. Committees, for example, sometimes hold 'hearings' and occasionally travel to member states for the precise purpose of meeting interest representatives, whilst political groups sometimes allow themselves to be addressed when they judge it to be appropriate.
4. Attempts can be made to encourage an MEP to seek permission to draw up an own initiative report which, if it makes progress, may possibly have the effect of pressurising the Commission and/or the Council into action of a desired sort.
5. Officials and MEPs engaged in preparing reports for EP committees often approach appropriate interests for their views, or allow themselves to be approached.
6. Attempts can be made to persuade individual MEPs to take matters up with governments and with the Commission.

Many possible avenues are thus available to interests to enable them to promote their causes. Which are the most suitable, the most available, and the most effective, naturally varies according to circumstances. A local authority, for example, wishing to attract ERDF funds, would be well advised to establish contacts with DGXVI (Regional Policy), but it should also court good relations with regional and national civil servants since the ERDF functions on a Community/national/regional partnership basis. By contrast, an environmental group in a country where the government is not noted for its sympathy to 'green issues' might be most effective working as part of a Euro-group: from the broad base of a Euro-group it might be possible to launch public information and relations campaigns that help persuade the EP to pass a resolution, it may be possible to pressurise the Commission to produce legislative proposals and to increase its efforts to ensure that existing legislation is properly implemented, and it may be possible to find a route to the Council of Ministers via at least some of the national affiliates being able to lean on their governments.

Influence

The factors which determine the influence exercised by interests in the Community are similar to those which apply at national levels. The more powerful and more effective interests tend to be those which have at least some of the following characteristics:

Control of key information and expertise. Effective policy-making and implementation requires a knowledge and understanding of matters which can often be provided to Community authorities only via interests. This obviously puts some interests in potentially very influential positions – as is seen, to some extent, in the way in which the influence interests exercise via official forums is often much greater in specialised advisory committees than it is in more general settings such as the ESC or the Standing Committee on Employment.

Adequate resources. The better resourced an interest is, the more likely it is to be able to make use of a variety of tactics and devices at a number of different potential access points. So, regarding proposed legislation, a well resourced interest is normally in a position to lobby the Commission from the initiation stage, the EP at the consultation stage, and the Council of Ministers – usually through national governments – at the decision-making stage. Similarly, a regional or local authority hoping for Community funds is more likely to be successful if it employs people who know what is available, how to apply, and with whom it is worth having an informal word.

Economic weight. Important economic interests – whether in the form of major companies or representational organisations – usually have to be listened to by Community decision-makers, not least because their co-operation is often necessary in connection with policies designed, for instance,to encourage Community-wide investment, to expand employment in the less prosperous regions, to stimulate cross border rationalisations, and to improve industrial efficiency. Examples of economic weight being an important factor in successful lobbying include: the chemical industry – via its Euro-group CEFIC – has managed to persuade the Commission to investigate numerous cases of alleged dumping, often by US industry; the Esprit programme to strengthen the European base in information technology stemmed in large part from major companies in the sector warning the Commission that unless something was done quickly the US and Japan would totally dominate the market; and EUROFER – the larger steel manufacturers' association – has worked closely with the Commission and governments to limit the damage to its members caused by the Community's steel rationalisation programme.

Political weight.   Many interests have political assets which can be used to advantage, usually via governments. So, for example, a national pressure group which is closely linked with a party in government may be able to get that government to virtually act on its behalf in the Council of Ministers. At a broader level, electoral factors can be important, with ministers in the Council not usually anxious to support anything which might upset key voters – especially if an important national or local election is looming. Farmers' organisations in France, Italy, Germany and elsewhere are the best examples of interests which have benefitted from having electoral significance.

Genuine representational claims.   National pressure groups and Eurogroups which genuinely represent a sizeable proportion of the interests in a given sector are naturally in a stronger position than those which do not.

Cohesion.   Some interests find it difficult to put forward clear and consistent views and are thereby weakened. As was noted earlier, this often applies to Euro-groups, especially umbrella Euro-groups, because of their varied membership and their loose confederal structures.

Access to decision-makers. Most of the characteristics just described play some part in determining which interests enjoy good access to decision-makers and which do not. Clearly, those interests which do have good access – especially if it is at both national and Community levels – are more likely than those which do not to be fully aware of thinking and developments in decision-making circles, and to be able to present their case to those who matter. At the Community level, COPA is the most obvious example of such an 'insider' interest, whilst at national levels COPA affiliates usually also enjoy advantageous positions.

Concluding Comments

There are both positive and negative aspects to the involvement of interests in Community processes. Of the positive aspects, two are especially worth emphasising. First, interest activity broadens the participatory base of the Community and ensures that policy and decision-making is not completely controlled by politicians and officials. Second, interests can provide Community authorities with information and viewpoints which improve the quality and effectiveness of their policies and decisions. Of the negative aspects, the most important is that some interests are much more powerful and influential than others. This lack of balance raises questions about whether interests unduly, perhaps even undemocratically, tilt Community policy and decision-making in certain directions – towards, for example, producing a legislative framework which tends to favour producers more than such 'natural' opponents as consumers and environmentalists.

But whether interest activity is judged to be, on the whole, beneficial or not, its importance is clear. Interests are central to many key information flows to and from Community authorities, and they bring considerable influence to bear on policy and decision-making processes from initiation right through to implementation. There are few, if any, Community policy sectors where interests of at least some significance are not to be found.

PART THREE

Policies and Policy Processes of the Community

Introduction

Part Three examines what the Community does and how it does it. Chapter 9 looks at Community policies. The origins, the range, and the context of the policies are all considered. Particular themes of the chapter are the breadth and diversity of Community policy interests, and the less than complete nature of many of the policies.

Chapter 10 focuses on patterns, practices and features of the Community's policy-making and decision-making machinery. Having examined the Community's institutions and political actors in Part Two, this chapter considers how the various pieces fit together. What sort of policy and decision-making system are they part of and have they helped to create? A central concern of the chapter is to emphasise that even the most general statements about how the Community operates normally have to be qualified. For one of the few things that can be said with certainty about Community processes is that they are many, complex, and varied. A truly accurate account of how the EC functions therefore requires something which just cannot be attempted here: an analysis of the procedures and practices applying in each policy and decision-making area.

In Chapter 11 the Community budget is examined. Where does the Community get its money from and what does it spend it on? The budgetary decision-making process, which in several important respects is distinctly different from the processes which apply in policy areas, is also examined.

Chapter 12 considers one particular policy area in depth. As such, the chapter offers something of a contrast to the necessarily rather general approach of Chapters 9 and 10. Agriculture has been selected for this special examination not because of any suggestion that it is typical – the variability of the Community's policy processes precludes any policy area being described as such – but simply because of its importance in the Community context.

Finally, Chapter 13 focuses on one of the most important, and certainly one of the most distinctive, features of Community processes: the mechanisms and arrangements used by the member states to control their relations with the Community and, insofar as it is possible, to control the Community itself.

9

Community Policies

The Origins of Community Policies

The origins of Community policies are to be found in a number of places. At a general level, the changed post-war mood in Western Europe has played a part. So also has the increasingly interdependent nature of the international system which has resulted in national borders becoming ever more ill-matched with political and economic forces and realities. This interdependence has helped to persuade West European states to transfer policy responsibilities to a 'higher' level in an attempt to shape, to manage, to control, to take advantage of, and to keep apace with, the modern world.

At a more specific level, the Treaties are generally seen as key determinants of Community policy. However, their influence is not as great as is commonly supposed. Certainly they are important stimuli to policy development and they also provide the legal base on which much policy activity occurs. So, for example, such 'core' Community policies as the Common Commercial Policy (CCP), the Common Agricultural Policy (CAP), and the Competition Policy find their roots – though by no means all their principles – in the EEC Treaty. Similarly, Community involvement with coal and steel cannot possibly be fully understood without reference to the Treaty of Paris. But Treaty provision for policy development does not guarantee that it will occur. The very limited progress made towards the establishment of a common transport policy, despite it being provided for in Part 2 Title 4 of the EEC Treaty, illustrates this. So too does the non-fulfilment of most of the hopes which were held out for Euratom. And a third, and in its implications for the nature of the Community crucially important, example of only limited development of Treaty provisions is the very partial implementation of Part 3 Title 2 of the EEC Treaty, under which member states are supposed to regard their macroeconomic policies 'as a matter of common concern' and are to co-ordinate, co-operate and consult with one another on key economic and financial questions. In practice, it is quite clear that although there has been co-operation and consultation in these areas – carried out mainly under the Ecofin Council of Ministers by committees of very senior national officials – the states have not worked and acted as closely together as the Treaty envisaged. Furthermore, one of the key steps towards financial co-operation – the creation in 1979 of the European Monetary System (EMS) which, amongst other things, fixes maximum and minimum rates of exchange for currencies in the system – was created outside the Treaty system because of concern in some quarters about the rigidities that a Treaty-based approach might entail, and also because not all member states (notably the UK) wished to be full participants. It was only in the late 1980s, thirty years after the EEC Treaty was signed, that clear, significant, formal, and Community-based moves towards economic and monetary integration between the member states began to be initiated and implemented.

If Treaty provision is no guarantee of policy development nor is lack of provision a guarantee of lack of development. Environmental policy illustrates this. Until it was given constitutional status by the Single European Act, environment was given no specific mention in the Treaties. Yet, from the early 1970s Community environmental policy programmes were formulated and legislation was approved. Legal authority for this was held to lie in the (almost) catch-all Articles 100 and 235 of the EEC Treaty. The former allows the Community to issue directives for the approximation of laws 'as directly affect the establishment or functioning of the common market' and the latter enables it to take 'appropriate measures' to 'attain in the course of the operation of the common market, one of the objectives of the Community'. Environmental policy was, therefore, able to find a tentative constitutional base. However, even the most liberal readings of Articles 100 and 235 cannot stretch to some policy areas, but this has not prevented policy development from occurring. Foreign policy co-operation prior to the SEA illustrates this. Aware that there were no Treaty provisions for such co-operation, and unenthusiastic about subjecting such a sensitive area to the formalities and restrictions of Treaty processes, the states in the early 1970s simply created a new European Political Co-operation (EPC) machinery alongside, but outside the formal framework of, the Treaties.

EPC points to the fact that the really crucial influence on policy development has not been so much the Treaties as the perception of the states of what is desirable, allied with their individual and collective capacities for translating these perceptions into practice.

Regarding the perceptions of the states – or, to be more precise, of national governments – a fundamental precondition of successful policy development is a judgement that the advantages of acting together outweigh the disadvantages. The advantages are mainly, though as EPC and recent initiatives on terrorism and drugs show, not entirely, economic in kind: those that stem from having, in an increasingly interdependent and competitive world, a single and protected market, a common external trading position, and some collective action and some pooling of resources in particular functional and sectoral areas. The principal disadvantage is the loss of national decision-making powers and sovereignty that transfers of power and responsibilities to the Community inevitably entail. Some states are more concerned about this than others, but even the most pro-integrationists are cautious about ceding powers that may, at a later stage, result in their own national room for manoeuvre being limited in areas that are important to them.

As for the capacities of the states to operationalise their perceptions of what is desirable, there are many problems. At the individual state level, a government may be favourably disposed towards a Community initiative but be inhibited from supporting it in the Council of Ministers because of opposition from a powerful domestic interest or because it could be electorally damaging. Following this through to the Community level, opposition from just one state, whether it is principled or pragmatic, can make policy development very difficult to achieve, given the Treaty requirement of unanimity in the Council of Ministers on many issues, and the preference in the Council for progress through consensus – especially on major issues – even where majority decisions are legally permissible.

The Community's Policy Interests and Responsibilities

The Community's main policy interests and responsibilities can be grouped under five headings: establishing the Common Market, economic and financial policies, functional policies, sectoral policies, and external policies.

Establishing the Common Market

The single most important reason why the dynamism and profile of the EC have been so raised in recent years is that since the mid-1980s the Community has been embarked on a programme to 'complete the internal market by 1992'.

This programme is really a development of the Community's long established goal of creating a common market. After years in which only modest progress had been made in this direction, a number of factors combined in the 1980s to convince the governments of the member states that a greater thrust was needed: the sluggish economic growth of the second half of the 1970s was continuing; the Community was clearly falling behind its competitors, notably Japan and the United States, in the new technologies; there was an increasing appreciation that the continuation of still essentially fragmented national markets was having a damaging effect on the economic performance of the member states; and the accession of three new countries (Greece in 1981, and Spain and Portugal in 1986) made it clear to all that to continue on the same path and in the same way would mean that the common market would never be properly established.

To this background the Commission in April 1985 produced the White Paper *Completing the Internal Market* (see also chapters 3, 7, and 10). What the White Paper did was to identify some 300 measures which would have to be taken to enable the internal market to be completed, and to suggest also that 31 December 1992 should be set as the deadline for the adoption of the measures. The European Council, at its June 1985 Milan meeting, accepted the White Paper, and at its December 1985 Luxembourg meeting agreed that both the internal market objective and the 1992 deadline be included in the Single European Act. Crucially, the inclusions in the SEA involved additions and amendments to the EEC Treaty. Article 13 of the

SEA, incorporating a new Article 8A of the EEC Treaty, was especially important:

> The Community shall adopt measures with the aim of progressively establishing the internal market over a period expiring on 31 December 1992 . . . . The internal market shall comprise an area without internal frontiers in which the free movement of goods, persons, services and capital is ensured in accordance with the provisions of this (the EEC) Treaty.

The Commission's White Paper sought, in essence, to establish the conditions in which market activities – buying and selling, lending and borrowing, producing and consuming – could be done as easily on a Community basis as they can on a national basis. The hope was that by removing the obstacles and barriers which sectionalise and fragment the Community market, efficiency, growth, trade, employment, and prosperity, could all be promoted.

The Commission was not, of course, starting from scratch with its internal market programme. A free and open market had been provided for in the EEC Treaty and much progress had been made. What the White Paper was intended to do was to inject a new focus, impetus, and dynamism into a fundamental Treaty objective which was proceeding far too slowly and, indeed, in some respects, had gone rather off the rails. Much of what was proposed in the White Paper, therefore, was not new, but had been around for some time – awaiting decisions by the Council of Ministers.

Based on a generally de-regulatory approach, the White Paper identified three sorts of barriers which needed to be removed for the completion of the market: physical, technical, and fiscal. Because, however, the proposals that were contained in the White Paper are best viewed as an outgrowth of an already established objective and course of development, they will be considered here in the context of an examination of the four main pillars on which the continuing process to establish the Common Market rests.

The first pillar is the guarantee of *free movement of goods, persons, services and capital* between the member states. Of these, the free movement of goods has received the greatest attention. It is a freedom which, it might be thought, could be fairly easily realised: all barriers to trade must be dismantled according to the guiding principles of the EEC Treaty which states that customs duties, quantitative restrictions, and measures having equivalent effect are not permitted. Great steps were quickly made in the 1960s with the first two of these and by 1968 customs duties and quantitative restrictions were removed. Measures having equivalent effect, however, have been more difficult to deal with and have frequently acted, and been used, as obstacles to trade. Attempts to eliminate such measures have generated a considerable amount of secondary legislation, much activity in the Court of Justice, and constitute an important part of the 1992 programme.

In seeking to establish the conditions for the free movement of persons, the Treaty provides for both the employed and the self-employed. The free movement of the former is to be attained by 'the abolition of any discrimination based on nationality between workers of the Member States as regards employment, remuneration and other conditions of work and employment' (Article 48 EEC). The free movement of the latter is concerned principally with rights of establishment, that is with the right of individuals and undertakings to establish businesses in the territory of other member states. As with the free movement of goods, secondary legislation and Court rulings have done much to clarify and extend the free movement of persons. They have done so in two main ways. First, by providing for mutual recognition of many educational, professional, and trade qualifications. Second, by providing key facilitators, notably in the form of the establishment of various legal entitlements, irrespective of nationality and place of domicile, to education and job training, health care, and social welfare payments

Some of the legislation and Court judgements which have promoted the free movement of persons, and more particularly rights of establishment, have, of course, also helped to give effect to the Treaty declaration that restrictions on the provisions of services within the Community should be abolished. Until recently financial services were a particular problem, but under the 1992 programme legislation has been passed – on, for example, banking, on insurance, and on insider trading – which should have the effect of opening up this hitherto highly protected and fragmented sector.

Establishing the free movement of capital has been extremely difficult. Treaty provisions partly explain this, since the elimination of restrictions on the movement of capital are required only 'to the extent necessary to ensure the proper functioning of the common market' (Article 67 EEC). More importantly, however, and notwithstanding the creation of the European Monetary System in the late

1970s (see below), the necessary political will did not exist until the late 1980s. For many states control of capital movements was an important economic and monetary instrument and they preferred it to remain largely in their own hands. However, as part of the 1992 programme, much of this former resistance was withdrawn or overcome, and all the major capital markets have – subject to some derogations and some national protective measures – been more or less open since 1990.

The second pillar of the Common Market involves the *approximation, or harmonisation, of such legal provisions in the member states as directly affect 'the establishment or functioning of the common market'* (Article 100 EEC). The need for harmonisation arises because, as noted above, the dismantling of barriers is not in itself sufficient to guarantee free movement. This is most clearly seen with regard to movement of goods where many non-tariff and non-quantitative barriers exist which inhibit, even prevent, free movement across Community borders. These barriers have, in the words of the Treaty, the 'equivalent effect' of tariffs and quantitative restrictions, and as such are obstacles to the creation of a market based on free and open competition. They tend, moreover, to be barriers of a kind that cannot be removed simply by issuing general prohibitions. Many take the form of different national standards, requirements, provisions and practices that have been adopted over the years, sometimes for perfectly good reasons, but sometimes as a deliberate attempt to protect a domestic market from unwanted competition without actually infringing Community law. Whatever the intent, the effect is often the same: because of the need to adapt products to meet the different national standards of different states, and because also of the need for products to be subject to retesting and recertification procedures, efficiency is not maximised and producers in one member state often cannot compete on an equal basis with producers in another state. Examples of non-tariff barriers include different national technical specifications for products, different health and safety standards, charges for inspections on categories of imported goods, and taxes which though nominally general in their scope are discriminatory against imported goods in their effect.

Harmonisation is concerned with the removal of barriers of this type and as such is vital if free movement across national boundaries is to be achieved. Council directives are the main instrument for achieving harmonisation, although Court of Justice rulings have also been supportive and helpful. Most harmonisation law is naturally to be found in relation to the free movement of goods, and consists largely of matters such as the setting of common standards on technical requirements, design specifications, product content, and necessary documentation. Critics of the Community often present such measures as harmonisation for harmonisation's sake, and from time to time proposals do indeed appear to smack of insensitivity to national customs and preferences. Sight should not be lost, however, of what harmonisation is all about: creating conditions which will allow, encourage and increase the uniform treatment of persons, goods, services and capital throughout the Community.

As was briefly explained in Chapter 6, and as is further explained in Chapter 10, the Community's approach to harmonisation has changed in recent years. Following the 'breakthrough' *Cassis de Dijon* case in 1979 – when the Court of Justice ruled that products which conform with the standards of one member state cannot be excluded from the markets of other member states unless they can be shown to be damaging to health, safety, the environment, or other aspects of the public interest – the Community has not concerned itself as much as formerly with harmonising technical details. Under the 'new approach' to harmonisation, which the Commission made part of the 1992 drive, a simpler and speedier process applies: wherever possible harmonisation legislation is restricted to laying down the essential requirements which national standards and specifications must meet – on health and safety requirements for example; as long as the essential conditions are met member states must mutually recognise each other's specifications and standards; and there is to be a movement away from national specifications and standards towards European specifications and standards – these to be drawn up by the appropriate European standards organisations.

Competition policy is the third pillar. The basic rules on competition are outlined in Articles 85–94 of the EEC Treaty. They have three principal aspects to them. First, under Article 85, 'all agreements between undertakings, decisions by associations of undertakings and concerted practices which may affect trade between Member States and which have as their object or effect the prevention, restriction or distortion of competition within the common market are prohibited'. Second, under Article 86, 'Any abuse by one or more undertakings of a dominant position within the common market or in a substantial part of it shall be prohibited or incompatible with the common market insofar as it may affect trade between Member States'. Third, under Article 92, state aid 'which distorts or threatens to distort competition by favouring certain undertakings or the production of certain goods shall, insofar as it affects trade between Member States, be incompatible with the common market'.

All of these Treaty prohibitions – on restrictive practices, dominant trading positions, and state aids – have been clarified by subsequent Community law, mainly in the form of Council legislation and Court judgements. It has been established, for example, that a 'dominant position' cannot be held to apply on the basis of an overall percentage market share, but only in relation to factors such as the particular product, the structure of its market, and substitutability. Similarly, exemptions to state aid prohibitions, which are only generally referred to in the Treaty, have been confirmed as legally permissible if they are for purposes such as regional development, retraining, and job creation in potential growth industries. Much of the work and time of DGIV (Competition) is taken up examining allegations of breaches in competition law and considering applications for exemptions.

An effective competition policy is, of course, necessary for an open and integrated market. To try and improve the policy and ensure that it is sufficiently effective the Community has adopted a twin approach in recent years. First, the Commission has become much more active in examining cases of apparent malpractice. For example, using its powers as investigator, prosecutor, judge, and jury (though with its decisions subject to appeal to the Court of Justice) it has been more willing to take action against member states in connection with state aids. Second, legislation designed to broaden the competition policy base has been approved. An example of such legislation is the 1989 Company Merger Regulation which gives considerable powers to the Commission to disallow mergers which it judges will have an adverse effect on competition. Other examples, in a very different area of competition policy, are the directives that are designed to open up public procurement – an area of activity that accounts for around fifteen per cent of Community GDP, but where only about two per cent of contracts in 1987 were awarded to firms in other member states.

The fourth pillar of the Common Market is the *Commom Customs Tariff* (CCT), or, as it is also known, the *Common External Tariff* (CET). The purpose of this is to further the course of fair and equal trading by surrounding all the member states with common trade barriers so that goods entering the Community via, say, Liverpool or Rotterdam, do so on exactly the same conditions as they do via Athens or Marseilles. No member state can therefore gain a competitive advantage by having access to cheaper raw materials and none can make a profit from exporting imported goods to a Community partner. The CCT takes the Community beyond being just a free trade area – where, at best, external tariffs are only approximated – and makes it a customs union.

Establishing the CCT was relatively easily achieved and maintaining it has not been too difficult. The external tariffs were in place by 1968, to coincide with the removal of the internal tariffs, and since then governments have had no independent legal authority over the tariffs to be charged on goods entering their country. The terms of trade of the member states are established and negotiated on a Community-wide basis via a Common Commercial Policy (CCP). If a member state wishes to seek exemptions from, or changes to, these terms of trade it must go through the appropriate Community decision-making processes. Naturally, there have been frequent disagreements between the states over different aspects of external trade and the CCP – tariff rates, trade protection measures, and alleged dumping are amongst the issues that have created difficulties – but the existence of a clear and binding legal framework has ensured that, for the most part, the external protection and common front system has worked.

Although much has been, and is being, achieved in establishing the Common Market, it is clear that it will be some years yet before the Community market is as open or as integrated as national markets. This is because not all of the barriers to free movement are being removed, and not all of the national policies which serve to fragment the market are being made common. The obstacles to a completely open and integrated market which will continue in at least some form for the forseeable future fall into three categories.

First, there are the somewhat intangible, but nonetheless very important, obstacles arising from different historical experiences, cultures, traditions, and languages. These obstacles are unquestionably being gradually broken down, but only slowly. EC laws may, for example, oblige public authorities to receive tenders for contracts from throughout the Community, but laws cannot control the many informal processes that often incline decision-makers to award contracts whenever possible to fellow national, or even locally-based, companies.

Second, some of the Commission's White Paper proposals do not meet with the approval of all the member states. They are sometimes therefore being loosened to overcome resistance, and in some cases – especially where the decision-making rules still require unanimity – are being held up altogether. Border controls are an example of such a problem area: procedures have been improved, but a minority of states (notably the UK) are concerned that the complete removal of frontier controls will make it more difficult to detect and track such undesirable practices as the illegal movement of drugs, terrorists, and immigrants. (In consequence of this inability to reach a Community-wide agreement, the Benelux countries, Germany, France, and later Italy, agreed in 1990 to the Schengen Agreement which provided for the eventual removal of border controls between the signatory states.) Another example of a problem area is the harmonisation of indirect taxation: differences between both national bases and rates of excise duties and VAT, and differences between states regarding the importance of indirect taxation for their exchequers, have made it very difficult for even watered down common bands – let alone common rates – to be agreed.

Third, there are many economic factors which were not included in the White Paper and which are not formally part of the internal market programme, which nonetheless exist as obstacles to a completely open and integrated market. Economists and politicians dispute exactly what economic factors do constitute such obstacles, and what their relative importance is, but prominent amongst the factors that are generally recognised are the following: the lack of closely co-ordinated – some would say the lack of common – economic and monetary policies; the lack of fixed exchange rates, and in the view of many the lack of a common currency; the only partial development of common regional, social, environmental, and consumer policies; and the diversity of personal and corporate direct taxation systems.

As is shown below many of these obstacles are increasingly being addressed, notably in the context of the movement towards Economic and Monetary Union, but their complete removal is not something for the short-term.

Economic and Financial Policies

Notwithstanding certain EEC Treaty provisions, and despite declarations by the Heads of Government in 1969 and 1972 that their intention was to establish an economic and monetary union by 1980, only limited practical progress has so far been made in approximating the economic and financial policies of the states.

Ministers and senior national officials do regularly convene to consult and to exchange ideas on macroeconomic policy, and at their meetings they periodically consider Commission submissions for the adoption of common guidelines and for short-term and medium-term strategies. But ultimately, it is up to the states themselves as to what they do. When, for example, the Commission, in its quarterly economic report published in February 1987, stated that Germany had the greatest margin for manoeuvre to stimulate domestic demand, and France and the UK could do more to boost productive capacity, there was no guarantee that national policies would thereby be adjusted. A state may be unwise to fall too much out of step with its partners – as the French government was in 1981–2 when it attempted to stimulate its economy against the general trend – but it is perfectly entitled, and able, to embark on such a course of action.

Financial policy (which, of course, in practice, is inextricably linked with economic policy) is also the subject of frequent contacts between the states – at ministerial, official and central bank levels – but, like economic policy, most of what comes out of such exchanges is of an exhortive rather than a directionist nature. That said, however, the existence of the EMS does give to Community financial policy some central structure and some powers, since amongst its features are: a common reserve fund to provide for market intervention (each country allocating 20 per cent of its reserves to the central pool); the European Currency Unit (Ecu) which acts as a reserve asset and a means of settlement; and, in the Exchange Rate Mechanism (ERM) of the EMS, fixed – though adjustable when necessary – bands of exchange for participating currencies.

The Community's macroeconomic and financial policies thus have only relatively weak policy instruments attached to them. Attempts to strengthen these instruments, so as to build up a more effective policy framework, have traditionally met with at least four obstacles. First, there have been genuine differences as to which – the economic or the financial – naturally comes first and should be accorded priority. Second, the Community's rather sectionalised policy-making mechanisms have inhibited an overall and co-ordinated approach. Third, different aspects of economic and monetary integration have different implications for the states, which has resulted in them being viewed with different degrees of enthusiasm. Fourth, for some states the possibility of ceding key macroeconomic and financial powers to the Community raises fundamental sovereignty questions.

But notwithstanding the many obstacles in the way of policy development, and notwithstanding either the rather limited practical progress that has been made to date, the situation is on the verge of being transformed. As a result of a number of factors – notably, an increasing appreciation by governments of the benefits for the internal market of economic and financial integration, the enthusiasm of the Commission for progress, and the amendment of the EEC Treaty by the SEA to include a new chapter on 'Co-operation in Economic and Monetary Policy' – the Community is now formally embarked on the road to Economic and Monetary Union (EMU). Differences remain between the states both as regards what precisely EMU should consist of, and what should be the timetable for its full implementation, but all (apart from the UK) subscribe to the broad outlines of the scheme that were put forward in April 1989 by the Delors Committee in its *Report on Economic and Monetary Union* (see Chapter 7 for the circumstances in which the Committee was established). The Committee proposed that the Community should move forward to EMU in three stages. In outline the stages were as follows:

Stage one would involve strengthening economic and monetary policy co-ordination within the existing institutional framework, and also would require the preparation and ratification of amendments to the Treaties which would be necessary for stage two. During stage one all countries would be expected to enter their currencies into the ERM of the EMS.

Stage two would come into force with the implementation of the new Treaty, and would involve the setting up of a European System of Central Banks in which a European Central Bank would coexist with the existing national Central Banks in a federal structure. During this stage the new Central Bank would assume important monetary responsibilities, and there would also be a strengthening of the provisions governing economic policy co-ordination.

Stage three would start with the irreversible locking of exchange rates and the transfer to Community institutions of key economic and monetary responsibilities. At some point the national currencies would be replaced by a single common currency.

Since the publication of the Delors Report there have been innumerable negotiations and discussions between the states – from European Council level downwards – on EMU. Many difficulties and differences have either continued to exist or have become newly apparent. Important progress has, nonetheless, been made. Up to the end of 1990 this progress was most marked in three particular respects. First, it was agreed at the June 1989 Madrid summit that stage one of EMU would begin on 1 July 1990. Under stage one the pound sterling entered the ERM in October 1990 – thus leaving only the Greek and Portuguese currencies outside the system. Second, it was agreed at the December 1989 Strasbourg summit that an intergovernmental conference would be necessary to propose the Treaty amendments that would be necessary for stage two, and in December 1990 the conference began its work. Third, at the special Rome summit in October 1990 eleven of the twelve agreed (the UK dissented) that stage two would begin on 1 January 1994.

Functional Policies

The Community has interests and responsibilities in many functional policies: policies, that is, which have a clear functional purpose, and which are more specific in nature than the policies considered under the previous heading.

The best known of the Community's functional policies, and in budgetary terms by far the most important, are the regional policy – which is financed by the European Regional Development Fund – and the social policy – which is mainly financed by the European Social Fund (there is some discussion of these funds in Chapters 3 and 11). Less prominent functional policies include educational policy, cultural policy, and consumer protection policy. Since it is not possible to examine all of the Community's functional policies here, four examples will be briefly considered to illustrate the range, and varying depth, of Community involvement in different functional areas.

Social Policy. The EEC Treaty, in Articles 117–122, provided for the development of a Community social policy. Until recently, not a great deal was done to give effect to this Treaty provision, although there were some developments – via both legislation and Court decisions – in areas such as working conditions, equal opportunities, and entitlements to social benefits.

The EEC Treaty also, in Articles 123–8, provided for a European Social Fund. This has been used primarily for employment training and retraining purposes, and has been directed particularly at young people.

In 1989 a major boost was given to Community social policy when the Commission – believing that the internal market programme should have a 'social dimension' – produced *The Community Charter of Fundamental Social Rights for Workers*. The Charter was inevitably somewhat general in its character and terminology but it contained the fundamental principles which should apply to twelve main themes. Amongst these themes were: free movement of workers on the basis of equal treatment in access to employment and social protection; employment on the basis of fair remuneration; improvement of living and working conditions; freedom of association and collective bargaining; and protection of children and adolescents. The Charter was adopted by eleven member states (the UK was the exception) at the December 1989 European Council meeting. The Strasbourg summit also took 'note of the fact that the Commission has drawn up an action programme on the application of the Charter and calls upon the Council to deliberate upon the Commission's proposals in the light of the social dimension of the internal market and having regard to the national and Community responsibilities' (Conclusions of the Presidency). Amongst the forty-seven measures which are listed in the Action Programme are proposals for directives on employment and working conditions, on employment contracts, on health and safety at work, on the protection of pregnant women and young people at work, and on the adaptation of working time.

Energy Policy. Given the existence of the ECSC and Euratom Treaties, given the centrality of energy to any modern economy, and given the disruption and damage that was caused by oil price increases in the 1970s, the very limited progress that has been made towards a single Community market in energy and a common energy policy – as opposed to policies for particular energy sectors – must be ranked as one of the Community's major failures. The Commission has long drawn attention to the immense advantages that would accrue from having an integrated energy market: if, for example, electricity was traded freely Community savings could be in the region of five billion Ecu per annum and generating costs could be sixteen per cent lower. The member states, however, with their differing domestic energy resources and their differing energy requirements, have preferred essentially national solutions.

The Commission has thus been forced to adopt a pragmatic and non-compulsory approach to energy issues, based on the identification of objectives around which national policies can converge. Amongst these objectives are the very general aims of promoting efficiency, slowing the growth in total energy consumption, and reducing the Community's dependence on imported energy.

Research and technological development policy. The Community's research and technological development (R & TD) policy and activities take four main forms:

1. Research is undertaken directly by the Community itself at the Community's Joint Research Centre (JRC). The JRC consists of four establishments and employs around 2250 people. Most of the work of the JRC is concentrated on nuclear energy (especially safety issues), materials, remote sensing, and, increasingly, industrial research related to the internal market.
2. The largest part of Community R & TD consists of shared-cost or contract research. This research is not undertaken by Commission employees but by tens of thousands of researchers in universities, research institutes, and public and private companies. The Community's role is to develop and agree the principles, aims, and conditions of the programmes under which the research is conducted, to co-ordinate activities, and to provide some of the finance (usually around 50 per cent of the total cost of the research). The better known programmes

in this approach to research activity include ESPRIT (information technology), BRITE (industrial technology), and RACE (advanced telecommunications).

3. There are concerted action-research projects where the Community does not finance the actual research, but facilitates and finances co-ordination of work being done at national level. The Community's medical research programme takes this form.

4. Some of the research activity takes none of the above three 'conventional' forms, but consists of arrangements in which, for example, only some member states participate, or in which the Community co-operates with non-member states and international organisations. A particularly important research activity of this type is the Joint European Torus (JET) project, in which non-Community states participate with the Community in joint-venture research into controlled nuclear fusion.

R & TD was not mentioned in the EEC Treaty but the SEA rectified this by amending the Treaty to add a new Title VI to Part Three entitled 'Research and Technological Development'. A particularly important aspect of the SEA amendments was that they legitimised, and gave a boost, to a development that the Community initiated in 1984: using multi-annual framework programmes to co-ordinate and give a strategic view to its many specific R & TD policies and activities. The first framework programme covered 1984–7, the second 1987–91, and the third (which overlapped with the second) 1990–4. The third framework programme was allocated 5700 million Ecu for its five years, and it has six major concerns. Amongst these concerns are: improving industrial competitiveness; meeting the challenges linked to the attainment of the internal market as regards norms and standards by strengthening pre-normative research; and introducing a European dimension into the training of scientific research and technological development staff.

Environmental Policy. Protection of the environment was not mentioned in the EEC Treaty but a separate chapter on the environment was included in the SEA. By 1990 around 200 legal instruments covering environmental matters had been adopted, many of them designed to give effect to the four Environmental

Action Programmes that the Community has adopted since 1973. Community environmental law now covers matters as important as water and air pollution, disposal of chemicals, waste treatment, and protection of species and natural resources. In 1990 the Council agreed to the establishment of a European Environment Agency to provide scientific information for preparing and carrying out an effective environmental policy.

Sectoral Policies

Some Community policies are directed towards specific economic sectors. A few such policies were explicitly provided for in the Treaties. Others have their origins in a combination of factors: difficulties in adjusting to changed trading conditions; rapid sectoral decline; and effective political lobbying by interested parties.

The most obvious example of a sectoral policy is the Common Agricultural Policy which consumes by far the largest proportion of Community expenditure and where most policy-making responsibilities have been transferred from the states to the Community. (The CAP is examined in some detail in Chapter 12.) Other – though more modest and less comprehensive – examples of sectoral policies include atomic energy, where important work is undertaken in areas such as research and safety standards, and shipbuilding, where a code of practice includes specified limitations on governmental subsidies and aids.

Two important sectoral policies will be taken to illustrate Community sectoral activity:

Fishing. Following years of discussion, and the periodic issuing of laws from 1970 regulating aspects of the industry, a legally enforceable Common Fisheries Policy (CFP) was eventually agreed in 1983. There are four main aspects to it. First, all waters within the Community's 200 mile zone are open to all Community fishermen, but within a 12 mile limit of their own shores member states may reserve fishing to their own fishermen and to those with traditional rights. Atlantic and North Sea fish stocks are controlled by the setting of total allowable catches that are divided into national quotas. All conservation measures are agreed at Community level. Second, there is a market organisation for fish covering a price system, marketing arrangements, and an external trade policy. Third, structural measures provide for matters such as processing and market development projects, conversion and modernisation schemes, and redeployment. Fourth, international negotiations – which mostly concern access to waters and conservation of fishing stocks – are conducted by Community representatives on behalf of all member states.

Steel. The Treaty of Paris is essentially based on a liberal economic philosophy in the sense that it is principally concerned with the removal of barriers to trade. So, for the products falling within its jurisdiction it provides for the removal of internal tariffs, quantitative restrictions and most state aids. It also forbids, subject to certain exemptions, price discrimination and cartels. However, some direct intervention is also permitted and powers are given to the Community authorities to grant loans for capital investment, to finance research and development, and, above all, to set mandatory minimum prices and production quotas when a 'manifest crisis' is deemed to exist. These policy instruments, developed and clarified by secondary legislation, do not add up to a comprehensive Community legal framework for steel – key decisions on individual enterprises, for example, are still taken primarily at national levels – but they do constitute a very important part of the sectoral law. The Community authorities have, indeed, potentially greater powers of intervention on steel than in any other sector apart from agriculture and fishing, and, from the mid-1970s, they used these powers to some effect to try and manage the Community's response to problems of falling demand. Initially the response relied mainly on voluntary measures, but from 1980 to 1988, during which a 'manifest crisis' was declared to exist, all producers were subject to mandatory price and quota restrictions. The purpose of these draconian powers was to effect a general restructuring of the industry.

External Policies

There are many different aspects to the Community's external relations and policies. Three are particularly important.

Trade Policy. The Community has trade agreements, or agreements in which a substantial part of the content is concerned with trade, with just about every country in the world. These agreements come in different forms: some are bilateral, some are multilateral; some are strict trade agreements, some are trade and economic co-operation agreements, and some are association agreements. Whatever the particular form of agreements, however, the Community states act as one in contracting the terms of agreements. That is to say, the members present a common external front to the world in respect of international trade. If they did not do so a unified internal market would not be possible. The main foundations of the common external front are the Common Customs Tariff and the Common Commercial Policy which enable, indeed oblige, the member states to act together on matters such as the fixing and adjusting of external customs tariffs, the negotiation of customs and trade agreements with non-member countries, and the taking of action to impede imports – this being especially likely where unfair trading practices, such as dumping and subsidies, are suspected.

Whether it is negotiating on a bilateral basis with another state, with another international regional grouping (such as EFTA or ASEAN), or in an international forum (such as GATT or UNCTAD), the Community, acting through the Commission, is usually in a very strong position to influence the outcome of trade negotiations. This is because, together, the member states constitute the world's largest economy (accounting for over 20 per cent of world gross domestic product), and they are also the world's largest trader (accounting for around 18 per cent of world trade, compared with 13 per cent for the USA and 11 per cent for Japan).

For the most part, this economic and commercial weight is used in the interests of a liberal trading policy, in which customs duties are set as low as possible and non-tariff barriers to trade are removed. (In 1990 the Community's average customs duties were 5.44 per cent, and were due to be reduced to 3.86 per cent after the conclusion of the GATT Uruguay Round of multilateral trade liberalisation negotiations.) This policy, however, is not always pursued with complete consistency, especially where economic circumstances or political pressures suggest a dose of protectionism. Most controversially in this regard, Community agriculture has long been sheltered from external competition – a fact that has strained trading relations with the USA. Furthermore, special protection measures – often in the form of export restraint agreements with cheaper competitors – have been sought and obtained in respect of certain Community industries, notably textiles and steel, experiencing difficulties.

Development Policy. The Community is actively engaged in helping to promote economic development in the Third World. Its reasons for being so engaged are a mixture of the moral: the belief that something should be done about world poverty and hunger; and the economic: the Community is highly dependent on the Third World for products such as rubber, copper and uranium, and also for markets – Third World countries account for around 35 per cent of Community exports.

Some of the forms of assistance made available by the Community apply to the whole of the Third World. Amongst these are:

1. Generalised preferences. All developing countries can export their industrial products to the Community without paying tariffs (subject to volume limits for some products). Additionally, many agricultural products can also be exported free of duty.
2. Food aid. Foodstuffs are sent to countries with serious food shortages.
3. Emergency aid. Aid of an appropriate sort is made available to countries stricken by natural disasters and other crises.
4. Aid to non-governmental organisations. The Community makes available aid to projects sponsored by non-governmental organisations in a number of Third World countries.

In addition to these general forms of assistance, the Community makes additional assistance and aid available to countries with which it has entered into special relationships. Most of these special relationships take the form of economic, trade, industrial, technical, and financial co-operation agreements. The most important, and most wide-ranging, co-operation agreement is the Lomé Convention which links the Community with African, Caribbean and Pacific countries (the ACP countries) with which some member states have historical links. Lomé IV (covering the years 1990–2000) was signed in 1989 and now involves 69 ACP states. It contains amongst its main features: duty-free access to the Community market for virtually all ACP exports; stabilisation of export earnings schemes (Stabex and Sysmin); and the European Development Fund (EDF) which, with resources of 12000 million Ecu for the period 1990–5, has as its main purpose financially assisting, on the basis of long-term concerted programmes, the development of ACP countries, especially as regards rural development, industrialisation, and economic infrastructure.

It should be stressed that these Community policies do not constitute the sum total of the Community's overall contribution to Third World development. This is because, unlike with trade policy, the Community itself does not enjoy exclusive policy competence in the development field but rather shares it with the member states. In some respects the Community takes the leading role, in other respects it aims to supplement, complement, and co-ordinate national development policies. So, the trade aspects of development policy are necessarily the Community's responsibility, but the states are much more prominent in respect of financial assistance – as is seen in the fact that the Community's own financial aid represents only about 13 per cent of the combined efforts of the member states. (In 1988 the Community's own aid totalled about 2.24billion Ecu – 1.04 billion financed by the Community budget, and 1.2 billion financed by the EDF which is funded by special contributions from the member states.)

Foreign Policy. There are many obstacles in the way of a developed, let alone a common, Community foreign policy. Amongst these obstacles are the following: many member states, especially those larger ones which have long histories of being influential on the world stage in their own right, prefer, at least in certain key areas, to conduct their own foreign policies; some member states have traditional and special relationships with particular parts of the world which they are anxious to maintain; important differences between the states on foreign policy questions arise from the ideological orientations of the national governments – differences, for example, over South Africa, over 'liberation'/'revolutionary' movements in South America, and over relations with the USA; and, finally, defence, which of course is inextricably linked with foreign policy, is largely outside the Community framework – and seems likely to remain so given the role and importance of NATO, and given too the doubts that some states (such as Ireland because of her traditional policy of neutrality) have of the wisdom of putting defence questions on the Community agenda.

But notwithstanding these obstacles important developments have occurred. Since 1970, when foreign policy co-operation, under the name European Political Co-operation (EPC), was first launched, the states have consulted with one another on virtually all important foreign policy issues. As is shown in Table 10.1 the consultation mechanisms are now extensive at both political and official levels, and are regular and institutionalised.

The developing importance of foreign policy co-operation was recognised when EPC was accorded its own section – Title III – in the SEA. Amongst other things Title III states: 'The High Contracting Parties (the member states), being members of the European Communities, shall endeavour jointly to formulate and implement a European foreign policy'. However, unlike certain other policy areas which were also recognised in the SEA, such as environment, Title III was not incorporated into the Treaties. This was mainly because the member states were unwilling to allow the normal Community decision-making processes to apply to foreign policy. As a result, EPC continues to be much looser, more voluntaristic in nature, than most other policy areas with which the Community concerns itself. No laws are made within EPC, most decisions are arrived at by consensus, and no state can be prevented from engaging in independent action if it so chooses.

Nonetheless, despite the lack of a Treaty base the pressures for member states to conduct their foreign policies within the EPC context are considerable, and the almost unceasing rounds of consultations which are at the heart of EPC are undoubtedly facilitating Community foreign policy co-operation and are assisting in the emergence of a distinctive European political voice. This is so in at least four ways. First, the member states have a better understanding of their partners' foreign policy stances. Second, the ability of the twelve to take a united approach in other international organisations and forums – such as the United Nations and its agencies – is improved. Third, the Community is increasingly in a position to engage in a political dialogue with non-Community states and organisations – as, for example, it does in periodic ministerial conferences with the countries of Central America and of the Contadora Group. And, fourth, the Community frequently is able to adopt common positions on international issues of contemporary importance. Many of these common positions are, it must be said, rather vague and fudged, but by no means all. In recent years, for instance, important joint statements and declarations, which have differed in important respects from the position of the major Western power, the USA, have been issued on subjects such as the Arab–Israeli conflict, the Falklands war, Poland, and arms control negotiations.

As long as defence and security issues are kept apart from foreign policy, EPC will, of course, always be restricted in its scope. The division between foreign policy and defence also weakens the potential effectiveness of what EPC can hope to achieve. This was illustrated in the Community's response to Iraq's invasion of Kuwait in 1990 – some joint statements and co-ordinated diplomatic responses on the Gulf crisis were agreed in the EPC context, but on the key issue of the Community's military response member states reacted in a piecemeal and unco-ordinated fashion.

Notwithstanding the limitations of the EPC system, however, it is, at a minimum, an important part of the framework in which the foreign policies of the member states are conducted. It seems, moreover, that it will increasingly become so in the future. One reason for this is that some of the obstacles mentioned above – such as the importance of special national relationships with particular parts of the world – are becoming less problematical as ties are loosened. A second reason is that there is a growing desire on the part of most of the states to improve the links, and where possible the match, between external economic relations and external political relations. And a third reason is that an increasing number of states, especially since the Gulf crisis and war, have expressed an interest in bringing foreign, security, and defence policies more into the Community system.

Characteristics of Community Policies

Three features of Community policies are particularly striking.

The Range and Diversity of Community Policies

The Community is often referred to as 'The Common Market' It is so because many of its policies and its laws centre on the promotion and defence of an internally free and externally protected market. So, there are the policies that are designed to encourage the free movement of goods, persons, services, and capital; there is the competition policy that seeks to facilitate fair and open competition within and across the borders of the member states; there is the common external tariff; and there is the common commercial policy. In practice, however, not all of these policies are complete or are wholly successful. There are, for example, still barriers related to company law and company taxation which can make it difficult for firms in different member states to be able to engage in joint commercial activities, and, despite strenuous activity on harmonisation, many non-tariff barriers to internal trade still exist. In consequence, the Community is, in some respects, less than the Common Market it is commonly supposed to be.

But in other respects it is more than the Common Market, in that many of its policy concerns range far beyond matters that are part and parcel of a common market's requirements. The policy concerns of the Community are not, in other words, just concerned with dismantling internal barriers and providing conditions for fair trade on the one hand, and presenting a common external front on the other. There are two main aspects to this.

First, as regards the Community's economic policies, many of these are not based solely on the non-interventionist/*laissez faire* principles that are often thought of as providing the ethos, the ideology even, of the Community. In some spheres the Community tends very much to interventionism/managerialism and in so doing it does not always restrict itself to 'market efficiency' policies. This is most obviously seen in the way in which the regional and social policies and much of the CAP have as their precise purpose the counteracting and softening of nationally unacceptable or socially inequitable market consequences. On a broader front, those policies which are designed to promote economic and financial co-operation at the macro level are part of a drive to take the Community beyond being 'just' a common market: they have as their ultimate purpose making it an economic and monetary union.

Second, the Community has developed many policies which are not only non-market policies but are non-economic policies. Of these the most obvious are those falling within the EPC framework, where the states consult and attempt to co-ordinate their positions on key foreign policy questions. In addition to EPC, there are also other areas – from education to broadcasting – for long thought of as not being the Community's concern, where important developments have occurred. An example of this at the highest level was seen in December 1986 when the Heads of Government, at the end of their London summit meeting, issued a communiqué that was much taken up with joint action they were proposing to combat terrorism, illegal immigration, and drug trafficking, and also with the co-ordination of public health campaigns on Aids and cancer.

The Differing Degrees of Community Policy Involvement

The Community's responsibility for policy-making and for policy-management varies enormously across its range of policy interests. In those spheres where significant responsibilities are exercised, arrangements are usually well established, and effective policy instruments – legal and financial – are usually available. Where, however, Community involvement is marginal, policy processes may be confined to little more than occasional exchanges of ideas and information between interested parties, whilst policy instruments may merely be of the exhortive and persuasive kind such as are common in many international organisations.

Examples of high Community involvement are the CCP, the CAP, and the CFP. Here, most major policy decisions, such as on external tariffs, agricultural prices, and fishing quotas, are taken at the Community level, whilst their detailed and supposed uniform implementation is left to the states acting as agents of the Community. In areas where these so-called common policies are not, in reality, totally common – and both the CAP and the CFP allow ample room for governments to provide national aids and assistance – decisions of any significance normally require at least clearance from Brussels.

Moving along the spectrum of Community policy involvement there are many spheres in which the Community's interests and competence, though less comprehensive than in the examples just given, remain very significant, and complement and supplement the activities of the states in important ways. Competition policy is an example. It seeks to encourage free and open competition throughout the Community by, for instance, setting out conditions under which firms can make and sell their products, by laying down conditions under which national authorities may assist firms, and by imposing restrictions on certain types of company merger. Social policy provides another example. Much of its concern is with job training and re-training, labour mobility, working conditions, and the general promotion of employment.

Turning, finally, to policy spheres where the Community's involvement is, at best, very limited, examples include education, health, and – a qualitatively different case – national defence. Interestingly, if one looks back to, say, 1970, many issues which would have been listed then as being in this category of very limited Community involvement – such as environment and foreign policy – are now no longer so marginal. As has already been indicated, environment has spawned policy programmes and legislation, foreign policy has evolved its own machinery and has seen some co-ordinated policy development, whilst both have been awarded constitutional recognition via the SEA. At the same time, some policy spheres which, in 1970, the Community would not have been thought of as having competence in at all, have crept onto the agenda. One such example is seen in the semi-secret Trevi process under which, since the mid-1970s, Interior and Justice officials, senior police and intelligence officers, and more recently ministers, have met to exchange information and further co-operation (often the first steps in policy development) on terrorism, drug trafficking and organised crime.

The Patchy and Somewhat Unco-ordinated Nature of Community Policies

Although the Community was given as one of its tasks in the EEC Treaty the promotion of 'a harmonious development of economic activities', the Community's overall policy framework can hardly be said to display a clear pattern or overall coherence. Some effort is now being made to give it a pattern, a coherence, and a rationale with the so-called subsidiarity principle, via which only those policies which it is agreed are best dealt with at Community level rather than national level do become the Community's concern. The problem with this principle, however, both as a description of the present reality and as a prescription for future action, is that it is vague and question-begging. Descriptions of the present and evolving policy framework as being centred on 'managed and tempered capitalism' or 'a controlled open market' are of more use in capturing the essence of the Community's policy interests, but they too are still far from wholly satisfactory in that they do not embrace the full flavour of the array and varying depths of Community policy interests, nor do they draw attention to the conflicting principles that underlie different parts of the policy network.

The fact is that in a Community in which there are considerable national and political differences, co-ordinated and coherent policy development that is based on shared principles and agreed objectives is very difficult. It is so because *any* policy development is usually only possible if searching questions are answered to the satisfaction of a large number of Community actors. From the viewpoint of the member states these questions include: is the national (or at least government) interest being served?; is the co-operation and integration that the policy development involves politically acceptable?; and, if the policy sphere does require closer relations with other states, is the Community the most desirable arena in which it should occur? As the Community's extensive range of policies demonstrates these questions have often been answered in the affirmative, though normally only after being subject to caveats and reservations which sit uneasily beside, and sometimes clash with, one another. But often, too, the responses have been in the negative, or at least have been so on the part of a sufficient number to prevent progress.

Policy development has consequently been as much about what is possible as what is desirable. In the absence of a centre of power with the authority and internal coherence to take an overall view of Community requirements and impose an ordered pattern, policies have tended to be the outcome of complex and laboured interactions where different, and often contrasting, requirements, preferences, reservations, and fears have all played a part. As a result, the Community's overall policy picture is inevitably patchy and rather ragged. A few spheres – such as the CAP and, increasingly, the operation of the internal market – are well developed. Other spheres, however, which might have been expected to be developed, are either developed only in unco-ordinated and partial ways, or are barely developed at all.

Industrial policy is a prime example of just such an unco-ordinated and underdeveloped policy. With industry employing 35 per cent of the Community's active population and accounting for 40 per cent of the gross value-added of the Community's economy, and with industrial growth in the Community lagging behind competitors, it might be expected that an industrial policy would be at the very centre of Community policy concerns. In practice, a fully developed, comprehensive, and coherent industrial policy does not exist. What do exist are a large number of policies, themselves usually only partially developed, which affect industry, but which do not in any sense constitute an integrated industrial framework with clear and consistent goals. The most obvious of these policies are those which are designed to promote the free movement of goods, persons, services and capital throughout the Community. Others include the competition policy, the research policy, aspects of the regional and social policies, and specific policies for some expanding and some contracting sectors.

Concluding Comments

A central theme of this chapter has been the range and diversity of the Community's policy responsibilities and interests. There are now few policy areas with which the Community does not have at least some sort of involvement.

But another theme has been that there are many deficiencies in Community policies. Economic and monetary policy, industrial policy, energy policy, and regional policy are but four examples of key policy areas where there are not, if Community effectiveness is to be maximised, sufficiently strong or integrated policy frameworks with clear and consistent goals. They are too partial and too fragmented. They are also, in general, underfunded.

Of course, similar critical comments about underdevelopment and lack of cohesion can also be levelled against most national policy frameworks. But not, usually, to the same extent. For, at individual state level, there is, even when the political system is weak and decentralised, more opportunity than there is in the Community for direction from the centre. This is partly because national decision-makers have access to more policy instruments than do Community decision-makers. It is mainly, however, because at state level there is normally some focus of political authority capable of imposing a degree of order: a Head of Government perhaps, a Cabinet or Council of Ministers, a Ministry of Economics or Finance, or a dominant party group. In the Community, the Council of Ministers and the European Council are the main foci of political authority, but neither is constituted or organised in such a way as to enable them to forge an overall policy coherence or specify a clear policy direction.

10

Policy Processes

Variations in Community Policy Processes

There can hardly be said to be a 'standard' or a 'typical' Community policy-making or decision-making process. A multiplicity of actors interact with one another via a myriad of channels.

The Actors

There are three main sets of actors: those associated with the Community institutions, with the member governments, and with Euro and national interests. As has been shown in previous chapters, each of these has responsibilities to fulfil and roles to perform. But so variable and fluid are Community policy processes that the nature of the responsibilities and roles may differ considerably according to circumstances. For instance, in one set of circumstances an actor may be anxious to play an active role and may have the power – legal and/or political – to do so. In a second set of circumstances it may not wish to be actively involved, perhaps because it has no particular interests at stake or because prominence may be politically damaging. And, in a third set of circumstances, it may wish for a leading part but not be able to attain it because of a lack of appropriate power resources.

The Channels

The channels vary in four principal respects.

In their complexity and exhaustiveness. Some types of decisions are made fairly quickly by a relatively small number of people using procedures that are easy to operate. By contrast, others are the subject of complex and exhaustive processes in which many different sorts of actors attempt to determine and shape outcomes.

In the relative importance of Community level processes and member state level processes and in the links between the two levels. One of the Community's major structural difficulties is that it is multi-layered and there are often no clear lines of authority or of hierarchy between the different layers or levels.

In their levels of seniority. This is seen in the many different forums in which the member states meet: Heads of Government in the European Council; Ministers in the Council of Ministers; Permanent Representatives and their deputies in COREPER; senior officials and national experts in working parties, management and regulatory committees, and expert groups.

In their degrees of formality and structure. By their very nature the fixed and set piece occasions of Community policy processes – such as meetings of the Council of Ministers, plenary sessions of the EP, Council of Ministers/EP delegation meetings called to resolve legislative and budgetary differences – tend to be formal and structured. Partly because of this, they are often, in themselves, not very well equipped to produce the trading, the concessions, and the compromises that are so often necessary to build majorities, create agreements, and further progress. As a result they have come to be supported by a vast network of informal and unstructured channels between Community actors. Examples of such channels are everywhere and range from the after dinner discussions that are held at European Council meetings to the continuous rounds of soundings, telephone calls, lunches, lobbying opportunities, and pre-meetings that are such a part of Community life in Brussels, Strasbourg, Luxembourg and national capitals.

An Illustration of Variations: External Relations

It is worth illustrating and reinforcing the central point made in the previous section, about the multi-faceted nature of Community processes, with a brief example. An outline sketch of some of the key policy and decision-making features involved in external relations will be taken. There are three main aspects to the Community's external relations.

External *commercial* relations involve the Community acting as a single unit in international trading negotiations. On the basis of Article 113 of the EEC Treaty, which provides for the Common Commercial Policy (CCP), trade policies are developed and decisions are taken by the Council and the Commission working – usually – closely with each other. So, in respect of trade negotiations which the Community conducts with non-member states, with groups of states, and in international forums (notably GATT), the normal pattern is as follows: on the basis of proposals that are presented to it by the Commission, the Council agrees a negotiating mandate; on the basis of this mandate, and under the watchful eye of, and in consultation with, the Article 113 Committee – which is made up of national officials and which meets at different levels – the Commision negotiates on behalf of all twelve Community states; the Commission can initial a negotiated agreement but the final decision as to whether to sign is up to the Council.

The powers of, and relations between, the Community's institutions in connection with the commercial policy are such that tensions of different sorts are by no means uncommon:

● The power balance between the Council and the Commission can be very delicate, with the Council wanting to ensure that the Commission remains under its control, and the Commission wanting and needing enough manoeuvrability to enable it to be an effective negotiator.

● Difficulties can arise within the Commission when DGs other than DGI (External Relations) believe they have an interest in particular external trade policies and agreements. Thus, in June 1990, the Farm Commissioner – Raymond MacSharry – stressing that he was determined to defend the Community position on farm reform in the GATT Uruguay Round of multilateral trade liberalisation talks, felt obliged to state publicly that he, not the Trade Commissioner – Frans Andriessen – was 'in charge of agricultural negotiations'.

● Most MEPs are dissatisfied that the Parliament has no automatic right to be consulted, let alone to insist that its views be considered, in connection with Article 113 agreements. In practice, the EP is notified about agreements, and the Commission, and to a lesser extent the Council, do discuss external trade matters with the EP – primarily in the forum of the Parliament's External Economic Relations Committee – but it is clear that Parliament's influence is very limited. At a minimum most MEPs would like to see the assent procedure powers that the EP enjoys in relation to Association Agreements under Article 238 of the EEC Treaty (as amended by the SEA) extended to cover all external agreements.

External *political* relations – in the form of European Political Co-operation (EPC) – are centred on a network of co-operative and consultative activities between the member states. As Table 10.1 shows, regular rounds of meetings at political and official levels are a central part of the EPC process: during a six month Council Presidency EPC business will be discussed at a European Council meeting, perhaps three or four meetings of Foreign Ministers, about six of political directors, and upwards of a hundred working group meetings. The aim of all this, and other EPC activity, is to try and ensure maximum information flow and co-operative effort between the member states, and, where possible, to enable the Foreign Ministers to issue joint Community statements on important foreign policy issues.

Because EPC developed outside of the framework of the Treaties, because of the politically sensitive nature of much of its subject material, and because it does not directly require Community legislation, EPC policy and decision-making processes have rather bypassed the usual Community institutions and processes and have been based primarily on intergovernmental, and in particular inter-Foreign Ministry, arrangements. The SEA did a little, but not much, to bring EPC more into the Community's framework, notably by according a formal role to the Commission and the EP: in language that could hardly have been vaguer, the Commission was to be 'fully associated' and the EP was to be 'closely associated' with EPC. The

TABLE 10.1

The decision-making structure of European Political Co-operation

European Council

- Composed of the twelve Heads of Government, the twelve Foreign Ministers, and the President and one Vice President of the Commission.
- Meets at least twice per year.
- Final communiqués usually contain statements on EPC matters; makes some contribution to setting out the guidelines of EPC.

Council of Ministers

- Composed of the twelve Foreign Ministers and a member of the Commission.
- Convenes at least twice during each Presidency, with special meetings called as and when they are necessary; in addition to EPC meetings Foreign Ministers also meet in other forums – in the General Affairs Council (where urgent EPC matters may be added to an agenda), at European Councils, at twice-yearly informal weekend gatherings.
- Functions as the main decision-making body of EPC in that it makes, or formalises, most final decisions.

Political Committee (**POCO**)

- Composed of the political directors and a senior Commission civil servant.
- Meets at least once each month, and in total about twenty times per year.
- Serves as the lynchpin of EPC – by preparing meetings of ministers, by drafting common declarations, and by directing the working groups.

Working groups

- Composed of senior diplomats – who are often department heads – and a Commission representative.
- Usually around twenty or so groups in existence, with each group meeting at least once during each Presidency, and with a total of around 120 meetings held each year.
- Some working groups deal with regions, e.g. the Middle East, Central and South America, Africa; some deal with themes, e.g. the CSCE, disarmament, human rights; and some deal with common operational matters, e.g. visas, EC representation in third countries, the EPC telecommunications system.
- Serve as the workhorses of the EPC.
- Include a special group – the correspondents group, the members of which serve as the co-ordinators of EPC inside Foreign Ministries and who meet at least one a month.

Other Mechanisms

- *The European Parliament* has monthly question time, special debates, committee meetings with the Council Presidency.
- The *Secretariat*, established in 1987, based in Brussels, is an instrument of the Presidency; membership rotates and is composed of diplomats from the member states.
- National *embassies, delegations*, and *missions* in the member states, in third countries, and attached to international organisations, promote co-operation.
- The *COREU Network* is a special telex link open 24 hours a day.

Source: Adapted from G. de Bassompierre, *Changing the Guard in Brussels* (Praeger, 1988).

SEA also established a small, permanent EPC Secretariat based in the Council of Ministers building in Brussels.

As part of its policy on *development co-operation* the Community has concluded numerous agreements with most of the countries of the Third World. As was shown in Chapter 9, the Lomé Convention is the most important of these agreements. The Convention has its own institutional structure which is made up of three principal bodies. The first is the ACP-EEC Council of Ministers, which is composed of the members of the Council of Ministers of the Community, a member of the Commission, and a member of the government of each ACP country. The Council meets at least once a year and takes the major political and policy decisions that are necessary during the life of a Convention. The second body is the Committee of Ambassadors, which is composed of a representative of each Community state, a representative of the Commission, and a representative of each ACP state. The Committee meets at least twice a year and is charged with assisting and advising the Council of Ministers, monitoring implementation of the Convention and progress towards achieving its objectives, and generally supervising and co-ordinating the work of the many committees and subsidiary bodies that exist under the general umbrella of the Convention. Finally, there is the Joint Assembly, which is made up of equal numbers of MEPs and ACP members of parliament or national representatives. It meets twice a year and acts as a general advisory and deliberating body.

Factors Determining Community Policy Processes

A number of factors can be identified as being especially important in determining the particular mix of actors and channels in Community policy-making and decision-making processes. (Factors applying to budgetary decision-making are not included in the following analysis as there is a separate chapter on the budget.)

The Proposed Status of the Matter Under Consideration

As a general rule, procedures tend to be more fixed when Community law is envisaged than when it is not. They are fixed by such factors as the Treaties (for example the requirement that a Commission proposal is needed), Court interpretations (the obligation on the Council to wait for the EP's Opinion), and conventions (the understanding that when a member state has genuine difficulties with a proposal the matter will not be rushed and an effort will be made to reach a compromise even when majority voting is permissible).

As for different types of Community law, Commission legislation is usually subject to much less review and discussion than Council legislation. The reason for this is that Commission legislation is normally of an administrative kind, more technical than political. Much of it, indeed, consists of updates, precisions, or amendments to already existing legislation – usually in the sphere of external trade or the CAP. As a result, Commission legislation, prior to being introduced, is often only fully discussed by appropriate officials in the Commission, and perhaps by national officials in a management or regulatory committee. Council legislation, on the other hand, because of its normally broader scope, usually becomes the subject of representations and pressures from many interests, is assessed by the EP and the ESC, and is scrutinised in detail in national capitals and in several Council forums in Brussels.

Where policy activity does not involve law making, considerable discretion is available to key decision-makers, especially governments, as to what policy processes will be used and who will be permitted to participate. A common procedure when states wish the Community to do something, but do not wish for it necessarily to involve making new law, (which may be because there is no agreement on what the law should be or because, as with foreign policy pronouncements, law is inappropriate), is to issue Council resolutions, declarations, or agreements. These can be as vague or as precise as the Council wishes them to be, and often they can have a very useful policy impact, even if it is just to keep dialogue going. But, because they are not legal instruments, they are not normally as subject as most Council legislation to examination and challenge by other Community institutions and actors.

The Degree of Generality or Specificity of the Policy Issue

At the generality end of the scale, Community policy-making may consist of little more than exchanges of ideas between interested parties to see whether there is common ground for policy co-ordination, for the setting of priorities, or for possible legislation. Such exchanges and discussions take place at many different levels on an almost continuous basis, but the most important, in the sense that their initiatives are the ones most likely to be followed up, are those which involve *les grands messieurs* of the Commission and the member states.

Far removed from *grands tours d'horizon* by *les grands messieurs* is the daily grind of preparing and drafting the mass of highly detailed and technical regulations that make up the great bulk of the Community's legislative output. Senior Community figures, especially ministers, are not normally directly involved in the processes which lead to such legislation. There may be a requirement that they give the legislation their formal approval, but it is Commission officials, aided in appropriate cases by national officials, who do the basic work.

The Newness, Importance, Controversiality or Political Sensitivity of the Issue in Question

The more these characteristics apply, and the perception of the extent to which they do may vary – what may be a technical question for one may be politically charged for another – the more complex policy processes are likely to be. If, for example, it seems likely that a proposal for a Council directive on some aspect of animal welfare will cause significant difficulties for farmers, it is probable that the accompanying decision-making process will display all or most of the following features: particularly extensive pre-proposal consultations by the Commission; the raising of voices from many sectional and promotional interest groups; very careful examination of the proposal by the EP and the ESC; long and exhaustive negotiations in the Council; considerable activity and manoeuvring on the fringes of formal meetings, and in between the meetings; and, overall, much delay and many alterations *en route* to the (possible) eventual adoption of the proposal.

The Balance of Policy Responsibilities between Community and National Levels

Where there has been a significant transfer of responsibilities to the EC – agriculture and commercial policy are the most obvious examples – Community level processes are naturally very important. In such policy spheres, Community institutions – and the Commission in particular – have many tasks to perform: monitoring developments, making adjustments, ensuring existing policies and programmes are replaced when necessary, and so on. On the other hand, where the Community's policy role is at best supplementary to that of the states – education policy and transport policy are examples – most significant policy and decision-making activity continues to be channelled through the customary national procedures and policy activity at Community level may be very limited in scope.

Circumstances and the Perceptions of Circumstances

This is seemingly rather vague, but it refers to the crucially important fact that policy development and decision-making processes in the Community are closely related to prevailing political and economic circumstances, to the perceptions by key actors – especially states – of their needs in the circumstances, and to perceptions of the potential of the Community to act as a problem solving organisation in regard to the circumstances. Do the advantages of acting at Community level, as opposed to national levels, and of acting in the Community in a particular way as opposed to another way, outweigh the disadvantages?

It is best to explain this point about circumstances with a specific example. Steel will be taken because it shows in a particularly clear manner how changing circumstances may bring about related changes in Community processes.

As was explained in Chapter 2, the Treaty of Paris gave considerable powers to the High Authority (later Commission). Until the mid-1970s these powers were used primarily to liberalise the market, with the High Authority/Commission expending much of its time and energy attempting to ensure that internal barriers were removed and cartels were eliminated. From 1974, however, market conditions began to deteriorate as a result of falling internal and external demand, reduced profit margins, and cost increases. This led the Commission to look more towards its hitherto largely neglected interventionist powers. Initially a largely voluntarist path was preferred, but when this proved to be ineffective a stronger approach was taken. By the end of 1980 an assortment of highly *dirigiste* policy instruments, some of which were mandatory, were in place. These included common external positions in the form of price agreements and export restraint agreements, strict controls on national subsidies, restrictions on the investment decisions of individual firms, and compulsory quotas (which became possible following the declaration by the Council of a 'manifest crisis' in October 1980).

The emphasis of Community steel policy thus switched between 1974–80, from promoting the freedom and efficiency of the market, to managing the market. This switch had very important implications for steel policy and decision-making processes. Four of these implications are particularly worth noting. First, there was now more policy responsibility and activity at Community level than previously. As a result of this, the overall policy picture as regards steel became a complicated mixture of Community and national processes, with not all of them pulling in the same direction. Second, the assumption by the Community of new and important policy powers, many of which had direct distributional consequences, inevitably created tensions in the Council. At the same time, it also resulted in the Council, as a collective body, taking greater care to ensure that on key decisions the Commission acted under its direction. (Although this did not stop governments from using the Commission as a useful device for deflecting the blame for necessary, but unpopular, decisions away from themselves.) Third, the Commission, notwithstanding its obligation to work within a Council-approved framework, extended its roles and functions in several important respects: as an initiator and proposer of policy; as a mediator amongst national and corporate interests (by, for example, putting together complicated production quota packages for the different types of steel product); as the Community's external negotiator (the Treaty of Paris did not establish a customs union and it was not until the late 1970s that the states began to adopt common external positions); and as a decision-maker (the Commission assumed more powers to act directly – for example, on investment aids subsidies). Fourth, non-institutional and non-governmental interests inevitably sought to become much more involved in decision-making as the Community developed policies with a very obvious and very direct impact on output, prices, profits, and employment. A striking illustration of this was the way in which EUROFER – the European Confederation of Iron and Steel Industries, which represents about 60 per cent of Community steel capacity – negotiated with the Commission on production quotas.

The Making of Community Legislation

Having established that there are considerable variations in Community policy and decision-making processes, it is necessary now to look at common, shared, and recurring features. For, except in the narrowest of senses, not every policy is formulated nor every decision taken, in a manner that is unique to it alone.

This is no more clearly seen than in relation to the making of Community legislation. Most legislation takes one of three 'set routes':

1. Administrative/management/regulatory/implementing legislation is issued mainly in the form of Commission regulations and decisions. The basic work on this type of legislation is undertaken by officials in the relevant Directorate General. Commissioners themselves only discuss such legislation when it is not straightforward or someone requests it.

   National officials usually have the opportunity to voice their comments in a committee, but whether they have the power to stop legislation to which they object depends on which committee procedure applies. As was explained in Chapter 3, the Commission is in a much stronger position when it works through advisory committees than it is when it works through management, and even more so regulatory, committees.

   When this type of legislation is issued as Council legislation, it naturally results in national officials playing a more active role, and formal ministerial approval is required.

2. Much of the legislation that is enacted in connection with the Community's external economic policies is based on agreements with third countries and is, therefore, subject to special decision-making procedures. An indication of some of these procedures was given above. Amongst the distinctive features are: the Commission usually acts as the Community's main negotiator in economic negotiations with third countries; the Council seeks to control and monitor what the Commission does during negotiations; the EP does not normally exercise much influence – except, following provisions included in the Single European Act, with regard to agreements establishing special relations negotiated under Article 238 of the EEC Treaty; most legislation produced as a result of negotiations,

including virtually all legislation which is intended to establish the principles of a legal framework, is enacted in the form of Council regulations and decisions and therefore requires formal ministerial approval.

3. Most of what remains consists of Council legislation that is deemed to require examination via a full legislative process. There are no hard and fast rules for deciding when proposals fall into this category, but, in general, they are those that are thought to be significant or concerned with establishing principles. The broader in scope they are, the more likely they are to be in the form of directives.

Because of its obvious importance, this full legislative process needs to be examined here. However, since much of the detail of how the Community institutions exercise their particular responsibilities has already been set out in Part II, a comprehensive account is not attempted in what follows. Attention is restricted to highlighting the principal features of each legislative stage.

Since the Single European Act came into force in 1987 there have been two different legislative processes: the consultation, or single reading, procedure, and the co-operation, or two readings, procedure. As can be seen from Table 5.1 both procedures are much used.

The Consultation Procedure

Initiation. The starting point of a legislative proposal is when somebody somewhere suggests that the Community should act on a matter. Most likely this will be the Commission or the Council: the Commission because it is the only body with the authority formally to table a legislative proposal, and because, too, of its special expertise in, and responsibility for, Community affairs; the Council because of its political weight, its position as the natural conduit for national claims and interests, and its unique legal power, under Article 152 EEC, to request the Commission 'to undertake any studies the Council considers desirable for the attainment of the common objectives, and to submit to it any appropriate proposals'. (A frequent complaint of the Commission is that requests made to it by the Council for policy proposals are rarely accompanied by promises of resources to finance whatever measures may be proposed.)

Beyond the Commission and the Council there are many other possible sources of Community legislation, but little progress can be made unless the Commission decides to take the issue up and draft proposals. Many circumstances may result in it deciding to do so, but often it is very difficult, in looking at specific proposals, to discover just why it decided to act and to identify precisely from where the initiative originated. For example, a Commission proposal that may seem to be a response to a Council request may, on inspection, be traced back beyond the Council to a national pressure group influencing a minister, who then gradually and informally introduced the issue into the Council as an option to be considered. Similarly, a Commission proposal may seem to be a response to an EP own initiative report or to representations from European-wide interests, but in fact the Commission may itself have dropped hints to the EP or to interests that they should look at the matter, (thus reinforcing the Commission's own position *vis-à-vis* the Council).

Preparation of a Text. Once it has been decided to produce a proposal (a decision that is usually taken at a senior level within the most relevant Directorate General), a text is prepared. The standard way in which this is done is as follows: officials in the appropriate DG write an initial draft; the draft is passed upwards through superiors; as it is passed upwards the draft is discussed with all DGs and specialised Commission services which have an interest; when all directly involved Commission interests have given their approval, the draft is sent to the *cabinet* of the Commissioner responsible for the subject; the *cabinet* may re-work the draft before submitting it to the Commissioner for his approval; when the Commissioner is satisfied, he asks the Secretariat General to submit the draft to the College of Commissioners; the draft is scrutinised, and possibly amended, by the *chefs des cabinets* at their weekly meeting; if the draft is judged to be uncontroversial the Commissioners may adopt it by written procedure; if it is controversial the Commissioners may, after debate, accept it, reject it, amend it, or refer it back to the relevant DG for further consideration.

In preparing a text officials usually find themselves the focus of attention from many directions. Knowing that the Commission's thinking is probably at its most flexible at this preliminary stage, and knowing, too, that once a proposal is formalised it is more difficult to change, interested parties use whatever means they can to press their views. Four factors most affect the extent to which the Commission is prepared to listen to outside interests at this pre-proposal stage. First, what contacts and channels have already been regularised in the sector and what ways of proceeding have proved to be effective in the past? Second, what political considerations arise and how important is it to incorporate different sectional and national views from the outset? Third, what degree of technical knowledge and outside expertise is called for? Fourth, how do the relevant Commission officials prefer to work?

Assuming, as it is normally reasonable to do, Commission receptivity, there are several ways in which 'external' views may be brought to the attention of those drafting a proposal. The Commission itself may request a report, perhaps from a university or a research institute. Interest groups may submit briefing documents. Professional lobbyists, politicians, and officials from the Permanent Representations may press preferences in informal meetings. EP committees and ESC sections may be sounded out. And use may be made of the extensive advisory committee system that clusters around the Commission and which was described in Chapter 3.

There is, therefore, no standard consultative pattern or procedure. An important consequence of this is that governmental involvement in the preparation of Commission texts varies considerably. Indeed, not only is there a variation in involvement, but there is a variation in knowledge of Commission intentions. Sometimes, governments are fully aware of Commission thinking, because national officials have been formally consulted in committees of experts. Sometimes, sectional interests represented on consultative committees will let their governments know what is going on. Sometimes, governments will be abreast of developments as a result of having tapped sources within the Commission, most probably through officials in their Permanent Representations. But sometimes, governments are not aware of proposals until they are published.

The time that elapses between the decision to initiate a proposal and the publication by the Commission of its text naturally depends on a number of factors: (1) is there any urgency? (2) how keen is the Commission to press ahead? (3) how widespread are the consultations? (4) does the Commission want the prior support of all key actors? (5) is there a consensus within the Commission itself? Not surprisingly periods of over a year are common.

The Opinions of the European Parliament and the Economic and Social Committee. On publication, the Commission's text is submitted to the Council of Ministers, which in turn refers it to the EP and, where appropriate, to the ESC, for their Opinions.

The EP is by far the more influential of the two bodies. Though it does not have the full legislative powers of national parliaments it has enough weaponry in its arsenal to ensure that its views are at least taken into consideration, particularly by the Commission. Its representational claims are one source of its influence. The quality of its arguments and its suggestions are another. And it has the power of delay, by virtue of the requirement that Parliament's Opinion must be known before the proposal can be formally adopted by the Council.

As was shown in Chapter 5, most of the detailed work undertaken by the EP on proposed legislation is handled by its specialised committees and, to a lesser extent, by its political groups. Both the committees and the groups advise MEPs how to vote in plenary.

The usual way in which plenaries act to bring influence to bear is to vote on amendments to the Commission's proposal, but not to vote on the draft legislative resolution – which constitutes the EP's Opinion – until the Commission states, as it is obliged to do, whether or not it will change its text to incorporate the amendments that have been approved by the EP. If the amendments are accepted by the Commission a favourable Opinion is issued, and the amended text becomes the text that the Council considers. If all or some of the amendments are not accepted, the EP can attempt to exert pressure by not issuing an Opinion and referring the proposal back to the committee responsible. A reference back can also be made if the whole proposal is judged to be unacceptable. Witholding of an Opinion does not, it should be emphasised, give the EP the power of veto, because it is legally obliged to issue Opinions and the Court, in several judgements, has referred to the duty of loyal co-operation between the Community institutions. What the witholding of Opinions does do, however, is to give the EP the often useful bargaining and pressurising tool of the power of delay.

For the reasons which were outlined in Chapter 5, and which are considered further below in the discussion on the co-operation procedure, it is difficult to estimate with any precision the impact the EP has on Community legislation. In general terms, however, it can be said that the record in the context of the consultation procedure is mixed:

● On the 'positive' side the Commission is normally sympathetic to the EP's views and accepts about three-quarters of its amendments. The Council is less sympathetic and accepts considerably less than half of the amendments, but that still means that many EP amendments, on many different policy matters, find their way into the final legislative texts.

● On the 'negative' side there are three main points to be made. First, there is not much the EP can do if the Council rejects its Opinion. The best it can normally hope for is a conciliation meeting with the Council (which is only available for legislation with significant financial implications), but such meetings do not usually achieve much – mainly because the Council has no wish to re-open questions which may put at risk its own, often exhaustively negotiated, agreements. Second, on occasions the Council takes a decision 'in principle' or 'subject to Parliament's Opinion', before the Opinion has even been delivered. Third, it is quite possible for the text of proposals to be changed after the EP has issued its Opinion. There is some safeguard against the potential implications of this insofar as the Court of Justice has indicated that the Council should refer a legislative proposal back to the EP if it (the Council) substantially amends the proposal after the EP has issued its Opinion. In practice, however, the question of what constitutes a substantial amendment is open to interpretation, and references back do not always occur.

The ESC is, generally, not so well placed as the EP to examine legislative proposals. As was explained in Chapter 8, a major reason for this is that its formal powers are not as great: while it must be consulted on draft legislation in some policy spheres, consultation is optional in others. Furthermore, when it is consulted, the Council or the Commission may lay down a very tight timetable, can go ahead if no Opinion is issued by a specified date, and cannot be frustrated by delays if the ESC wants changes to the text. Other sources of weakness include the part-time capacity of its members, the personal rather than representational nature of much of its membership, and the perception by many interests that advisory committees and direct forms of lobbying are more effective channels of influence.

As a result of these weaknesses the ESC's influence over Community legislation is considerably less than that of the EP. Nonetheless, some note is taken of its Opinion, though exactly how much is impossible to say, for even when ESC views do appear to have been taken into account, closer inspection often reveals that the really decisive influence has probably come from elsewhere. For example, a Council directive concerned with the implementation of the principle of equal treatment for men and women in occupational social security schemes, which was listed in the 1986 ESC Annual Report as being influenced 'to a large extent' by an ESC Opinion, was also the subject of strong representations by sectional interests and member governments. In the 1987 Annual Report, a similar claim was made for a Council directive on the legal protection of original topographies of semi-conductor products, but on this very same proposal the EP made much the same claim and suggested that the Council had accepted eight of the twelve amendments it had adopted.

Decision-making in the Council. As has just been noted the Council does not necessarily wait on the EP or the ESC before proceeding with a proposal. Indeed, governments may begin preparing their positions for the Council, and informal discussions and deliberations may even take place within the Council itself, before the formal referral from the Commission.

The standard procedure in the Council is for the proposal to be referred initially to a working party of national representatives for detailed examination. The representatives have two principal tasks: on the one hand, to ensure that the interests of their country are safeguarded; on the other, to try to reach an agreement on a text. Inevitably these two responsibilities do not always coincide, with the consequence that working party deliberations can be highly protracted. Progress depends on many factors: the controversiality of the proposal; the extent to which it benefits or damages states differentially; the number of countries, especially large countries, pressing for progress; the enthusiasm and competence of the Presidency; the tactical skills of the national representatives and their capacity to trade disputed points (both of which are dependent on personal abilities and the sort of briefs laid down for representatives by their governments); and the flexibility of the Commission in agreeing to change its text.

Once a working party has gone as far as it can with a proposal – which can mean reaching a general agreement, agreeing on most points but with reservations entered by some countries on particular points, or very little agreement at all on the main issues – reference is made upwards to COREPER or, in the case of agriculture, to the Special Committee on Agriculture. At this level, the Permanent Representatives (in COREPER II), their deputies (in COREPER I), or senior agriculture officials (in the SCA) concern themselves not so much with the technical details of a proposal as with its policy and political implications. So far as is possible differences left over from the working party are sorted out. Where this cannot be done, bases for possible agreement may be identified, and the proposal is then either referred back to the working party for further detailed consideration, or forwarded to the ministers for political resolution.

All proposals must be formally approved by the ministers. Those that have been agreed at a lower level of the Council machinery are placed on the ministers' agenda as 'A' points and are normally quickly ratified. Where, however, outstanding problems and differences have to be considered a number of things can happen. One is that the political authority that ministers carry, and the preparatory work undertaken by officials prior to ministerial meetings, may clear the way for an agreed settlement: perhaps reached quickly over lunch, perhaps hammered out in long and frequently adjourned Council sessions. A second, and increasingly utilised, possibility is that a vote may be taken. This does not mean that the traditional preference for proceeding by consensus no longer applies, but it does mean that it is not quite the obstacle it formerly was. A third possibility is that no agreement can be reached, a vote is not possible under the Treaties or is not judged to be appropriate, or if a vote is judged to be possible and appropriate no qualified majority exists. This may lead to the proposal being referred back down the Council machinery, being referred back to the Commission accompanied with a request for changes to the existing text, or being referred to a future meeting in the hope that shifts will take place in the meantime and the basis of a solution will be found.

As is shown in Figure 10.1, under the consultation procedure the decision-making process at Community level ends with the Council's adoption of a text.

The Co-operation Procedure

As was seen in Table 5.1 a substantial proportion of Community legislation is now made via the co-operation procedure, even though the procedure applies to only ten articles of the EEC Treaty. The main reason for the heavy use of the procedure is that under Article 100A of the EEC Treaty (which was incorporated by the SEA) one of the ten articles is Article 8A (which was also incorporated by the SEA). Article 8A states that the 'Community shall adopt measures with the aim of progressively establishing the internal market over a period expiring on 31 December 1992'. In other words, most (though not quite all) of the priority 1992 programme – the programme which is concerned with the harmonisation of laws, legislation and administrative action to bring about the establishment and functioning of the internal market – is subject to the co-operation procedure.

The provisions of the co-operation procedure are set out in Article 7 of the SEA and are incorporated into a new Article 149 of the EEC Treaty. As can be seen from Figure 10.1 the route taken by legislative proposals under the co-operation procedure is much more complex than the route taken under the consultation procedure. The main stages of the co-operation procedure are as follows:

EP First Reading. After the Commission has published its proposal the EP examines the text and issues an Opinion. The process by which the examination is conducted is broadly similar to the process of examination under the consultation procedure.

Council First Reading. After obtaining the EP's Opinion the Council does not, as in the consultation procedure, take a final decision on the proposal, but rather adopts, by a qualified majority vote if need be, what is known as its common position. As is the practice on single reading proposals, unanimity is required for any amendments with which the Commission does not agree. (The Commission, of course, can alter its text at any time, and is likely to have done so after the EP's first reading in order to incorporate at least some EP amendments.)

EP Second Reading. The common position is communicated to the EP for what becomes its second reading of the Commission's proposal. The Council must inform Parliament of the reasons which led it to

*The Consultation (Single   The Co-operation (Two
Reading) Procedure   Reading) Procedure*

FIGURE 10.1
Main stages in the making of Council legislation

adopt the common position in its particular form. The EP has three months to take one of four courses of action:

1. It can approve the common position.
2. It can reject the common position by an absolute majority of all members.
3. It can amend the common position by an absolute majority of all members.
4. It can choose, or fail, to act in none of the three ways just listed.

Council Second Reading. What the Council does at its second reading depends on what has happened at the EP second reading. Taking, in turn, the four options available to the EP that have just been outlined:

1. In the event of EP approval of the common position, the Council may adopt the common position as a Community legislative act.
2. In the event of EP rejection of the common position by an absolute majority the Council can adopt the proposal only by acting unanimously within three months.
3. In the event of EP amendment of the common position by an absolute majority the Commission must decide within one month whether or not it wishes to incorporate the amendments into the version of the text that is referred back to the Council. If they are incorporated the Council can approve them by a qualified majority; if they are not incorporated the Council can only approve them by acting unanimously. Whether they are incorporated or not, all EP amendments not accepted by the Commission must be forwarded to the Council. If the Council does nothing within three months of receiving the re-examined text from the Commission, the proposal is deemed not to have been adopted.
4. In the event of the EP not acting in any of the three above ways the Council may adopt the proposal in accordance with the common position.

The co-operation procedure has naturally had several implications, in terms of both functioning and influence, for the institutions which have to operate it. The main implications are these:

●   The Commission, the Council, and the EP are working much more closely with one another on legislative matters. This is seen in the development of new channels of communication and negotiation between the three institutions, the increased willingness of the three to keep each other informed about the progress of proposals in the individual institutions, and in the practice which began in 1988 by which the Commission attempts to agree its annual legislative programme and timetable with the EP.

●   When presenting legislative proposals the Commission has to ensure that it is using the correct legal base, for this determines whether the co-operation procedure applies at all. A proposal which could, for example, give rise to a possible dispute would be an internal market measure having environmental aspects: if the legal base chosen by the Commission is Article 100A (measures necessary for establishing the internal market) the co-operation procedure applies; if the legal base is Article 130S (action by the Community relating to the environment) the procedure does not apply. Because it wishes to see its proposals adopted, preferably without being amended too much, the Commission's own order of procedural preference is almost invariably: (1) consultation procedure with provision for majority voting; (2) co-operation procedure; (3) consultation procedure with unanimous voting. Knowing, however, that many subjects where the legal base is open to possible dispute are politically sensitive, knowing that the Legal Services Departments of the Council and the EP will thoroughly examine each legal base, and knowing too that its decisions on the legal base are subject to challenge in the Court of Justice, the Commission necessarily acts with great care. The taking of care does, not, however always satisfy everyone: the Council, the EP, and individual governments have all at times been aggrieved, there have been references to the Court, and the Council has changed some legal bases so as to avoid the co-operation procedure.

●   The Commission has an even more difficult task than it has under the consultation procedure in exercising its judgement as to whether, and if so at what stage, it should amend its text so as to get proposals through in a reasonably acceptable form. At the second reading stage, in particular, a delicate balance may have to be struck: between, on the one hand, being sufficiently sympathetic to EP amendments so as not to upset MEPs too much, and, on the other hand, being aware that a revised text might break-up a majority attained in the Council at first reading.

● Decision-making in the Council has been speeded up. This is partly accounted for by the provisions for Council qualified majority voting, partly by the timetable limitations which come into effect after the Council has agreed its common position, and partly by the fact that so much of the legislation that is subject to the co-operation procedure is part of the priority 1992 programme. Decisions on particular proposals can still be delayed by the Council's preference – whatever the legal position – for decision-making by consensus, but looking at the picture as a whole, decision-making in policy areas now subject to the co-operation procedure is much quicker than it was before the procedure applied. The extent of the speeding up varies between policy areas, but drops from around 36–48 months to 12–15 months are common.

● The Council has the problem of now having to be unanimous not just at one legislative stage but at two, if it wishes to avoid incorporating Commission accepted EP amendments into the final text. Moreover, since amendments at the EP second reading require the support of an absolute majority of MEPs and are therefore hardly the reflection of minority interests, the EP – theoretically at least – has a reasonable chance of finding the only ally it needs when the Council holds its second reading. To try and get round this problem one thing the Council is now doing at its first reading, on proposals where the EP appears likely to cause 'difficulties' at its second reading, is to take time to see if unanimity can be achieved: if it can – and that may be possible only after considerable horse-trading and compromising – the EP is very unlikely to be able to divide the Council and prevent unanimity at the second reading.

● The EP has had to adjust its working methods in several ways: (1) MEPs, and especially *rapporteurs* and committee chairman, have had to develop a fuller grasp of the technical implications of Commission proposals. (2) The texts embodying Parliament's Opinions have had to become more substantial and detailed documents. (3) There is pressure, especially on the group whips, to muster absolute majorities at second readings. (When such majorities are clearly not going to be achieved there are sometimes references back to committees, and there have been instances of an absolute majority having been declared on a show of hands when there have been less than 260 in the

Chamber – in such instances there has been little opposition to the proposal in question, or opponents have been too slow to call for a roll-call vote.) (4) As noted in previous paragraphs, there is much more liaising and negotiating to be done with the Commission and the Council.

● Regarding the distribution of power between the institutions, the EP is the most obvious beneficiary of the co-operation procedure, for it is placed in a much more advantageous position than it is under the consultation procedure to pressurise the Commission and the Council to accept its views. Whilst the EP is still, under the co-operation procedure, some way short of being a co-decision maker with the Council, it can do, and is doing, various things to ensure its potential influence is maximised: committees are preparing detailed reports on Commission texts; the increased channels of communication the EP now has with the Commission and the Council are being exploited; and texts are being amended by absolute majority vote at second reading whenever that seems to be necessary and proves to be politically possible. Some indication of the influence the EP is exercising under the co-operation procedure is seen in the following:

1. About 40 per cent of common positions are being approved by the EP at its second reading. An important reason for this in some ways surprisingly high figure, is that the Council is often willing to incorporate EP amendments into the common position so as to appease MEPs and/or so as to secure quick approval for proposals.

2. There have been few serious attempts to reject common positions, and in the first three and a half years of the co-operation procedure (that is to say, up to the end of 1990) only one common position was rejected. Four main factors account for this reluctance on the part of the Parliament to vote for rejections: (a) Although the EP usually wishes to amend proposals it is rarely opposed to them in principle and so is not normally desirous of seeing them stopped altogether. (b) On the few occasions when rejection of the common position has seemed possible, the Commission has normally amended its proposal to reach an accommodation with the EP (as happened on a directive dealing with emissions from small motor vehicles where the EP was pressing for the mandatory fitting of catalytic converters). (c) The Council has usually incorporated a

reasonable proportion of EP amendments into its common position on proposals that the EP has demonstrated it feels strongly about. (d) As part of the long-standing campaign to be given more powers, the EP prefers to project itself in a positive rather than a negative manner, to be seen to be constructive rather than destructive.

Potentially, of course, rejection of the common position may well spell the end for a proposal because the Council can then only approve it by acting unanimously – and unanimity is always likely to be difficult to achieve if the issue is so contentious as to stir an absolute majority of MEPs to reject it completely. Such indeed was the case in 1988 with the very first common position to be rejected. Events unfolded in the following way: the Commission proposed a directive – the so-called 'benzene directive' – on the protection of workers from the risks related to exposure to benzene at work; at its first reading the EP amended and 'stiffened' the proposal; at the Council's first reading the Commission's text, now incorporating EP amendments, was supported by only two member states, so the Commission – after the Commissioner himself had appeared before the responsible parliamentary committee to try and seek a compromise – watered down its proposal in order to attain majority Council support; at the EP's second reading amendments were approved by an absolute majority which restored restrictions on exposure to benzene which had been deleted by the Council; the Commission informed the EP that it was unable to incorporate the second reading amendments into its text because it felt they would fail to find qualified majority support in the Council, and, as a consequence, the EP took the view that the proposal had become too weak and rejected the common position by 274 votes to 47 with 3 abstentions; the Council at its second reading was unable to find the unanimity that was necessary to overrule the EP and the proposal fell; subsequently, in 1989, the Commission brought forward further proposals as part of another directive.

3. As has been noted previously (see Chapter 5), figures on the incorporation of EP amendments into legislative texts have to be interpreted cautiously: some amendments are intended for bargaining purposes rather than with the realistic hope of being incorporated; the Commission or the Council sometimes let it

be known that amendments which are not being incorporated will appear as part of a future legislative proposal; and crude figures do not indicate the relative importance of amendments. Bearing these interpretative difficulties in mind, the evidence does, nonetheless, appear to indicate some considerable measure of EP success. Taking the 112 proposals that were adopted up to the end of 1989 under the co-operation procedure, 66 per cent of the amendments requested by the EP at first reading were accepted by the Commission and 48 per cent by the Council; at second reading – when the number of proposals had effectively been reduced to 68 because of the acceptance of 44 common positions – 49 per cent of EP amendments were accepted by the Commission and 14 per cent by the Council.

Community Legislation After Adoption

What happens to proposals after they are adopted as Community legislation, what use is made of them, and how they are applied, varies considerably. Many of these variations are considered on an individual basis in other chapters – notably in Chapters 3, 6, and 13 – but it will be useful to briefly pull the more important variations together here so as to give an indication of the overall picture. The more significant of the variations are as follows:

● Whereas regulations and most decisions do not require any measures to be taken at national level before they apply, directives do not assume legislative force until after they have been incorporated into national law by the appropriate national authorities. The member states themselves determine which are the appropriate national authorities in their case, and by what process the incorporation is to be made. As a result the mechanisms by which directives are incorporated at national level varies between member states according to both differing national legislative procedures and differing perceptions of how important particular directives are judged to be. The general pattern, however, is for incorporation to be achieved either by attaching appropriate administrative measures to existing primary or secondary legislation, introducing new secondary legislation, or adding new clauses to already planned primary legislation. States are given anything from a few months to a few years to effect the incorporation – the final date being specified in the directives – and are obliged to notify the Commission of the national legislation, regulations, or administrative provisions they have adopted to give formal effect to each directive.

● Much Council legislation needs to be supplemented by implementing legislation so as to fit it to particular circumstances and keep it up to date. Indeed, on a quantitative basis, the vast bulk of Community legislation is implementing legislation – issued usually in the form of Commission regulations.

● Some Council legislation needs to be followed up not just with implementing legislation, but with further 'policy' Council legislation. This is most obviously the case in respect of 'framework' legislation, which is legislation that lays down general principles for an area of activity and basic rules which states have to follow, but which needs usually to be complemented by more narrowly focused legislation that covers in a reasonably detailed manner policies/issues/initiatives that fall within the remit of the framework. An example of framework legislation is the *Council Directive of 12 June 1989 on the introduction of measures to encourage improvements in the safety and health of workers at work* (89/391/EEC). That this legislation was intended to be a base and a focus for further legislation is seen in Article 16 of the Directive which states: 'The Council acting on a proposal from the Commission, based on 118a of the Treaty, shall adopt individual Directives, *inter alia*, in the areas listed in the Annex'.

● Legislation which also requires further measures, but measures which are very different in character to those that have just been outlined, is the 'new approach' legislation that constitutes an important part of the internal market programme. Under the 'new approach', the Community does not try to harmonise all the specifications and technical standards of marketed goods, as it formerly did, but confines itself to producing relatively short texts which lay down 'essential requirements' – in particular, requirements relating to health and safety matters, and consumer and environmental protection. As long as member states conform to the 'essential requirements' they can have their own national standards, which are subject to mutual recognition by other states, but the intention is that national standards are replaced as quickly as possible by European standards which are agreed by European standards bodies. The main such bodies are the European Committee for Standardisation (CEN) and the European Committee for Electrotechnical Standardisation

(CENELEC). Both CEN and CENELEC have eighteen members (the EC and EFTA countries) and both use weighted voting procedures for the taking of final decisions on standards. Once European standards are agreed Community states must adopt them within a fixed time limit, and within the same time limit must remove all conflicting national standards.

● Issues arising in connection with the implementation of Community legislation were well aired in Chapter 3 in the examination of the Commission's executive and legal guardianship functions. Attention here will, therefore, be restricted to just a few key points on the two main problem areas:

1. Regarding the incorporation of directives into national law, the Commission has – as was noted above – to be informed of the measures member states take. It therefore has a reasonably good picture of what is happening. Notwithstanding this, however, some states have a considerably better record of incorporating directives than do others (the UK, Denmark, and Germany have the best records). In consequence, there are variations between the states in terms of the speed at which, and extent to which, directives are applied, and variations too in terms of the frequency with which states are subject to Commission and Court action for non/incomplete/incorrect incorporation of Community law (see Table 10.2)

2. Regarding the application of Community legislation, that is dependent on a number of factors, not least the competence and goodwill of the many different national authorities and officials whose responsibility it is to collect excise duties, to read tachographs, to check that beef for which payments are being made is of the quality that is being claimed etc. The Community does make use of a range of administrative controlling mechanisms – these being exercised by the DGs that are responsible for particular policies, by DGXX (Financial Control), by the Commission's anti-fraud unit, by the Court of Auditors, by the EP's Budgetary Control Committee, and by the member states themselves. Nonetheless, despite this range of agencies which have some responsibility for administrative control, it is evident that all is not well with the implementation of some Community policies. The problem is partly one of fraud – the head of the Commission's anti-fraud unit has

estimated that fraud accounts for 10–20 per cent of the Community budget. The problem is also, however, partly one of irregularities: that is to say, not of deliberate deception but of incorrect understanding and application of Community law. Doubtless the control mechanisms, and administrative procedures, could be improved – not least in respect of flows of information between the Commission and the multitude of national agencies that undertake the front line implementation of policies. But the fact is that with the Commission being unable to do very much direct surveillance of its own because of limited powers and limited resources, and with much Community legislation being so complicated that it is barely comprehensible even to the expert, it will probably never be possible to ensure that all laws are fully, properly and uniformly implemented.

Characteristic Features of Community Policy Processes

A number of general features are characteristic of much Community policy and decision-making. They include compromises and linkages, difficulties in effecting radical change, tactical manoeuvring, and protracted processes.

Compromises and Linkages

The diversity of competing interests across the twelve member states, coupled with the nature of the Community's decision-making system, means that successful policy development is usually heavily dependent on key actors, especially governments, being prepared to compromise. If they are not so prepared, effective decision-making becomes all but impossible.

As part of the process wherein compromises provide the bases for agreements, deals are frequently formulated in which different, and sometimes seemingly unrelated, policy issues are linked. Linking issues together in 'package deals' can open the door to agreements by ensuring that there are prizes for everybody and not, as might be the case when only a specific issue is taken, for just a few.

TABLE 10.2

Number of infringement proceedings initiated between 1986 and 1989 classified by member state, legal basis, and stage of proceedings

Member State	Stage of the infringement proceeding	1986 Directives				1987 Directives	
		No measures notified	Not properly incorporated	Not properly applied	Treaties and Regulations	No measures notified	Not properly incorporated
Belgium	FN	39	4	6	7	22	6
	RO	13	3	1	8	12	1
	RCJ	6	2	2	5	4	–
Germany	FN	14	6	5	15	23	5
	RO	8	–	2	7	2	4
	RCJ	2	1	1	7	–	–
Denmark	FN	13	4	2	7	22	1
	RO	1	2	–	–	1	1
	RCJ	–	–	–	1	–	–
Greece	FN	63	6	1	36	46	5
	RO	7	–	2	15	13	1
	RCJ	4	–	1	6	3	–
Spain	FN	–	–	1	21	21	–
	RO	–	–	–	–	–	–
	RCJ	–	–	–	–	–	–
France	FN	19	9	7	34	19	9
	RO	11	4	6	9	7	–
	RCJ	3	2	–	3	2	–
Ireland	FN	31	8	13	9	29	6
	RO	10	4	6	11	9	–
	RCJ	8	2	2	6	1	–
Italy	FN	26	3	8	7	32	5
	RO	6	–	–	2	14	–
	RCJ	2	–	–	2	9	1
Luxembourg	FN	35	2	2	4	18	–
	RO	10	2	–	–	7	–
	RCJ	3	1	–	–	2	–
Netherlands	FN	15	2	4	9	22	1
	RO	6	–	2	1	4	1
	RCJ	–	–	–	–	–	1
Portugal	FN	–	–	–	–	3	–
	RO	–	–	–	–	–	–
	RCJ	–	–	–	–	–	–
United Kingdom	FN	13	7	5	12	20	4
	RO	1	1	2	1	2	2
	RCJ	–	1	–	–	1	–

Key: FN: Formal Notice
RO: Reasoned Opinion   } These different stages are
RCJ: Reference to the Court of Justice   explained in Chapter 3.

Not properly applied	Treaties and Regulations	1988 Directives		Not properly applied	Treaties and Regulations	1989 Directives		Not properly applied	Treaties and Regulations
		No measures notified	Not properly incorporated			No measures notified	Not properly incorporated		
13	14	30	4	7	11	38	2	12	15
6	9	5	5	6	7	6	1	4	71
1	2	4	–	3	3	3	2	3	4
21	16	27	3	12	16	19	3	16	16
2	9	4	2	12	6	1	3	5	3
–	2	1	3	2	2	–	1	2	1
10	3	20	1	6	2	21	1	8	4
2	2	–	1	2	3	–	1	2	1
–	–	–	–	2	1	–	–	1	–
8	18	37	2	11	14	63	2	11	16
–	14	12	6	3	11	6	–	6	7
–	8	5	2	–	7	2	1	2	5
10	22	–	3	3	15	13	4	22	12
3	5	–	–	5	6	–	1	3	4
1	–	–	–	–	1	–	1	2	2
12	26	22	1	19	16	21	2	11	28
4	18	8	5	3	11	–	2	6	11
3	3	3	1	1	5	1	1	1	5
5	6	27	3	4	7	31	3	6	6
8	7	6	4	–	–	4	1	4	3
1	1	4	2	1	1	–	–	–	2
19	17	53	6	23	25	48	4	42	16
4	9	17	7	19	9	16	4	20	13
5	6	5	2	1	6	8	3	14	10
6	2	28	2	3	3	26	1	4	7
–	3	5	1	1	1	5	–	1	3
–	–	2	–	–	–	5	–	–	1
6	12	22	4	6	10	32	3	14	8
–	6	3	1	4	4	3	–	3	4
1	1	2	–	–	1	1	–	1	3
5	3	–	1	4	13	4	–	12	10
–	–	–	–	3	4	–	–	4	1
–	–	–	–	–	–	–	–	1	–
10	10	16	3	9	5	21	–	11	5
2	3	1	6	3	5	3	–	4	4
–	–	–	–	–	–	–	1	1	3

Source: Official Journal of the European Communities C232, 17 September 1990.

The European Council has been instrumental in formulating some of the Community's grander compromises and linked deals. For example, it was centrally involved in the bargain which, in 1978, saw Ireland and Italy extract a range of 'compensating' resource transfers in exchange for their agreeing to join the European Monetary System. Again, in 1984, at the Fontainebleau summit, it put together the package that included increasing the Community's budget revenue, decreasing the UK's budgetary contribution, and establishing budgetary discipline guidelines.

One of the reasons the European Council has become involved in the construction of overarching deals of the kind just described is that other Community institutions and actors, and Community processes as a whole, are ill-adapted to linking different policy areas and constructing complex package deals. The Foreign Ministers have a theoretical potential in this regard but, in practice, they tend not to have the political authority or status to impose global solutions on sectoral Councils. As for the sectoral Councils, they do not normally become involved in discussions beyond their immediate policy concern, and they certainly do not have the effective means – except perhaps occasionally in joint Councils – of linking difficulties in their own areas with difficulties being experienced by other ministers elsewhere.

Much Community policy and decision-making thus tends to be rather compartmentalised, and it is within, rather than across, policy compartments that the trading, bargaining, linkaging and compromising that is so characteristic of Community processes are mainly to be found. At Council working party level, trading may consist of little more than an official conceding a point on line 8 of a proposed legal instrument in exchange for support received on line 3. At ministerial level, it may result in a wide-ranging and interconnected package, such as is agreed annually between Agriculture Ministers to make up the farm price settlement.

Difficulties in Effecting Radical Change

Partly as a consequence of the prevalence of compromise, much Community policy and decision-making displays a deep gradualism and incrementalism. It is just not possible for the Commission, the Council Presidency, a national government, or anyone else, to initiate a clear and comprehensive policy proposal, incorporating bold new plans and significant departures from the *status quo*, and expect it to be accepted without being modified significantly – which usually means being watered down. Ambitious proposals customarily find themselves being smothered with modifications, escape clauses, and long transitional periods before full implementation.

The obstacles to innovation and radical change are powerful, and some of them have increased in force over the years. They have done so for four principal reasons. First, the way forward is not as clear as it was in the 1960s, when specific Treaty obligations were being honoured and 'negative integration' (that is, the dismantling of barriers and the encouragement of trade liberalisation) was generally accepted as the main policy priority. Second, international economic uncertainties have made states – some much more than others – cautious about ceding too many decision-making powers to the Community. The uncertainties have also exacerbated the pre-existing tension between a Community founded on an essentially liberal model of integration and states that have traditionally sought to regulate economic life by intervention. Third, the Community has become more politically and ideologically heterogeneous. This is partly because of enlargement and partly because the broad Keynesian consensus on social and economic policy that existed in most Western European countries until the mid-1970s has been called into question by high rates of inflation, high unemployment, and low economic growth. Finally, policy development has inevitably created and attracted interests which have a stake in the *status quo*. This is most obviously the case in agriculture, where Commission proposals for reform invariably produce protests from powerful sectional groups and from electorally sensitive governments. The ability of the farmers' lobby to defend its interests has helped agriculture to dominate the Community budget, which in turn – given the determination of some governments to restrain overall expenditure – has seriously limited policy development in other fields.

All this is not to suggest that the Community is condemned to stagnation and sclerosis. The increased pace of integration since the mid 1980s – which is seen most obviously in the internal market momentum and in the moves towards Economic and Monetary Union – demonstrates that Community policy development can vary according to time and circumstances. But it is to suggest that since just about any policy innovation meets with at least some resistance from some quarter(s), bold initiatives are always likely to be weakened and/or checked.

Tactical Manoeuvring

Tactical manoeuvring and jockeying for positions are universal characteristics of policy and decision-making processes. However, they are especially apparent in the Community as a result of the multiplicity of its actors and channels and the diversity of its interests.

It is not possible to attempt a comprehensive catalogue of tactical options here, but a sample of the questions that often have to be considered by one category of key Community actors – national representatives in the Council – will serve to give a flavour of the intricacies and potential importance of tactical considerations:

● Can a coalition be built to create a positive majority or a negative minority? If so, should it be done via bilateral meetings or in a Community forum?

● Is it necessary to make an intervention for domestic political purposes? (Although Council meetings are not open to the public or the media most of what goes on – especially in ministerial meetings – gets reported back.)

● Is it possible to disguise an opposition to a proposal by 'hiding' behind another state?

● Should concessions be made in a working party or in COR-EPER to ensure progress, or should they be held back until the ministers meet in the hope that this will be seen as conciliatory and reap dividends elsewhere?

● How is the necessary balance to be struck between being seen to be tough in the defence of the national interest and being seen to be Community minded and ready to compromise? (Often, on a particular issue, some states have a vested interest in an agreement being reached, whilst the interests of others are best served by the absence of any agreement and, as a result, the absence of Community obligations.)

Protracted Processes

Community processes are often criticised for being cumbersome and slow. Unquestionably they can be, but it should be recognised that they are not always so. Procedures exist that allow certain types of decisions to be made as and when they are necessary. So, farm price and budgetary decisions are made (more or less) according to a predetermined annual timetable; Commission legislation can be issued almost immediately; and Council regulations and decisions can be pushed through via urgent procedures if the circumstances require it.

The problems arise principally with issues which, for whatever reason, cause difficulties for a state or states, and which are not subject to the dictates of a timetable. In such cases, it may take years for an idea, or even a formally tabled Commission proposal, to achieve legislative status. Such, for example, was the case with the very important *Council Regulation (EEC) No.4046/89 of 21 December 1989 on the control of concentrations between undertakings* (commonly referred to as the Merger Control Regulation): it was first formulated by the Commission in July 1973 and had undergone repeated redrafting before its eventual adoption *sixteen* years later. The main reason processes can be so slow is that the Council is, in many respects, weak in its decision-making capability. If just one state decides to dig in its heels against a proposal it can be very difficult for progress to be made. There may not even be much of a concerted attempt to force progress if it is felt that the minority state genuinely has difficulties with the proposal, for governments tend to be very sensitive to one anothers needs – not least because they are aware that they themselves may be in a minority one day.

The increasing use of majority voting is quickening the pace in some policy areas. However, speedy and decisive decision-making across the whole policy spectrum will be possible only when it is generally accepted that effective decision-making is as much about the making of decisions as it is about accommodating and safeguarding national interests.

The Efficiency of Community Policy Processes

The Community lacks a fixed, central authoritative point where general priorities can be set out and choices between competing options can be made. In other words, there is no adequate framework or mechanism for determining and implementing an overall policy view in which the requirements of agriculture, industry, the environment and so on, are weighed and evaluated in relation to one another and in relation to resources. The Commission, it is true, attempts to set general priorities but it does not itself have the decision-making power to carry them through. In the Council of Ministers, the sectoral Councils do not link up with one another in a wholly satisfactory manner, and although incoming Presidential states do set priorities, these are essentially short-term in nature and in most policy sectors are not part of a properly integrated long-term programme. As for the European Council, it has had some limited success in co-ordinating policies, notably at the 1988 Brussels summit when a five year reference framework for expenditure was agreed (see below and Chapter 11), but it has never attempted to set out anything like a comprehensive Community policy programme.

Within individual policy sectors, there are, as has been shown, many obstacles to coherent and properly ordered policy development. For example, resistance by states to what they regard as an excessive transfer of powers to the Community has undoubtably resulted in many policy spheres being less integrated and comprehensive in their approach than is – from a policy efficiency perspective – ideally desirable. Regional policy, industrial policy, environmental policy, and policy on social security systems are examples of policy areas where policy responsibilities are shared between the Community and the states – with the former usually in a junior role – and where frequently the activities of the two levels are not properly co-ordinated, and sometimes are not even mutually complementary.

Community policy thus tends not to be the outcome of a rational model of decision-making. That is to say, policy is not normally made via a procedure in which problems are identified, objectives are set, all possible alternatives for achieving the goals are carefully evaluated, and the best alternatives are then adopted and proceeded with. Rather other models of decision-making are often more useful for highlighting key features of Community processes. For example:

The political interests model of decision-making draws attention to the interaction of competing interests in the Community, to the variable power exercised by these interests in different decision-making situations, and to the ways in which decisional outcomes are frequently a consequence of bargains and compromises between interests.

Political elite models highlight the considerable concentrations of power, at official and political levels, that exist across the Community's decision-making processes. Concentrations are especially marked in areas such as monetary policy and foreign policy, where processes are more secret and more closed than they are, for example, in steel or agriculture. Political elite models also draw attention to the absence of mechanisms available to Community citizens for exercising direct accountability over Community decision-makers.

The organisational process model of decision-making emphasises how the rules and understandings via which Community decisions are made do much to shape the nature of the decisions themselves. The organisational processes, that is to say, are not neutral. So where, to use Jacques Delors' phrase, policy can only 'make progress twelve abreast', and where every conceivable national, regional and sectional interest is entitled to be consulted before policy can be developed, progress is frequently slow and outcomes are often little more than lowest common denominators. Where, on the other hand, processes are more streamlined – and permit, for example, majority voting in the Council of Ministers, or the Commission to disburse funds directly – then decision-making is likely to be more decisive and, perhaps, more coherent.

Having identified weaknesses in the quality of Community policy and decision-making processes, some re-balancing is now in order lest the impression be left of a system that is wholly and uniquely disordered and undemocratic. There are three main points to be made.

The first point is that, in many respects, Community policy and decision-making processes are not so different from national processes. That is not to say that differences do not exist. The international nature of the Community, for example, makes for more diverse and more powerful opposition to its initiatives than customarily exists within states. It is also the case that Community decision-makers are less directly accountable than are national decision-makers to those who are subject to their decisions: the power of the European Council, the Council of Ministers, and the Commission, on the one hand, and the comparative weakness of the EP on the other, does make, as many have observed, for a 'democratic deficit' in the Community. Another difference is that the Community's institutions, taken collectively, are much weaker than their national counterparts. But recognition of these and other differences should not obscure similarities of type – if not perhaps intensity – between Community and national processes: political interest, political elite, and organisational process models of decision-making can throw light on features of the latter, as well as the former. So, for example, in all member states, especially those where there are coalition governments (which is the norm in most Community states), political accommodations are an everyday occurrence and policy trimming is common. Furthermore, in those countries where there is a considerable geographical decentralisation of power (as, for example, there is in Germany's quasi-federal system), tensions between levels of government over who does what, and who pays for what, are by no means unusual. In short, many of the Community's decision-making 'problems' – such as the prevalance of incrementalism, and of policy slippages – are by no means unknown in national political systems.

The second point is that not all Community policy and decision-making processes are completely a matter of cobbling together deals which can satisfy the current complexion of political forces. These certainly are crucially important features, but they do not amount to the complete picture. In recent years, greater efforts have been made, especially by the Commission, to initiate rather than just to react, to look to the medium-term rather than just tomorrow, and to pull at least some of the pieces together into co-ordinated programmes.

At the level of overarching policy co-ordination, progress in the direction of more forward-looking and more co-ordinated policy planning has, it must be said, been only modest. But there have been some potentially significant developments. One important example of such a development is seen in the Commission's 1987 document *The Single Act: a new frontier* which made recommendations for dealing with what it saw to be the Community's central priorities over the period up to 1992. The programme outlined in the document became the subject of exhaustive Council and European Council negotiations. These negotiations led, at the 1988 Brussels summit, to a package deal which, though the outcome of the usual political trading, did at least address, in an interlinking five year financial programme, some, though by no means all, of the Community's most pressing problems (see Chapter 11). Another example is seen in the process, which began to get seriously underway in 1988, to move towards Economic and Monetary Union.

There has been an enormous amount of effort to ensure that this is properly planned and co-ordinated. The process – the main stages of which were outlined in Chapter 7 – has seen constant rounds of meetings and negotiations at the highest levels, involving, amongst others, the European Council, the Ecofin Council, the Monetary Committee, the Committee of Governors of Central Banks, and the Intergovernmental Conference which was opened in December 1990.

Below the level of overarching policy co-ordination, within certain policy sectors clear medium to long-term policy objectives and rounded programmes are to be found. These are drawn up by the Commission, usually in consultation with appropriate consultative committees and committees of experts, and have to be approved by the Council. They appear in various forms: policy documents (for example, '*A future for Community agriculture*' which was approved by the Council in December 1985); White Papers, (for example, the 1985 Paper that contained detailed proposals for the completion of the internal market); framework legislation and programmes (for example, the major overhaul of the structural funds which was set out in Council Regulation (EEC) No.2052/88 of 24 June 1988); and action programmes.

It is worth saying a little about action programmes to illustrate how, within specified fields of activity, a measure of co-ordinated development over a planned medium-term period is possible. Action programmes vary in nature, from the broad and general to the highly specific. The broad and general typically include measures for improving the monitoring and supervision of existing legislation, ideas for new legislation, running a pilot scheme, and spending programmes. Such an action programme, aimed at improving 'equal opportunities for girls and boys in education' was approved by the Education Ministers in June 1985. The ten point programme was rather modest, as it had to be to attract the support of those governments which are not especially committed to such concerns and/or have little national legislation in the sphere themselves, but the provisions were not without significance. They included: educational and vocational guidance to be provided as a service to all pupils to encourage girls and boys to diversify their career choices; opening schools to working life and the outside world; eradicating persistent stereotypes from school textbooks, teaching materials in general, and guidance and assessment materials; and special measures to help the underprivileged. By contrast with the broad and general action programmes, the specific action programmes are naturally much more specialised in their areas of concern and tighter in their provisions. Examples are the ECSC social research programmes which are given appropriations for a given period and which provide up to about 60 per cent of the costs of approved research projects. Amongst such programmes approved in the 1980s was one on safety in mines, which was given a total appropriation of 12.5 million Ecu spread over five years, and one on industrial hygiene in mines, which was allocated an appropriation of 11 million Ecu over five years.

The third, and final, 'rebalancing' point to be made about Community processes is that critical jugements about how the Community functions ought to be placed in the context of the considerable degree of co-operation and integration that has been achieved. There is no comparable international development where individual states have voluntarily transferred so many policy responsibilities to a collective organisation of states and, in so doing, have surrendered so much of their national sovereignty. It is hardly surprising, given the enormity of the exercise, that pressures and desires for co-operation and integration should so often be challenged, and held in check, by caution, uncertainties, conflicts, and competition.

11

The Budget

The Community raises and spends money in many different ways. Mostly it does so within the framework of the annual budget and it is with the budget that this chapter is concerned.

Before examining the budget, however, the Community's non-budgetary revenue raising and spending operations will be outlined. This will enable a full picture of the Community's financial activities and instruments to be presented. The non-budgetary revenue raising and spending operations fall into four main categories:

● The Community borrows sums on capital markets which are then made available, in the form of loans, to both public and private undertakings for investment. The European Investment Bank, which is the principal source of Community investment finance, has already been discussed in this connection (see Chapter 8). Borrowing and lending operations, to assist projects of many different sorts, are also conducted in respect of the ECSC, Euratom, and the New Community Instrument (NCI) which has as its general purpose assisting the financing of investments which make for greater convergence and integration in member states' economic policies.

● Borrowing and lending activities, of a different sort, are also undertaken to enable member states to cope with balance of payments difficulties. The Community Loan Instrument was established for this purpose in 1975, and in 1979 standby arrangements between the Central Banks were created within the framework of the European Monetary System.

● The European Development Fund, which finances aid to the African, Caribbean and Pacific countries under the Lomé

313

Convention, is not resourced from the budget but from direct contributions by the member states.

● The ECSC is resourced from its own funds, the principal component of which is a levy on coal and steel production.

Turning now to the Community budget, one point needs to be emphasised at the outset: despite the considerable attention it has received over the years, and despite the enormous amount of political acrimony it has generated, the budget is, in fact, relatively small. In 1990 it totalled 46.7 billion Ecu in payment appropriations: about £34.5 billion and $57 billion at April 1990 exchange rates. This represented only 1.2 per cent of the Gross Domestic Product of the member states and about 3.3 per cent of the total of their national budgets. The reason why the budget is so small is that most of the policy sectors which make up the bulk of public expenditure – defence, education, health, social welfare etc., – remain primarily the responsibility of national governments. Many of the Community's policy activities, such as those designed to open up the internal market, do not involve much in the way of operational costs. When Community policies do involve significant operational costs, for example where they impose obligations to introduce measures so as to conform with Community environmental legislation, the financial impact often falls not on the Community's budget but on private firms and public authorities in the member states.

The modesty of the size of the Community's budget should, therefore, be borne in mind when assessing its financial and policy impact. Clearly the budget cannot, and does not, serve to effect a major transfer of financial resources from national exchequers to the Community, or *vice versa*.

The Composition of the Budget

Revenue

Following a decision taken by the member states in 1970, the funding of the Community's budget was changed between 1970 and 1975 from a system based on national contributions to one based on 'own resources'. A major reason for bringing about this change was that it would give to the Community an increased financial independence. The member states would determine the upper limit of the own resources, but the resources themselves would belong to the Community and not the states.

At the time of the introduction of the new arrangements the own resources consisted of customs duties, agricultural levies, and a proportion of Value Added Tax (VAT) up to a one per cent ceiling. At the beginning of the 1980s, however, it became apparent that these resources were not capable of generating enough income to meet the Community's increasing financial obligations. The member states could, in theory, have resolved this problem easily enough by raising the own resources limit, but some states – the UK in particular – were reluctant to do this. The consequence was that the Community experienced a series of budgetary crises in the early 1980s. These crises led, eventually, to the conclusion of a complicated deal at the 1984 Fontainebleau European Council. Key elements of the deal included new rules on budgetary discipline, a formula for reducing UK budgetary contributions, (which were generally recognised as being excessive), and an expansion of own resources through the setting of a new 1.4 per cent ceiling for VAT from 1986. The Fontainebleau agreement was, however, too little too late, in that no sooner had the 1.4 per cent ceiling been introduced in 1986 than it was exhausted and the Commission was forced to open a new campaign for a further expansion of the revenue base.

That campaign culminated in the 1988 Brussels summit which saw a further, but as compared with Fontainebleau, much more radical, package deal designed to deal with the Community's recurring budgetary difficulties. Included in the deal were provisions for expanding certain categories of expenditure, a continuation of special arrangements for the UK, a much tighter framework for ensuring budgetary discipline, and a significant expansion of own resources through the creation of a new own resource.

A financial perspective for the years 1988 to 1992 was agreed as part of the Brussels package and it was within the context of this perspective that the expansion of own resources was to occur. Own resources were to be linked to an expanding spending programme, subject to the limitation that the total amount of own resources for any one year could not exceed the following percentages of the total GNP of the Community for the year in question – 1988: 1.15; 1989: 1.17; 1990: 1.18; 1991: 1.19; 1992: 1.20.

The creation of the new resource at the Brussels summit means that the own resources now consist of the following:

● *Common Customs Tariff duties and other duties* which are collected in respect of trade with non-member countries.

● *Agricultural levies, premiums and other duties* which are collected in respect of trade with non-member countries within the framework of the CAP. These differ from customs duties in that they are not fixed import taxes, but are fluctuating charges designed to have the effect of raising import prices to Community levels. There are also certain internal agricultural levies and duties, notably within the framework of the common organisation of the market in sugar, which have as their purpose limiting surplus production.

● *The application of a 1.4 per cent rate to the VAT assessment base* which is determined in a uniform manner for member states. So as to protect countries whose VAT base is high, the assessment base for VAT may not exceed 55 per cent of the Gross National Product at market prices. (It should be emphasised that these VAT rules still allow countries to vary their specific national VAT rates).

● *The application of a rate to a base representing the sum of member states' Gross National Product at market prices.* This is the Brussels-agreed fourth own resource. The rate is determined under the budgetary procedure in the light of the total of all other revenue and the total expenditure agreed. Since this resource is very much like a national contribution, it has been suggested by many observers that it does not have quite the own resource character of the other resources. Key features of this resource are that it introduces into the Community's revenue system a link with ability to pay, and it also creates a resource which can be easily adjusted to bring budgetary revenue into balance with budgetary expenditure.

Precisely what proportion of total budgetary revenue comes from each resource naturally varies a little from year to year according to such factors as trade flows, world agricultural prices, and national growth rates. In the first three years of the new system, 1988–90, the proportions averaged as follows – VAT: 58.6 per cent; customs duties: 22.2 per cent; GNP resource: 9.8 per cent; agricultural levies: 5.6 per cent. (The remaining 3.7 per cent was accounted for by balances and miscellaneous income).

Expenditure

The Community makes a distinction between expenditure which is a direct result of Treaty application or acts adopted on the basis of the Treaties – called compulsory (or obligatory) expenditure – and that which is not – called non-compulsory (or non-obligatory) expenditure. As Table 11.1 shows the former accounts for around two-thirds of the total budget. Of this two-thirds, over 80 per cent is used for the purpose of farm price guarantees. Two main factors account for this dominant role of agriculture in Community expenditure. First, agriculture has seen a greater transfer of financial responsibility from national budgets to the Community budget than any other major policy area. Second, as is explained in Chapter 12, an agricultural price guarantee policy has been pursued that has kept Community prices well above world prices, and in a number of product sectors this has resulted in production levels well in excess of the capacity of the market. In consequence, the Community has had to pay for agricultural produce it does not require: by buying up surplus production; by storing it; by selling it at subsidised rates on domestic and world markets; and by converting it into animal feed.

On a 'rational' and 'commonsense' basis this can hardly be justified. Agriculture is clearly overfunded, whilst policy areas drawing on non-compulsory expenditure – such as regional policy, research policy and energy policy – are (most would argue) underfunded. However, budgetary expenditure, like budgetary income, is not determined by 'objective' criteria but by political interplay. And in that interplay there are many powerful forces which wish to maintain high levels of spending on agriculture: governments anxious to receive farmers' votes do not normally wish to upset this often volatile section of the electorate, and net beneficiaries of the CAP (both states and sectional interests) are not inclined voluntarily to surrender their gains.

However, notwithstanding these obstacles to reform, the pressures for radical change became intense by the mid to late 1980s: previous schemes for reducing agricultural expenditure were having only a marginal effect; ever-larger surpluses for some products were being predicted; and some states were becoming increasingly anxious to increase non-agricultural spending. As a result, important measures designed to bring about a gradual shift in the Community's pattern

TABLE 11.1

The 1990 Community Budget: breakdown according to main headings and at main decision-making stages (Commitment appropriations)*

	1990 financial perspective	Preliminary draft budget	Council first reading	Parliament first reading	Council second reading	1990 budget
(1) *European Agriculture Guidance and Guarantee Fund-Guarantee*	30 700	26 858	26 522	26 818	26 522	26 522
(2) *Structural Operations*						
European Social Fund		4 075	4 075	4 075	4 075	4 075
European Agriculture Guidance and Guarantee Fund-Guidance		1 700	1 700	1 700	1 700	1 700
European Regional Development Fund		5 408	5 408	5 408	5 408	5 408
Other		197	123	125	119	125
Total 2	11 555	11 530	11 527	11 555	11 527	11 533
(3) *Policies with multiannual allocations*						
Integrated Mediterranean Programmes		344	344	344	344	344
Research		1 723	1 614	1 727	1 686	1 727
Total 3	2 071	2 067	1 957	2 071	2 031	2 071

(4)	*Other Policies*					
	Education, training, youth		145	139	160	141	150
	Fisheries		406	395	431	415	421
	Energy		64	41	99	56	59
	Industry, internal market		164	145	164	152	164
	Co-operation with developing and Third World countries		1 396	1 321	1 713	1 352	1 664
	Others		494	458	596	497	548
	Total 4	3 029	2 669	2 500	3 163	2 614	3 005
(5)	*Repayments and administration*	4 930	4 778	4 688	4 790	4 682	4 716
(6)	*Monetary reserves*	1 000	1 000	1 000	1 000	1 000	1 000
	TOTALS						
	Compulsory expenditure	35 454	31 623	31 275	31 588	31 237	31 248
	Non-compulsory expenditure	17 831	17 279	16 920	17 809	17 138	17 599
	Grand total	53 285	48 902	48 194	49 397	48 375	48 847

* (a) Figures are presented in millions of Ecu. The value of the Ecu in April 1990 was: 1 Ecu = £0.74 = $1.22.

(b) The financial year runs from 1 January to 31 December.

(c) The budget is always broken down into payment appropriations and commitment appropriations. Payment appropriations, which totalled 46716 Ecu in 1990, cover expenditure during the financial year. Commitment appropriations, which are listed here, cover expenditure during the financial year plus liabilities extending beyond the year. Commitment appropriations are naturally always higher, but only slightly higher, than payment appropriations.

Source: Adapted from the *Bulletin of the European Communities* 12-1989 of expenditure were agreed to as part of the package deal that was agreed at the 1988 Brussels European Council meeting.

Central to these expenditure measures was a five-year programme for reducing agricultural spending on the one hand (see Chapter 12 for details), and a programme for doubling spending on the structural funds (mainly the Regional Fund and the Social Fund) by 1993 on the other. These programmes were given added force when, in June 1988, the Presidents of the Council of Ministers, the Commission, and the European Parliament, signed, on behalf of their respective institutions, the *Interinstitutional Agreement on Budgetary Discipline and Improvement of the Budgetary Procedure* (see Document 11.1). The importance of the *Interinstitutional Agreement* was that it contained a formal commitment by all three Community institutions to the framework of the financial perspective for the years 1988 to 1992 that was attached to the Agreement. The financial perspective was based on the Brussels agreement and envisaged the proportion of agricultural expenditure over the period of the perspective being reduced to around 60 per cent of total budgetary expenditure, and the proportion of expenditure on structural operations being almost doubled.

So as to present a more detailed picture than is shown in the financial perspective of particular budget allocations, the main headings of the 1990 budget (the third year in which the financial perspective was applied) are presented in Table 11.1. The most striking feature about the distribution of the funds is the relatively modest sums available in all categories other than that for agricultural price guarantees. So, to take three key areas of non-compulsory expenditure: the European Regional Development Fund (ERDF), which has as its aim the correction of serious disparities in levels of development and prosperity in different regions of the Community, is allocated 11 per cent; the European Social Fund, which is primarily concerned with vocational training and employment promotion activities, especially amongst youth, is allocated 8 per cent; and research activities are allocated just over 3 per cent. As is explained above, and is apparent from Document 11.1, these potentially very important areas are all being expanded under the financial perspective, but even when they have reached their limits in 1992 the Community's financial capability to effectively act as an agent for tackling pressing problems such as under-investment,

DOCUMENT 11.1

Extracts from the

INTERINSTITUTIONAL AGREEMENT

ON BUDGETARY DISCIPLINE

AND IMPROVEMENT OF THE BUDGETARY PROCEDURE

I. BASIC PRINCIPLES OF THE AGREEMENT

1. The main purpose of the Interinstitutional Agreement is to achieve the objectives of the Single European Act, to give effect to the conclusions of the Brussels European Council on budgetary discipline and accordingly to improve the functioning of the annual budgetary procedure.

2. Budgetary discipline under the Interinstitutional Agreement covers all expenditure and is binding on all the institutions involved for as long as the Agreement is in force.

3. This Agreement does not alter the respective budgetary powers of the various institutions as laid down in the Treaty.

4. The contents of the Interinstitutional Agreement may not be changed without the consent of all the institutions which are party to it.

II. BUDGET FORECASTS: FINANCIAL PERSPECTIVE 1988 to 1992

A. Contents

5. The financial perspective 1988 to 1992 constitutes the reference framework for interinstitutional budgetary discipline. Its contents are consistent with the conclusions of the Brussels European Council; it forms an integral part of the agreement . . . .

B. Nature

7. The European Parliament, the Council and the Commission recognize that each of the financial objectives laid down in the persperctive 1988 to 1992 represents an annual expenditure ceiling for the Community. They undertake to observe the different ceilings during the corresponding budgetary procedure.

8. The European Parliament, the Council and the Commission will join in the effort undertaken by the Community gradually to achieve a better balance between the various categories of expenditure.

    They give an undertaking that any revision of the compulsory expenditure figure given in the financial perspective will not cause the amount of noncompulsory expenditure shown in the perspective to be reduced . . . .

III. BUDGETARY DISCIPLINE FOR COMPULSORY EXPENDITURE

14. (a) The European Parliament, the Council and the Commission are in agreement on the conclusions of the European Council concerning budgetary discipline for compulsory expenditure in the EAGGF Guarantee Section.

    The three institutions undertake, within this Agreement, to respect these conclusions.

    (b) The European Parliament, the Council and the Commission confirm the principles and the mechanisms for the agricultural guideline and the monetary reserve.

    (c) As regards the other compulsory expenditure, the three institutions undertake to honour the Community's legal obligations in a manner consistent with the financial perspective.

IV. BUDGETARY DISCIPLINE FOR NON-COMPULSORY EXPENDITURE AND IMPROVEMENT OF THE BUDGETARY PROCEDURE

15. The two arms of the budgetary authority agree to accept, for the financial years 1988 to 1992, the maximum rates of increase for non-compulsory expenditure deriving from the budgets established within the ceilings set by the financial perspective.

16. The Commission will present each year, within the limits of the financial perspective, a preliminary draft budget based on the Community's actual financing requirements.

    It will take into account:

    – the capacity for utilizing appropriations, endeavouring to maintain a strict relationship between commitment appropriations and payment appropriations;

    the possibilities for starting up new policies or continuing multiannual operations which are coming to an end, after assessing whether it will be possible to secure a proper legal base.

17. Within the maximum rates of increase for non-compulsory expenditure specified in paragraph 15 of this Agreement, the European Parliament and the Council undertake to respect the allocations of commitment appropriations provided in the financial perspective for the Structural Funds, the Specific Industrial Development Programme for Portugal (PEDIP), the Integrated Mediterranean Programmes (IMPs) and the Research-Technology-Development (RTD) framework programme.

    They also undertake to bear in mind the assessment of the possibilities for executing the budget made by the Commission in its preliminary drafts...

FINANCIAL PERSPECTIVE

Commitment appropriations

(million ECU at 1988 prices)

	1988	1989	1990	1991	1992
1. EAGGF Guarantee	27 500	27 700	28 400	29 000	29 000
2. Structural operations	7 790	9 200	10 600	12 100	13 450
3. Policies with multiannual allocations	1 210	1 650	1 900	2 150	2 400
(IMPs, research)					
4. Other policies	2 103	1 385	2 500	2 700	2 800
of which non-compulsory	1 646	1 801	1 860	1 910	1 970
5. Repayments and administration	5 700	4 950	4 500	4 000	3 550
(including financing of stock disposal)	1 240	1 400	1 400	1 400	1 400
6. Monetary reserve	1 000	1 000	1 000	1 000	1 000
TOTAL	45 303	46 885	48 900	50 950	52 800
of which compulsory	33 698	32 607	32 810	32 980	33 400
non-compulsory	11 605	14 278	16 090	17 970	19 400
Payment appropriations required	43 779	45 300	46 900	48 600	50 100
of which compulsory	33 640	32 604	32 740	32 910	33 110
non-compulsory	10 139	12 696	14 160	15 690	16 990
Payment appropriations as % of GNP	1,12	1,14	1,15	1,16	1,17
Margin for unforeseen expenditure	0,03	0,03	0,03	0,03	0,03
Own resources required as % of GNP	1,15	1,17	1,18	1,19	1,20

Source: *Official Journal of the European Communities* L185, 15 July 1988

technological change, unemployment, and regional imbalances will remain very limited.

Budgetary Decision-making

The Budgetary Process

A timetable and set of procedures for drawing up and approving the annual budget is laid down in Article 203 of the EEC Treaty (as amended in 1970 and 1975). However, in practice, Article 203 gives only an approximate and rather formal guide to what actually happens. It provides a framework which has been fleshed out and adapted over time in response to pressures, necessities, and convenience.

Because variations occur from year to year it is difficult to describe the 'typical' way in which the budget is made. In broad terms, however, and assuming no major problems exist or arise to severely disrupt the process, the pattern is as follows.

Preparation of the Preliminary Draft Budget. The Commission gets down to work on the budget in the late winter/early spring of the year before which it is due to come into effect. In attempting to look this far ahead – almost twelve months to the beginning of the financial year (in January) and twenty-four months to its close – the Commission is necessarily faced with many uncertainties on both the revenue and expenditure sides. Agriculture causes particular difficulties. For example, crop yields cannot be foreseen: a small change in weather conditions might raise production in a particular product from 101 per cent of consumer demand to 102 per cent, thus resulting in a considerable underestimate of the amount of budget support required for that product. Another problem is that agriculture expenditure is highly dependent on world agricultural prices and currency movements which cannot be controlled: a falling dollar can have a drastic effect on Community finances because export subsidies for farm products are linked to dollar-denominated international market prices. (The fall of the dollar in December 1986–January 1987 alone added more than 1 billion Ecu to spending commitments.)

The Commission has, therefore, to make many assumptions, some of which, in the event, may not be realised. If changed situations become apparent during the course of the budgetary cycle corrections can be made fairly easily, by sending rectifying or amending letters to the Council and the Parliament. If, however, the financial situation changes for the worse during the budgetary year itself, that is more serious. In the past, 'temporary' solutions, such as postponement of payments, delays in the introduction of new programmes, and supplementary budgets have been used. Since the 1988 Brussels summit, however, the Commission has had available, and has used, a range of stronger management powers to enable it to take approriate action at an early stage if agricultural expenditure – the main problem – gets out of hand: it can, for example, impose levies and price support cuts on certain products if designated production ceilings are exceeded.

The prime responsibility within the Commission for drawing up what is known as the Preliminary Draft Budget (PDB) falls to the Directorate General for Budgets (DGXIX). Inevitably it is subject to pressures from many sides: from other DGs who forward their own estimates and bids; from national representatives – both through the Council and on a direct lobbying basis; from the EP, especially leading figures of its Committee on Budgets; and from sectional interests. The Budget Commissioner and officials from DGXIX have many meetings, of both a formal and informal kind, to enable many of these interested parties to have their say. Naturally, those that have the most chance of achieving some satisfaction are those that carry political weight and/or are already in tune with the Commission's thinking.

Once DGXIX has its proposals ready they must be presented by the Commissioner to his fellow Commissioners and all must agree on the package. When they do, the proposals officially become the Preliminary Draft Budget.

In the past, the PDB usually disappointed those who wanted to see the budget used as the motor for change in Community priorities. The Commission did, in the 1980s, make several attempts to use the PDB to effect at least modest shifts in policy emphases – notably by proposing the containment of agricultural expenditure and the expansion of the structural funds – but its manoeuvrability was always severely restricted by existing expenditure commitments, and also by the knowledge that any significant change that it might propose from the *status quo* would be fiercely resisted in the Council. The 1988 Brussels summit agreement and the *Interinstitutional Agreement* have changed this situation by setting out a framework and a programme for using the budget to effect change.

Three interrelated aspects of the 1988 agreements are especially crucial. First, the budget must conform with the principles of the agricultural guideline – which means that the rate of increase in agriculture guarantee expenditure in any one year must not exceed 74 per cent of the annual rate of increase in Community Gross National Product (see Chapter 12 for further details). Second, the budget must be set within the framework of the financial perspective 1988 to 1992. As Document 11.1 shows the perspective contains a financial programme for altering the balance of Community expenditure. Third, the Commission, the Council, and the EP, are strictly bound to respect the ceilings set out in the financial perspective.

Apart from technical adjustments the financial perspective can only be revised by a joint decision of the Council and the EP, acting on a proposal from the Commission – as, for example, it was in June 1990 when new funding (200 million Ecu in 1990, 1225 million Ecu in 1991, and 1478 million Ecu in 1992) was made available for a number of purposes, notably assistance to Eastern Europe.

The financial perspective does not, it should be emphasised, totally constrain the Commission when it draws up the PDB. It does have manoeuvrability below the ceilings, and it does have options within expenditure headings. The financial perspective, in other words, is not a straightjacket. But it does place very clear limits on what the Commission can do.

Council First Reading.   Assuming there are no major or special problems, the PDB is referred to the Council at the end of May or in early June.

Most of the Council's detailed examination of the budget is undertaken by the Budget Committee, a working group of national officials who, in what are frequently long and exhaustive sessions, examine the PDB chapter by chapter, line by line. As the date of the Ministers' meeting in the Budget Council approaches, the Committee is likely to meet with increasing frequency in order to resolve as many issues as possible. The negotiators are in almost constant contact with their national capitals about what transpires in the Committee, and so they mostly have a prepared view when items come up for discussion. When this produces a rigidity in negotiating positions, much responsibility is thrown on the chairman to find a solution. The Commission can assist him in this task.

From the Committee the draft proceeds to COREPER. The number of unresolved items put before the Permanent Representatives naturally depends on what has happened in the Committee. Normally, much remains to be done, and COREPER attempts, like the Committee, to clear as many items as possible before the Ministers meet. It is usually most successful with those issues which do not have a potentially conflictual political aspect attached to them.

The Ministers customarily meet in mid-July, although there have been occasions when they have not gathered until September. Before beginning their deliberations they meet a delegation from the EP which is comprised, usually, of the Parliament's President, the chairman of the Committee on Budgets, half a dozen or so Committee members, and perhaps two or three other committee chairmen. The main purpose of this meeting, which is the first of two formal occasions when the Council and the EP meet under the budgetary procedure, is to enable the EP to outline its thinking on the budget and to voice its early reactions to the PDB. The MEPs' observations do not normally have much effect: at this stage the Ministers are primarily concerned with reaching an agreement between themselves.

Prior to the Brussels summit, the Budget Council normally lasted for a couple days and involved 15 to 20 hours of negotiations in formal sessions, plus extensive informal discussions and manoeuvrings in the wings. Qualified majority voting usually allowed a draft to be eventually agreed, but on controversial proposals a blocking minority sometimes existed. On two occasions the divisions between the member states were such that the July meeting was unable to approve a draft, which meant that there had to be a reference back to officials. The officials then produced a new package for the Ministers to consider when they returned in September – by which time the timetable was pressing and an agreement had to be reached.

The reason why the July meeting was often so difficult was that the states differed, both in their views about the balance to be struck between restraint and expansion, and in their perceptions of problems and priorities. What emerged, therefore, was a draft reflecting accommodations and compromises. Almost invariably, however, the general thrust of the draft was, on the one hand, to propose a tighter overall budget than that envisaged in the PDB, and, on the other hand, to propose some shift from non-compulsory expenditure to compulsory expenditure, that is, from items such as regional, social and research expenditure (which were relatively 'soft' because of their non-compulsory character) to agriculture (which was difficult to touch given existing commitments).

The Brussels summit package and the *Interinstitutional Agreement* have constrained the Council, as they have the Commission, in what it can do. This has had two effects on the Council's first reading stage. First, the decision-making process is less divisive and troublesome than in the past. Second, the Council is obliged to produce a draft that is very similar to the PDB.

Parliament First Reading. On being approved, the Council's first draft is referred to the Parliament. If the timing is suitable the President of the Budget Council may formally present the draft himself: to the Budget Committee and/or in an address to the plenary.

Although this presentation of the Council's draft marks the first formal point at which the EP becomes involved in the budgetary process, it always, in practice, has been attempting to exert influence for some time: key Parliamentary figures feed views into the Commission and the Council as best they can; the PDB is sent by the Commission to the EP at the same time as it is referred to the Council, and the Committee on Budgets begins its considerations almost immediately; and, as was indicated above, an EP delegation meets the Budget Council before the latter's first reading.

Now, with the Council's draft available, the pace is stepped up. There is a brief debate in plenary session, but the detailed work is given over to committees. The Committee on Budgets naturally has most responsibility. It examines the budget in detail itself, and it also acts as a co-ordinating agency for reports submitted to it by other EP committees which look at the budget to see how their sectors are affected. The Committee on Budgets does not, however, have the power completely to control what goes forward to the plenary: it cannot, for example, stop an amendment that has support elsewhere, especially if it is backed by any of the larger political groups. Partly in consequence of this, hundreds of proposed changes are usually put forward (500 for the 1989 budget), many of which conflict with one another, or are even mutually exclusive. Much, therefore, rests on the liaising, organising, and leadership skills of the chairman of the Committee on Budgets and the appointed *rapporteur*.

The intention is normally to hold the plenary session dealing with the budget in October, but if the submission of the Council's draft is delayed it may have to be put off until November. At the plenary MEPs can do three things with the contents of the Council's draft: accept them; propose amendments to non-compulsory expenditure (which requires majority support of members); propose modifications to compulsory expenditure (which requires majority support of votes cast).

As with both the drafting of the PDB and the Council's first reading, the EP's first reading has been affected by the Brussels summit and the *Interinstitutional Agreement*. In the past, the customary pattern at this stage was for the EP to propose increases in non-compulsory expenditure (over which, as explained in Chapter 5, it has greater power than it does over compulsory expenditure) and often, also, to raise general points of principle. So, for instance, in 1984 – re the 1985 budget – the Parliament complained about the lack of provision for a projected budget deficit; in 1985 – re the 1986 budget – it criticised the inadequate provision for the accession of Spain and Portugal and for the 'weight of the past'; and in 1986 – re the 1987 budget – it stressed the urgent need to tackle agricultural overexpenditure. The position since the Brussels summit and the *Interinstitutional Agreement* is that there is not such a gap between the Council and the EP. This is because of the obligations and constraints of the financial perspective which, in addition to partly satisfying some of the EP's policy ambitions – through the changes in projected expenditure patterns – also reduces, though it by no means eliminates, the significance of the distinction between compulsory and non-compulsory expenditure.

Prior to the *Interinstitutional Agreement* there was frequently a disagreement during the budgetary process between the Council and the EP over the 'maximum rate of increase'. This is a figure calculated annually by the Commission according to a complex formula based on inflation, growth of national budgets, and the overall level of economic growth, and it was applied to non-compulsory expenditure. After the *Interinstitutional Agreement* the Council attempted to continue to apply the maximum rate of increase to what it called the 'non-privileged' element of non-compulsory expenditure. (This non-privileged element was to include transport, energy and fisheries; the privileged element was to include the structural funds, research, and the Integrated Mediterranean Programmes.) The EP resisted the Council's attempts to make this distinction between types of non-compulsory expenditure and insisted that it was the ceilings set out in the financial perspective that counted. The resistance was successful, with the consequence that the maximum rate of increase, though still calculated and published, has lost most of its former significance. Since 1988 disagreements between the Council and the EP in the budgetary process have mainly focused on EP efforts to ensure: (1) that funds are allocated up to the level of the ceilings set out in the financial perspective (the EP is in a stronger position to ensure this for non-compulsory expenditure than it is for compulsory); (2) that unforeseen and emergency expenditure (such as to help meet the cost of

German unification) is met by revisions of the financial perspective and not by diverting funds from existing allocations.

After the EP has debated the draft budget in plenary session, and after all amendments and modifications have been voted upon, a resolution on the budget is adopted by the Parliament.

Council Second Reading. From Parliament the draft goes back to the Council where officials prepare for the ministerial second reading which is usually held in mid to late November. If issues remain to be settled activity can be feverish, and many meetings may be held to try and achieve progress. Amongst such meetings could be one under the 'Tripartite Dialogue' (or Trialogue as it is commonly called), by which the Presidents of the Council, the EP, and the Commission can meet at any time during the budgetary procedure to consider unresolved problems.

At some point the second formal meeting with an EP delegation is held. In taking their decisions the Ministers are thus well aware of what is likely to meet with EP approval, and what is likely to produce a full scale row and endanger possible adoption.

In looking at the EP's proposed changes, the Budget Council can, within the financial perspective, take three sorts of decisions:

● Acting by a qualified majority, it can modify amendments to non-compulsory expenditure.

● Acting by a qualified majority, it can reject modifications to compulsory expenditure that do not have the effect of increasing total expenditure. In the absence of decisions to reject them, proposed modifications stand as accepted.

● Acting by a qualified majority, it can accept modifications to compulsory expenditure that have the effect of increasing total expenditure. In the absence of decisions to accept them, proposed modifications are rejected.

Where it is clear that Parliament's views have not been fully met, and particularly where significant funds are involved or possible points of principle are at stake – such as on the classification of a certain type of expenditure – then the Council has to decide whether it wishes to close the door on the matter (and hope for the best at the EP's second reading) or leave it ajar for a possible compromise. In the past this has produced sharp divisions in the Council, because it raises the possibility of budgetary rejection.

Parliament Second Reading. The EP holds its second reading on the budget in December. What happens before, at, and after the plenary depends very much on the extent to which contentious issues remain unresolved.

If the situation is relatively straightforward and most problems have been sorted out, then the normal procedure is for the Committee on Budgets to meet, to reinsert such non-compulsory expenditure as it legally can, and, on this basis, to recommend adoption. The plenary then votes, and if the budget is approved the President formally signs it and declares it to be adopted.

But where, as prior to the Brussels summit was frequently the case, major differences between the Council and the EP remain, the two sides are obliged to get down to negotiations. Various procedures can come into play: the President of the Budget Council, accompanied by the Budget Commissioner, may meet with the Committee on Budgets; the President of the Budget Council may make an appeal to the plenary; a Trialogue meeting may be held; or a special Budget Council may be hurriedly called, perhaps to meet again with an EP delegation, perhaps to give the budget what is, in effect, a third reading. If all efforts to reach a Council–EP agreement fail, the latter can reject the budget by a majority of its members, including two-thirds of the votes cast.

Non-Approval of the Budget. In five of the first nine years following the introduction of direct elections in 1979, budgets were not approved in time to be implemented at the beginning of the financial year on 1 January. These were the budgets of 1980 and of 1984–8.

If a legal budget is not approved by the EP before 1 January a fall back position applies. This allows for funding to continue, but only on the basis of what are known as 'provisional twelfths', which means that spending is limited to the monthly average expenditure of the previous year. Policies do not therefore collapse, but some payments may have to be suspended, and programmes, especially those that are new, may have to be delayed. A speedy agreement on the budget of what is, by this stage, the current financial year, is thus desirable.

There is no formal procedure or set pattern regarding what happens in the event of non-adoption. The expectation and assumption is that the process is resumed at the point at which it broke down, but practice has shown matters not to be so simple. Developments following non-adoptions have varied considerably, depending principally on the reasons for the non-adoption. So, for example, the 1986 budget was, like those for 1985 and 1988, not approved until halfway through the financial year. The problem with the 1986 budget was not that a budget was not approved by the EP in December 1985, but rather that the Council judged the budget that had been adopted by the EP to be illegal on the grounds that it included more non-compulsory expenditure than was legally permissible. The Council, therefore, asked the Court of Justice for a ruling. On 3 July 1986 the Court eventually delivered its judgement and, in essence, upheld the Council's claim that the budget was illegal. The next week then saw hectic activity, a truncated budgetary procedure, and, on 10 July, the adoption of a budget in which creative accountancy and financial ingenuity played prominent parts.

The Brussels summit package and the *Interinstitutional Agreement* removed, or at least blunted the sharpness of, many of the problems that occasioned non-adoption of budgets in the 1980s. In particular, agricultural expenditure was made subject to stronger budgetary discipline, the size of the structural funds was increased, and mechanisms were established to improve the match between income and expenditure. Of course, not all differences or potential problems were totally erased. But the prospect of budgets normally being adopted at December plenaries was considerably enhanced, and the first three budgets to come forward under the new system – those for 1989, 1990 and 1991 – were indeed so adopted.

Characteristic Features of the Budgetary Process

Some features of the process that has just been described merit particular comment.

First, the budget, like the annual agriculture price review, is unusual in the Community decision-making context in the sense that it is supposed to operate according to a clear timetable. Legislative proposals can be pushed along if they are strongly supported, and the 1992 momentum and the greater use of majority voting have quickened the pace of some legislative decision-making, but it is only in the later stages of the co-operation procedure that a timetable applies. It is still the case that many legislative proposals drag on in the Council until some sort of agreement is reached, and if this proves not to be possible they may be indefinitely postponed or even dropped altogether. With the budget such a relaxed and open-ended approach is not possible, since expenditure and resource decisions have to be made each year. The existence and exigencies of the timetable thus introduce an urgency into budgetary decision-making that is not usually found in other spheres of Community decision-making.

Second, the power balance between the institutions is not the same on the budget as it is elsewhere. Whereas the Council and the Commission are the main decision-makers in most policy sectors, with the EP often struggling to make its voice heard, in respect of the budget the Council and the EP jointly constitute the budgetary authority and are co-decision-makers. The Commission remains important, but after the presentation of the PDB it is cast in an essentially servicing capacity: responding to what happens in the Council and the Parliament and doing what it can to bring the two sides together. As for the particular nature of the balance between the Council and the EP, the former is unquestionably the stronger, but the *Interinstitutional Agreement* does open the way for some tilting in the direction of the EP. It does so by binding the institutions into a financial framework which can only be revised by common agreement, by giving the EP a glimpse of shared control over compulsory expenditure, and by establishing a precedent of the EP being party to a general accord on future expenditure patterns.

Third, budgetary decision-making is the only significant decision-making area where Council majority voting has long been common. This has enabled decisions to be made more easily, but it has not necessarily improved their quality. With a blocking minority in the Council needing 23 votes out of 76, and a qualified majority requiring 54, states inevitably have had to look for allies, have had to agree to reciprocal arrangements, and have had to give support in return for support received. This has resulted in budgetary decisions being heavily dependent on the outcome of pushing and pulling between different institutions and interests.

Fourth, many of the arguments and confrontations that have occurred during the budgetary process have been occasioned not so much by the financial sums involved – which have usually been relatively small – but more by a broader institutional struggle, especially between the Council and the EP. With the EP dissatisfied with its overall position in the Community system, it is only natural that it should have sought to use the budget, where it does have real powers, to maximum advantage. There are a number of ways in which it has gone about this. One has been its increased willingness since 1979 to reject the budget. Another has been interpreting the Treaties, along with agreements and understandings about budgetary decision-making, in ways which are advantageous to itself – as on matters such as the bases for budgetary calculations, and the classification of expenditure in terms of compulsory and non-compulsory. And a third way has been by attempting to exploit differences within the Council – by, for example, seeking to exert pressure in a particular direction through the indication of preferences in plenary votes or, less formally, in interinstitutional exchanges such as conciliation meetings.

Fifth, certain fundamental budgetary decisions are not taken via the annual budgetary process. As has been shown, decisions on resource ceilings, on 'rebates' for countries making excessive budgetary contributions, and on budgetary discipline, have all been taken by European Councils. (Although, of course, these European Council decisions have had to be given legal form by the Council of Ministers.)

Sixth, and finally, the effectiveness of the budgetary process has, like virtually all Community decision-making, tended to be weakened by the absence of a consensus amongst decision-makers as to how the Community should develop, and also by the lack of any single body that has been in a position to impose a framework based on clear and coherent budgetary long-term, or even medium-term, priorities. Until the 1988 *Interinstitutional Agreement* this resulted in budgetary outcomes being highly incremental in nature. In terms of the Community's policy balance, they effected, at best, only marginal adjustments to the *status quo*. The *Interinstitutional Agreement* allowed for some modest changes in this situation. It did not, perhaps, bring 'cohesive' or 'objective' budgetary planning much closer, but it did at least enable the budget to become the instrument for important, though not fundamental, reform.

12

Agricultural Policy and Policy Processes: A Detailed Study

Despite the fact that it accounts for only 2.7 per cent of Community GDP and 7.7 per cent of Community employment, agriculture looms large in the life of the Community. It does so in three main ways. First, the Community carries, via the Common Agricultural Policy (CAP), major policy-making and decision-making responsibilities for agriculture. Second, as the major recipient of EC funds, agriculture dominates Community financial deliberations and serves to restrict policy development in non-agricultural spheres. And third, there is a greater institutional presence and activity in the agricultural field than in any other: the Agriculture Ministers meet more frequently than all other Councils except for the Foreign Ministers; uniquely, Agriculture Council meetings are prepared not by COREPER but by a special body, the Special Committee on Agriculture (SCA); DGVI (Agriculture) is the second largest of the Commission's twenty-three Directorates General (only DGIX is larger and that deals not with a policy sector but with Personnel and Administration); and there are far more Council working parties and Commission management and advisory groups in the sphere of agriculture than in any other single policy area.

For its supporters, the CAP is important both in itself – the benefits accruing from joint policy-making and common management are seen as far outweighing the disadvantages – and important, too, as a symbol and indicator that real policy integration is possible at

Community level. Those who criticise the CAP are thus liable to be attacked, both on technical and efficiency grounds (with the claim that national solutions would be much less satisfactory), and more broadly for being *non communautaire* (with the assertion that the only true Community policy should not be undermined). For opponents of the CAP, economic efficiency is the key issue. Subsidisation of wealthy farmers, high prices for consumers, and production of farm surpluses which nobody wants are the most frequently heard criticisms.

Yet even amongst those who are most critical of the CAP few seriously challenge the view that there should be a Community agriculture policy of some kind. Certainly no member state believes that the agricultural edifice should be uprooted and policy returned to national capitals. The view that there is something special about agriculture, something that distinguishes it from other sectoral activities and merits it receiving advantageous treatment, whilst not commanding such strong support as in the early days of the Community, still strikes a chord with Community decision-makers.

Why Does Agriculture have a Special Place in the Community?

The attention given to agriculture in the EEC Treaty, and the subsequent creation of the CAP through long and often tortuous negotiations, is often seen as being part of a trade-off between France and Germany. There is something in this view. In exchange for the creation of a common market in industrial goods, which the French feared would be greatly to Germany's advantage, France – with her large, but rather uneconomic, agricultural sector – would benefit from an agricultural system which, though also in the form of a common market, would be based not on free and open market principles, but on foundations which would protect farmers from too much competition.

Important though it was, however, the Franco-German 'deal' provides only part of the explanation for why agriculture, from the earliest days of the Community, was given an elevated policy status. For the fact is that when the CAP was being created in the late 1950s and 1960s, none of the then six member states seriously objected to it in principle, though there were differences on the pace of its construction and the precise nature of its policies. This consensus on the general principle was a result of a shared recognition that agriculture required special treatment.

Today, despite the EC having increased in size from six to twelve, despite the circumstances and conditions of agriculture having dramatically changed, and despite the CAP having caused major difficulties and disruptions to the whole Community system, agriculture is still generally regarded by the national governments as requiring special treatment. Many of the reasons for this are much the same as they were in the EC's early days. Others are more recent. They can be grouped under two general headings: the distinctive nature of agriculture, and political factors.

The Distinctive Nature of Agriculture

For many years, but especially since the Second World War, most governments of the industrialised world have taken the view that agriculture is not like other areas of economic activity. It is special and merits special treatment to encourage, to assist and to protect it. In the Community four main arguments are advanced in support of this.

(1) If they are not controlled by public authorities agricultural prices are more subject to fluctuation than are the prices of most other goods. Agricultural price instability is undesirable for two reasons. First, if prices suddenly go up, inflation will be immediately fuelled (given that food constitutes around 24 per cent of the budget of the average Community citizen). Second, if prices fall too low, farmers may not be able to make an adequate living and may be forced off the land. Even those who are able to stay in farming may experience severe difficulties as a result of the high debt loads carried by many farmers on land and capital purchases.

(2) Reliance on imports for vital foodstuffs creates a potential political vulnerability to outside pressures. It is a particular source of weakness during periods of strained international relations.

This factor is not, perhaps, so important now, but in the early years of the EC, when memories of wartime shortages and of the vulnerability and misery this occasioned were fresh, it played an important part in encouraging a drive for greater self-sufficiency.

(3) Because people must have food, insufficient domestic production means that the gap between output and demand has to be met

by imports, with potentially damaging consequences for the balance of payments. Moreover, since the demand for food is fairly inelastic up to necessity levels – as long as income allows it, food will still be bought even if prices go up – the economic vulnerability of an importing state is high.

Naturally, as certain vital food products in the Community have moved into surplus – notably dairy produce, cereals, and meat – this self-sufficiency argument for increased farm production has lost much of its force; all the more so since the disposal of the surpluses is expensive owing to world prices being lower than Community prices.

(4) Social reasons for keeping farmers on the land have been increasingly heard in recent years. Sometimes these have an idealistic tone to them, with pleas that a populated countryside is part of the natural fabric, or the suggestion that management of the land is a desirable end in itself. Rather more hard-headed perhaps is the argument that, with relatively high levels of unemployment in the EC – the overall average was 10.3 per cent in 1988 – it is both undesirable and potentially dangerous to allow farm incomes to deteriorate to the point that poor farmers and agricultural workers are forced to move to the towns in search of employment that often does not exist.

Political Factors

Farmers enjoy political assets that they have been able to translate into influence on Community policy. Three of these assets are especially important.

(1) At the national decision-making level, Ministries of Agriculture have tended traditionally to be slightly apart from mainstream policy processes, and since 1958 this has been reproduced at the Community level. All policy areas, of course, attempt to use their own expertise, knowledge and information to provide themselves with some insulation from the rest of the decision-making system, but agriculture is particularly well placed to be able to do this. Its supposed special nature, the complexity of much of its subject matter, and the customary close relations between agricultural decision-makers and producers, all combine to make it difficult for 'outside' decision-makers to offer an effective challenge or alternative to what is presented to them. At the Community level, this is

compounded by the particular strength of DGVI and the fact that co-ordination of policy areas has never been a strong point of either the Commission or the Council of Ministers.

(2) Farmers enjoy considerable electoral weight. Even though their relative numerical importance has declined sharply over the years – in 1958 around 25 per cent of total Community employment was in agriculture, by 1990 it was around 8 per cent – the agricultural vote is still very significant. The significance varies from state to state. The size of the domestic population engaged in agriculture is one important factor in determining this significance: proportions range from around 30 per cent in Greece and 24 per cent in Portugal to 3 per cent in Belgium and the UK. Another consideration is the direction of the agricultural vote. On the whole farmers, especially richer farmers, incline to Centre-Right and Right parties, with the consequence that it is they, rather than parties of the Left, which are usually the strongest defenders of agricultural interests in Community forums. But this inclination to the Right does not, in most countries, amount to an exclusive loyalty, so few parties can afford to ignore the farmers altogether: at a minimum they must give the impression of being concerned and solicitous.

(3) Farmers have long had very strong domestic organisations to represent and articulate their views. When it became clear after the signing of the EEC Treaty that much agricultural policy and decision-making was to be transferred to Brussels, similar organisations were quickly established at Community level. As early as 1963, some 100 Community-wide agriculture groups had been formed. By the early 1990s, this number had grown to over 150. The most important of these groups is COPA which is an umbrella or peak organisation representing all types of farmers on the basis of affiliation through national farming groups. Beyond COPA and a few other overarching organisations, specialist bodies exist to represent virtually every product that is produced and consumed in the Community, and every stage of the agricultural process – farmers most obviously, but also processors, traders, retailers etc.

There can be no doubt that this agricultural lobby has been, and remains, a very powerful force in the Community. It is worth setting out the reasons why.

The sheer size of the lobby is formidable. It operates at two levels, the national and the Community.

At the national level there are considerable variations in the pattern and strength of agricultural representation. But, in all member states, there are groups of some kind which have as part of their purpose the utilisation of whatever devices and channels are available to them to influence both national agricultural policy (within the general principles of the CAP, states still enjoy a considerable policy discretion) and Community agricultural policy. Thus, the National Farmers' Union for England and Wales employs a full-time professional staff of around 240 at its London headquarters and 600 or so in the regions. Additionally it funds, in conjunction with the NFU of Scotland and the Ulster Farmers' Union, a Brussels office, known as the British Office of Agriculture, which has a regular staff of between five and ten who are topped up as required.

At the Community level the large number of Euro-agric groups means that lobbying activities across the agricultural sector are almost continuous. COPA moves on the broadest front and, with some 45 full-time officials, is by far the best resourced and staffed organisation. (See Chapter 8 for further information on COPA.) The more specialised groups – the mustard makers (CIMCEE) for example, or the butchers (COBCCEE) – are much more modestly provided for and may have, at best, one full-time member of staff working in an office made available by a national affiliate. But since the interests of these small groups is usually narrowly drawn this may be enough to allow basic lobbying requirements to be fulfilled – meetings and consultations with decision-makers, feeding information through to the Community institutions, preparing policy and briefing documents. If circumstances require it reinforcements are usually available from national and Euro-umbrella associations.

Agricultural interests generally enjoy good contacts with, and access to, decision-makers. Again, this factor operates at both national and Community levels.

At the national level, influence with governments is vital, not only because of their control over nationally determined policies but also because they are the route to the Council of Ministers. Most governments are at least prepared to listen to representations from national agricultural interests, and some engage in a virtual automatic consultation on important issues. There are a number of reasons why governments are generally approachable in this way: there may be a pre-existing sympathy for the interests' views; a fuller picture of what is going on in the agricultural world is made possible; policy implementation may be made easier; and political support may be generated by being sympathetic, or at least by giving the impression that the government and the interest are as one. If, despite being sympathetically listened to by its government, a national agricultural interest is dissatisfied with what is agreed in the Council of Ministers, the government can always try to blame 'the awkward Italians', 'the impossible Greeks', or 'the immovable Germans'.

At the Community level, the Commission is the prime target for agricultural interests. For the most part it is only too willing to listen. Indeed, it has encouraged the establishment of Euro-agric groups and readily makes itself available to them. They are seen as useful channels for a number of purposes, and close Commission–group relations are viewed by the Commission as being as useful to it as to the groups: the interests can contribute their knowledge and their experience which may improve policy; the Commission can explain to the interests why it is engaging in certain actions and thus seek to sensitise them to Commission concerns and aims; face-to-face meetings can help break down barriers and resistance arising from suspicions that 'the bureaucrats in the Berlaymont' do not really understand farming practicalities; and if Euro-groups can do something to aggregate the conflicting national interests and demands that arise in relation to most proposals, they can considerably simplify the Commission's task of developing policies that are acceptable and can help to legitimate the Commission as a decision-maker in the eyes of the Council and the EP.

The agricultural organisations are not counterbalanced by strong and vigorous groups advancing contrary attitudes and claims. 'Natural opponents' do exist – consumers and environmentalists most notably – but they are weak by contrast. A major reason for their weakness is that whereas farmers constitute a clear section of the population with a readily identifiable common sectoral interest, consumers and environmentalists do not have such a group consciousness, are dispersed, and, in consequence, are just not so easy to mobilise or organise. So, though there are many more consumers than there are farmers in the EC, the largest of the Euro-consumer groups – the Bureau of Consumer Associations (BEUC) – carries a staff of only seven or eight. This is respectable enough when compared with most Euro-groups, but it pales when compared with the massed ranks of the agriculture associations. Moreover, the BEUC has to cover the whole spectrum of relevant Community policies; agriculture takes up only part of its time.

In terms of access to decision-makers, the farmers' 'rivals' do not, as a rule, enjoy the 'insider status' granted to the agriculture lobby. They rarely have a 'sponsoring' ministry in the way that agricultural interests do. Nor are they consulted by the Commission on agricultural matters as a matter of routine, or automatically called in for discussions when something of importance or potential interest arises. The fact is that they do not have the political and economic power of farmers, they cannot offer trade-offs in the way of co-operation on policy implementation, they are – in some instances – relative latecomers, and a few – notably the more radical 'Greens' – are seen as not quite conforming with established values and the rules of the game. Some of the more respectable of these 'oppositional' agriculture groups have their foot in the Community door, but none has quite entered the room.

Agriculture has powerful friends. While farmers and those directly engaged in the agricultural industries have been the most obvious beneficiaries of the CAP, others have gained too, notably the owners of land. Huge profits have been made by investment institutions, financiers, banks, industrial corporations and private landlords from the rising value of land that has been triggered by the CAP. Many of these interests have direct access to decision-makers, indeed are themselves numbered amongst the decision-makers in some governments, and have sought to use their influence accordingly.

Until the mid-1980s unity was a considerable source of strength. Despite the great range of interests represented, the agriculture lobby was, until the mid-1980s, more or less united in its aims: it pressed for comprehensive market regimes for as much produce as possible, and it sought the largest price increases it could get. In recent years, however, as the first significant steps to bring agriculture spending under proper control have been taken, the unity of the lobby has been subject to increasing strains and its effectiveness has accordingly been weakened a little. Sectors have vied with one another as more careful attention has had to be paid, not only to the size of the cake, but also to the way in which it is cut.

How the Common Agricultural Policy Works

Title II of the EEC Treaty (Articles 38–47) sets out the general principles of the Community's agricultural policy. The objectives are laid down in Article 39:

(a) to increase agricultural productivity by promoting technical progress and by ensuring the rational development of agricultural production and the optimum utilisation of the factors of production, in particular labour;

(b) thus to ensure a fair standard of living for the agricultural community, in particular by increasing the individual earnings of persons engaged in agriculture;

(c) to stabilise markets;

(d) to assure the availability of supplies;

(e) to ensure that supplies reach consumers at reasonable prices.

Many matters are barely touched on in Title II and were deliberately left aside for later consideration by representatives of the states. Amongst the first fruits of these deliberations was the adoption by the Council of Ministers in December 1960 of the three major operating principles of the CAP. These still apply today.

A Single Internal Market with Common Prices

Agricultural goods are supposed to be able to flow freely across Community borders, unhindered by barriers to trade and unhampered by devices such as subsidies or administrative regulations which might distort or limit competition. However, it is not a free trade system based on pure market principles because certain common prices are set by the Council for most important products. These prices include a target price, which is the price it is hoped farmers will be able to obtain on the open market, a threshold price which is the price to which Community imports are raised, and a guaranteed or intervention price, which is the price at which the Commission will take produce off the market by stepping in and buying it up (see Figure 12.1). The amount of support a product is given is a consequence of how high these prices are set, the size of the gap between the prices, and the way in which price and currency mechanisms (see below) and intervention practices function.

Source: Adapted from *The Common Agricultural Policy and its Reform*, European Documentation, 1987.

FIGURE 12.1
Outline of the different price levels and the levy and refund system for a full market regime product

The price support system, which exists primarily to maintain farm incomes, dominates the CAP. It does so mainly because it is so costly to finance.

There are three principal reasons why it is expensive. First, many goods are produced in amounts that are surplus to Community requirements. Between 1973–4 and 1986–7 the Community's level of self-sufficiency increased from 98 per cent to 105 per cent for butter, from 91 per cent to 111 per cent for cereals, from 96 per cent to 106 per cent for beef, and from 100 per cent to 127 per cent for sugar. High guaranteed prices are the main reason for these surpluses, but improved farming techniques and the concentrated use of fertilisers and additives have also played a part. Second, the range of products protected by a market regime has gradually been extended so that now 94 per cent of all Community produce is covered in some way. Different regimes provide different forms of protection – so that in practice there are several agricultural policies rather than just one – but most (around 70 per cent) are the beneficiaries of support prices. For some products the support prices are available on an unconditional and open-ended basis, but more commonly, following a series of Council decisions in the 1980s designed to tackle the problem of surpluses and reduce CAP expenditure, they are subject to restrictions. The precise nature of the restrictions varies from product to product, but they usually take one of, or some combination of, three main forms: quotas; co-responsibility levies; and stabilisers – which consist of a mechanism in which production thresholds (maximum guaranteed quantities) are set, and if these are exceeded the guaranteed payments are automatically reduced. Third, apart from a brief interlude in 1974–5, Community agricultural prices have consistently been above world prices, which has meant that it has not been possible to export surpluses without suffering a financial loss: the loss being the difference in price between what the Community has agreed to pay the farmer and what it can sell the product at on world markets. Many devices are used to dispose of the surpluses – exporting and providing a refund (a 'restitution' in Community jargon) to the exporter to ensure he incurs no loss on the transaction, storing until Community prices rise, food aid, converting to animal foodstuffs – but they all have to be financed from the Community budget.

In addition to its cost, another major problem with the agricultural price system is that, apart from a short initial period, it has never been truly based, as intended, on common prices. This stems from the absence of a single European currency. As a result, the prices that are agreed annually by the Agriculture Ministers for products that are covered by a market regime are set in European Currency Units (Ecus) – which are based on a 'basket' or weighted average of the national currencies. For payments purposes Ecus are then converted into national currencies. (Following an agreement made in April 1984 support prices are set not in 'standard' Ecu but in a special 'green' Ecu called the agricultural unit of account which is linked to the deutschmark.)

If the exchange rates at which Ecu are converted into national currencies were the same as those which obtain on the open market common agricultural prices would exist. In practice, they are not. This is principally because market rates in the late 1960s and early

1970s became subject to sharp and rapid fluctuations, and this had implications for agriculture which governments were not prepared to accept: farmers' incomes and food prices were affected and trade patterns became distorted. As a result, it was decided to try and stabilise agricultural incomes, prices, and markets by the use of 'green' rates of exchange which would be set by the Agriculture Ministers and which would remain fixed whatever happened to the market rates of exchange. To ensure that differences between market rates and green rates would not distort intra-Community flows in agricultural products a system of border levies and subsidies, known as monetary compensation amounts (MCAs) was also introduced.

As a result of this system, the setting of agriculture prices cannot be viewed in isolation from exchange rates. Indeed, governments – especially in recent years, as Ecu prices have been kept down as part of the attempt to reduce CAP expenditure – have tended to look at the price–exchange rate linkage as a useful device both for protecting their farmers or consumers and for giving themselves a greater flexibility in Council negotiations. Trade-offs in the Council are common, with, for example, a government that feels pressurised by its farmers, agreeing to low price increases only on the condition of being allowed to devalue its green rate on specified products. (Each currency has not one green rate but several.) Convenient though it has sometimes been to governments, however, the agri-monetary system has undermined common prices, has been a major stumbling block in the way of a unified agricultural market, has weakened the attractions of product specialisation, and has been a drain on the Community budget. As a result, and after constant pressing by the Commission, it has been agreed that MCAs will be dismantled by 1992: whether, in the event, they actually will completely disappear, will depend on a number of factors, not least developments and decisions regarding currency alignments.

Community Preference

A necessary consequence of the guaranteed price system is that the Community market should be protected from the international market. Since world prices are normally lower than Community prices free access onto the Community market would clearly destroy the whole CAP system. Community preference is, therefore, required.

Whether, however, it is required at quite such preferential levels as in practice apply is a matter of dispute.

The mechanics of the preference system vary according to the market regime for the product concerned. For the 21 per cent of produce which has a market regime but not one based on guaranteed prices (wines other than table wines, some fruit and vegetables, some cereals, eggs and poultry), external protection takes the form of levies, customs duties, and a combination of the two. For the 70 per cent of produce which does enjoy guaranteed prices (most cereals, dairy produce, milk, beef, lamb) the system is such as to prevent imports entering the Community at prices below the agreed target prices. This exclusion is, as is shown in Figure 12.1, achieved by the threshold price which is calculated at a level to bring the world price up to the Community's target price, minus an allowance for unloading and transport costs. The gap between world prices and the threshold price is bridged by the imposition of a levy, which is adjusted according to variations in Community and world prices. The levies become part of the Community's own resources.

The exclusion procedures just described do not apply to all the imports into the Community from all states. As was explained in Chapter 9, the EC has negotiated arrangements by which a large number of countries, most of them underdeveloped, are given special access to Community markets for at least some of their products, including agricultural products. So, the Community grants 'generalised preferences' to more than 120 developing countries and one effect of this has been the abolition or reduction of levies on about 300 agricultural products intended for processing. Under the Lomé Convention virtually all of the exports of the 69 ACP countries have free access to the Community. (It should perhaps be pointed out here that these 'concessions' do not stem simply from generosity and goodwill. Much of the produce falling under the generalised preferences and Lomé agreements is tropical in nature and not in competition with EC produce.)

Joint Financing

The cost of the CAP is financed jointly by the member states through the European Agricultural Guidance and Guarantee Fund (EAGGF) of the Community budget. This is divided into two sections: the Guarantee section which finances markets and prices, and the Guidance section which finances structural policy. The early intention was that the Guarantee section would be larger than the Guidance section by a ratio of two or three to one, but, in practice, this has never been even remotely approached, and the Guidance section hovers somewhere in the region of only six per cent of total EAGGF expenditure. The demands on the Guarantee section occasioned by high Community prices is the main reason for this imbalance. A second reason is that, unlike expenditure on price support, expenditure on structural measures is not wholly financed by the EAGGF but is co-financed – usually by the Community in partnership with either member states or regions. And a third reason is that member states have often not been much interested in supporting Community agricultural structural policy – mainly because it usually involves contraction or bringing about changes to which agricultural interests are opposed.

But notwithstanding the limited size of the EAGGF Guidance section, there is still a very considerable amount of non-price related agricultural expenditure in the EC. Some of this comes from other Community sources – in particular the Regional Fund, Integrated Mediterranean Programmes, and the European Investment Bank. By far the most of it, however, comes from national exchequers: member states are allowed to assist their farmers in almost whatever way they like as long as they do not – in the judgement of the Commission – distort competition or infringe the principles of the market. In some states national subsidies to agriculture far outstrip those of the Community.

The Impact and Effects of the Common Agricultural Policy

Whether the CAP is to be regarded as a success or not obviously depends on the priorities and interests of those making the judgement. Since, however, the issue raises so much controversy it is worth examining some of the major development under the CAP system. This will be done via the five aims that were set out in Article 39 of the EEC Treaty and which were listed above.

Agricultural efficiency has increased enormously as a result of modernisation and rationalisation. Furthermore, despite the popular impression in some places that the CAP is little more than a device to cushion farmers, agriculture, both as a proportion of GNP and as a source of employment, has more than halved amongst the original six since 1958. That said, it may still be asked whether the overproduction of certain products at great cost, and the encouragement that high prices have given to many who would otherwise have left the land to stay, is wholly consistent with 'ensuring the rational development of agricultural production . . .'.

Under the CAP *agricultural incomes have grown roughly in parallel with incomes in other sectors*. However, this overall average masks enormous variations, both between large farmers (who have done very well for the most part) and small farmers, and also between producers of northern temperate products (notably dairy produce, cereals and beef which are the main product beneficiaries of the price support system) and producers of other – mainly Mediterranean – products.

Markets have been stabilised, in the sense that there have been no major food shortages and Community prices have escaped the fluctuations that have occurred in world market prices on some products.

The Community *is now self-sufficient in virtually all of those foodstuffs its climate allows it to raise and grow*. (In 1958 it produced about 85 per cent of its food requirements.) However, as was noted earlier, in some sectors it is much more than self-sufficient and, because domestic prices are high, the surpluses can be disposed of only at considerable cost.

The exclusion of cheaper (and often much cheaper) produce from outside the Community means that *the aim of 'reasonable prices' to the consumer has had a low priority*. The undeniable fact is that, within the Community, the principal beneficiaries of CAP's pricing system have been rich farmers, whilst the main losers have been poor consumers. (It might also be added that the exclusion of efficient non-Community producers has had an impact at the international level too – notably in distorting the international division of labour and the rational utilisation of resources, and in fuelling trading hostilities.)

Policy and Decision-making Processes

In many respects, policy and decision-making processes for agriculture are much the same as in other policy sectors. However, the importance, the range, and the complexity of the CAP, plus the ever-changing nature of the world's agricultural markets, means that there are significant variations from the 'standard' Community model. The principal variations are as follows.

Commission Initiation and Formulation

Whereas the policy initiation and formulation responsibilities of the Commission in most sectors are much concerned with creating a policy framework, in agriculture they are inevitably directed more towards improving the efficiency of one that already exists.

But, as has been indicated above, there are formidable obstacles in the way of the Commission if it is to come forward with proposals that both go to the heart of the agricultural problem and are also acceptable to the Council. As long ago as 1968 the then Commissioner for Agriculture, Sicco Mansholt, launched a major plan to reduce the size of the agriculture sector and improve the efficiency of what remained, but his proposals had little effect and were not followed up by enough Council legislation. As a result the Commission in the 1970s approached its policy initiation and formulation responsibilities in a very cautious way. It became reluctant to advance wide-ranging schemes aimed at fundamental reform and concentrated more on short-term measures of an essentially reactive nature: reacting, that is, to specific problems in particular market sectors.

In the 1980s circumstances changed in such a way that they enabled, even obliged, the Commission to bring a longer-term view back onto the agenda and force real and properly integrated reform to be at least seriously discussed. The most important of these circumstances were deteriorating market conditions and increasing surpluses, recurring budgetary problems, international pressures against the EC's high levels of protectionism and subsidisation, and the enlargement of the Community to states which would not do especially well out of the CAP as constituted. It was to this background that in 1985 the Commission launched a consultative Green Paper – *Perspectives for the Common Agricultural Policy* – which outlined policy options and the future of agriculture until the end of the century. After wide ranging discussions with interested parties the Green Paper was followed up with more detailed guidelines in the form of a communication to the Council and the EP entitled *A future for European agriculture*. At the heart of the Commission's proposals lay an ambitious long term strategy for a movement to a more market-based and restrictive pricing policy, more flexibility in guarantees and intervention mechanisms, and a much greater degree of producer co-responsibility for surpluses. These objectives were restated in the Commission's influential 1987 document *The Single Act: A new frontier for Europe*, and constituted the basis for the important agricultural reforms that the Agriculture Ministers agreed to in December 1986 and the Heads of Government agreed to in February 1988 (both of these agreements are considered below).

Council Decision-making

Of all the Councils, the Agriculture Council is the one which is most reliant on issue linkages and package deals for conducting its business (see Exhibit 4.1 for an indication of the range of business which is covered by Agriculture Ministers).

One reason it *has* to be so reliant is that whereas in some sectors issues can be allowed to drift almost indefinitely, in agriculture certain decisions, most obviously those taken as part of the annual price review, cannot be continually postponed. They must be resolved, but a resolution is normally possible only if it is based on a recognition of the different interests and priorities of the states: most states, for example, are net exporters of agricultural produce, but a minority are net importers; some have temperate climates, some Mediterranean; some have mainly large and efficient farms, others still carry many small and inefficient family based units; and some have vast tracts of 'less favoured' land, whilst others have very little.

A major reason the Council is *able* to make use of linkages and packages is that it has available to it a variety of possible policy instruments. By bringing these together in carefully weighted combinations the way can often be opened to agreements in which there is something for everyone.

An example of a package deal is the one which was struck on beef and dairy products in December 1986 when the ministers responded to Commission initiatives (noted above) and Council Presidency (UK) pressure to tackle surplus production. A range of measures were agreed (see Exhibit 12.1), but only after days of negotiations involving ministers and senior officials, after some of the Commission's more radical measures were watered down, and after 'softening' and 'compensating' devices of various kinds were approved. With the agreement still leaving a projected dairy surplus of around

EXHIBIT 12.1

Package agreed by Ministers of Agriculture, December 1986*

1) A commitment to achieve a 9½ per cent reduction in milk production over a two year period by a mixture of voluntary and mandatory cuts in quotas. Farmers to be paid compensation. (Some of the measures in this part of the deal – notably the temporary nature of a proportion of the quota cuts and the high level at which compensation was set – were included primarily to pacify the Germans who had an election due. Ireland succeeded in persuading the Council to instruct the Commission to note the 'unique dependence' of Ireland upon the dairy sector, especially in relation to intervention. Unofficial estimates by the Commission put the real size of the reduction at around only 6 per cent.)

2) An agreed 13 per cent reduction in the guaranteed price for beef, and changes in the operation of the beef intervention system. (Ireland threatened to veto the whole package if, as was initially proposed, it was excluded from receiving a new form of compensatory payment for beef producers on the grounds that its farmers were already being adequately supported. A compromise resulted in Ireland receiving a scaled down version of the new funds.)

3) Green rate devaluations: 14.5 per cent on Greek sheepmeat; 4.8 per cent on French beef and veal and 3.185 per cent on sheepmeat; 6 per cent on Portuguese sheepmeat; 3.2 per cent on Spanish sheepmeat. (The effect of these devaluations would be to boost farmers' incomes in the five countries concerned.)

4) Structural measures. The details of these were left to be worked out at a later stage but it was agreed they would include encouragement for early retirement, provisions for less intensive farming, and the adoption of a flexible attitude towards any government which wished to top up Community funds with contributions of its own.

*Only the four main elements of the package are set out here.

12 per cent above total domestic consumption, (even on the extremely doubtful assumption that the new quotas would be properly applied in all the states), and with the decisions on beef really doing little more than adjusting market support to changes in beef production, the package hardly merited the description of 'historic importance' which some of the participating ministers attached to it. Rather was it a typical Agriculture Council compromise.

What the exhaustive negotiations of December 1986 produced was essentially a political deal. As with many agreements/pronouncements/resolutions/declarations in the Community, translating the deal into implementing legislation subsequently proved to be very difficult. A particular problem was that some governments, on analysing the implications of the deal in detail and at greater leisure, readjusted their positions. The Danes, the French, the Germans and the Irish – all perhaps influenced by the implications of what was becoming known would be very restrictive Commission price proposals for 1987–8 – decided they had been hard done by. Later Council meetings were thus obliged to debate again issues supposedly resolved at the December meeting.

A rather different example of extensive political wheeling and dealing in the Council of Ministers being necessary before an agreement on agriculture matters could be reached occurred in the autumn of 1990 in connection with the negotiating mandate to be given to the Commission in the Uruguay Round of GATT negotiations. Agriculture had proved to be the major problem in the Uruguay Round because of an insistence by most of the Community's major trading partners, notably the United States and the Cairns group of fourteen farm exporting countries, that the Community's system of subsidising agriculture should be virtually dismantled: the US wanted the internal farm subsidies cut by 75 per cent, and the export subsidies cut by 90 per cent, over a ten year period. The Council of Ministers was quite unable to accept this, but France and Germany, with some support from Ireland, were instrumental in preventing the Council from even agreeing to a compromise negotiating formula put forward by the Commission whereby Community farm subsidies as a whole would be cut by 30 per cent over a ten year period backdated to 1986 – which, since the post-1986 reforms had already had some effect in cutting subsidies, meant a real cut of only about 15 per cent between 1990 and 1995. As a result, the Community was unable to meet the mid-October 1990 deadline by which time it had been agreed that all the participating parties in GATT should formally table their negotiating positions. It was not until early November – after extensive negotiations on the matter in seven different Council of Ministers meetings involving Agriculture, Foreign, and Trade Ministers – that a marathon joint session of Agriculture and Trade Ministers was eventually able to agree a negotiating brief for the Commission. Almost inevitably the agreement bore all the hallmarks of both a fudge and a compromise, combining a commitment to cut subsidies by 30 per cent with other commitments to cushion farmers from loss of incomes, to protect them against any sudden increase in cheap food imports, and to introduce import levies on some products hitherto allowed free access to the Community. (In the event, the Community's position was still seen as being too protectionist by the US, and the GATT negotiations were suspended – with the hope, on both sides, that informal contacts and soundings, coupled with reflections on the potentially dire consequences for all of international trade if no agreement could be reached, would produce a greater flexibility when negotiations resumed.)

Management and Implementation of the Common Agricultural Policy

Because of the nature of the CAP, the Community is much more involved in the management and implementation of agricultural policy than it is in other policy spheres. The Commission, and particularly DGVI, are central in this regard. They oversee the general operation of the whole system, they adjust it as necessary, and, insofar as it is possible, they try to ensure that the national agencies which undertake the front line implementation of policy – Ministries of Agriculture, intervention agencies, customs and excise authorities etc. – fulfil their obligations in a proper manner.

In exercising these duties the Commission must operate within Community law and Council guidelines. This means that much of what it does in managing the CAP is of an essentially technical nature: adjusting regulators to match ever-changing market conditions. But in some spheres it can do this in ways which amount to rather more than simply applying tightly drawn rules. Many of its decisions – for example on the operation of the intervention and support systems, on refunds, on storage – are taken within margins of manoeuvre that give it at least some flexibility. It is a flexibility that can result in the Commission's choices having important financial implications for producers, traders, processors, and the Community budget.

Where payments and charges have to be adjusted almost daily, and in other instances where quick management decisions have to be taken, the Commission is authorised to act without reference to any other body. However, as was explained in Chapter 3, the Commission's general agricultural management responsibilities are not exercised by Commission officials alone but via management committees made up of civil servants from the member states. There are over twenty such committees, including one for each product that has a market regime, and the Commission would not normally go ahead with anything important – in relation to export refunds for example – without referring to the appropriate committee, and to the Council if necessary. It is generally accepted that the Commission determines the direction and sets the pace in the committees but the existence of the committees does mean that the member states have a direct input to, and ultimately a control over, all but the fine details of agricultural policy and the management of that policy.

The Annual Price Review

A distinguishing feature of agriculture decision-making is that many of the key decisions are made as part of a regular annual process: in the price review. Contrary to what the name suggests, prices are not the only element of the reviews. Many non-price elements get swept up and become components of what is usually a highly complex and interconnected package by the time the final agreement is made. The core of the package usually consists of a range of different product price increases, agri-monetary adjustments, structural measures, and statements of intent about future action.

The date of the beginning of the marketing year varies between products, but as some begin on 1 April the intention of the Commission is always to have a settlement before this date. To achieve this a timetable exists that is supposed to culminate with the Agriculture Council making decisions in March. In practice, it has not usually been possible to keep to the later parts of the timetable in recent years and agreements have been delayed into April, May, and even later. This has obliged the Council to prolong the previous year's allocations in order to permit payments still to be made.

There is an important sense in which price reviews are a constant part of the work of DGVI, since market situations are subject to constant monitoring, whilst medium to long-term schemes for agricultural reform have to be implemented, to some extent at least, via reviews. The systematic work on particular reviews, however, is concentrated into the six to seven month period before they are due to come into effect. The main stages are as follows:

(1) In September the directorates and divisions, working with the management committees, begin to analyse and draw up reports on such matters as quantities, state of stocks, prices, and exports in their market sectors. This is essentially a technical exercise.

(2) During October and November consultations occur between the Commission and interested parties. Some of these are in the structured settings of management and advisory committees, others are more informal exchanges between DGVI officials and representatives of governments and sectional interests. Amongst the sectional interests which feed their views into the Commission are farmers organisations (notably COPA), consumers organisations (notably BEUC), trade organisations (such as COCERAL – which represents the grain trade), and food industry organisations (such as ASSILEC – which represents the dairy industry).

(3) The first drafts from the various sectors should be ready by mid-November. The process of integrating them necessitates several rounds of meetings involving the Commissioner for Agriculture, members of his *cabinet*, the director general, assistant directors general, directors, and senior officials representing the three main product areas of the review – livestock, crops, wine. In attempting to bring everything together the Commissioner and his advisers have to bear in mind a number of considerations:

● Commission and Council policy preferences drawn from both rolling programmes and continuing commitments.

● The limitations imposed by the agricultural reference framework. Recognising that previous attempts to control agricultural expenditure via budgetary discipline guidelines had not been successful, and faced with growing agricultural surpluses and (another) impending budgetary crisis, the Heads of Government, as part of their February 1988 Brussels 'package deal' (see Chapter 11), agreed to a five year reference framework for agricultural expenditure which had as its aim a significant decrease in the proportion of the Community budget devoted to agriculture. The agreement at Brussels was given effect by the *Interinstitutional Agreement* of June 1988 (see Document 11.1) which specified that from a reference base of 27.5 billion Ecu EAGGF Guarantee expenditure for 1988, annual growth rates in subsequent years should not exceed 74 per cent of the annual rate of increase in Community Gross National Product.

● The likely effect of penalties, some of the more important of which were also agreed at the Brussels summit, for particular products where guarantee production thresholds set for those products are exceeded. Some penalties come into force in the current financial year, and some in the next. So, for example, in the important case of cereals, if the agreed threshold (set at 160 million tonnes up to the 1991–2 marketing year) is exceeded, then a co-responsibility levy of up to three per cent is imposed in the current financial year and a price cut of up to three per cent is introduced in the next financial year.

● Political factors and the implications proposals may have for states. If, for example, an important national election is coming up, a decision may have to be made over whether to draw up the budget early in an attempt to minimise its political impact or deliberately delay it.

(4) On being agreed in DGVI a draft is submitted to the Commissioners for their approval. Ideally this submission is made by mid-December, although often the timetable slips and it may be later.

The Commissioners' deliberations are preceded by meetings of members of their *cabinets* assisted by senior officials from DGVI. If all goes well a general agreement on most key points can be reached at this stage. The Commissioners themselves, however, have to approve the final proposals. Whether this is largely a formality or involves difficult negotiations depends on what has happened at the pre-meetings.

(5) As soon as they are agreed – which should be in early January – the Commission's proposals are sent to the Council, and also to the ESC and the EP for Opinions.

The influence of the ESC is very marginal. This reflects its limited role in the Community as a whole, though such potential for exerting influence on the review as it does have is not helped by its customary inability to take a united view on agricultural questions. So, its Opinion on the 1987–8 Commission proposals – which incorporated agreements, disagreements, and agreements subject to conditions – was adopted (at the April plenary because of a timetable slippage) by 94 votes to 53 with 12 abstentions; that is, only half of the ESC's 189 members supported the Opinion.

The EP, by virtue of its greater power and authority, is listened to rather more seriously – or, at least, the Commission and the Council strive harder to give the impression that they are listening. Most MEPs, however, fully realise that they are hardly central actors in the price review exercise. Indeed, largely because of this, the EP has abandoned its former practice of holding a special session on the review and now incorporates its debate and the delivery of its Opinion into the March plenary, or, if there has been a timetable slippage, as soon as is practicable thereafter. The proceedings are conducted on the basis of reports drawn up by the Agriculture Committee in consultation with other interested committees. In the plenary, many amendments to the Commission's proposals are voted upon, and usually MEPs follow the recommendations which are made to them by the Agriculture Committee's *rapporteur*: at the March 1990 plenary, in respect of the 1990/91 review, it took three and a half hours to vote on the 300 or so amendments which had been laid. (The Commissioner for Agriculture, however, quickly made it clear that he would not alter his proposals to accommodate the two major revisions proposed by the EP – the establishment of a preferential pricing system to favour small producers, and the abolition of co-responsibility levies for milk and cereals.)

In the Council, ministers are likely to have an early meeting to give their first reactions to the Commission proposals. All will arrive well armed with briefs and analyses as to how the proposals will affect their farmers, their consumers, their budgetary contributions, their balance of payments and so on. In all probability most will say the proposals are too restrictive, and all twelve will put down markers for future meetings by identifying particular points that are unacceptable as they stand. Subsequent ministerial meetings will be arranged as necessary, by which time new points may have arisen and others may have been resolved as a result of meetings at lower Council levels: most of the agricultural working parties (of which there are around 25, including one for each of the principal commodity regimes), will meet at least twice to consider the Commission's proposals as they affect their areas; and the SCA (see Chapter 4) will try to pull the working parties' reports together and give them an overall coherence.

(6) In the light of views expressed – and quite apart from formal pronouncements by the ESC, the EP, and the Council, intense lobbying campaigns are conducted by national and sectional

interests – the Commission makes adjustments to its proposals. These are designed to improve the prospects of a settlement in the Council, whilst clinging to as much of the original proposals as possible.

(7) Towards the end of March, or later if proceedings have fallen behind schedule, the Agriculture Council meets to try and agree a settlement. Marathon sessions are common, and meetings may have to be reconvened if solutions cannot be found at the first time of asking.

Each minister naturally tries to get the best terms he can and wishes also to be seen to be putting up a vigorous defence of national interests. This makes for extremely difficult negotiations, with much posturing and striking of attitudes sitting alongside genuine differences on such matters as price preferences, Community budgetary implications, elimination of surpluses, and commitments to farmers and consumers. Complicated package deals, with many non-price factors being dragged in to increase flexibility, are usually the only means by which a solution can be found. (Exhibit 12.2 is an example of a typical price review package.) Voting is common, and ministers may well make their vote of approval on one issue dependent on guarantees of support on another. Frequently those who are dissatisfied with the proposed settlement on a matter – say cereal price increases – seek 'compensation' elsewhere – perhaps in the form of permission to offer national subsidies of some kind. Wheeling and dealing and the trading of points can thus usually give to all participants something to identify in the way of national benefits when they leave the negotiating table.

As was noted earlier, the final package which constitutes the annual price review should be agreed by the end of March, but it has not been so in recent years. In 1987, for example, the timetable fell behind schedule from an early stage when, as a result of differences over cereal prices, green currency devaluations, and a proposed tax on oils and fats, the Commission's draft proposals were delayed. When they were made available, negotiations in the Council, on these same issues, proved to be extremely difficult and it was only after intense diplomatic activity in national capitals, and after the issues were discussed at the European Council meeting at the end of June, that the impasse was eventually broken. The Heads of Government indicated the basis of a deal and the Agriculture Ministers, meeting the very next day, then finalised it. Another example of the March deadline being missed occurred in 1990 when

EXHIBIT 12.2

Major decisions taken as part of the 1986/7 Farm Price Review

		Price Increase* (%)
Wheat	–	
	Target Price	+ 0.5
	Intervention Price – bread making quality	0.0
Maize	–	
	Intervention Price	0.0
	Feed Quality Grains	– 5.0
	except Rye	– 5.9
Durum Wheat	–	
	Intervention Price	– 4.0
	Aid	+ 12.3
Olive Oil	–	
	Intervention Price	– 5
Rice, Sugar, Rapeseed, Sunflower Seed, Soya, Dried Fodder, Hemp, Cotton, Wine		0
Peas, Field Beans, Lupins		+ 1.0
Dairy Products, Beef, Sheep, Pigmeat		0
Tobacco		0 to – 6

* Spain and Portugal are not due to become full members of the price and aid system until 1996.

Other measures of the 1986/7 'package' to include:

1. All countries except West Germany and the Netherlands to devalue their green currencies.
2. A 3 per cent co-responsibility on cereal production. Member states to be allowed to make various direct payments to farmers to compensate them for this.
3. Higher quality standards to apply on grain bought up for intervention.
4. A 3 per cent cut in milk quotas for all 12 member states spread over three years

The overall effect of the above settlement was that the Commission's desire for a tight review was broadly satisfied. It did, however, have to make some important concessions, for example, the milk quota reductions were to be spread over three years rather than one, the price of butter was to be frozen rather than cut by 4 per cent, and the green currency devaluations softened the blow of the prices restraint.

Germany – and to a lesser extent Ireland, Luxembourg and Spain – had most reservations about the agreement. A consequence of this was that Germany agreed to compensate its farmers for the real cuts in their income and in May persuaded the Council to allow it to re-classify nearly half of its farm acreage as poor areas, and thus eligible for higher levels of government support. Another consequence was that Germany adopted a very tough position in the 1987–8 negotiations and was openly critical both of the Commission as a whole – which again approved a tight review – and of the President and the two German Commissioners in particular.

almost four days of negotiations in the Agriculture Council at the end of March failed to produce a settlement for 1990–1. The talks broke down mainly over the question of whether or not to reduce the co-responsibility levies for cereals and milk. The deadlock was only broken at another marathon Agriculture Council meeting at the end of April when green currency realignments were used to bring about a settlement.

The 1988 Brussels summit has had three important implications for the annual agricultural price review. First, by establishing restrictive guidelines for agricultural expenditure it has meant that price settlements have had to be tight. As can be seen from Table 12.1 a restrictive price increase policy was already underway before the Brussels summit, but since the summit price increases have been even lower. Second, it has assisted another process which was also underway before the summit, namely that there be a close alignment between the original Commission proposals and the final settlement. And, third, by placing greater limits on the Council's range of

TABLE 12.1

Annual average percentage changes in agricultural support prices in Ecus and national currencies

| Year | Council Decision | | Commission Proposal | |
	Ecu	National Currency	Ecu	National Currency
1978–9	2.1	8.5	2.0	8.4
1979–80	1.3	7.4	0.0	6.1
1980–1	4.8	10.5	2.5	8.2
1981–2	9.2	10.8	7.8	9.4
1982–3	10.4	12.1	8.4	10.1
1983–4	4.2	6.9	4.2	6.9
1984–5	−0.4	3.2	0.8	4.4
1985–6	0.0	1.3	−0.3	1.0
1986–7	−0.3	2.2	−0.1	0.9
1987–8	−0.2	2.6	−0.5	0.2
1988–9	0.0	1.6	0.0	0.3
1989–90	−0.1	1.3	−0.2	0.7
1990–1	−1.1	0.3	−1.1	0.2

Source: A. Fearne, 'The Administration of EC Agricultural Policies by National Agencies'. Paper given to the *Annual Conference of the Public Administration Committee* 1990; and *Bulletin of the European Communities*.

options, it has made observance of the timetable just a little easier to achieve. As was shown above, with reference to the 1990–1 settlement, there is still ample room for disputes, and there is certainly no guarantee that all can be settled by March (indeed the first two reviews to fall fully under the new system – those of 1989–90 and 1990–1 – were not settled until April), but the narrowing of the range of possible courses of action has eased, if only slightly, the complexities of the CAP decision-making process.

Concluding Remarks

The CAP is not quite as common or as integrated as it is often thought to be. On the one hand, at the Community level, the supposed common pricing system is distorted by the mechanisms of green currencies and monetary compensation amounts. On the other hand, at the national level, governments still have the option of making various forms of special assistance available to their farmers. Some of the richer states, especially Germany, have, in response to the restrictive price policy of recent years, considerably extended the assistance they give. This has happened on such a scale that some observers have even spoken of there having been a movement towards a 'renationalisation' of agricultural policy.

Nonetheless, the CAP is, in many respects, still the most important sectoral policy of the EC. But clearly, as the continuing existence of surpluses demonstrates, the policy does not work completely satisfactorily. A key reason for this is that agriculture is not excluded from, indeed is characterised to an enhanced degree by, the central problem associated with policy and decision-making throughout the Community: competing interests make it very difficult for matters to be decided on a rational basis. Progress and change have thus tended to be circumspect and piecemeal rather than comprehensive and sweeping. But progress and change there have been, as is most obviously seen in the introduction of a series of measures since the early 1980s designed to cut back on the previously open-ended commitment to high levels of support for farmers. Low price increases, respect for budgetary discipline, quotas, co-responsibility levies, stabilisers, the phasing out of MCAs, and schemes for taking agricultural land out of production (so called 'set aside'), are all designed to make the CAP more market oriented.

These more restrictive policies have, however, far from solved all of the CAP's problems, and sharp differences still exist over the balance to be struck between market efficiency on the one hand and support – and whether the emphasis should be on price support or direct income support – on the other. Since these are differences which cannot be easily reconciled it seems likely that agriculture will continue to loom large in the life of the Community for some time to come.

13

National Influences and Controls on Community Processes

It is generally agreed that the highest price states have to pay for their membership of the Community is a substantial loss of their own law-making powers. In some policy spheres – agriculture and external trade in particular – autonomous national powers have been very largely removed. The reason the states are prepared to countenance this loss of sovereignty and are willing to participate in collective decision-making is that their national decision-makers, supported by large sections of their populations, believe it to be in their national interest to do so. The particular balance of advantages and disadvantages varies from state to state, but each judges that there is more to be gained from being in the Community than being out.

But belonging to the Community is seen to require care and vigilance so as to ensure that national interests are fully articulated and properly defended. Since, however, there are competing views within the member states about what these interests are, and since too there are a variety of domestic institutions, movements, interests, and parties which wish to be heard, there are many inputs from each of the states into Community policy and decision-making processes.

The precise nature of these inputs varies from state to state – reflecting such factors as different national political systems, traditions, and cultures – but they can all, in broad terms, be seen as being directed through six principal channels: governments, parliaments, courts, public opinion, political parties, and interests.

Governments

Governments are naturally in the strongest position to exercise national controls and influence on Community processes. This is most obviously seen in their relationships with the Commission and the Council.

There are many opportunities for governments to bring pressure to bear on the Commission. Formal opportunities include experts groups, management committees, and Council meetings. Informal opportunities can range from a minister ringing up a Commissioner, to a working party representative meeting a Commission official for lunch.

Appointments to the Commission, which all governments watch closely so as to ensure that fellow nationals are well represented and well placed, can also be used to advantage. At the level of the Commissioners themselves, the practice of appointment by national nomination institutionalises national inputs. Below the Commissioners, a similar function is performed by the informal national quota system that exists for senior grades.

This potential for Council influence on the Commission is not to suggest that Commissioners or Commission officials act as governmental representatives. As was shown in Chapter 3, they do, for the most part, look to the Community-wide interest and are not open to instructions from national capitals. But they may, quite naturally, be inclined to take a particular interest in the impact of proposals on their own country. And governments looking for sympathetic ears in the Commission may well make fellow nationals their first port of call. (Though not necessarily: competent national officials, especially from the Permanent Representations, cultivate a broad range of contacts in the Commission.)

It should also be recognised that governmental influence on Commission thinking is not necessarily a bad thing. On the contrary, it can be positively helpful, by, for example, improving the prospects for the eventual adoption of proposals for Council legislation. Where, however, it can become unhealthy is when governments try to lean too heavily on their fellow nationals in the Commission, and when clusters of nationals have a disproportionate influence on policy development in a key sector.

The potential for any single government to exercise control over what happens in the Council depends on a number of factors:

The size of the state it represents. No matter what is being discussed the larger countries, especially France and Germany, are always likely to carry more weight than the smaller countries, such as Portugal and Luxembourg.

The importance of the state to particular negotiations. On the Common Fisheries Policy, for example, the Spanish government represents many more interests and is likely to be a much more central actor than Belgium.

The desire of the government to play an active role. An illustration of the importance of this factor is seen in the way German governments, until the late 1960s, acted very much as political lightweights, even though their country was clearly an economic heavyweight. This was partly because of Germany's historical legacy and partly because of the delicacies involved in the 'normalisation' of her relations with Eastern Europe and especially the German Democratic Republic. In more recent years, as Germany's position has come to be seen as not so unique or so special, her governments have increasingly asserted themselves across the Community's policy spectrum, and have not been unwilling to adopt 'awkward' and even isolated positions.

The capacity of the government to play an active role. A government may have clear views on a Community initiative, and may wish to play an active role in supporting or opposing it, but it could be restrained from doing so by domestic political considerations such as a finely balanced coalition government, opposition from key interest groups, or possible electoral damage.

Relations with other governments. Cohesive and fixed alliances *within* the Community between *particular* governments do not exist. Rather, governments tend to divide and join in different combinations on different issues. However, some governments do make more conscious efforts than others to seek general understandings and co-operation with Community partners, and where they are successful they do appear often to increase their influence as a consequence. The best example of this is the close relationship that has been consciously fostered between most French and German governments since the early 1960s. The so-called Franco-German axis is not so commanding now as it was when there were only six Community members, or when Chancellor Schmidt and President Giscard d'Estaing worked closely together in the 1970s, but it still plays an important part in helping to shape and set the pace of Community developments.

The procedures applying. Of particular importance is whether majority voting is constitutionally permissible and politically acceptable. If it is, concessions and compromises might be preferable to being out-voted. If it is not, any government can cause indefinite delay, though by so doing it may weaken goodwill towards it and so damage its long-term interests.

The competence of governmental negotiators. Given the extensive tactical manoeuvrings involved in Community processes, and given too that many negotiations are not about the broad sweep of policy but are about highly technical matters, the competence of individual nego-tiators can be crucial. Are they well briefed and able to master details? Can they judge how far their negotiating partners can be pushed? Can they avoid being isolated? Can they build coalitions? Can they time their interventions so as to clinch points? The evidence suggests that variations in such competencies are not so much between states as between individual negotiators.

The arrangements for linking representatives in the Council with national capitals. This point is worth developing in a little detail because there are significant variations in the ways in which governments attempt, and are able, to control their inputs into the Council via their representatives. Two aspects of the control are particularly worth mentioning:

First, some countries – including Belgium, Italy, Luxembourg and the Netherlands – appear generally to allow their representatives to work within a fairly loose framework. That is to say, representatives are often able to negotiate on important policy matters not just at ministerial level but also in working parties and in COREPER. As well as assisting the functioning of the Council as a whole – by reducing the need for awkward issues to be referred upwards – manoeuvrability and flexibility of this kind can be used to the national advantage by competent negotiators. At the same time, however, too much independence for representatives can lead to the necessity for awkward backtracking at a later negotiating stage if a misjudgement is made. By contrast, representatives from other states – including France, Greece, Ireland and the UK – tend to have less room for manoeuvre in working parties and in COREPER and are generally reluctant to negotiate on policy issues below ministerial level. Whether, as is sometimes claimed, this greater rigidity improves the consistency and effectiveness of a country's negotiating position is doubtful. Undoubtedly, the more that countries lean in this direction, and all do at times, the more negotiations at the Council's lower levels are limited to technical matters and the more the overall Council process is protracted.

At the most senior Council level – ministerial meetings – there is, of course, not such a problem of control from national capitals. It is important to ensure that the minister is fully briefed on the national implications of proposals, and is accompanied by national officials who fully understand all aspects of agenda items, but the political weight of the participants usually means that, if the will is there, commitments can be entered into without having to refer back to the relevant ministry for clearance. This is not to say that those in attendance at ministerial meetings can do as they like. At a minimum they are obliged to operate within the general guidelines of their government's policies. They may also be subject to special national constraints: perhaps occasioned by an inability of the minister himself to attend; perhaps linked to domestic political difficulties caused by the existence of a coalition government; or perhaps a consequence of a particular national interest having resulted in the establishment of a rigid governmental position in advance.

Second, the ability of governments to co-ordinate their national position across different sectoral Councils is important. Unless there is some particular advantgage, no government wishes its representatives in one policy sphere to be contradicting or undermining the efforts of its representatives in another. All member states have, therefore, established internal co-ordinating mechanisms of some kind. These work with varying degrees of efficiency, depending largely on the nature of the domestic political and governmental system and the sophistication of the mechanisms that are established.

In the UK, the centralised governmental system and the majority party political system provide a favourable base for effective co-ordinating mechanisms. The mechanisms themselves are formalised, structured, and seemingly well integrated. At the general policy level, the Foreign and Commonwealth Office (FCO), the Cabinet Office, and the UK Permanent Representation are the key bodies: the FCO has two European Community Departments – Internal and External; the Cabinet Office contains a European Secretariat which, amongst other things, convenes each year around 200 interdepartmental meetings of civil servants attended by representatives from appropriate ministries, including one regular weekly meeting which is attended by the Permanent Representative; and the Permanent Representation Office – which is formally an FCO overseas post – acts as the eyes and ears of the UK in Brussels. Together these three attempt to monitor, co-ordinate and control overall Community developments: by giving general consideration to important matters due to come up at forthcoming meetings; by looking at whether a broadly consistent line is being pursued across different policy areas; by trying to ensure that ministries have issued sufficiently clear guidelines for representatives in Council meetings; and, in the cases of the FCO and the UK Permanent Representation, giving briefings themselves to representatives where appropriate. 'Above' these three bodies, but not involved in such a continuous manner, there is a Cabinet Committee on the European Community, the Cabinet itself, and the Prime Minister. 'Below' them, each ministry has its own arrangements for examining proposals that fall within its competence and for ensuring that specialist negotiators are well briefed and fully aware of departmental thinking. Where Community matters loom large in a ministry's work special divisions or units exist for co-ordination purposes.

In Germany, by contrast, all sorts of factors make effective co-ordination very difficult: the existence of a coalition government and the need to satisfy – though not on a consistent basis across policy areas – the different elements of the coalition; the relative autonomy of ministers and ministries within the federal government (seen, most notably, in the long running and open disagreement between the Finance Ministry and the Agriculture Ministry over the cost of the CAP); the lack of an authoritative co-ordinating centre – the Foreign Ministry has a rather imprecise responsibility for general integration policy, and the Economics Ministry has responsibility for routine matters; the relative independence from government of the Bundesbank (which has resulted in open differences between the government – or at least parts of the government – and the Bank, on

Economic and Monetary Union); the strong powers of the federal states – the *Länder* – in certain policy areas; and strong sectoral specialisation, allied with loyalties to different federal ministries, amongst the staff of the German Permanent Representation in Brussels. As a result, Germany's European policies are sometimes less than consistent. Fortunately for Germany, its position as the strongest single Community state seemingly enables it to avoid being too seriously damaged by this internal weakness.

Whatever the particulars of their arrangements for controlling and influencing Community activities all governments have found the task becoming increasingly difficult in recent years. Three factors are especially important in accounting for this:

● Many more decisions are now being taken by the Community. This applies to both major and long-term decisions – on EMU, on institutional reform, on the social dimension etc. – and to more small scale and specific decisions – such as the great volume of internal market legislation.

● Not only are more decisions being made but many are being made much more quickly. The much greater use of majority voting means that governments cannot now always delay progress on a proposal until they are ready and satisfied.

● The increased scope of Community policy interests means that there are now no longer just a few domestic ministries – agriculture, trade, finance and so forth – which are directly involved with the Community. The 'Europeanisation' of domestic politics and administration has resulted in most ministries in most states becoming actively involved in Community affairs.

Parliaments

Parliaments are much less influential than governments in influencing Community developments. Of course, governments normally reflect the political composition of their national legislatures and must retain their confidence, so, in an indirect sense, governmental activity in relation to the Community could be said to be reflective of parliamentary will. But that is a quite different matter to direct parliamentary control.

One of the major reasons for the lack of much direct parliamentary control is that national parliaments have no formal Treaty powers, so governments can choose what to consult their parliaments about. All governments do consult their parliaments on fundamental matters where the Treaties refer to ratification in accordance with 'respective constitutional requirements' (enlargements, Treaty amendments, and the Community's budgetary base carry this provision), but otherwise there are variations between the states. Another reason for weakness is the particular difficulties that arise in relation to what might be expected to be the major sphere of influence of national parliaments: advising on Community legislation. The difficulties here are legion: a high proportion of Community legislation is, or is regarded by governments as being, 'administrative' legislation and not, therefore, within parliamentary competences; much Community legislation is so technical that it is almost incomprehensible to the average legislator; there is little opportunity for considering even the most important legislation at the formative and crucial pre-proposal stage; proposed legislation that is considered is often well advanced in, and may even be through, the Council system before it is examined by parliaments; and majority voting in the Council means that a parliament whose government has been outvoted has no way at all of calling the real decision-makers to any sort of account.

But notwithstanding these problems and difficulties all national parliaments have established some sort of specialised arrangements for attempting to deal with Community affairs. They are arrangements which, in different ways and with different degrees of effectiveness, are focused on examining proposed Community legislation, scrutinising ministerial positions and performance, producing reports on Community related matters, and generally monitoring Community developments. Amongst the many differences that exist between the national arrangements three are particularly worth noting:

(1) Virtually all parliaments have established European committees of some sort, but whereas in some cases these serve as the main forum for dealing with Community matters, in others they serve more as co-ordinating committees and the detailed work is undertaken by appropriate 'domestic' committees.

(2) The appearance of ministers before the appropriate parliamentary bodies varies considerably.

(3) In three parliaments – the Belgian, German, and Greek – the specialised parliamentary organs include MEPs, and in a growing number of parliaments use is being made of MEPs as experts when appropriate.

Despite the changes and adjustments made by parliaments in recognition of the importance of the Community, it is still the case, however, that parliaments are mostly confined to a relatively minor role.

The position of the Irish Parliament is fairly typical. Following accession in 1973, arrangements were made which were supposed to give Parliament monitoring, advisory, and deliberating responsibilities in respect of Irish participation in the Community. These arrangements were to consist, in particular, of an obligation on the part of the government to present a six-monthly report to Parliament on developments in the Community, and the creation of a new committee – the Joint Committee on Secondary Legislation comprising 26 Dail Deputies and Senators – with the brief of examining Community proposals and advising the government on their implications and suitability for Ireland. The evidence indicates that these arrangements have had but a marginal effect. Certainly Irish Community policy is not made, and can hardly be said to be properly examined, by the Dail or the Senate. Rather, it tends to be in the hands of a small, government-dominated, network of politicians and officials who listen to others only as they see fit. So, in the case of agriculture for example, the Minister of Agriculture, senior officials in the Department of Agriculture, and leaders of appropriate organisations – particularly the Irish Farmers Association – hold the key to decision-making and decision implementation, and they are not unduly inconvenienced by parliamentary probing.

The major exception to the general pattern of legislative weakness is the Danish Folketing. Two principal factors combine to put the Folketing in a rather special position. First, there has been a powerful anti-Community movement and a strong anti-Community popular sentiment in Denmark since accession in 1973. No Danish government has been able to ignore this – especially since all governments have been coalitions or minorities: Social Democratic led between 1973–82, and Centre-Right since 1982. Second, the Folketing has a very strong Market Relations Committee comprised of senior politicians which meets weekly to review the forthcoming business in the Council of Ministers and to hear reports from ministers on their proposed negotiating positions. The Committee does not vote or formally grant negotiating mandates, but it does tender advice, and it is necessary that a 'negative' clearance is given to the minister's position in the sense that there is no majority against it. The principal advantage of the Market Relations Committee procedure is that it helps to ensure that agreements reached by Danish ministers in the Council are not subsequently queried or endangered at home. The principal disadvantage is that it can make it difficult for Danish representatives to be flexible in the Council and can result in them being isolated if new solutions to problems are advanced during the course of negotiations.

Courts

National courts might be thought to have a significant role to play as the guarantors and defenders of national rights against Community encroachment. In practice, they do not.

The reason for this, as explained in Chapter 6, is that the principle of the primacy of Community law is now accepted. There were some initial teething problems in this regard, but it is now extremely rare for national courts to question the legality of Community proceedings and decisions. The Treaties, Community legislation, and even case law of the Court of Justice are seen as taking precedence when they clash with national law. The increasing practice of national courts to seek preliminary rulings from the Court of Justice in cases where there is uncertainty over an aspect of Community law is testimony to the general desire of national courts not to be out of step with Community law.

That said, national courts have occasionally sought to assert national rights and interests against the Community. For example, there have been a few instances where national courts have refused to acknowledge the legality of directives that have not been incorporated into national law by the due date, even though the Court of Justice has ruled that in such circumstances they may become directly applicable. Constitutional law, especially as applied to individual rights, has been another area where some assertion of national independence has been attempted by national courts, though not so much since the principle of the precedence of Community law over national constitutional law was confirmed in Court of Justice rulings in the early 1970s.

In recent years the most celebrated instance of national court intervention occurred in December 1986 when the Irish Supreme Court, by a vote of three to two, found in favour of a Raymond Crotty who challenged the constitutional validity of the Single European Act. The judges ruled that Title III of the Act, which puts foreign policy co-operation on a legal basis, could restrict Ireland's sovereignty and might inhibit it from pursuing its traditionally neutral foreign policy. The Act must therefore, they indicated, be endorsed by a referendum. As a result, the SEA was unable to come into effect in any of the twelve EC states on 1 January 1987, as had been intended, and was delayed until the Irish gave their approval in the duly held referendum. The Act eventually entered into force on 1 July 1987.

Public Opinion

National public opinion exercises both a direct and an indirect influence on Community decision-making.

The most direct means by which the populace can have their say is in referenda. Several of these have been held on Community-related matters. However, it is hard to sustain a case that they have added very much to the democratic base of the Community: partly because of their infrequency, and partly because at least three of them were not genuine attempts to consult the citizenry but were the consequences of internal politicking. Those to have been held are:

● In 1972 France held a referendum to ratify the enlargement of the Community. In reality it was designed to boost the legitimacy and status of President Pompidou and produce a public split in the Socialist-Communist opposition.

● In 1972 Denmark and Ireland each held a referendum on Community membership after their governments signed the Treaties of Accession. (Norway held a 'consultative' referendum after also signing a Treaty of Accession. A majority voted against membership and Norway withdrew its application.)

● In 1975 a referendum was held in the UK on continued Community membership following the renegotiation of UK membership terms at the Heads of Government meeting in Dublin. The real purpose of the referendum was to settle a split in the Labour Cabinet on the principle of EC membership.

● In 1986 Denmark held a referendum on the ratification of the SEA. This was brought about after the Folketing had rejected the Act, nominally on the grounds that it undermined national sovereignty, but partly too because the Left thought rejection would force an election they might win. The Conservative Prime Minister, Poul Schlüter, outmanoeuvred them by calling a referendum rather than an election.

● In 1987, in circumstances described above, Ireland held a referendum on the ratification of the Single European Act.

● In 1989, on the same day as the EP elections, a referendum was held in Italy on whether the European Community 'should be transformed into an effective Union'. The referendum had been proposed by senators and deputies in the European Federalist Movement and was designed to reinforce the authority of Italian ministers and MEPs in giving the process of European integration a push.

In all of these referenda, with the exception of Norway in 1972, majority votes were cast for the 'pro-Community' side of the question.

By contrast with the only occasional and localised opportunities for participation offered by referenda, the elections to the EP are regular and European-wide (see Chapter 5 for details). For some observers, these elections provide the Community with a democratic base and, through the involvement of political parties and the election of MEPs, serve to link the peoples of the Community with Community processes. This view, however, must be counterbalanced by a recognition of the fact that since the elections are not contested by European parties standing on European issues, but are more second-order national elections, they can hardly be regarded as occasions when the populace indicate their European policy preferences. That voter turnout is, in most cases, low by national standards, and that those who are elected to be MEPs have only limited powers, raises further doubts about the participatory and democratic impact of the elections.

The most obvious way in which public opinion exercises an influence is via national elections. This is because most important Community decisions are taken by the elected representatives of the member states in the Council of Ministers. It is an influence, however, that is indirect, in the sense that it is exercised at two or three stages removed: voters in national elections elect legislatures, from which governments are formed, which send representatives to Council meetings. It is an influence too that is somewhat tangential, in the sense that in national elections voters are not much concerned with 'European issues' or with the competence of candidates in dealing with European affairs.

As for the extent to which governments respond to public opinion – as measured by public opinion polls and as interpreted by politicians – that depends very much on their own ideological and policy preferences, their perceptions of the importance and durability of issues, and the time remaining until the next election. Certainly there is no automatic relationship between what the people think about Community matters and what governments do: Mrs Thatcher's government, for example, made no move to withdraw from the Community in the early 1980s even though a majority of the British population thought it should, and it did not weaken its opposition in the late 1980s to the Social Charter even though polls suggested the Charter was supported by about two-thirds of the British people.

That said, where an issue is generally accepted as constituting a national interest, or at least commands strong domestic support, then governments of whatever political persuasion are likely to pursue it in the Council. Even if they themselves do not wish to be too rigid, they may well be forced, by electoral considerations and domestic pressures, to strike postures and make public displays of not being pushed around. So, for example, Irish and French governments invariably favour generous settlements for farmers, Danish and German governments press for strict environmental controls, and Greek and Portuguese governments argue for larger structural funds to enable them to modernise their economies.

Where no very clear national interest is at stake, or national opinion is unformed or divided, then the positions adopted by governments in the Council may be more reflective of domestic partisan divisions. So, for example, from 1974 to 1979 the attitude of the UK government to the Community budget was largely conditioned by Labour objections to the resources devoted to the

CAP. After 1979, however, and the election of the Conservatives to power, the attitude came to mirror a more general ideological distaste for high public expenditure.

Political Parties

Political parties normally wish to exercise power which, in liberal democratic states, means they must be able to command popular support. This, in turn, means they must be able to articulate and aggregate national opinions and interests. At the same time, parties are not normally content simply to act as mirror images of the popular will. Drawing on their traditions, and guided by leaders and activists, they also seek to direct society by mobilising support behind preferred ideological/policy positions. Judgements thus have to be made about the balance to be struck between 'reflecting' society and 'leading' it. Those parties which lean too much towards the latter have little chance of winning elections, although in multi-party systems they may well still find themselves with strong negotiating hands.

Of course, the precise extent to which parties are, on the one hand, reflecting and channelling opinions on particular issues and are, on the other hand, shaping and determining them, is very difficult to judge since, in most instances, the processes are two-way and interrelated. But whatever the exact balance may be between the processes, both are very much in operation in relation to the Community. The recent experience of Denmark, Greece and the UK illustrates this. In each of these countries widespread popular scepticism in the early to mid-1980s about Community membership found both expression and encouragement at the party political level, with some parties advocating a complete withdrawal from Community membership, and others expressing a considerable concern about aspects of the implications of membership – especially in relation to sovereignty. As the 'realities' of Community membership began to seep through, however, both public opinion and party attitudes began to change. So much so that by the beginning of the 1990s Greece had become one of the more enthusiastic Community states in terms of public opinion, and a 'typical' one in terms of the attitudes of its political parties, whilst Denmark and the UK were not lagging

MAP 13.1

Attitudes to membership of the EC*

Percentage of population believing
membership is 'a good thing'

● 71% – 82%

◉ 61% – 70%

○ 49% – 60%

*The question asked was: 'Generally speaking, do you think that (your country's) membership of the Common Market is a good thing, a bad thing, or neither good nor bad?'
Minimum believing a good thing: Denmark = 49%; maximum: Netherlands = 82%; EC weighted average = 65%
Source: Eurobarometer, Number 33, June 1990

too far behind the Community 'average' on either count (see Maps 13.1 and 13.2 for indicators of public opinion in the member states).

Apart from their interactive relationship with the attitudinal climate in which Community processes work, political parties feed also directly into Community decision-making. First, by providing much of the ideological base of the ideas of governments, and by providing most – if not all – of the leading personnel of governments, they do much to determine and shape the attitudes, priorities and stances of the member states in the Council. While it is true that

MAP 13.2

Feelings on whether membership of the EC has been beneficial*

Percentage of population believing membership has been beneficial

● 71% – 80%

◕ 58% – 70%

○ 47% – 57%

*The question asked was: 'Taking everything into consideration, would you say that (your country) has on balance benefited or not from being a member of the European Community (Common Market)?
Minimum believing 'has benefited': UK = 47%; maximum: Ireland = 80%; EC weighted average = 59%
Source: Eurobarometer, Number 33, June 1990

many policy positions are barely altered by changes of government, shifts of emphasis do occur and these can be significant. Second, even when they are in domestic opposition, political parties can influence government behaviour in the Council because governments do not wish to be accused of being weak or not strongly defending national interests. Third, national political parties are the main contestants of the European elections and their successful candidates become the national representatives in the EP.

Interests

Acting either by themselves or through an appropriate Euro-group, national interest groupings – be they sectional, promotional, or regional – have a number of possible avenues available to them to try and influence Community policies and decisions. Some avenues are at the domestic level – such as approaches through fellow national MEPs, government officials and ministers. Others are at the Community level – such as contacts with the Commission, EP officials, or taking a case to the Court of Justice. These avenues were discussed in some detail in Chapter 8.

In very general terms the most successful national interests of the sectional or promotional type tend to fulfil at least one of two conditions. Either they are able to persuade their government that there is little distinction between the group's interests and the national interest. Or, they have power resources that persuades at least some Community decision-makers that they ought to be listened to. A major reason why farmers have been so influential is that both of these conditions have applied to them in some countries. In France, Germany, Ireland, and elsewhere, this has resulted in Ministries of Agriculture perceiving a major part of their responsibility in the Council being to act virtually as a spokesman for the farmers.

For regional and local institutional interests, the mark of success is usually their ability to attract allocations from Community funds. This can necessitate lobbying, or at least 'keeping in touch', with key national and Community officials. It also requires, and this is a factor that is often not sufficiently recognised, a good knowledge of what is available and how to apply. Even today many institutional interests are not fully aware of what the Community has to offer.

Concluding Remarks

The existence of different and frequently conflicting inputs from member states is the major obstacle in the way of the creation of a smooth, efficient and decisive Community policy and decision-making machinery. But that national views and requirements should be able to be articulated, and incorporated into decisions, is vital if the Community is to work at all. For, ultimately, the EC exists to further the interests of those who live in the member states. If the citizens of the states and, more particularly, the political elites in governments and in parliaments, were to feel that the Community was no longer serving that purpose, then there would be no reason for continued membership. The Community must, therefore, be responsive to its constituent parts.

14

Conclusion: Present Realities and Future Prospects

The Community and the Changing Nature of the International System

The Community should not be viewed in too narrow a context. Whilst many of the factors which have influenced its development have applied to it alone, many have not. This is most clearly seen in the ways in which modernisation and interdependence, which have been crucial in the creation of many of the central features of the Community, have produced similar effects elsewhere in the international system – albeit usually to a more modest degree. There has, for example, been a steady increase in the number and variety of international actors, and some corresponding weakening in the dominance of states. An increasing range of methods and channels are used by international actors to pursue their goals. Relationships between governments are no longer so controlled as they used to be by Foreign Offices and Ministries of External Affairs. The range of issues on international agendas has grown with, in particular, traditional 'high' policy issues – those concerned with security and the defence of the state – being joined by an array of 'low' policy issues – those concerned with the wealth and welfare of citizens. And there has been a decline, in the Western industrialised world at least, in the use of physical force as a policy instrument – conflicts over trade imbalances and currency exchange rates are not solved by armed conflict but by bargaining, adjusting, and compromising.

382

The Community must, therefore, be set within the context of the rapid changes that are occurring throughout the international system. It is a system that is becoming, like the Community system itself, increasingly multilayered and interconnected. Whether the purpose is to regulate international trade, to promote the efficient functioning of the international monetary system, to set international standards on packaging for the transportation of hazardous material, or to control the hunting and killing of whales, states now come together in many different ways, in many different combinations, for many different purposes. To take just formalised interstate forums and linkages, in Western Europe alone there are now many of these, quite apart from those which occur within the framework of the Community. States, for instance, co-operate with one another in joint projects, such as the European Fighter Aircraft, and EUREKA (the European technology programme). On a more institutionalised basis, Western European organisations include the Council of Europe, the European Free Trade Association, the Western European Union, the European Space Agency, and the European Patent Organisation.

This development of many different types of cross-border relations, in response to the different requirements and propensities of states, has also occurred within the Community. When the 'standard' Community method has been judged to be inappropriate or over-rigid, interstate relations have taken other forms. This is seen, for example, in the development of European Political Co-operation alongside, but outside, the formal Community structure, in the creation of the European Monetary System on a partial member-ship basis, and in the willingness of the Community to open up some of the programmes it sponsors to non-Community states – Sweden and Switzerland, for example, are associated with the JET (Joint European Torus) nuclear fusion project. As is increasingly the case with interstate relations in the international system as a whole, flexibility and diversity are thus key Community characteristics.

The Uniqueness of the Community

Three Unique Characteristics

Compared with other international organisations, the Community is in many respects unique. Three aspects of this uniqueness are particularly worth emphasising.

First, the Community has a much more developed and complex institutional structure than is found in other international bodies. The standard pattern of international organisations – permanent secretariats and attached delegations – is perhaps, in a much grander and more elaborated form, replicated in the EC with the Commission and the Permanent Representations, but to these are added many other features. Among the more obvious of such features are: the regular and frequent meetings between member governments at the very highest political levels; the constant and many varied forms of contact between national officials; the Court of Justice; and the European Parliament – the only directly elected multi-state assembly in the world.

Second, no other international organisation has anything like the policy responsibilities of the Community. In terms of width, there are now few significant policy areas which have completely escaped the Community's attentions. In terms of depth the pattern varies, but in many important areas, such as external trade, agriculture, and competition policy, key initiating and decision-making powers have been transferred from the member states to Community authorities.

Third, the Community has progressed far beyond the essentially intergovernmental nature of most international organisations and has incorporated many supranational characteristics into its structure and operation. Since the nature of the balance between intergovernmentalism and supranationalism in the Community has not been directly examined in any of the previous chapters, and since also hostility to too much supranationalism – and the loss of sovereignty it is perceived as entailing – is a major reason why governments (especially the UK) are often reluctant to accept integrationist initiatives, it is appropriate at this point to give some consideration to intergovernmentalism, supranationalism, and the Community.

Intergovernmentalism and Supranationalism

In the 1960s, the governments of five of the Community's then six member states were willing to permit, even to encourage, some movement in the direction of supranationalism. President de Gaulle, however, who wished to preserve 'the indivisible sovereignty of the nation state', was not. In order to emphasise this point, and more particularly to prevent certain supranational developments which were due to be introduced, he withdrew France in 1965 from most of the Community's key decision-making forums. The outcome of the crisis which this occasioned was the 1966 Luxembourg Compromise which, though it had no legal force, had as its effect the general imposition of intergovernmentalism on Community decision-making processes: the powers of the Commission and of the European Parliament were contained, and decisions in the Council came customarily to be made – even where the Treaties allowed for majority voting – by unanimous agreements.

The first enlargement of the Community in 1973 reinforced intergovernmentalism, bringing in as it did two countries – Denmark and the UK – where there was strong domestic opposition to Community membership and where supranationalism was viewed with suspicion. The Greek accession in 1981 had a similar effect. The onset of the international economic recession in 1973–4 also encouraged intergovernmentalism, since it made states look rather more critically at the distributive consequences of Community policies, produced a temptation to look for national solutions to pressing problems, and resulted in a greater caution with regard to the transfer of powers to Community institutions.

However, intergovernmental attachments and pressures were never able, and have never been able, completely to stop the development of supranationalism in the Community. The Treaties, the ever-changing political and economic environments in which the Community exists, and the logic of the Community itself, have all ensured that in terms of both decision-making processes and decision-making outcomes, national sovereignties have been progressively undermined. Indeed, not only has supranationalism become more embedded in the Community system, but since the mid-1980s it has been given a considerable boost as most of the states have adopted a much more positive attitude towards its development. They have done so partly because the effects of the delays and the inaction that intergovernmentalism sponsors have become more obvious and more damaging, and partly because it has been recognised that in the larger and more diverse Community of the twelve, over-rigid intergovernmentalism is a greater recipe than ever before for stagnation and sclerosis.

The Community thus displays both intergovernmental and supranational characteristics.

The principal intergovernmental characteristics are as follows:

● In most of the major areas of public policy – including foreign affairs, defence, macroeconomic policy, financial and monetary policy, education, health, and law and order – decisions are still mainly taken at the national level. Each state consults and co-ordinates with its Community partners on aspects of these policies, and is sometimes subject to constraints as a result of Community membership, but usually, in the last analysis, a state can decide for itself what is to be done.

● Virtually all major decisions of the Community are taken by the European Council or the Council of Ministers. These institutions bring together the political representatives of the member states.

● In the European Council and the Council of Ministers most major decisions are taken on the basis of consensus and unanimity. Where, in the Council of Ministers, there is constitutional provision for majority voting it is still theoretically possible (although it may be politically difficult) for any state, as a result of the Luxembourg Compromise, to veto a policy proposal if it has a 'vital national interest' at stake.

● The Commission and the Parliament, the two most obvious supranational power rivals to the European Council and the Council of Ministers, are restricted in their decision-making powers, and have had only very limited success in imposing policies on the Council which it did not really want.

Of the supranational characteristics of the Community, the following are particularly important:

● The Commission may have to defer to the European Council and the Council of Ministers with respect to the taking of major decisions, but it is an extremely important decision-maker in its own right when it comes to secondary and regulatory decision-making. Indeed in quantitative terms most Community legislation is issued in the name of the Commission and not the Council.

● In the Council of Ministers, majority voting has always been an acceptable practice for budgetary decision-making, but, since the mid-1980s, it has come to be increasingly used in other areas too. By extending the spheres in which majority voting is constitutionally permissible – including to the crucial sphere of the internal market – the Single European Act gave a considerable impetus to this growth in the use of majority voting.

● The European Parliament's constitutional powers may be limited, but its role in Community decision-making should not be dismissed altogether: it has important powers over the budget, and it exercises a by no means inconsiderable influence on legislative proposals – especially where the two reading co-operation procedure applies.

● The force and status of decision-making outcomes is crucial to Community supranationalism for, clearly, the Community could hardly be described as supranational at all if its decisions had no binding force. Some, indeed, do not and are merely advisory and exhortive. But many do, and constitute Community law. It is a law that constitutes an increasingly prominent part of the legal systems of all member states. It is a law, too, that takes precedence over national law should the two conflict, and a law that, in the event of a dispute, finds its final authority not in national courts, but in the interpretations of the Community's own Court of Justice.

A Pooling of Sovereignty?

The three aspects of Community uniqueness which are referred to above – the complex institutional structure, the range of policy responsibilities, and the combination of intergovernmental and supranational characteristics – have combined, and are combining, to produce a system which is quite unique in the extent to which it involves states engaging in *joint* action to formulate *common* policies and to make *binding* decisions. As the words 'joint', 'common', and 'binding' imply, the process of working together is resulting in the Community states becoming ever more intermeshed and interdependent. This is no more clearly seen than in the ratchet-like effect of many aspects of their relationships and their shared activities: ratchet-like in the sense that it will not be possible for them to be reversed without creating major constitutional, legal, political and economic difficulties at both Community and national levels.

Clearly a central aspect of the intermeshing and the interdependence, and one of the principal distinguishing characteristics of the Community, is the way in which the member states have voluntarily surrendered some of their national sovereignty and independence to collective institutions. Indeed, in a few policy sectors, such as agriculture and external commercial policy, the requirements of the Community system have resulted in the role of the states being relegated almost to that of intermediaries. However, viewed from a broader perspective, the Community is not only the cause of a decline in national powers, but is also a response to decline. This is so because much of the rationale of the Community lies in an attempt – an attempt for which there is no international parallel – on the part of the twelve states to increase their control of, and their strength and influence in, a rapidly changing world. Although all of the states have reservations, and some have fundamental criticisms, about aspects of the Community, each has made the judgement that membership enhances its ability to achieve certain objectives. The precise nature of these objectives varies from state to state, but, in virtually all cases, the main priorities are the promotion of economic growth and prosperity, the control of economic and financial forces which are not confined to national boundaries, and the strengthening of political influence. Insofar as these objectives are being attained, it can be argued that the diminution in the role of the state and the loss of sovereignty that arises from supranationalism is counterbalanced by the collective strength of the Community as a whole.

Indeed, since international change has resulted in all of the member states experiencing a considerable *de facto*, if not *de jure*, loss of national sovereignty quite irrespective of the loss which is attributable to Community membership, it can be argued that discussions of national sovereignty, in the classic sense of the term at least, are no longer very meaningful. Rather should it be recognised that the only way in which medium-sized and small states, such as those which make up the membership of the Community, can retain control of their operating environments is by pooling and sharing their power and their sovereignty.

The Future of the Community

Factors Affecting Prospects

The Community has not evolved in quite the way, or as quickly, as was envisaged by many of its early founders. The expectation that policy interests and responsibilities would grow, with achievements in initially selected sectors leading to developments in other sectors, has been partly borne out, but only up to a point, and certainly not consistently – in the 1970s and early 1980s policy development was extremely sluggish. The anticipation that national institutions and political and economic actors would become progressively entwined with one another has been similarly partially realised, but it has also been partially frustrated – not least because of the persisting reluctance of some governments to transfer responsibilities and powers to Community institutions. The assumption that the focus of political activities and attentions would switch from national capitals to Europe has happened to an extent – but in most policy areas the national level is still more important than the Community level. And, finally, the belief that a European spirit would emerge, based on shared perceptions of a common interest, has proved to be over-optimistic.

There has, in short, been no semi-automatic movement in an integrationist direction. But if integration has not inevitably, and of itself, led to more integration, it has certainly stimulated pressures for more integration. It has done so, for example, by creating 'client groups' – of which, in the Community context, Eurocrats are not the least prominent – that have strong vested interests in sustaining and extending integration. Integration has also provided an institutional framework into which integrationist pressures, of many different sorts, have been channelled. Among such pressures on the Community today are: the international trade challenge of the USA, Japan, and the newly-industrialising countries; the increasingly perceived need for monetary stability; the transnational character of problem areas such as the environment and terrorism; and the need to respond to the integration that is occurring outside formal Community processes through developments as diverse as industrial mergers, closer cross-border banking and other financial arrangements, and population movements.

How, in the future, the Community will respond to these and other pressures will depend on a number of factors, the most important of which are perceptions, support and leadership.

The importance of *perceptions* is seen in the way prospects for progress are considerably enhanced when all of the member states perceive an initiative to be broadly desirable, or at least regard the costs of not proceeding as being too high. Very frequently, of course, there is no such common perception, especially where new types of development are envisaged and/or when initiatives have sovereignty or clear distributional implications.

The extent to which key actors are motivated to *support* or oppose an initiative is dependent on many things. Perception of merit is obviously central, but this can be offset by other considerations. A government, for example, may fiercely resist a proposal in the Council of Ministers not because it regards it as being innately unsound, but because acceptance would be electorally damaging or would lead to problems with an important domestic pressure group.

Leadership has long been a weakness of the Community in that there is no strong and central focus of decision-making authority. The Commission, the European Council, and the Council of Ministers are in many ways the key decision-making bodies, but their ability to get things done is subject to limitations. When attempts are made to provide leadership – by, perhaps, an informal coalition of states, by an ambitious Council Presidency, or by a forceful Commission President – there is usually resistance from some quarter.

Perceptions, support, and leadership are, of course, not static, but rather are in constant transition. Since the early to mid-1980s they have undergone significant changes, in ways which have facilitated integrationist developments. Factors accounting for the changes are many and varied, and range from the specific – such as the appointment of the highly dynamic Jacques Delors to the Commission Presidency in 1985 – to the general – such as the opening up of the internal market, and the increasingly obvious interdependence of international economic and political life. The changes have helped to produce a climate wherein, for example, the European Council and the Commission are both offering bolder policy leadership than formerly they did, and in government circles there is now an increased perception of the need of, and also increased support for, further integration.

But if the internal market and other developments are resulting in a new sense of dynamism being inserted into integration processes, they have not removed all of the obstacles. This is no more clearly seen than in the different public positions taken by governments on the future shape of the Community. On the one hand, there are the 'maximalists', such as the Italians and the Belgians, who are enthusiastic about economic, monetary and political union, and who do not automatically recoil at the prospect of a federal Europe. On the other hand there are the 'minimalists', with the UK in the vanguard, who talk more of co-operation than they do of integration and who still make much of the importance of preserving national independence and sovereignty.

Of course, rhetoric is one thing and actual deeds are another. The statements of national politicians may do something to capture the many different ideas which exist about the future of the Community, but they sometimes also serve to mask as well as to reveal. So, UK governments have done much – even when Mrs. Thatcher was Prime Minister – to facilitate integration through such acts as approval of the SEA, acceptance of the 1988 Brussels summit package, and strong support for the dismantling of barriers which prevent the free movement of goods, services, capital and labour. At the same time, those governments which are highly vocal in their support for integration processes are often quite prepared to drag their feet and create difficulties when specific proposals do not accord with their own preferences or national interests.

Deepening and Widening

Of critical importance in determining the future evolution of the Community will be how the many pressures for expansion are handled. These pressures for expansion take the form of both pressures for further integration – which will bring about a deepening of the Community – and pressures for further enlargements – which will bring about a widening of the Community.

A deepening of the Community. A deepening of the Community can be expected to occur via both policy and institutional developments.

Regarding policy developments, particular attention can be expected to be given to a number of areas. Prominent amongst these are the following:

● The 1992 momentum and the much publicised programme of completing the internal market will continue to be given a high priority. Since not all barriers to free movement will in fact be removed by 1992, and since too there is still far from complete accord between the member states over what needs to be harmonised for genuinely free and open competition to exist, the market issue can be expected to remain on the agenda well beyond 1992 itself.

● Economic and Monetary Union will receive considerable attention. With virtually all interested parties now having accepted the need for monetary stability on a market-wide basis, the EMU debate has moved on to the issues of a common currency, a European Central Bank, and consistency in economic policies. The Delors Report, the opening of Stage 1 of EMU in 1990, and the setting of 1 January 1994 as the date for the opening of Stage 2, have done much to get the whole EMU process well off the ground. Doubtless the Intergovernmental Conference on EMU, which was opened in December 1990, will help to take it much further.

● Paralleling the economic, monetary, and market-based integrationist developments, increasing attention is now being paid, and is likely to continue being paid, to the 'social dimension' of the Community; that is, to areas such as social welfare provision, health and safety at work, and industrial democracy. The Commission's Social Charter, which the European Council accepted in 1989, will continue to be gradually given legislative effect.

● Foreign policy co-operation is likely to be extended and strengthened. The Community may be an international economic giant – a situation largely attained by economic strength being harnessed to agreed goals via the Common Commercial Policy – but it is something of a political pygmy. On many issues which have very important implications for Western Europe – including arms control and regional conflicts – the United States and the Soviet Union tend to negotiate directly with one another, and Western Europe's voice – even in a consultative capacity with its major ally – counts for little. Many in the Community would like to see this situation of international political weakness – which was further emphasised in the period leading up to and during the Gulf War when the United States took most of the initiative – rectified by the further development of EPC and by the incorporation of security and defence issues into the Community's policy framework.

It is, of course, not possible to predict the Community's future policy evolution with precision, for whatever the mix of pressures for development and action prove to be, it is quite certain that many of them will be strongly resisted. The reasons for the resistance will be found in the familiar barrage of barriers which explain why so much policy activity is slow, uneven, and uncertain: differences over the merits of proposals, over the costs of proposals, over the distributional consequences of proposals, over whether proposals are appropriate Community business, and over whether or not loss of national controls and sovereignty are acceptable. Conceivably such obstacles to progress may have the effect of causing the states to divide in certain respects into fast and slow integration streams. Certainly they will ensure that many initiatives, which command a fair measure of support among the states and in Community institutions, will nonetheless be put on indefinite hold, will be watered down, or will be diverted away from the making of legislation into relatively harmless liaising and co-ordinating channels.

Regarding institutional developments, the Community has long been criticised for persisting with a policy and decision-making institutional framework that is slow, inefficient, and insufficiently subject to democratic controls. Many schemes and proposals for reform have been put forward over the years, most of which have focused on two main themes. First, the need for a stronger executive – among specific measures advocated have been a merging of the Commission and the Council of Ministers, a more independent Commission, and more majority voting in the Council of Ministers. Second, the need for a stronger Parliament – measures advocated here have ranged from modest extensions of the EP's consultative rights, to granting the EP real and effective legislative powers.

Clearly the adoption of almost any of these proposed measures would extend political integration in the Community. It is for this very reason that national governments, or at least a sufficient number of them, have been inclined to resist calls for significant institutional reforms and have preferred to cede to Community institutions only such powers as have seemed to be necessary. But what has seemed to be necessary has changed over the years, and this has brought about integrationist developments in the Community's institutional structures and decision-making processes. Some of these developments, such as the increasing use of majority voting in the Council of Ministers in the early 1980s, were not a consequence of formal political agreements or constitutional amendments but came about gradually, almost imperceptibly, as the Community adjusted to evolving circumstances and requirements. Other devel-
as the budgetary reforms of the 1970s and the SEA (
formally contracted and ratified Treaty amendm
further integrationist developments of a similar kin

in the 1990s; indeed, they are guaranteed by the Intergovernmental Conference on Political Union which opened in December 1990.

A widening of the Community. German unification in 1990 brought about a widening of the Community in that the unification made the territory of the former German Democratic Republic not only part of Germany but also part of the Community. However, as was explained in Chapter 2, this was a very special sort of widening, not least since it did not involve the usual protracted accession procedures of formal application, Commission investigation, Council decision in principle, exhaustive negotiations on the terms of accession, final Council decision by unanimous agreement, and – since the SEA – assent of the European Parliament. Rather was the whole process pushed through in a few weeks via special arrangements.

Such special consideration is not being, and will not be, accorded to the increasingly long queue of states which wish to be members of the Community. In 1987 Turkey applied for membership – an application which was rejected in 1989. In 1989 Austria applied. In 1990 Cyprus and Malta applied. Also in 1990, Hungary signalled that it would like to be a member by the mid-1990s, and both Norway and Sweden indicated that applications from them would probably be forthcoming before too long.

This interest in Community membership stems from three main factors. First, there is the economic strength of the Community. There are obvious attractions for medium and small sized states to be members of a powerful international bloc. Second, there is the increasingly integrated Community market. For states which conduct a large part of their trade with the Community, such as the EFTA countries, there are considerable disadvantages in having to meet Community rules and regulations without having a direct say in determining what those rules and regulations are. Third, there are the processes of democratisation and economic liberalisation in Eastern Europe, which have not only made the previously Communist countries theoretically eligible for membership, but have encouraged them to look to the Community for markets, for economic assistance, and – in some cases – for possible bolstering of their fledgling democracies. The changes in Eastern Europe have also – by removing the East–West division that existed in Europe from the late 1940s – made it possible for the neutralism of countries such as

Austria and Sweden to no longer be an insuperable barrier to Community membership.

In all probability applicant states will have to wait until the mid-1990s before negotiations on their possible accession are opened, and until at least the late 1990s before Community membership is granted. This is because moves to widen the Community are seen by many as potentially slowing down moves to deepen it, and for most of those within the Community who wish to see integration further developed deepening takes priority over widening.

But if a widening of the Community in the form of new accessions is unlikely for some while, the Community has shown that it is willing to open up and broaden its relations with non-Community European states in other ways. With the EFTA countries the projected European Economic Area is being sought and if this is realised it should have the effect of extending the internal market to nineteen European countries. (Liechtenstein, which is neither an EC nor an EFTA member, is also involved.) With the East European countries the Community is willing to extend the trade and co-operation agreements which already exist to more ambitious and wide-ranging association agreements – which could be the path to free trade, to increased financial and economic assistance, to joint projects, and to a much closer political dialogue.

The Re-shaping of Europe

A major re-shaping of Europe's organisational arrangements is clearly underway. As some have put it, the political architecture is being changed.

The deepening and widening of the Community are, of course, key features of the re-shaping. But there are also other important developments: in 1990 Hungary became the first former Communist country to join the Council of Europe, and others are following; also in 1990, and at the Community's initiative, a new international bank, the European Bank for Reconstruction and Development (EBRD), was founded with the purpose of helping the East European countries to establish market oriented economies – all significant European countries, apart from Albania but including the USSR, have become members of the EBRD; early in 1991 the Council for Mutual Economic Assistance (Comecon), the East European trading bloc which had been established under Soviet leadership in 1949, dissolved itself; and, in the sphere of defence and security, the East's Warsaw Pact is being dismantled, the West's NATO and Western Europe's WEU are having to reassess their roles, and the thirty-four nation Conference on Security and Co-operation in Europe (CSCE) is emerging as a potentially important pillar of a new European security order.

The impartial and detached observer, noting the many organisational changes which are taking place across Europe, and noting perhaps particularly the desire of EFTA and Eastern European countries to have close relations with the Community, might conclude that what is required is a new pan-European organisation bringing together all those states which wish to co-operate and integrate with one another. In the long term such an organisation may indeed emerge. It is hardly likely, however, in the foreseeable future. Amongst the obstacles in the way of such a root and branch restructuring are uncertainties in Western Europe about the future development of what is now a very heterogeneous Eastern Europe, differences between West European states regarding what organisational developments are desirable, and a reluctance in some quarters – especially EC quarters – to disentangle established, and in many respects successful, structures and relationships.

For some years yet the organisational shape of Europe is thus likely to continue to be based on a number of different organisations, each with their own – often overlapping – memberships and functions. Doubtless the European Community will continue to be, in many respects, the most important and most dominant of these organisations.

Postscript: The Treaty on European Union

The Making of the Treaty

The Intergovernmental Conferences (IGCs) on Political Union and on Economic and Monetary Union, which had been formally launched at the Rome meeting of the European Council in December 1990, met throughout 1991. As scheduled they presented their reports to the December 1991 Maastricht European Council meeting. The IGC on Economic and Monetary Union was able to reach agreement on virtually all issues within its remit and to present clear recommendations on Treaty reform to the summit. The IGC on Political Union, however, was not so successful, in that although agreements were eventually hammered out on most issues, a number of particularly contentious matters – regarding both institutional and policy reform – had to be referred to the summit for final resolution.

At Maastricht the intention on all sides was to try and ensure that the proposed new treaty – the Treaty on European Union which embodied the outcomes of the two IGCs – could be agreed. This required concessions from all participants. Such concessions were forthcoming but on one matter – the Community's competence in the social sphere – no agreement could be reached. Eleven of the national governments wished to see the Community's policy competence, and ability to take decisions by qualified majority vote, extended in the social sphere, whilst the UK government was opposed to both of these proposed developments. After much discussion the social chapter was removed from the main body of the European Union Treaty but was annexed to it in the form of a separate protocol and an agreement on social policy between the eleven member states.

397

After being carefully examined by a working party of legal and linguistic experts the Treaty on European Union was formally signed by Foreign and Finance Ministers at Maastricht in February 1992.

The Objectives of the Treaty

The general objectives of the Treaty on European Union are set out in Articles A and B:

ARTICLE A
By this Treaty, the High Contracting Parties establish among themselves a European Union, hereinafter called 'the Union'.
This Treaty marks a new stage in the process of creating an ever closer union among the peoples of Europe, in which decisions are taken as closely as possible to the citizen.
The Union shall be founded on the European Communities, supplemented by the policies and forms of cooperation established by this Treaty. Its task shall be to organize, in a manner demonstrating consistency and solidarity, relations between the Member States and between their peoples.

ARTICLE B
The Union shall set itself the following objectives:
—   to promote economic and social progress which is balanced and sustainable, in particular through the creation of an area without internal frontiers, through the strengthening of economic and social cohesion and through the establishment of economic and monetary union, ultimately including a single currency in accordance with the provisions of this Treaty;
—   to assert its identity on the international scene, in particular through the implementation of a common foreign and security policy including the eventual framing of a common defence policy, which might in time lead to a common defence;
—   to strengthen the protection of the rights and interests of the nationals of its Member States through the introduction of a citizenship of the Union;
—   to develop close cooperation on justice and home affairs;

— to maintain in full the *acquis communautaire* and build on it with a view to considering, through the procedure referred to in Article N(2) [an intergovernmental conference to be convened in 1996 to examine revision of the European Union Treaty], to what extent the policies and forms of cooperation introduced by this Treaty may need to be revised with the aim of ensuring the effectiveness of the mechanisms and the institutions of the Community.

The objectives of the Union shall be achieved as provided in this Treaty and in accordance with the conditions and the timetable set out therein while respecting the principle of susidiarity as defined in Article 3b of the Treaty establishing the European Community.

The Three Pillars of the Treaty

Further to the first sentence of the third paragraph of Article A, provisions are laid down in the Treaty for the Union to be based on three pillars: the European Communities, a Common Foreign and Security Policy, and Cooperation in the Fields of Justice and Home Affairs. The principal features of these pillars are as follows:

(A) The European Communities

This is by far the most important pillar since it incorporates most of the Union's policy responsibilities and institutional arrangements. Under the Treaty the existing Community *acquis* is to be preserved, and in several important respects the Community is to be extended and strengthened by revisions of the EEC, ECSC, and Euratom Treaties.

Two important new principles are introduced into the EEC Treaty. First, the much discussed principle of subsidiarity is formally incorporated by a new Article 3b:

ARTICLE 3b
The Community shall act within the limits of the powers conferred upon it by this Treaty and of the objectives assigned to it therein.

In areas which do not fall within its exclusive competence, the
Community shall take action, in accordance with the principle of
subsidiarity, only if and in so far as the objectives of the proposed
action cannot be sufficiently achieved by the Member States and
can therefore, by reason of the scale or effects of the proposed
action, be better achieved by the Community.
Any action by the Community shall not go beyond what is
necessary to achieve the objectives of this Treaty.

Second, Union citizenship is established, with every national of a
member state being a citizen of the Union. Union citizens are
formally given the right to live and work anywhere in the Community. They are further given the right to vote and stand as candidates
in European Parliament and local elections, subject to detailed
arrangements which are to be adopted by the Council, and subject
too to any derogation for EP elections which may be warranted by
problems specific to a member state.

Apart from these two new principles other revisions of the Treaties
can be grouped under two broad headings.

(1) Institutional changes.   The revisions which fall under this heading
are mostly designed to improve the efficiency and democratic nature
of the Community's institutional structures and decision-making
processes. Overall, the greatest impact is on the Council of Ministers, which becomes empowered to take a greater range of decisions
on the basis of qualified majority votes, and on the European
Parliament, which is given increased powers and influence in several
respects – notably regarding legislation.
   The following list indicates the most significant institutional
changes.
   ● A new legislative procedure – the co-decision procedure – is
established. Like the cooperation procedure it provides for two readings by the Parliament and the Council. It differs, however, from the
cooperation procedure in regard to what happens if the EP cannot
accept the Council's common position. In brief, the main differences
are that: (a) Lack of agreement between the Council and the EP,
can, but need not always, result in the convening of a Conciliation
Committee made up of an equal number of representatives from the

Council and the EP. The task of the Conciliation Committee is to reach agreement on a joint text. (b) If an absolute majority of MEPs vote to reject the common position (which could be after the Council has called a Conciliation Committee to explain its position), or if MEPs vote by an absolute majority to reject a text which the Council has approved by a qualified majority but on which no agreement could be reached in the Conciliation Committee, or if MEPs by a majority of the votes cast reject a text which has been agreed by the Conciliation Committee, then a proposal cannot be adopted. The co-decision procedure thus gives the EP a veto power over legislation which is subject to the procedure. The policy areas covered by the procedure are freedom of movement, freedom of establishment, internal market, research and development framework programmes, environmental action programmes, trans-European network guidelines, education and training, public health, culture, and consumer protection. (In a variation of the co-decision procedure, Council decisions on research framework programmes and on culture must be taken by unanimity.)

● The legislative spheres covered by the cooperation procedure are extended to include development policy, education and training, aspects of transport, competition, social, and environmental policies, and implementation of the regional development fund.

● The scope of the assent procedure (which requires proposed measures to be approved by an absolute majority of MEPs) is extended to cover citizenship issues, the reform and general rules of the structural funds, the role of the European Central Bank, the (eventual?) uniform electoral system, and international agreements which set up institutions, which have major financial implications, or which require legislation under co-decision.

● From January 1995 the term of office of Commissioners is to be extended from four to five years so as to bring the lifespan of a Commission closely into line with the lifespan of a Parliament. The national governments are to nominate by common accord, after consulting the EP, the person they intend to appoint as the President of the Commission. Other members of the Commission are to be nominated by the national governments in the established manner, but now in consultation with the nominee for Commission President. The entire prospective Commission is to be subject to a vote of approval by the EP before being formally appointed by common accord of the national governments.

● A Committee of the Regions is to be established for the purpose of providing the Council and the Commission with advice on matters of major importance for the regions. The Committee is to be of the same size (189) and to have the same distribution of national representatives as the Economic and Social Committee, but its members are to be representatives of regional and local authorities.

● The Court of Justice may impose fines on member states not complying with its judgements or failing to implement Community law.

● The EP is to appoint an Ombudsman to receive complaints from citizens 'covering instances of maladministration in the activities of the Community institutions or bodies, with the exception of the Court of Justice and the Court of First Instance acting in their judicial role'.

(2) Policy changes.   The Community's policy competence is extended and strengthened. It is so in three main ways:

● The main features of Economic and Monetary Union are defined and a timetable for establishing EMU is specified.

Regarding the features, EMU is to include the irrevocable fixing of exchange rates leading to the introduction of the Ecu as a single currency and to the establishment of a European Central Bank (ECB) which will operate within the framework of a European System of Central Banks (ESCB). The main objectives of the ESCB will be to maintain price stability. In so doing it shall support the general economic aims and policies of the Community. The basic tasks to be carried out through the ESCB shall be: to define and implement the monetary policy of the Community; to conduct foreign exchange operations; to hold and manage the official foreign reserves of the member states; and to promote the smooth operation of payment systems. Under EMU, member states are to regard their economic policies as a matter of common concern and are to co-ordinate them within the Council.

Regarding the timetable, EMU is to be established in three stages. The transitional stages one and two (stage one began in 1990 and stage two is to begin in 1994) are essentially concerned with promoting economic and monetary co-operation, co-ordination, and convergence between the member states. By the end of 1996 the Council, acting by qualified majority, shall decide: (1) whether a majority of the member states meet the convergence criteria for the adoption of a single currency (the criteria involve low rates of inflation, low government deficits, currency stability, and low interest rates); (2) whether a majority of the member states wish to enter stage three. If a date for the beginning of stage three has not been set by the end of 1997, the third stage will start automatically on 1 January 1999 for those states which meet the convergence criteria. In a protocol attached to the Treaty it is recognised that the UK 'shall not be obliged or committed to move to the third stage of Economic and Monetary Union without a separate decision to do so by its government and Parliament'. In another protocol the Danish government reserves the right to hold a national referendum before participating in the third stage of EMU.

● Some policy areas in which the Community has not been previously involved, or in which its involvement has not had an explicit Treaty base, are brought into the EEC Treaty for the first time. For example, a new chapter of the Treaty confirms the Community's commitment to help developing countries and to do so by providing multi-annual programmes. Beyond development policy, most of the other policy areas newly introduced into the EEC Treaty are brought in only a rather tentative manner, in the sense that the Community's responsibilities are carefully restricted. Policy areas thus identified include education, public health, consumer protection, trans-European networks, and competitiveness of industry.

● Community responsibilities in some policy areas which were first given Treaty recognition by the Single European Act are further developed. This applies particularly to research and technological development, the environment, and economic and social cohesion. As part of the strengthening of economic and social cohesion a new fund – the Cohesion Fund – is to be set up by December 1993 to provide financial assistance in the fields of environment and trans-European transport infrastructures.

(B)   A Common Foreign and Security Policy

The SEA stated that the member states 'shall endeavour jointly to formulate and implement a European foreign policy'. The Treaty on European Union greatly stiffens this aim by specifying that the Union and its member states 'shall define and implement a common foreign and security policy . . . covering all areas of foreign and security policy', and by further specifying that the common policy 'shall include all questions related to the security of the Union, including the eventual framing of a common defence policy, which might in time lead to a common defence'.

The objectives of the Common Foreign and Security Policy (CFSP) are defined only in general terms: for example, 'to safeguard the common values, fundamental interests and independence of the Union', and 'to develop and consolidate democracy and the rule of law, and respect for human rights and fundamental freedoms'. More specific definition and elaboration of the principles and general guidelines of the CFSP are to be the responsibility of the European Council.

There are to be three principal ways in which the objectives of the CFSP are to be pursued:

● Systematic co-operation is to be established between the member states on any matter of foreign and security policy that is of general interest. Whenever it deems it necessary the Council shall, on the basis of unanimity, define common positions. Member states shall ensure that their national policies conform to such common positions.

● On the basis of general guidelines from the European Council, the Council may decide that a matter is to be the subject of joint action. (In a separate Declaration the European Council stated that the implementation of joint action was proposed as being possible from the entry into force of the Treaty in areas connected with security, and in particular in the following areas: the CSCE process; the policy of disarmament and arms control in Europe; nuclear non-proliferation issues; the economic aspects of security.) In deciding on joint action, or at any stage during the development of a joint action, the Council may determine that implementation decisions should be taken by qualified majority vote.

● The Western European Union, which 'is an integral part of the development of the Union', is requested 'to elaborate and implement decisions and actions of the Union which have defence implications. The Council shall, in agreement with the institutions of the WEU, adopt the necessary practical arrangements.' There is no provision for qualified majority voting on issues which have defence implications. In a Declaration annexed to the Treaty the nine Community members of the WEU state that the WEU 'will be developed as the defence component of the European Union and as the means to strengthen the European pillar of the Atlantic Alliance'.

This second pillar of the Treaty on European Union thus puts European Political Co-operation (EPC), which has been well-established for some time, within the broader framework of a Common Foreign and Security Policy. The pillar is also extremely significant in that it introduces two important new elements into the West European integration process. First, although foreign policy remains essentially intergovernmental in character, it does none-theless become potentially subject to some qualified majority voting, if only for 'second-order' decisions. Second, defence makes its first formal appearance on the 'Community' (strictly speaking 'Union') policy agenda, albeit very tentatively.

(C)   Co-operation in the Spheres of Justice and Home Affairs

The member states are to regard the following areas as matters of common interest:

1. asylum policy (in a Declaration annexed to the Treaty the member states agreed to try and adopt a common asylum policy by the beginning of 1993);
2. rules governing, and controls on, the crossing by persons of the external borders of the member states;
3. immigration policy and residence rights of third-country nationals;
4. combatting drug addiction;
5. combatting international fraud;
6. judicial co-operation in civil matters;
7. judicial co-operation in criminal matters;
8. customs co-operation;
9. police co-operation to combat terrorism. drug trafficking and other serious crime through a union-wide police intelligence office (Europol).

Any measures taken in regard to these matters must be in compliance with the European Convention of Human Rights.

To bring about co-operation in these policy areas the member states are expected to establish co-ordinating mechanisms between the relevant departments of their administrations. In addition the Council may, by unanimity:

(a)   Adopt joint positions and promote any suitable form of co-operation.
(b)   Adopt joint actions. It may decide that measures implementing joint action are to be adopted by a qualified majority.
(c)   Draw up conventions which it shall recommend to the member states for adoption in accordance with their respective constitutional requirements. Unless otherwise provided by such conventions, implementing measures shall be adopted within the Council by a majority of two-thirds of the member states.

As with the CFSP pillar of the European Union the significance of this Justice and Home Affairs pillar lies not only in the substantive content of its provisions but also in the broader contribution which it makes to the integration process in Europe. There are, as there are with the CFSP pillar, policy and institutional aspects to this. Regarding the policy aspects, a legal base is given to co-operation in areas of activity which in the past have either been dealt with purely on a national basis or have been the subject of only rather loose and informal co-operation between the member states. Regarding the institutional aspects, whilst intergovernmentalism continues to prevail, a small hole in the dyke has appeared with the possibility of qualified majority decisions on certain aspects of policy implementation, and a rather big hole with provision for visa policy to be determined by qualified majority from 1996.

The Protocol on Social Policy and the Agreement Amongst Eleven Member States on Social Policy

It is to be emphasised that, contrary to the impression given by much of the media, the protocol on social policy and the agreement made between eleven member states on social policy do not have the effect of removing social policy from the Community or Union Treaty framework. On the contrary, it is explicitly stated that 'this Protocol and . . . Agreement are without prejudice to the provisions of this Treaty, particularly those which relate to social policy which constitute an integral part of the *acquis communautaire*'.

Just what this will mean in practice will not be clear for some considerable time. In broad terms, however, it would seem to imply that many social policy proposals, including attempts to give further effect to the Community's Social Charter, will continue, in the first instance at least, to be brought forward on the basis of trying to get full agreement by all twelve member states. If it then becomes apparent that the UK cannot accept a proposal, it will opt out of deliberations and decisions and the eleven member states will proceed on the basis of the protocol and agreement.

In so proceeding the eleven will use the Community's existing institutions, procedures, and mechanisms. For the following issues the co-operation procedure will apply, with a qualified majority in the Council consisting of 44 votes out of 66: health and safety at work; working conditions; information and consultation of workers; equality at work between men and women; and the integration of persons excluded from the labour market. For the following issues unanimity will be required: social security and social protection of workers; protection of workers made redundant; representation and the collective defence of the interests of workers and employers; conditions of employment for third-country nationals; and financial contributions for promotion of employment and job creation.

All measures adopted by the eleven are to 'take account of the diverse forms of national practices, in particular in the field of contractual relations, and the need to maintain the competitiveness of the Community economy'. Measures are not to be taken which 'apply to pay, the right of association, the right to strike or the right to lock-outs'.

Clearly the protocol and agreement on social policy break new institutional ground. In so doing they raise a number of issues – on, for example, the precise status of decisions made under their auspices – which may require legal clarification. Assuming, therefore, that the UK stance on social policy does not change, and the protocol and agreement remain part of the Union Treaty, it may well be that much will be heard of social policy issues in national courts and in the Court of Justice.

The Significance of the Treaty on European Union

Clearly the Treaty on European Union significantly advances the integration process in Western Europe. As a result of the Treaty more policy competences are passed from the member states to the Community/Union level, the power of Community institutions is strengthened, and supranationalism is given a further boost.

It is to be emphasised, however, that the Treaty does only *advance* the cause of integration: it does not, in any sense, mark the end of the integration process or even identify where that end might be. The discussions and negotiations which took place before and at Maastricht were marked – as have been all such previous post-war discussions and negotiations – by considerable differences between the participants on the nature and pace of integration. What emerged was a compromise: a compromise which did not advance integration as much as some governments (notably the German, Italian, and Benelux) had hoped, but did advance it further than at least one government (the UK) would have liked.

In so advancing the cause of integration the Treaty highlighted once again what has long been one of the most important characteristics of the Community: its flexibility. When, in the past, the member states, or a sufficient number of them, have wished to act together in a policy area and the established mechanisms have been judged to be not suitable for the purpose then alternative ways of proceeding have been found. This, for example, was the case with the establishment and development of EPC and the EMS. The Treaty on European Union continued with this tradition of adaptability and innovation, most notably in regard to the framework set out for the two 'non-Community' pillars (some states regarded it as premature to bring the policy areas covered by the pillars into the Community), and in regard also to the protocol and agreement on social policy.

With another intergovernmental conference already scheduled for 1996, with many of the provisions of the Treaty on European Union specifically earmarked for review in that conference, and with the Community committed to moving beyond the deepening questions which were the focus of the Maastricht Treaty to widening questions, it can be confidently anticipated that the 1990s will see continuing rounds of discussions and negotiations on the next steps of the integration process.

Chronology of Main Events in the Development of the European Community

1947 March   Belgium, Luxembourg and the Netherlands agree to establish a customs union. Subsequently an economic union is established in October 1947 and a common customs tariff is introduced in January 1948.

      March   France and the UK sign a military alliance, the Treaty of Dunkirk.

      June   General George Marshall, United States Secretary of State, offers American aid for the economic recovery of Europe.

      September   Sixteen nations join the European Recovery Programme.

1948 March   Brussels Treaty concluded between France, the UK and the Benelux states. Aim is to promote collective defence and to improve co-operation in the economic, social and cultural fields.

      April   Founding of the Organisation for European Economic Co-operation (OEEC) by sixteen states.

      May   A Congress is held in the Hague attended by many leading supporters of European co-operation and integration. It issues a resolution asserting 'that it is the urgent duty of the nations of Europe to create an economic and political union in order to assure security and social progress'.

1949	April	Treaty establishing North Atlantic Treaty Organisation (NATO) signed in Washington by twelve states.
	May	Statute of Council of Europe signed in Strasbourg by ten states.
1950	May	Robert Schuman, the French Foreign Minister, puts forward his proposals to place French and German coal and steel under a common authority. He declares 'it is no longer the moment for vain words, but for a bold act – a constructive act'.
	October	René Pleven, the French Prime Minister, proposes a European Defence Community (EDC).
1951	April	European Coal and Steel Community (ECSC) Treaty signed in Paris by six states: Belgium, France, Germany, Italy, Luxembourg and the Netherlands.
1952	May	EDC Treaty signed in Paris by the six ECSC states.
	July	ECSC comes into operation.
1954	August	French National Assembly rejects EDC Treaty.
	October	WEU Treaty signed by the six ECSC states plus the UK.
1955	June	Messina Conference of the Foreign Ministers of the six ECSC states to discuss further European integration. The Spaak Committee established to study ways in which a fresh advance towards the building of Europe could be achieved.
1956	June	Negotiations formally open between the six with a view to creating an Economic Community and an Atomic Energy Community.
1957	March	The Treaties of Rome signed establishing the European Economic Community (EEC) and the European Atomic Energy Community (Euratom).

1958 January   EEC and Euratom come into operation.

1959 January   First EEC tariff cuts and increases in quotas.

1960 January   European Free Trade Association (EFTA) Convention signed at Stockholm by Austria, Denmark, Norway, Portugal, Sweden, Switzerland and UK. EFTA comes into force in May 1960.

        December   Organisation for Economic Co-operation and Development (OECD) Treaty signed in Paris. OECD replaces OEEC and includes Canada and USA.

1961 July   Signing of Association Agreement between Greece and EEC. Comes into effect November 1962.

        July–August   Ireland, Denmark and the UK request membership negotiations with the Community.

1962 January   Basic features of Common Agricultural Policy (CAP) agreed.

        July   Norway requests negotiations on Community membership.

1963 January   General de Gaulle announces his veto on UK membership.

        January   Signing of Franco-German Treaty of Friendship and Co-operation.

        July   A wide ranging association agreement is signed between the Community and 18 underdeveloped countries in Africa – the Yaoundé Convention. The Convention enters into force in June 1964.

1964 May   The GATT Kennedy Round of international tariff negotiations opens in Geneva. The Community states participate as a single delegation.

1965	April	Signing of *Treaty establishing a Single Council and a Single Commission of the European Communities* (The Merger Treaty).
	July	France begins a boycott of Community institutions to register its opposition to various proposed supranational developments.
1966	January	Foreign Ministers agree to the *Luxembourg Compromise*. Normal Community processes are resumed.
1967	May	Denmark, Ireland and UK re-apply for Community membership.
	July	1965 Merger Treaty takes effect.
	July	Norway re-applies for Community membership.
	December	The Council of Ministers fails to reach agreement on the re-opening of membership negotiations with the applicant states because of continued French opposition to UK membership.
1968	July	The Customs Union is completed. All internal customs duties and quotas are removed and the common external tariff is established.
1969	July	President Pompidou (who succeeds de Gaulle after his resignation in April) announces he does not oppose UK membership in principle.
1969	July	Signing of the second Yaoundé Convention. Enters into force in January 1971.
	December	Hague summit agrees on a number of important matters: strengthening the Community institutions; enlargement; establishing an 'economic and monetary union' by 1980; and developing political co-operation (i.e. foreign policy).
1970	April	The financial base of the Community is changed by the *Decision of 21 April 1970 on the replacement of financial*

contributions from Member States by the Communities' own resources. The Community's budgetary procedures are regularised and the European Parliament's budgetary powers are increased by the *Treaty amending Certain Budgetary Provisions of the Treaties.*

June   Preferential trade agreement signed between Community and Spain. Comes into effect in October 1970.

June   Community opens membership negotiations with Denmark, Ireland, Norway and UK.

October   The six accept the Davignon report on political co-operation. This provides the basis for co-operation on foreign policy matters.

1972 January   Negotiations between Community and the four applicant countries concluded. Signing of Treaties of Accession.

May   Irish approve Community accession in a referendum.

July   Conclusion of Special Relations Agreement between Community and EFTA countries.

September   Majority vote against Community accession in a referendum in Norway.

October   Danes approve Community accession in a referendum.

October   Paris summit. Heads of government set guidelines for the future, including a reaffirmation of the goal of achieving an economic and monetary union by 1980.

1973 January   Accession of Denmark, Ireland and UK to the Community.

January   Preferential trade agreement between Community and most EFTA countries comes into effect. Agreements with other EFTA countries come into force later.

1974 December   Paris summit agrees to the principle of direct elections to the European Parliament and to the details of a European Regional Development Fund (the establishment of which had been agreed at the 1972 Paris and

1973 Copenhagen summits). In addition it is agreed to institutionalise summit meetings by establishing the European Council.

1975	February	Signing of the first Lomé Convention between the Community and 46 underdeveloped countries in Africa, the Caribbean and the Pacific (the ACP states). The Convention replaces and extends the Yaoundé Convention.
	March	First meeting of the European Council at Dublin.
	June	A majority vote in favour of continued Community membership in UK referendum.
	June	Greece applies for Community membership.
	July	Signing of the *Treaty amending Certain Financial Provisions of the Treaties*. This strengthens the European Parliament's budgetary powers and also establishes the Court of Auditors.
1976	July	Opening of negotiations on Greek accession to the Community.
1977	March	Portugal applies for Community membership.
	July	Spain applies for Community membership.
1978	October	Community opens accession negotiations with Portugal.
1979	February	Community opens accession negotiations with Spain.
	March	European Monetary System (which had been the subject of high level negotiations for over a year) comes into operation.
	May	Signing of Accession Treaty between Community and Greece.
	June	First direct elections to the EP.

October	Signing of the second Lomé Convention between the Community and 58 ACP states.
December	For the first time the EP does not approve the Community budget. As a result the Community has to operate on the basis of 'one twelfths' from 1 January 1980.

1981	January	Accession of Greece to Community.
	October	Community foreign ministers reach agreement on the 'London Report' which strengthens and extends European Political Co-operation.

1983	January	A Common Fisheries Policy is agreed.
	June	At the Stuttgart European Council meeting approval is given to a 'Solemn Declaration on European Union'.

1984	January	Free trade area between Community and EFTA established.
	February	The European Parliament approves *The Draft Treaty establishing the European Union.*
	June	Second set of direct elections to the EP.
	June	Fontainebleau European Council meeting. Agreement to reduce UK budgetary contributions (which Mrs. Thatcher had been demanding since 1979) and agreement also to increase Community resources by raising the VAT percentage from 1% to 1.4%.
	December	Signing of the third Lomé Convention between the Community and 66 ACP countries.
	December	Dublin European Council meeting agrees budgetary discipline measures.

1985	June	Signing of Accession Treaties between the Community and Spain and Portugal.
	June	The Commission publishes its White Paper *Completing the Internal Market.*

	June	Milan European Council meeting approves the Commission's White Paper. It also establishes an Intergovernmental Conference to examine various matters including Treaty reform. The decision to establish the Conference is the first time at a summit meeting a decision is taken by a majority vote.
	December	Luxembourg European Council meeting agrees the principles of the *Single European Act*. Amongst other things the Act incorporates various Treaty revisions – including confirming the objective of completing the internal market by 1992.
1986	January	Accession of Spain and Portugal to Community.
1987	June	Turkey applies for Community membership.
	July	After several months delay caused by ratification problems in Ireland the SEA comes into force.
1988	February	A special European Council meeting at Brussels agrees to increase and widen the Community's budgetary base. Measures are also agreed to significantly reduce expenditure on the CAP and to double expenditure on the regional and social funds.
	June	The Community and Comecon (the East European trading bloc) sign an agreement enabling the two organisations to recognise each other. As part of the agreement the Comecon states officially recognise, for the first time, the authority of the Community to negotiate on behalf of its member states.
	June	Hanover European Council meeting entrusts to a committee chaired by Jacques Delors the task of studying how the Community might progress to Economic and Monetary Union (EMU).
1989	April	The 'Delors Committee' presents its report (the 'Delors Report'). It outlines a scheme for a three-stage progression to EMU.

June   Third set of direct elections to the EP.

June   Madrid European Council meeting agrees that Stage 1
                 of the programme to bring about EMU will begin on
                 1 July 1990.

July   Austria applies for Community membership.

September–   The collapse of Communist governments in Eastern
December   Europe. The process 'begins' with the appointment of a
                 non-Communist Prime Minister in Poland in September
                 and 'ends' with the overthrow of the Ceausescu regime
                 in Romania in December.

December   Signing of the fourth Lomé Convention between the
                 Community and 68 ACP countries.

December   Community and USSR sign a ten year trade and
                 economic co-operation agreement.

December   Commission advises Council of Ministers to reject
                 Turkey's application for Community membership.

December   Strasbourg European Council meeting accepts Social
                 Charter and agrees to establish an Intergovernmental
                 Conference (IGC) on EMU at the end of 1990. Both
                 decisions taken by eleven votes to one, with the UK
                 dissenting in each case.

1990 April   Special Dublin European Council meeting confirms the
                 Community's commitment to Political Union.

      June   Dublin European Council meeting formally agrees that
                 an IGC on Political Union will be convened.

      July   Cyprus and Malta apply for Community membership.

      October   Unification of Germany. Territory of former East
                 Germany becomes part of the Community.

      October   Special Rome European Council meeting agrees that
                 Stage 2 of EMU will begin on 1 January 1994.

      December   The two IGC's on EMU and on Political Union are
                 opened at the Rome summit.

1991 July   Sweden applies for Community membership.

      December   Maastricht European Council meeting agrees to The
                 Treaty on European Union. The Treaty is to be based
                 on three pillars: the European Communities, a Common
                 Foreign and Security Policy and Cooperation in the
                 Fields of Justice and Home Affairs. The European
                 Communities pillar includes the strengthening of Com-
                 munity institutions, the extension of the Community's
                 legal policy competence, and a timetable leading to
                 EMU and a single currency.

Selected Further Reading

Reference Sources and Information Guides

A wide variety of reference and information material is available on the Community. Leaving aside specialist works, the following are among the most useful:

Budd, S.A., and Jones, A., *The EEC: A Guide to the Maze*, 3rd edn (Kogan Page, 1989).

Directory of Community Legislation in Force and Other Acts of the Community Institutions (Office for Official Publications of the European Communities, twice yearly).

Directory of EEC Information Sources (Euroconfidential, annual). A guide to information sources and Community activities.

Documents (Office for Official Publications of the European Communities, monthly plus cumulated and annual catalogues). Lists Commission Documents, EP Reports and ESC Opinions. *Publications of the European Communities* (issued quarterly and annually) is a companion catalogue listing monographs, serials and periodicals issued by the Community institutions. The name of both of these publications has been changed from time to time.

EEC Update (Eurofi, updated bimonthly). Provides a summary of Commission policy statements and proposals for legislation.

European Access (Chadwyck-Healey, bimonthly). Contains: (a) updating articles; (b) information developments; (c) listings of recent references from a wide range of EC and non-EC documentation.

Europe (Croner, updated monthly). A looseleaf handbook mainly covering Community law – especially as it applies to business.

Hopkins, M., *European Communities Information: Its Use and Users* (Mansell, 1985).

Index to Documents of the Commission of the European Communities (Eurofi, annual). A guide to Commission proposals for Council legislation and to reports presented by the Commission to the Council and the EP.

Inglis, A., and Hoskyns, C., *The Europe 1992 Directory*, 2nd edn (HMSO, 1990).

International Organisations Catalogue (HMSO, annual).

Jefferies, J., *A Guide to Official Publications of the European Communities*, 2nd edn (Mansell, 1981).

Myles, G., *EEC Brief* (Locksley Press, updated annually). A handbook, in looseleaf form, covering Community institutions, policies and laws.

Overton, D., *Common Market Digest* (Library Association, 1983).

Paxton, J., *A Dictionary of the European Communities*, 2nd edn (Macmillan, 1984).

Recent Publications on the European Communities (Office for Official Publications of the European Communities, monthly). Compiled by Commission library. Covers EC publications and documents, books from the commercial and academic presses, and articles from certain periodicals.

SCAD Bulletin (Office for Official Publications of the European Communities, weekly). Catalogues principal Community publications and documents, and presents summaries of articles on the Community taken from a wide range of journals and periodicals.

Thomson, I., *The Documentation of the European Communities* (Mansell, 1989). An extensive guide to EC documentation.

Yearbook of the European Communities and of other European Organisations (Editions Delta, annual). Gives an account of the role and structure of EC institutions and of other European organisations. Also gives detailed listings of personnel in these institutions and organisations.

In addition to published documentation, reference information about the Community is also available on several EC databases. The best known of these is CELEX, which is the official database of Community law. CELEX is organised into sectors which deal, for example, with the Treaties, secondary legislation, preparatory documentation, and case law of the Court of Justice.

Official Community Sources

The Community issues a vast amount of material, from brief information leaflets to weighty reports. Most of this material is available from the Office for Official Publications of the European Communities and/or directly from the appropriate Community institution. A good way of attaining a direct acquaintance of what is available is to browse at a European Documentation Centre (EDC). EDCs receive copies of most of the Community's published documents and are located throughout the member states. Usually they are attached to academic libraries.

Clearly a detailed review of Community publications is not possible here. For that, readers should refer to the various guides and catalogues that were itemised in the previous section. What follows is an outline guide to major publications.

The Treaties Establishing the European Communities should naturally be consulted by all those who wish to understand the nature and functioning of the EC. They have been published in several editions by, amongst others, the Office for Official Publications of the European Communities, HMSO, and Sweet and Maxwell.

The Official Journal of the European Communities (OJ) is issued on most weekdays and provides the authoritative record of decisions and activities of various kinds. It is divided into three series. The 'L' (Legislation) series is the vehicle for the publication of Community legislation. The 'C' (Information and Notices) series contains a range of information, including appointments to advisory committees, minutes of EP plenary proceedings and resolutions adopted by plenaries, ESC Opinions, Court of Auditors reports, cases referred to the Court of Justice and Court judgements, Commission communications and notices, and Commission proposals for Council legislation. The 'S' (Supplement) series is mainly concerned with public contract and tendering announcements. Debates of the EP are published in *Annex. Debates of the European Parliament*. An Index to the 'L' and 'C' series of the OJ is available in monthly and annual editions.

The monthly *Bulletin of the European Communities* provides a general account of most significant developments. Some of the information contained amounts to a summary of material included in the OJ (with appropriate references). Much else is additional: there are, for example, reports – albeit rather brief ones – of Council of Ministers meetings; there are updates on policy developments; there is a monitoring of progress in the annual budgetary cycle; and there is information on initiatives, meetings and agreements in the sphere of external relations.

The *General Report on the Activities of the European Communities* is published annually and provides an excellent summary of both institutional and policy developments. Where necessary it can be supplemented by the annual reports that are also published by most of the institutions.

Information about the annual budget is available in a number of places. The budget itself is published in the *Official Journal* (L series) about one month after it has been approved by the EP. Other useful sources are *Community Public Finance: the European Budget After the 1988 Reform* and, an annual publication, *The Community Budget: the Facts in Figures*.

The most detailed analysis and information about Community policies is usually to be found in documentation produced by the Commission. Leaving aside one-off publications this appears in three main forms. First, in serialised reports which are issued on a regular basis and which cover just about every aspect of Community affairs. As an indication of the sort of reports that are produced three might be mentioned: *European Economy* covers economic trends and proposals and is issued quarterly, with monthly supplements; *Eurobarometer* reports on public opinion in the Community and appears twice a year; the *Agricultural Situation in the Community* is an annual report. Second, an enormous volume of information is issued by the Statistical Office: on matters ranging from energy consumption patterns to agricultural prices. It all bears the *Eurostat* logo imprint. Third, there are Commission Documents (COMDOCS) which are made up principally of monitoring reports, policy reviews, and – most importantly – proposals for Council legislation.

Useful material stemming from other institutions on a regular basis includes: *Reports* (formerly called *Working Documents*), *Dossiers*, and *Research Documents* of the EP; the monthly *Bulletin* of the ESC; and *Reports of Cases Before the Court*.

Finally, it is worth mentioning that a number of Community publications are available without charge. Most of these are rather slight and are intended

primarily for those who know very little about the Community, but some do
go beyond basics and can be used to build up a useful collection. All of the
institutions, for example, produce pamphlets or booklets describing how they
are organised and what they do. The *European File* series – which is available
from the Office for Official Publications of the European Communities –
consists of around twenty pamphlets per year covering a variety of topics.
The *European Documentation* series – which is also available from the Office for
Official Publications – consists of four or five quite substantial booklets per
year on a range of Community matters.

Other Sources

The governments of the member states produce a considerable volume of
documentation on the Community. The precise nature of this material varies
from state to state, but mostly it consists of a mixture of 'state of play' reports,
reports from relevant parliamentary committees, and information pamph-
lets/booklets/packs. Because many of the latter are intended to stimulate a
greater public awareness about the Community, or are designed to
encourage business to take advantage of Community policies, they are often
available free of charge.

Several sources contain detailed and regular information about the work of
the Community. A daily bulletin of events is provided by *Europe* – commonly
known as *Agence Europe* – which is published by Agence Internationale
D'Information Pour La Presse. *European Report*, which is published by
Europe Information Service, also provides a detailed monitoring of events,
in its case on a twice-weekly basis.

In most member states the 'quality' press provides a reasonable review of
Community affairs. In the UK the most comprehensive coverage is to be
found in the *Financial Times*.

Academic articles on the Community are to be found in a number of
places. Particularly useful academic journals include the *Journal of Common
Market Studies* (which includes an annual review of activities in the
Community), the *Journal of European Integration*, *Common Market Law Review*,
and *European Law Review*.

The number of books published on the Community is now voluminous.
Since only a brief indication of what is available can be attempted here,
references have been confined to texts in English and preference has tended
to be given to recent publications. The titles listed are grouped into broad
sections but it must be emphasised that the boundaries between the sections
are far from watertight. Comments on books are entered only where
particularly distinctive features apply.

(a)Historical Development

Archer, C., *Organizing Western Europe* (Edward Arnold, 1990). Looks at the
development and functioning not just of the EC but also of the other main
West European organisations.

Blacksell, M., *Post-War Europe*, 2nd edn (Hutchinson, 1981).
Burgess, M., *Federalism and European Union* (Routledge, 1989).
Hallstein, W., *Europe in the Making* (Allen & Unwin, 1972). Now largely outdated, but useful in capturing the idealism that characterised many of the Community's founders.
Joll, J., *Europe Since 1870*, 3rd edn (Penguin, 1983).
Jones, R.B., The Making of Contemporary Europe (Hodder & Stoughton, 1980).
Milward, A.S., *The Reconstruction of Western Europe 1945–51* (Methuen, 1984). An extremely detailed analysis of the early post-war years that challenges some aspects of the interpretations of the 'standard' accounts.
Monnet, J., *Memoirs* (Collins, 1978). The memoirs of the 'father' of West European integration.
Nicholson, F., and East, R., *From the Six to the Twelve: the Enlargement of the European Communities* (Longman, 1987).
Pollard, S., *The Integration of the European Economy Since 1815* (Allen & Unwin, 1981).
Pryce, R., *The Dynamics of European Union* (Croom Helm, 1987).
Urwin, D.W., *Western Europe Since 1945*, 4th edn (Longman, 1989).

(b) General Books on the Government and Politics of the European Community

Arbuthnott, H., and Edwards, G., *A Common Man's Guide to the Common Market*, 2nd edn (Macmillan, 1989).
Butler, M., *Europe: More Than a Continent* (Heinemann, 1986). An 'insider' account, by the former UK Permanent Representative.
Daltrop, A., *Politics and the European Community*, 2nd edn (Longman, 1986).
Freestone, D., and Davidstone, J.S., *The Institutional Framework of the European Communities* (Croom Helm, 1988).
George, S., *Politics and Policy in the European Community* (Clarendon Press, 1985).
Henig, S., *Power and Decision in Europe* (Europotentials, 1980).
Kerr, A., *The Common Market and How it Works*, 3rd edn (Pergamon, 1986).
Leonard, D., *Pocket Guide to the European Community* (Blackwell, 1988).
Lodge, J., (ed.), *The European Community and the Challenge of the Future* (Pinter Publishers, 1989).
Nicoll, W., and Salmon, T.C., *Understanding the European Communities* (Philip Allan, 1990).
Taylor, P., *The Limits of European Integration* (Croom Helm, 1983).
Tugendhat, C., *Making Sense of Europe* (Viking, 1986). Another 'insider' account, this time by the former Budget Commissioner.

(c) Institutions and Actors

Not many books focus exclusively on particular Community institutions and actors. Many of the sources listed in sections (b), (d) and (e) do, however, contain relevant chapters and sections.

Barnouin, B., *The European Labour Movement and European Integration* (Frances Pinter, 1986).

Bassompierre, G. de, *Changing the Guard in Brussels: An Insider's View of the EC Presidency* (Praeger, 1988).

Bulmer, S., and Wessels, W., *The European Council* (Macmillan, 1987).

Butt Philip, A., *Pressure Groups in the European Community* (University Association for Contemporary European Studies, Occasional Papers No. 2, 1985).

Jacobs, F., and Corbett, R., *The European Parliament* (Longman, 1990).

Jenkins, R., *European Diary 1977–1981* (Collins, 1981). An 'insider' view by the former President of the Commission. Gives an excellent flavour of the many informal processes at work in Brussels.

Kirchner, E., and Schwaiger, K., *The Role of Interest Groups in the European Community* (Gower, 1981).

Nuallain, C.O., (ed.), *The Presidency of the European Council of Ministers* (Croom Helm, 1985).

Palmer, M., *The European Parliament* (Pergamon, 1981).

Robinson, A., and Webb, A., *The European Parliament in the EC Policy Process* (Policy Studies Institute, 1985).

Siedentopf, H., and Ziller, J., *Making European Policies Work: The Implementation of Community Legislation in the Member States*, 2 vols (Sage, 1988).

(d) The Court of Justice and Community Law

Brown, L.N., *The Court of Justice of the European Communities*, 3rd edn (Sweet and Maxwell, 1989).

Hartley, T.C., *The Foundations of European Community Law*, 2nd edn (Clarendon Press, 1989).

Lasok, D., and Bridge, J.W., *Law and Institutions of the European Communities*, 4th edn (Butterworths, 1987).

Mathijsen, P.S.M.F., *A Guide to European Community Law*, 4th edn (Sweet and Maxwell, 1985).

Millet, T., *The Court of First Instance of the European Communities* (Butterworths, 1990).

Olmi, G. et al., *Thirty Years of Community Law* (Office for Official Publications of the European Communities, 1983).

Wyatt, D., and Dashwood, A., *The Substantive Law of the EEC*, 2nd edn (Sweet and Maxwell, 1987).

(e) Policies and Policy-Making

Preference has been given in this section to books which examine not only policy content but also policy processes.

Brewster, C., and Teague, P., *European Community Social Policy* (Institute of Personnel Management, 1989).

El-Agraa, A.M., *The Economics of the European Community*, 3rd edn (Philip Allan, 1990).

Harris, S. et al, *The Food and Farm Policies of the European Community* (Wiley, 1983).

Harrop, J., *The Political Economy of Integration in the European Community* (Elgar, 1989).

Hine, R.C., *The Political Economy of European Trade* (Harvester Wheatsheaf, 1985).

Hitiris, T., *European Community Economics* (Harvester Wheatsheaf, 1988).

Holland, M., *The European Community and South Africa* (Pinter Publishers, 1988).

Ifestos, P., *European Political Co-operation* (Avebury, 1987).

Leigh, M., *European Integration and the Common Fisheries Policy* (Croom Helm, 1983).

Ludlow, P., *The Making of the European Monetary System* (Butterworths, 1982).

Meny, Y., and Wright, V., *The Politics of Steel* (Walter de Gruyter, 1987).

Moyer, H.W., and Josling, T.E., *Agricultural Policy Reform: Politics and Process in the EC and the USA* (Iowa State University Press, 1990).

Neville-Rolfe, E., *The Politics of Agriculture in the European Community* (Croom Helm, 1983).

Pearce, J., *The Common Agriculture Policy* (Routledge & Kegan Paul, 1981).

Shackleton, M., *Financing the European Community* (Pinter, 1990).

Swann, D., *Competition and Industrial Policy in the European Community* (Methuen, 1983).

Swann, D., *The Economics of the Common Market*, 6th edn (Penguin, 1988).

Wallace, H., Wallace, W., and Webb, C., *Policy-Making in the European Community*, 2nd edn (Wiley, 1983).

(f) Member States and the Community

Bulmer, S., and Paterson, W., *The Federal Republic of Germany and the European Community* (Allen & Unwin, 1987).

Coombes, D., *Ireland and the European Communities* (Gill & Macmillan, 1983).

El-Agraa, A.M., (ed.), *Britain Within the European Community* (Macmillan, 1983).

George, S., *An Awkward Partner: Britain in the European Community* (Oxford University Press, 1990).

Gregory, F.E.C., *Dilemmas of Government* (Martin Robertson, 1983).

Hill, C., *National Foreign Policies and European Political Co-operation* (Allen & Unwin, 1983).

Jenkins, R., (ed.), *Britain and the EEC* (Macmillan, 1983).

Simonian, H., *The Privileged Partnership: Franco-German Relations in the European Community 1969–1984* (Oxford University Press, 1985).

Twitchett, C., and Twitchett, K., *Building Europe* (Europa, 1981).

Yanopoulos, G., (ed.), *Greece and the EEC: Integration and Convergence* (Macmillan, 1986).

Index

Accession, Treaties of *see* Treaties
Adenauer, Konrad 27, 35
advisory committees 74–6, 84–5,
    286
Advisory Committee on the
    Development and Conversion
    of Regions 80
African, Caribbean and Pacific
    (ACP) countries 264, 278,
    313, 414
agriculture 41–2, 44–5, 56, 83,
    200–1, 225–6, 261, 269, 316,
    335–63 *passim*
  advisory committees 74–6
  Agriculture Ministers 106,
      116–17, 335, 345–6, 351–4,
      358–61
  Annual Price Review 355–62
  Committee on Agricultural
      Structures and Rural
      Development 80
  Common Agricultural Policy
      (principles of) 343–8
  decision-making
      processes 349–55
  Directorate-General vi, 66, 335,
      338, 355–7
  European Agricultural Guidance
      and Guarantee Fund
      (EAGGF) 79, 318, 323,
      347–8
  management committees 84–7,
      354–5
  Special Committee on
      Agriculture *see* Council of
      Ministers
Albania 395
Andriessen, Frans 276

Article 113 Committee 95, 108,
    275
Assembly (of EC) *see* European
    Parliament
Assembly (of ECSC) *see* Common
    Assembly
assent procedure 49, 276, 394
association agreements 136, 276,
    395
Australia 20
Austria 20, 29, 394, 411, 417

Bank for International
    Settlements 23
Barber v. *Guardian Royal Exchange
    Assistance Group* case 179
Basic Research in Industrial
    Technologies in Europe
    (BRITE) 260
Belgium 6, 20, 25–6, 35, 41, 90,
    339, 367, 372, 409–10
Benelux countries 26, 37, 40, 41,
    409
    see also under Belgium,
        Luxembourg,
        Netherlands
Benelux Customs Union 409
benzene directive 297
Bevin, Ernest 16
Bretton Woods Conference 18
Briand, Aristide 7
Britain *see* United Kingdom
Brittan, Sir Leon 92
Brussels, Treaty of (1948) *see*
    Treaties
budget (of the EC) 79–81, 136–8,
    161, 300–1, 313–34 *passim*, 412,
    413, 414, 416

Budget Ministers 106, 326–30
Bulgaria 82
Bundesbank 369–70

Cabinet (of UK) 369
Cabinet Office (of UK) 369
Cairns group 353
Canada 17, 20, 411
capital, free movement of *see*
    internal market
Cassis de Dijon case 179–80
Christian Democracy, Christian
    Democratic parties 26, 45,
    149
Churchill, Winston 16, 28
Cockfield, Lord 62, 76
Cold War 16–18, 39
Commission (of EC) 46, 54–5,
    61–402 *passim* (*but especially*
    61–99, 123–36, 139–40, 207,
    225, 233–5, 252, 283–9, 324–6,
    333, 341, 350–62, 365, 386,
    401)
  advisory committees 74–6
  appointment and
      composition 61–6
  organisation 66–72
  Presidency 11,63–4, 70–2
  responsibilities and
      powers 72–98
Commission v. *Germany* case 180
Committee of Governors of Central
    Banks 109, 311
Committee of Permanent
    Representatives
    (COREPER) *see* Council of
    Ministers
Committee of Professional
    Agricultural Organisations
    (COPA) 75, 227, 229–31,
    235, 239, 339–40
Committee of the European Social
    Fund 80
Committee on Agricultural
    Structures and Rural
    Development *see* agriculture
Common Agricultural Policy
    (CAP) *see* agriculture

Common Assembly (of EC) 46–7
  see also European Parliament
Common Assembly
    (of ECSC) 37–8
  see also European Parliament
Common Commercial Policy
    (CCP) 44, 134–5, 253, 263,
    275–6
Common Customs Tariff 44, 78,
    252–3, 263, 316
Common External Tariff
    (CET) *see* Common Customs
    Tariff
Common Fisheries Policy
    (CFP) 30, 83, 261–2, 269
Common Market 44–5, 56,
    247–54, 267–8
  see also internal market
Communism, communist
    parties 16, 26, 42, 150–1
Community Charter of the
    Fundamental Social Rights of
    Workers 77, 197, 258, 376,
    392, 417
Community Loan Instrument 313
Community Support
    Frameworks 80–1
competition policy 251–2, 269
Completing the Internal Market (White
    Paper 1985) 76–7, 247–8,
    254, 415–16
Confederation of the Socialist
    Parties of the European
    Community (CSP) 146
Conference on Security and Co-
    operation in Europe
    (CSCE) 396
Conservative Party (of the
    UK) 149
consultation procedure 131–5,
    284–90
Consultative Committee (of
    ECSC) 38, 78, 210, 214
consultative committees *see*
    advisory committees
co-operation procedure 48–9,
    132–3, 135, 161, 291–8
Correspondents Group 109

Costa v. *ENEL* case 176–7
Council of Europe 15–16, 20–1,
    25, 30, 34, 94, 383, 410
Council of Ministers (of EC) 46–9,
    54–5, 61–407 *passim* (*but*
    especially 76, 100–28, 131–6,
    140–2, 207, 277, 289–96, 306,
    326–33, 340–1, 350–62, 366–70,
    386–7)
  committees and working
    parties 107–10, 112–14,
    289–90
  composition 103–11
  Committee of Permanent
    Representatives
    (COREPER) 106–14, 290,
    326
  decision-making
    processes 111–28
  organisation 103–28
  Presidency 104–5, 111, 124–8,
    141
  responsibilities 101–2
  Secretariat 110–11
  Special Committee on
    Agriculture 107, 112, 290,
    335
Council of Ministers (of
    ECSC) 37–8
Council for Mutual Economic
    Assistance
    (COMECON) 395–6, 416
Court of Auditors 48, 222–6
Court of First Instance 49, 189
Court of Justice (of EC) 46, 49,
    54–5, 87–93, 131, 166–92
    passim, 208, 249–52, 288, 332,
    387
  membership and
    organisation 187–9
  powers and
    responsibilities 178–87
  President 188
  procedure 190–1
Court of Justice (of ECSC) 38
Crotty, Raymond 374
Cyprus 20, 394, 417
Czechoslovakia 20, 82

Davignon, Etienne 413
decisions, definition of 171
deepening (of EC) 391–4
defence policy 39–40, 267
Delors, Jacques 63, 70–1, 202, 309,
    390, 416
Delors Report (1989) 202, 256–7,
    416
democratic deficit 165, 309
Democratic Party of the Left 150
Denmark 20, 28–30, 50–1, 120,
    122, 300, 372, 374, 375–8,
    411–13
development policy 264–5, 278
direct applicability (of EC
    law) 177
direct effect (of EC law) 177
Directorates-General 66–72
    see also Commission
directives, definition of 169–71
Dooge Committee Report 204
Draft Treaty Establishing the
    European Union 165, 204,
    415
Dunkirk, Treaty of (1947) *see*
    Treaties

Economic and Finance Ministers
    (Ecofin) 106, 109, 245, 311
economic and financial
    policy 244–75 (*but especially*
    245, 255–7)
Economic and Monetary
    Union 109, 202–3, 254–7,
    310–11, 392, 402–3, 416–18
Economic and Social Committee
    (ESC) 210–17, 235, 287–9,
    357, 358
Education Ministers 311
energy policy 39, 259
enlargement (of EC) 50–4, 94–5,
    122–3
Environment Ministers 106
environmental policy 48, 89–90,
    245, 260–1, 270
European Agricultural Guidance
    and Guarantee Fund
    (EAGGF) *see* agriculture

European Atomic Energy
Community (Euratom) 4, 25,
28
European Central Bank 256–7, 392
European Bank for Reconstruction
and Development
(EBRD) 395
European Bureau of Consumers'
Associations (BEUC) 228,
341, 356
European Coal and Steel
Community (ECSC) 4, 22,
25–8, 34–9, 46, 78, 262, 281–2,
312, 314, 410
European Committee for
Electrotechnical
Standardisation
(CENELEC) 299–300
European Committee for
Standardisation
(CEN) 299–300
European Confederation of Iron
and Steel Industries
(EUROFER) 238, 282
European Convention on Human
Rights 16
European Council 11, 49, 55,
76–7, 115, 118, 193–209, 277,
304, 308, 359, 386, 413–14
activities 201–6
membership 195
origins 193–5
organisation 196–201
Presidency 196–200, 207–8
summits: Brussels (1977) 203;
Brussels (1978) 204;
Brussels (1987) 200;
Brussels (1988) 81, 115,
137, 200–1, 205–6, 308, 310,
320, 332, 356–7, 416;
Copenhagen (1987) 200;
Dublin (1975) 375, 414;
Dublin (1984) 204, 415;
Dublin 1 (1990) 197, 198,
205, 417; Dublin 2
(1990) 198, 203, 205, 417;
Fontainebleau (1984) 115,
204, 304, 315, 415; Hanover

(1988) 202, 416; London
(1977) 194; London
(1986) 268–9; Luxembourg
(1985) 115, 197, 199–200,
202, 204, 416; Maastricht
(1991) 397–8; Madrid
(1989) 202, 257, 417;
Milan (1985) 197, 199,
202, 416; Rome 1
(1990) 198, 203, 257, 417;
Rome 2 (1990) 197, 198,
199, 203, 205, 257, 417;
Strasbourg (1989) 197,
203, 204, 257, 258, 417;
Stuttgart (1983) 194, 204,
415; Venice (1980) 203
European Court of Human
Rights 178
European Court of Justice *see*
Court of Justice
European Currency Unit (Ecu),
definition of 255, 345–6
European Defence Community 25,
28, 39–40, 410
European Democratic Group (in
EP) 148–9, 153
European Development
Fund 264–5, 313
European Economic Area
(EEA) 31–2
European Economic Community
(EEC) 4, 25–8, 39–425 *passim*
(*but especially* 39–49)
European Economic Space
(EES) *see* European
Economic Area
European Environment
Agency 261
European Environmental Bureau
(EEB) 228
European Federalist
Movement 375
European Fighter Aircraft 383
European Free Trade Association
(EFTA) 20–1, 29, 31–2, 52,
81, 383, 394–6, 411, 413
European Investment Bank 96,
218–22, 313

European Monetary System
  (EMS)   23, 109, 202, 245,
  255–7, 304, 313, 383, 414
European Parliament   48–9, 54–5,
  129–65 *passim*, 222, 224–5,
  235–7, 287–9, 291–98, 328–33,
  358, 386–7, 400–2, 414–17
  committees   133, 159–63
  composition   154–6
  elections   142–5
  intergroups   152
  organisations and
     operation   156–64
  plenary sessions   163–4
  political groups   146–53
  powers and influence   129–42,
     207–8, 224–5, 276
  Presidency   158
European Patent
  Organisation   383
European People's Party –
  Federation of Christian
  Democratic Parties of the
  European Community
  (EPP)   145
European People's Party (in
  EP)   *see* Group of European
  People's Party
European Political Community   40
European Political
  Co-operation   24, 49, 109,
  141, 246, 265–6, 268, 276–8,
  383, 392, 405, 413, 415
European Programme for High
  Technology Research and
  Development
  (EUREKA)   383
European Recovery
  Programme   409
  see also Marshall Aid
European Regional Development
  Fund (ERDF)   79–81, 236,
  257, 320, 413
European Right   *see* Technical
  Group of the European Right
European Social Fund   79, 257–8,
  320
European Space Agency   383

European Strategic Programme for
  Research and Development in
  Information Technology
  (ESPRIT)   260
European Trade Union
  Confederation (ETUC)   75,
  228, 229, 234
Exchange Rate Mechanism
  (ERM)   *see* European
  Monetary System
expenditure (of EC)   317–23
expert committees   74–6

Falklands   120, 267
Fascism   6, 8
Federation of Liberal and
  Democratic Parties of the
  European Community
  (LDP)   145–6
Fianna Fail   150
Finland   20, 30
fishing   *see* Common Fisheries
  Policy
Folketing   372–3, 375
Foreign and Commonwealth
  Office   369
Foreign Ministers   103, 106,
  111–12, 114–15, 195–6, 276–7,
  304
  see also European Political Co-
     operation
foreign policy   *see* European
  Political Co-operation
France   5–7, 20, 25–7, 35, 39–42,
  50, 54, 89–90, 119, 122, 255,
  336, 368, 374, 376, 409–10
Franco, General   52

Gaulle, Charles de   25, 50, 384–5,
  411
Gaullists   150
General Agreement on Tariffs and
  Trade (GATT)   18–19, 94, 95,
  263, 275–6
General Council   *see* Foreign
  Ministers
Generalised Preferences   264

German Democratic Republic 18, 54, 82, 366, 394, 417
German unification 54, 394, 417
Germany (pre-1949) 6–8, 16, 17
Germany, Federal Republic of 16, 17–18, 20, 25–7, 35, 39–42, 50, 54, 120, 300, 336, 362, 366, 367, 369–70, 372, 409–10
Giscard d'Estaing, Valèry 193, 201, 367
goods, free movement of *see* internal market
Greece 6, 20, 28, 51–2, 89–90, 120, 121, 122, 182, 339, 368, 372, 376–8, 411, 414–15
Group for the European Unitarian Left (in EP) 148, 150, 153
Group of the European Democratic Alliance (in EP) 148, 150, 153
Group of European People's Party (in EP) 148–9, 153
Group of the Greens in the European Parliament,
Gulf crisis and war 197, 267, 392

Hague Congress (1948) 15, 409
Hallstein, Walter 12
Hauer v. *Land Rheinland Pfalz* case 174
Heath, Edward 51
High Authority (of ECSC) 36–9
Hoechst v. *Commission* case 90
Holland *see* Netherlands
Hungary 20, 394, 395

Iceland 20, 30
implementation (of EC law) 82–4, 87–93, 225–6, 298–301, 354–5
industrial policy 271–2
Industry Ministers 106
Integrated Mediterranean Programmes (IMPs) 203–4
interests and interest groups 226–39, 339–42
see also under names of individual interest groups
Intergovernmental Conference (1985) 197, 199

Intergovernmental Conference on Economic and Monetary Union 197, 199, 392, 397, 417
Intergovernmental Conference on Political Union 165, 197, 205, 394, 397, 417
intergovernmentalism 100–1, 191, 384–7
intergroups (in EP) *see* European Parliament
Interinstitutional Agreement on Budgetary Discipline ... (1988) 137–8, 320–3, 325–30, 332–4, 356
internal market 44–5, 48, 49, 56, 202, 247–54, 391
Internal Market Ministers 106
International Bank for Reconstruction and Development 18, 222
International Energy Agency (IEA) 94
International Monetary Fund (IMF) 18, 23
Ireland 5, 6, 8, 20, 50–1, 122, 265, 368, 372, 374–5, 376, 411–13
Irish Farmers' Association 372
Irish Parliament 372
Irish Supreme Court 374
Isoglucose case 131, 180
Israel 136
Italy 6–8, 20, 25–6, 40–2, 54, 89–90, 367, 375, 409–10

Japan 21, 202, 238, 247, 263, 389
Joint European Torus (JET) 383
Joint Research Centre 65, 259

Kohl, Helmut 200
Korean War 39, 40
Kuwait 267

labour, free movement of *see* internal market
Labour Party (of UK) 375, 376
law (of the EC) 166–92 *passim*, 387
League of Nations 8, 15
Left Unity Group (in EP) 153

Liberal Democratic and Reformist
    Group (in EP)   148–9, 153
liberalism, Liberal parties   146,
    148–9
Liechtenstein   21, 395
Lomé Conventions   264, 313–4,
    347, 414–17
Luxembourg   21, 25–6, 35, 41, 367,
    409–10
Luxembourg Compromise   119–21,
    127–8, 385, 412

MacSharry, Raymond   275
Malta   21, 394, 417
management committees   84–7
Mansholt, Sicco   350
Marshall Aid and Marshall
    Plan   17, 19, 409
member states (of EC)   364–81
    passim
    national courts   178, 186–7,
        373–4
    national governments   100–1,
        232–3, 365–70; *see also under*
        Council of Ministers
    national interest groups   227,
        380; *see also under names of
        individual interest groups*
    national parliaments   370–3
    national political parties   154,
        377–9
    national public opinion   374–7
    *see also under names of individual
        countries*
Merger Treaty   *see* Treaties
Messina Conference   40–1, 410
Monetary Committee   109, 311
monetary compensation amounts
    (MCAs)   346, 362
Monnet, Jean   34–5
multinational corporations   23,
    227–8
mutual recognition   180, 251

National Farmers' Union
    (of UK)   340
Nazism   6, 8

Netherlands, The   21, 25–6, 35, 41,
    367, 409–10
New Community Instrument
    (NCI)   203, 218, 220, 313
New Zealand   21
Nordic Council   20–1, 30–1
North Atlantic Treaty Organisation
    (NATO)   9, 17, 20–1, 39–40,
    53, 265, 410
Norway   21, 29, 30, 50, 374–5,
    411–13

Organisation for Economic
    Co-operation and Development
    (OECD)   19–21, 30, 94, 411
Organisation for European
    Economic Co-operation
    (OEEC)   19, 22, 25, 34, 409,
    411

Palestine Liberation
    Organisation   203
Paris, Treaty of (1951)   *see* Treaties
Pleven, René   39, 410
Poland   417
Poland and Hungary: Aid for the
    Restructuring of Economies
    (PHARE)   82
Political Committee   109, 277
political parties
    national   154, 377–9; *see also
        under names of individual parties*
    political groups in the
        EP   146–53
    transnational   145–6
Pompidou, Georges   50–1, 374, 412
Portugal   8, 21, 27–9, 52–3, 95,
    339, 376, 411, 414–16
pressure groups   *see* interests and
    interest groups
primacy (of EC Law)   178
public opinion   374–7

Rainbow Group (in EP)   149–51
recommendations, definition
    of   171
referenda   374–5

regional policy 48, 49, 257 *see also* European Regional Development Fund
regulations, definition of 168–9
regulatory committees 84–7
Renault case 92
Report of the Three Wise Men 204
Research and Development in Advance Communications Technologies for Europe (RACE) 260
research and technological development policy 48, 49, 259–60
revenue (of EC) 314–16
Rocard, Michel 92
Romania 82, 417
Rome, Treaties of (1957) *see* Treaties

San Marino 21
Savings Bank Group of the EEC (GCECEE) 229
Schengen Agreement 254
Schlüter, Poul 375
Schmidt, Helmut 193, 201, 367
Schuman, Robert, and Schuman Plan 34–5, 40, 410
services, free movement of *see* internal market
shipbuilding policy 261
Simmenthal v. *Commission* case 178
Single European Act *see* Treaties
skimmed milk cases 186
Social Charter *see* Community Charter of Fundamental Social Rights for Workers
Social Democracy 45
Social Fund *see* European Social Fund
social policy 41, 49, 257–8, 269, 392, 397, 406–7
Socialist Group (in EP) 147–9
Solemn Declaration on European Union 204, 415
South Africa 197
sovereignty 2–3, 121, 364, 384–8

Soviet Union 8, 16, 18, 392, 395–6, 417
Spaak, Paul Henri, and Spaak Committee 41, 410
Spain 6, 8, 24, 27–8, 52–3, 413, 414, 415
Special Committee on Agriculture (SCA) *see* Council of Ministers
Spinelli, Altiero 9
Stalin, Joseph 40
Standing Committee on Employment 108, 235
steel policy 78, 262, 281–2
Stockholm Convention 29, 411
Streseman, Gustav 7
structural funds 79–81, 311, 318, 320
see also EAGGF (Guidance), ERDF, and ESF
subsidiarity 270, 399–400
summits 193
Copenhagen (1973) 414
Hague (1969) 204, 412
Paris (1972) 413
Paris (1974) 193–4, 413–14
see also European Council
supranationalism 120, 100–1, 119–21, 191, 384–8
Sweden 8, 21, 29, 30, 383, 411
Switzerland 8, 21, 29, 383, 411

Technical Councils 103, 106, 111–12, 114–15, 304
see also under names of individual sectoral Councils
Technical Group of the European Right (in EP) 148, 150–1
Thatcher, Margaret 62, 149, 200, 201, 376, 391, 415
Third World *see* development policy
trade
Ministers 353
trade policy 41, 262–3; *see also* Common Commercial Policy
see also internal market
transport policy 45, 183

Treaties and Acts   42–9, 167–8,
    244–6
  Act concerning the election of the
    representatives of the
    Assembly (1976)   48, 156
  decision on the replacement of
    financial contributions from
    Member States by the
    Communities' own
    resources   314, 412–13
  Single European Act   48–9, 77,
    79–80, 84, 121, 123, 131–2,
    136, 189 194–5, 204–5,
    247–8, 260, 266, 291, 374–5,
    416
  Treaties of Accession: (1972)   48,
    374; (1979)   48; (1985)   48
  Treaty amending Certain
    Budgetary Provisions
    (1970)   47–8, 136–7, 413
  Treaty amending Certain
    Financial provisions
    (1975)   47–8, 136–7, 222, 414
  Treaty establishing a Single
    Council and a Single
    Commission of the European
    Communities (1965,
    commonly known as the
    Merger Treaty)   47, 107,
    412
  Treaty of Brussels (1948)   40, 409
  Treaty of Dunkirk (1947)   409
  Treaty of Paris (1951)   4, 25,
    35–8, 42, 78, 262, 281, 410
  Treaty of Rome (1957, EEC)   4,
    26, 41–420 *passim (but
    especially* 41–9)
  Treaty of Rome (1957,
    Euratom)   4, 26, 41–2, 45–7
  Treaty of Versailles (1919)   7–8
  Treaty on European Union
    (1992)   397–408
Trevi Group and Trevi
    process   110, 270
Truman, Harry, and Truman
    Doctrine   17
Tugendhat, Christopher   98
Turkey   21, 394, 416–17

Union of Industries of the European
    Community (UNICE)   75,
    228, 229, 234
United Kingdom (UK)   6–8, 16,
    18, 21, 28–9, 41, 50–1, 54,
    89–90, 120, 122, 300, 315, 339,
    368–9, 375, 376–8, 409–14
United Nations (UN)   15, 94, 266
United Nations Conference on
    Trade and Development
    (UNCTAD)   263
United States of America
    (USA)   16–19, 21, 23, 50, 202,
    247, 263, 353–4, 389, 392, 411

Val Duchesse dialogue   2, 3, 4
Value Added Tax (VAT)   81, 254,
    315–16
Van Gend en Loos case   177
Venice Declaration   203
Versailles, Treaty of (1919)   *see*
    Treaties

Warsaw Pact   396
Western Economic Summits   11,
    23, 81–2, 194, 202
Western European Union
    (WEU)   20–1, 40, 383, 396,
    404–5, 410
West Germany   *see* Germany,
    Federal Republic of
widening (of EC)   391, 394–5
wood pulp case   180–1
workers, free movement of   *see*
    internal market
working parties (of Council of
    Ministers)   *see* Council of
    Ministers
World Bank   *see* International
    Bank for Reconstruction and
    Development
World War, First (1914–18)   7
World War, Second
    (1939–45)   7–8, 14–22

Yaoundé Conventions   411, 412
Yugoslavia   21, 82